CW00422467

THE STAR AND
THE SCEPTER

UNIVERSITY OF NEBRASKA PRESS ‖ LINCOLN

THE STAR AND THE SCEPTER

A Diplomatic History of Israel

EMMANUEL NAVON

THE JEWISH PUBLICATION SOCIETY ‖ PHILADELPHIA

© 2020 by Emmanuel Navon.

All rights reserved. Published by the University of
Nebraska Press as a Jewish Publication Society book.
Manufactured in the United States of America. ∞

Library of Congress Cataloging-in-Publication Data
Names: Navon, Emmanuel, author.
Title: The star and the scepter : a diplomatic history of
Israel / Emmanuel Navon, the Jewish Publication Society,
Philadelphia.
Description: Lincoln: University of Nebraska Press,
[2020] | Includes bibliographical references and index. |
Summary: "The first all-encompassing book on
Israel's foreign policy and the diplomatic history of the
Jewish people, The Star and the Scepter retraces and
explains the Jews' interactions with other nations from
the ancient kingdoms of Israel to modernity"
—Provided by publisher.
Identifiers: LCCN 2020001888
ISBN 9780827615069 (hardback)
ISBN 9780827618589 (epub)
ISBN 9780827618596 (mobi)
ISBN 9780827618602 (pdf)
Subjects: LCSH: Israel—Foreign relations. | Arab-Israeli
conflict. | Jews—History.
Classification: LCC DS119.6 .N375 2020 |
DDC 327.5694—dc23
LC record available at https://lccn.loc.gov/2020001888

Set in Merope by Mikala R. Kolander.

In memory of my grandparents,
Joseph & Jamila (née Levy) Mréjen and
Claude & Jacqueline (née Weinberg) Blum,
and of my mother, Martine Blum

A star rises from Jacob, a scepter
comes forth from Israel.

—NUMBERS 24:17

Man is immortal; his salvation
is hereafter. The state has
no immortality; its salvation
is now or never.

—CARDINAL DE RICHELIEU

Contents

Maps

Acknowledgments

This book originated in a class on Israel's foreign policy, which I have been teaching for many years at Tel Aviv University (TAU) and at the Interdisciplinary Center Herzliya (IDC). I owe special thanks to colleagues who have given me the opportunity to teach at those prestigious institutions: Prof. Aharon Klieman, Prof. Yossi Shain, and Prof. Azar Gat for TAU; Dr. Lesley Terris, Prof. Boaz Ganor, and Dr. Amichai Magen for IDC. I also extend anonymous but heartfelt thanks to the countless students whose feedback, questions, and constructive criticism have refined my teaching and, as a result, the quality of this book.

I am thankful to Yossi Klein Halevi for suggesting The Jewish Publication Society (JPS) as a publisher, to JPS director Rabbi Barry Schwartz for being forthcoming, and to the University of Nebraska Press (UNP) for copublishing this volume.

I also wish to thank the people who have helped improve the original manuscript: Prof. Sasson Sofer, Prof. Aharon Klieman, and Rabbi Barry Schwartz for their useful feedback and suggestions; Channah Koppel for her meticulous proofing of the first draft; JPS managing editor Joy Weinberg for her rigorous and diligent editing; UNP editor Ann Baker; and copyeditor Debra Hirsch Corman for polishing and fine-tuning the final version of the book.

My ultimate thanks go to my beloved wife, Sima, without whom none of my endeavors and achievement—including this book—would be possible.

Introduction

Eighteenth-century Genevan philosopher Jean-Jacques Rousseau expressed thus his bewilderment at Jewish history:

> The Jews provide us with an astonishing spectacle. . . . Athens, Sparta, Rome have perished and no longer have children left on earth; Zion, destroyed, has not lost its children. . . . What must be the strength of legislation capable of working such wonders, capable of braving conquests, dispersions, revolutions, exiles, capable of surviving the customs, laws, empire of all the nations . . . to last as long as the world? . . . Any man whosoever he is, must acknowledge this as a unique marvel, the causes of which, divine or human, certainly deserve the study and admiration of the sages.[1]

This book follows Rousseau's advice by studying the diplomatic history of the Jewish people. It retraces and explains the Jews' interactions with other nations from the ancient Kingdom of Israel to the modern State of Israel today.

Such an endeavor is as ambitious as it is necessary. Books on Israel's foreign policy understandably begin with Israel's independence in 1948, but in doing so they have lacked the wider perspective of Jewish history. They have also tended to focus exclusively on certain aspects of Israel's foreign policy, most typically the Arab-Israeli conflict or the U.S.-Israel relationship. Seven decades after Israel's independence, an updated and comprehensive account of Israel's foreign policy was missing. The present book was written to fill that void.

Writing a diplomatic history of Israel is complicated by the uniqueness of that history. The astounding survival of the Jewish people throughout the centuries, after the Roman destruction of Jewish sovereignty in 70 CE, defies logic. In the words of Prof. Ruth Wisse, Jews are "comeback kids of a saga that defies historical probability."[2] British historian Arnold Toynbee had used the word "fossil" to describe the Jewish people precisely because he could not make sense of the Jews' unexplainable survival. Pressed about the national rebirth of the Jews in the twentieth century, Toynbee conceded that "Israel has become defossilized as you can defrost a car."[3] The "defrosted car" is by now a thriving and successful country; the "fossil" has come back to life.

Diplomatic history is about statesmanship, yet the Jews were stateless for two-thirds of their three-millennia history. In antiquity, Jews were sovereign for about a millennium: under the United Monarchy (1050–930 BCE); under the kingdoms of Israel (930–720 BCE) and of Judah (930–586 BCE); under the Yehud (Judea) Province of the Babylonian Empire (586–539 BCE), the Assyrian Empire (539–332 BCE), and the Greek Empire (332–140 BCE); under the Hasmonean Dynasty (140–37 BCE); and under the Judean province of the Roman Empire (37 BCE–70 CE). With Rome's merciless repression of the Bar Kokhba revolt in 135 CE, the Jews became stateless and dispersed. Even in exile, however, Jewish leaders negotiated with heads of states to advance Jewish interests. Fifteenth-century Spanish Jewish scholar and financier Isaac Abarbanel used his fortune to free the Jews of Arzila (Morocco) from slavery; he loaned large sums of money to the king of Spain during the Reconquista. After settling in Venice (in 1503), Abarbanel negotiated a trade treaty between the Venetian Republic and Portugal. In 1655 the Portuguese Jewish scholar and diplomat Menashe Ben-Israel convinced Oliver Cromwell to allow Jews back in England. In 1840 European Jewish politicians, such as Adolphe Crémieux in France, and financiers, such as the Rothschilds in England, convinced their respective governments to pressure the Turkish sultan into ending the "Damascus Affair," a blood libel against the Jews of Damascus. The Rothschilds served the diplomatic interests of Great Britain in the nineteenth century: they helped the British government pay for both the Crimean War (1853–56) and the Suez Canal (in 1875). Benjamin Disraeli, a British prime minister proud of his Jewish origins, advocated Jewish national revival in the Land of Israel. The Zionist movement established by Theodor Herzl in 1897 turned its leaders into diplomats decades before the establishment of the State of Israel, as Zionist activists lobbied world leaders to support the idea of Jewish statehood in the Jews' ancient homeland. In other words, despite the lack of Jewish sovereignty for much of the Jewish people's history, there was a "Jewish diplomacy," and it must be addressed.

About This Book

The book is divided into four parts. Part 1, "Israel and the Nations in the Hebrew Bible," analyzes the theme of "Israel and the Nations" via exegetical readings of the Pentateuch (chapter 1), the Prophets (chapter 2), and the Writings (chapter 3). There is much to learn from the Hebrew Bible about the foreign policy of the ancient kingdoms of Israel. Furthermore, I believe one cannot understand Israel's interaction with the world without a basic knowledge of the Hebrew Bible. The Jewish psyche was shaped and continues to be influenced by the founding document of Judaism and Jewish peoplehood. Concepts such as "a people that dwells alone," the eternal enmity of Amalek, or messianic redemption are not comprehensible without biblical knowledge. Those concepts are intertwined with the Jews' self-perceived historical role and their interactions with other nations. As the Bible scholar Jon Levenson argues, in the study of Jewish history "the whole truth is larger than either traditional memory or modern critical historiography can accommodate alone."[4]

Part 2, "Jewish Diplomacy from Antiquity to Modernity," includes the foreign policy of the ancient kingdoms of Israel until the Romans' destruction of the Judean province in 70 CE (chapter 4); the diplomacy of Jewish Diasporas in Europe from the Middle Ages to Emancipation (chapter 5); the emergence of the Zionist movement in the late nineteenth century and its efforts to gather international support (chapter 6); Zionist diplomacy in the post–World War I international system (chapter 7); and the foreign policy dilemmas of the Zionist leadership in the 1930s and during World War II (chapter 8).

Part 3, "The Rebirth of Israel and the Arab-Israeli Conflict," surveys Israel's independence and struggle in the unwelcoming Middle East. It explains Israel's foreign policy dilemmas at the beginning of the Cold War (chapter 9); Israel's attempts to build alliances in a hostile Middle East (chapter 10); Israel's wars and peace agreements with the Arab states (chapter 11); and Israel's unresolved conflict with the Palestinians (chapter 12).

Part 4, "Israel on the World Scene," describes and explains Israel's foreign policy from 1948 to our days. It covers Israel's relations with Europe (chapter 13), the United States (chapter 14), Russia (chapter 15), Asia (chapter 16), Africa (chapter 17), Latin America (chapter 18), the United Nations (chapter 19), and the Jewish Diasporas (chapter 20). The last chapter (chapter 21) explains how Israel's foreign relations are being transformed by the changing geopolitics of energy.

The volume is necessarily not exhaustive, given the wide range of topics and long period of time covered. Rather, a central idea—or thesis—emerges from this historical survey: the Jews have survived and succeeded in their interactions with other nations thanks to a strong sense of historical mission, as well as to the constant adaptation of that mission to the real world.

This idea is encapsulated by the book's two epigraphs.

The verse from the book of Numbers ("A star rises from Jacob, a scepter comes forth from Israel," Num. 24:17) raises two questions:

(1) if Jacob was renamed Israel, why do both names continue to appear alternatively throughout the biblical text, sometimes in the same verse; and (2) what do the star and the scepter signify? The book of Genesis describes Jacob as "a mild man who stayed in camp" and his twin brother Esau as "a skillful hunter, a man of the outdoors" (Gen. 25:27). The former was Athenian and the latter Spartan, so to speak, but individually neither man possessed the two qualities needed to carry on the legacy of Abraham and Isaac: faith and power. The Star of David symbolizes the Jewish faith, while the scepter is a symbol of power. Jacob had faith but lacked strength. He was renamed Israel only after proving his ability and willingness to fight in the real world. Yet, then as now, the balancing act between faith and power is never to be taken for granted; it is constantly challenged. Hence, it seems, the back-and-forth use of the names Jacob and Israel.

Cardinal Richelieu's quote ("Man is immortal; his salvation is hereafter. The state has no immortality; its salvation is now or never") also relates to the dilemma between faith and power, though admittedly not from a Jewish perspective. Richelieu was both a clergyman and a statesman. As a high-ranking member of the Catholic Church, he should have sided with the Catholics in the Thirty Years' War between Catholics and Protestants. Yet Richelieu allied with the Protestants so as to weaken the Holy Roman Empire and to secure France's domination of the European continent. He put *raison d'État* (national interest) before theological preferences and even produced a formula to justify himself: because statesmen are responsible not only for their soul but also for the survival and well-being of their country, they have no other choice but to separate between faith and power. This logical twist enabled Richelieu to be ruthless and cynical while preserving his religious garments.

Diplomacy involves compromise between ideals and realpolitik, between principles and interests. Israeli diplomacy is no exception in this regard, but the diplomatic history of Israel is unique. Drawing lessons from this exceptional history is prerequisite to guaranteeing Israel's future.

THE STAR AND
THE SCEPTER

PART 1. Israel and the Nations in the Hebrew Bible

1. The Pentateuch

The Lord will scatter you among all the peoples from one end of the earth to the other. . . . Yet even among those nations you shall find no peace, nor shall your foot find a place to rest.

DEUT. 28:64–65

A People Born in Struggle

The Hebrew word for "nation/people" appears for the first time in its singular form in chapter 12 of the book of Genesis, when God tells Abraham, "Go forth from your native land and from your father's house to the land that I will show you. I will make of you a great nation" (Gen. 12:1–2). The reader is left in the dark about the purpose of Abraham's journey. Only ten chapters later are we told why Abraham became the founding father of a new nation: because of his unconditional willingness to accept God's will and to act upon it (Gen. 22:17–18).

The birth of this nation, however, is fraught with division, jealousy, and even hatred. Abraham's two sons, Ishmael and Isaac, are respectively born from two rival women: Hagar and Sarah. While Ishmael, says the Bible, is a "wild ass of a man; his hand against everyone" (Gen. 16:12), the Abrahamic alliance is transmitted through Isaac: "But my covenant I will maintain with Isaac" (Gen. 17:21).

Like his father, Isaac has two rival sons, Esau and Jacob, who are described as two separate nations (Gen. 25:23). Esau is the firstborn. Once an adult, however, Esau agrees to sell his birthright to Jacob because, says he, "I am at the point of death, so of what use is my birthright to me?" (Gen. 25:32). When Isaac feels that he is about to die, he asks Esau—not Jacob—to get ready for the fatherly blessing. Following his mother's advice, Jacob deceives his blind father and receives the blessing intended for Esau. After realizing his mistake, Isaac confesses to an enraged Esau that Jacob is the blessed one. Consequently, Esau swears to kill Jacob (Gen. 27:41).

Jacob literally runs away with the legacy he received in dubious circumstances, and he needs to fight hard to deserve it. A penniless refugee in Mesopotamia, he works for twenty years for Laban, his deceitful and abusive uncle (and father-in-law). After building his own wealth and founding a family, Jacob decides to return to his homeland. But he cannot do so without confronting Esau's wrath and is therefore compelled to fight for the inheritance he grabbed. On his way back home, Jacob is unexpectedly and mysteriously assaulted by an unnamed man (or angel) during the night. Failing to subdue Jacob, the unsuccessful assaulter begs to be released before dawn and asks Jacob his name. When Jacob responds, the man (or angel) tells him, "Your name shall no longer be Jacob, but Israel, for you have striven with beings divine and human, and have prevailed" (Gen. 32:29). God later confirms Jacob's new name: "'You whose name is Jacob, / You shall be called Jacob no more, / But Israel shall be your name.' / Thus He named him Israel" (Gen. 35:10).

If the Bible recounts the origins of the people of Israel, how does it explain their purpose as a nation? The Pentateuch (Five Books of Moses) provides a recurring answer to that question: Israel bears the historical responsibility of bringing to humanity the testimony of God's existence by remaining faithful to the Sinai covenant. If the people do so, they will be free and live in peace in the land promised to Abraham, Isaac, and Jacob. Should Israel, on the other hand, forgo its obligations, the people will be exiled from their land, subjugated by foreign nations, and suffer until Israel returns to the Sinai covenant.

Israel's connection to its land is, therefore, contractual. The founding act of the Hebrew nation is Abraham's *emigration* from his homeland. Furthermore, the biblical laws of sabbatical and jubilee years are meant to remind the Jewish people that the land, ultimately, is not theirs (Lev. 25:23). Every seven years, Hebrew farmers are commanded to let their land rest, and they are forbidden from cultivating it (sabbatical). Every forty-nine years, all slaves and prisoners are freed, and all debts are forgiven (jubilee).

In Greek mythology, by contrast, the first king of Athens, Cecrops, was an "autochthon," a half-human, half-serpent creature that symbolized the Athenians' connection to their earthly origin. The word "autochthonous" refers to a land's natives. While in the Bible, Adam's creation from the earth symbolizes the universality of man, the autochthonous myth depicts an inherent link between nations and their respective motherlands. Even today, some nations describe their link to their land as organic. Ethnic Malaysians, for example, call themselves *bumiputra*, or "sons of the soil." Like other nations, the Jews are granted their own share of land, but the Jews' right to their attributed land remains dependent on the preservation of the Sinai covenant. Israel's right to its land may thus be suspended, but not repealed: "I give all the land that you see to you and your offspring forever" (Gen. 13:15).

Between Assertiveness and Submissiveness

Abraham leaves civilization for the wilderness in the name of an ideal. He does not, however, get to escape from the real world. When confronted with rivalry, Abraham chooses peace when possible and war when necessary: to his nephew Lot, Abraham offers territorial compromise; to the kings who kidnapped Lot and stole his property, Abraham declares war and fights until the enemy's total surrender. He uses war as a means to achieve justice in an unjust and violent world, and not as a tool for personal gain ("I will not take so much as a thread or a sandal strap" [Gen. 14:23]).

As a nomad, Avraham is compelled to deal with foreign leaders. King Abimelech, who is described in the book of Genesis as "king of the Philistines," asks Abraham to sign an agreement meant to grant him the right to live in the land (Gen. 21:23). Abraham, however, does not hesitate to remind the king of his subjects' disrespect for property rights: Abimelech's servants had unjustly taken possession of Abraham's wells—a critical source of daily survival in the desert. Because the king insists on sealing an alliance, Abraham puts aside seven lambs and explains to Abimelech, "You are to accept these seven ewes from me as proof that I dug this well" (Gen. 21:30).

The alliance with Abimelech turns out to be of questionable value. After Abraham's death, a famine hits the land of Canaan again. Abraham's anointed successor, Isaac, subsequently decides to go to Abimelech—apparently to benefit from the favors Abimelech had promised to Abraham and his descendants. Isaac does not ask for handouts from Abimelech, but sows his lands (Gen. 26:12). Isaac becomes so successful and wealthy that the Philistines become jealous and clog up Abraham's wells with dirt (Gen. 26:15). Abimelech himself asks Isaac to leave, "for you have become far too big for us" (Gen. 26:16), in violation of Abimelech and Abraham's alliance. Isaac does not argue with Abimelech. He leaves, and he rebuilds, one by one, his father's wells, thus bringing water to a desolate land. Once the water flows, the Philistines claim it belongs to them.

Although Isaac first complies with Abimelech's injunction to leave, he then shows determination in front of the Philistines' vandalism and bad faith. Isaac reopens his father's wells without giving in to the Philistines' false claims, and his resilience eventually pays off: after the fights for the wells of Esek and Sitnah, Isaac digs a third well, but the Philistines "did not quarrel over it" (Gen. 26:22). Obviously impressed by Isaac's determination and inner strength, Abimelech comes to him and admits candidly, "We now see plainly that the Lord has been with you, and we thought: Let there be a sworn treaty between our two parties, between you and us. Let us make a pact with you" (Gen. 26:28). Abimelech then displays the same bad faith he did with Abraham, by claiming that he and his people "have always dealt kindly with you" (Gen. 26:29). Isaac agrees to seal an alliance with Abimelech nonetheless.

Eventually, an aging and blind Isaac unwittingly transmits the fatherly blessing to Jacob rather than Esau. This blessing is full of significance with regard to the fate of Jacob's descendants among the nations: "Cursed be they who curse you, / Blessed they who bless you" (Gen. 27:29). Jacob becomes a foreigner in exile. He serves his uncle Laban for two decades, learning how to make a living and how to deal with an abusive and manipulative master. As he grows in wealth and sophistication, Jacob arouses Laban's ire, the same way that Isaac's achievements had caused Abimelech to resent him. When Jacob decides to return to his country, Laban pursues him with revengeful intentions, claiming that Jacob's belongings are his.

Having survived Laban, Jacob must now face his resentful and avenging brother Esau. While Esau is "a skillful hunter, a man of the outdoors," Jacob is "a mild man who stayed in camp" (Gen. 25:27). Does Jacob have the will to overcome his foes? His mother Rebekah had counseled him to outsmart Esau. After twenty years of abuse and treachery at the hands of his uncle, Jacob finally stood up for himself with Laban. Now the true trial comes: the dramatic encounter with Esau.

Jacob tries to appease his brother by sending him messengers and presents. Jacob prays for safety, and he divides his family into two camps to improve the chances of partial survival in case Esau decides to unleash his wrath. Diplomacy, faith, and strategy do not suffice, however. Jacob needs to prove he is willing to fight physically in order to survive in the real world. Hence the mysterious encounter with a man (or angel) who wrestles with him in the middle of the night. Jacob fights valiantly and "passes the test." He receives the name Israel (meaning "God's fighter").

Israel may be a fighter, but Jacob is hesitant to use force and has a tendency for appeasement. He is exceedingly apologetic and self-debasing with Esau, calling his brother "my lord" and calling himself "your servant." He tries to buy Esau's goodwill with presents. The midrash (a compilation of early rabbinic interpretations and commentaries on the Bible) strongly condemns Jacob's self-debasing attitude toward Esau and even states that eight nations shall subjugate the people of Israel because Jacob called Esau "my lord" eight times (*Bereshit Rabbah* 75:11). The thirteenth-century rabbi and scholar Nachmanides (Ramban) concurs with the above midrash and adds that Israel's defeat by the Roman Empire was caused by Jewish submissiveness. By contrast, Rabbi Yehuda Hanassi, the second-century Jewish leader and editor of the Mishnah (Jewish codex of oral law), taught that being accommodating with the Romans was a matter of realism and of survival. A friend of the Roman emperor Antonius, Rabbi Yehuda Hanassi addressed him with the words "your servant" and justified this reverence with Jacob's similar uttering vis-à-vis Esau.

Jacob's uneasiness with power is fully revealed by his reaction to Prince Shechem's rape of his daughter Dinah. Two of Jacob's sons, Simeon and Levi, avenge their sister's rape by murdering Prince Shechem, his father King Hamor, and all their male subjects. In addition, Simeon and Levi plunder the property of their victims. When he learns of their deeds, Jacob castigates Simeon and Levi out of fear for his image and the family's safety among people who outnumber them: "You have brought trouble on me, making me odious among the inhabitants of the land, the Canaanites and the Perizzites; my men are few in number, so that if they unite against me and attack me, I and my house will be destroyed" (Gen. 34:30). To Simeon and Levi's protest—"Should our sister be treated like a whore?" (Gen. 34:31)—Jacob gives no answer.

Indeed, Jacob's uneasiness with his new role as a fighter may explain why the Bible keeps using the names "Jacob" and "Israel" interchangeably even after Jacob is given his new name. By contrast, the Bible never reverts to the former names of Abraham and Sarah, who used to be called Avram and Sarai respectively.

Like his grandfather and his father, Jacob/Israel suffers from drought and famine in the land of Canaan, and the need to find food brings him in contact with foreign nations and leaders. In Jacob's days, however, food is to be found in Egypt alone. Whereas Abraham and Isaac had to deal with the deceitful Abimelech, Jacob needs to ask for food from the leader of the great kingdom of Egypt. Yet God's "invisible hand" has been at work to make Jacob's favorite son, Joseph, viceroy of Egypt. Jacob thus arrives in Egypt as the honored father of the country's strongman, even as he and his sons are ultimately at the mercy of Pharaoh, the king of Egypt.

After painstakingly and hesitantly learning the importance of power to sustain ideals in the real world, Jacob is now compelled to relinquish power in order to survive. As a guest of Pharaoh, he loses the freedom he enjoyed in Canaan. In exile, Jacob's descendants lose the physical power that is a perquisite for sovereignty. Survival now depends on intellectual power, which Joseph masters: Pharaoh had elevated him precisely because Joseph understands the world and knows how to improve the lives of others. Ultimately, however, Pharaoh can dismiss him, send him back to jail, or kill him.

Indeed, Joseph's submissiveness to Pharaoh becomes evident when Jacob dies: even though he is supposedly powerful, Joseph barely dares to ask Pharaoh's permission to fulfill his father's desire to be buried in Canaan. In fact, the reader might expect Joseph and his brothers to return to Canaan and resettle there after burying Jacob in Hebron; the famine, after all, was over.[1] But Jacob and his sons are no longer free; they are the subjects of Pharaoh, who sustained them in time of need and who can therefore decide their fate.

That the fate of Jacob's descendants is in Pharaoh's hands is trag-ically confirmed as soon as Joseph dies. A new Pharaoh is anointed, and he decides to turn the Hebrews into slaves and to kill their male newborns. Faced with such cruelty and arbitrary use of power, the Hebrews are powerless.

The saga of the Ten Plagues is the story of Pharaoh's stubborn and foolish attempt to push his luck to its limits. As time passes, Pharaoh loses the trust and support of his own people because of the ruin he brings upon Egypt. Eventually, Moses becomes "much esteemed in the land of Egypt, among Pharaoh's courtiers and among the people" (Exod. 11:3), and the Hebrews are set free.

However, after freeing the Hebrews, Pharaoh makes a last desperate attempt to recapture them. Seeing Pharaoh on their trail, the Hebrews display early signs of Jewish chutzpah (or humor?) by sarcastically asking Moses if he took them out of Egypt for lack of graveyards there. Freedom, however, comes at a price: Israel's archetype enemy, Ama-lek, appears in the Sinai desert and fights Israel (Exod. 17:8). Israel's ability to prevail over this mysterious enemy seems to be based on inner will and determination, as allegorically suggested by the text: "Whenever Moses held up his hand, Israel prevailed; but whenever he let down his hand, Amalek prevailed. But Moses' hands grew heavy" (Exod. 17:11–12). Only after Israel's temporary victory are we told why Amalek was attacking Israel: Amalek's issue is not with Israel per se, but with Israel's message to the world. Amalek struggles with God through Israel, and therefore "the Lord will be at war with Amalek throughout the ages" (Exod. 17:16). Indeed, the Bible later enjoins the Hebrews to "remember what Amalek did to you" and elucidates the true cause of Amalek's enmity toward Israel: he was "undeterred by fear of God" (Deut. 25:17–18).

Israel also has enemies from within: the "mixed multitude" (*erev rav* in Hebrew), which is always eager to spread demoralization and to question the very wisdom of leaving Egypt. The "mixed multitude" are a group of demagogues who do not hesitate to describe the hellish past of Egyptian slavery as a lost paradise: "If only we had meat to eat! We remember the fish that we used to eat free in Egypt" (Num. 11:4–5). With or without the "mixed multitude," doubt and demoralization often jeopardize the journey toward freedom. When Moses sends out spies to gather intelligence about the land that the Hebrews have been ordered to conquer, ten of the twelve spies come back with a dark picture. "We came to the land you sent us to," they tell Moses and the people. "It does indeed flow with milk and honey. . . . However, the people who inhabit the country are powerful. . . . We cannot attack that people, for it is stronger than we. . . . We looked like grasshoppers to ourselves, and so we must have looked to them" (Num. 13:27–33). Claiming that Israel will not be able to overcome the inhabitants of the land is an opinion, however, not an intelligence report. Indeed, the minority opinion of Caleb (one of the twelve spies sent out by Moses) is different: "We shall surely overcome [the enemy]" (Num. 13:30). But the majority opinion stems from the spies' perception of themselves as "grasshoppers."

The ten spies spread both division and doubt among the people. Indeed, "the people wept that night. All the Israelites railed against Moses and Aaron. . . . And they said to one another, 'Let us head back for Egypt.'" (Num. 14:1–4). The two spies who did believe in conquering the land, Joshua and Caleb, reply, "Have no fear then of the people of the country. . . . The Lord is with us. Have no fear of them!" (Num. 14:9). Both leaders are nearly lynched for their message, and the people are sentenced to forty years of wandering in the desert. Once the sentence is pronounced, and once the bad-mouthing evil spies suddenly die of illness, the Hebrews realize they have gone a step too far and decide to make up for their mistakes. After nearly lynching Joshua and Caleb for recommending the conquest of the land, the Hebrews now decide to follow their advice. Yet it is too late. As Moses tells them, "Do not go up, lest you be routed by your enemies, for the Lord is not in your midst" (Num. 14:42). The former rebels-turned-zealots ignore Moses' advice, and their adventure turns into a military debacle.

Demoralization leads to rebellion. A mutiny organized by Korah, a great-grandson of the patriarch Levi and a cousin of Moses and Aaron, threatens to overthrow Moses. If he has failed to bring them to the Promised Land, they claim, then he should resign: "Is it not enough that you brought us from a land flowing with milk and honey to have us die in the wilderness, that you would also lord it over us?" (Num. 16:13). The revolutionaries' sophistry is pushed to its limits: there was no reason to leave Egypt and it really is Moses' fault if the people are now turning in circles in the desert.

After containing Korah's mutiny and the people's endless complaints, Moses needs to make military and diplomatic preparations for the conquest of the land. He reverently asks the king of Edom (himself a descendant of Esau) for permission to go through his land. Just like Jacob had sent messengers to his brother Esau in the "country of Edom" (Gen. 32:4) and had uttered the words "I pray thee" for Esau to accept his presents, so too does Moses approach the king of Edom, presenting himself as "your brother" and imploring him to allow the Hebrews to walk through his land on their way to the Promised Land (Num. 20:14–21). Moses tries to arouse the king's pity for the Hebrews—the journey is necessary because the Hebrews suffered in Egypt—and promises not to cause any harm whatsoever to his land (they will not even drink from the wells of Edom). The king, however, flatly rejects Moses' request and threatens to smite the Hebrews—who subsequently retreat (Num. 20:21). Israel's submissive attitude lifts the spirits of its enemies: upon hearing the Hebrews' capitulation to the king of Edom, the king of Arad declares war on them and takes many prisoners.

Moses learns some lessons from the failure of his diplomatic niceties with the king of Edom. When he approaches the king of the Amorites, Moses does not ask for permission to walk through his land;

instead, he notifies the king that the Hebrews will be passing through but will cause no damage to his land (Num. 21:21). Like the king of Edom, the king of the Amorites rejects Israel's announcement and prepares for battle. This time, however, the Hebrews decide to fight, and they achieve victory (Num. 21:24–32). This victory does not convince another local monarch, King Og of Bashan, to seek conciliation. Og, who knows that the Hebrews are planning on walking through his land as well, decides to use military force against them, but they overcome him (Num. 21:35).

Israel's two military victories spread panic among other potential enemies. Among them is Balak, king of Moab, who is said to be afraid of Israel (Num. 22:3). King Balak decides to hire Balaam the sorcerer to curse Israel. Yet instead of cursing the Hebrews, Balaam utters meaningful words about Israel's place among the nations: "There is a people that dwells apart, / Not reckoned among the nations" (Num. 23:9). He then declares about Israel, "Blessed are they who bless you, / Accursed they who curse you!" (Num. 24:9). Finally, Balaam predicts Israel's ultimate victory against the nation's enemies: "What I see for them is not yet, / What I behold will not be soon: / A star rises from Jacob, / A scepter comes forth from Israel; / It smashes the brow of Moab, / The foundation of all children of Seth. / Edom becomes a possession, / Yea, Seir a possession of its enemies; / But Israel is triumphant" (Num. 24:17–18).

Conditional Sovereignty, Unconditional Survival

As we have seen, the Bible describes the relationship between God and Israel in contractual terms: Israel shall testify to the world of God's existence through compliance with God's commandments; in exchange, Israel will enjoy sovereignty and peace in the land promised to Abraham, Isaac, and Jacob (Lev. 26:3–8). If, on the other hand, Israel decides to abandon the Sinai covenant, the consequences shall

be dire: "But if you do not obey Me and do not observe all these commandments. . . . I in turn will do this to you: I will wreak misery upon
you. . . . I will set My face against you: you shall be routed by your
enemies, and your foes shall dominate you. . . . And you I will scatter
among the nations" (Lev. 26:14–33). Eventually, suffering and exile will
bring repentance: "Those of you who survive shall be heartsick over
their iniquity in the land of your enemies. . . . Then at last shall their
obdurate heart humble itself, and they shall atone for their iniquity.
Then will I remember My covenant with Jacob; I will remember also
My covenant with Isaac, and also My covenant with Abraham; and I
will remember the land" (Lev. 26:39–44). Israel can technically abandon the Sinai covenant, but the nation will be doomed for doing so
because "the Lord will scatter you among all the peoples from one end
of the earth to the other. . . . Yet even among those nations you shall
find no peace, nor shall your foot find a place to rest" (Deut. 28:64–65).

The fifteenth-century Spanish rabbi and author Isaac Arama argues
in his book *Akedat Yitzhak* that the verse "you shall find no peace, nor
shall your foot find a place to rest" is a reference to the time when
Jews will try to assimilate to avoid persecution. According to Arama,
the verse teaches us that the nations will not let the Jews forget who
they are. Even when they live as gentiles, they will be persecuted and
killed as Jews. Similarly, a midrash (*Bereshit Rabbah* 33:8) juxtaposes
this verse with the one describing the dove's return to Noah's ark ("But
the dove could not find a resting place for its foot, and returned to him
to the ark" [Gen. 8:9]), teaching us that the curse of "you shall find
no peace, nor shall your foot find a place to rest" can be turned into
a blessing: had the Jews been able to assimilate, they would not have
returned to their faith and to their land, just as the dove would not
have returned to the ark had it found a resting for the sole of its foot.

Likewise, argues the Babylonian Talmud, the curse of Ahijah the
Shilonite in the first book of Kings may be understood as a blessing.
Ahijah tried to curse Israel by saying, "The Lord will strike Israel until

it sways like a reed in water" (1 Kings 14:15). And yet, as the Talmud explains, "The reed stays put in the water: its stock renews itself and its roots are many, and all the winds in the world cannot make it budge from its place, for it bends with them" (*Ta'anit* 20a). In other words, Israel may bow and be humiliated for its sins, but the nation will always come back to its original glory, thanks to the depth of its roots.

Among the last verses of the book of Deuteronomy is the line "Thus Israel dwells in safety, / Untroubled is Jacob's abode" (Deut. 33:28). The sixteenth-century Talmud scholar Rabbi Samuel Eidels (also known as the Maharsha) argues that Jacob's abode being "untroubled" was originally meant as a blessing: The Israelite nation would be untroubled by its enemies who, out of fear, would leave the people alone. However, because of their sins, the Jews would also be "alone" in the negative sense of being ostracized by other nations. This curse, however, is reversible if the Jews return to the covenant they were warned not to abandon. The Bible's eschatology of Jewish history can therefore be understood thus: defeat is a temporary and deserved payback from the Ruler of the universe, but it is never a final blow.

Conclusion

The name Israel is given to Jacob after he proves his ability and willingness to fight for his spiritual legacy in the real world. Yet even after receiving his new name, Jacob/Israel continues to oscillate between assertiveness and submissiveness. Even after Jacob is renamed Israel, the Torah continues to use both names alternatively. This apparent contradiction suggests that the name Israel is an ideal to be fought for by way of a delicate and never-ending balancing act between idealism and realism, between values and power.

The fact that the Torah describes the relationship between Israel and its land as a contractual one shaped the Jews' self-perceived historical role, their interpretation of historical setbacks, and their relations with other nations. Precisely because the Jews perceived their sovereignty as a reward and their subjugation as a punishment, they did not interpret national defeats and humiliations as the end of their history, but as a well-deserved penalty that would eventually be followed by forgiveness and redemption. This self-perceived historical role and unique relationship with the nations of the world may well explain why the Jews never vanished from the annals of history.

2. The Prophets

We hoped for good fortune, but no happiness came;
For a time of relief—instead there is terror!

JEREMIAH 8:15

Diplomacy and War

The book of Judges describes a recurrent pattern: the Hebrews sin, thus provoking divine rebuke; foreign nations subjugate Israel; the Children of Israel pray to God and obtain temporary relief from the foreign yoke; and yet soon the same scenario repeats itself all over again. Eventually, God sarcastically answers Israel's prayers thus: "Go and cry to the gods which you have chosen; let them deliver you in your time of distress!" (Judg. 10:14). Yet God does send a savior to Israel: Samson (Shimshon), who terrifies the Philistines with his strength and vigor. The Hebrews, however, are so used to being subjugated to the Philistines that betraying their own hero seems more natural to them than letting him fight the enemy. Ordered by the Philistines to deliver Samson, the Children of Israel say to him, "You knew that the Philistines rule over us; why have you done this to us? . . . We have come down to take you prisoner and to hand you over to the Philistines" (Judg. 15:11–12).

Israel may have had good reasons to fear the Philistines, who slaughtered thirty thousand Hebrews in Shilo and captured the Ark of the Covenant (1 Sam. 4:10–11). But, as Samuel (Shmuel) argues, the Hebrews can only blame themselves for the Philistines' might, which can be overcome through faithfulness to the Sinai covenant (1 Sam. 7:3). With the people's temporary repentance comes temporary victory and a peace between the nation of Israel and its neighbors (1 Sam. 7:15). When the Hebrews ask Samuel for a king, however, they do so in order to be "like all the other nations" (1 Sam. 8:20).

The reign of Israel's first king, Saul (Shaul) is unsuccessful, and the Philistines continue to terrify the Hebrews—especially with their mighty warrior Goliath. Saul's disgrace is partly the result of his failure to carry out the divine order of wiping out Amalek (1 Sam. 28:18).

David, on the other hand, mercilessly pursues and kills the descendants of Amalek who burned down the city of Ziklag (1 Samuel 30). Anointed king of Israel, David transfers the kingdom's capital from Hebron to Jerusalem. While the Philistines had terrorized Israel during the reign of Saul, David smites and subdues them, as well as the rest of Israel's enemies (2 Sam. 8:6). This strength and greatness draw the respect and admiration of Israel's neighbors, such as King Hiram from the neighboring land of Tyre in Lebanon (2 Sam. 5:11) and King Toi of Hamath, both of whom send David messages of peace upon hearing of his victories (2 Sam. 8:9). Israel's military victories convince the nation's foes to ask for peace (2 Sam. 10:19).

One of King David's sons, Solomon (Shlomo), succeeds him. Solomon begins his reign by eliminating his internal enemies and neutralizing his external ones. Egypt is a powerful and menacing neighbor, but Solomon makes it a tacit ally by marrying the daughter of Pharaoh (1 Kings 3:1). During his reign, Israel enjoys peace and tranquility (1 Kings 5:4–5). King Hiram, who had offered peace to David because of his victories, seeks to maintain peace with Solomon upon hearing his wisdom. After securing peace with Egypt, Solomon establishes an alliance with Lebanon (1 Kings 5:26). Solomon is admired and respected for his wisdom (1 Kings 10:24), but he has a human weakness: his love for women, especially foreign ones. As he grows older, Solomon drifts away from the Sinai covenant under the influence of his foreign wives. The eleventh chapter of the first book of Kings relates that King Solomon practiced idolatry at the end of his life and that, as a result, God "awoke" Israel's old enemies: Hadad the Edomite (who, after his surrender to King David, fled to Egypt and became Pharaoh's protégé and brother-in-law); Rezon son of Eliada (who, after his defeat by King David, fled to Damascus); and Jeroboam (Yarovam) son of Nebat (who became a Hebrew refugee in Egypt after King Solomon tried to eliminate him upon hearing the prophecy of Ahijah the Shilonite that Jeroboam would inherit his kingdom).

One of King Solomon's sons, Rehoboam (Rehavam), succeeds him. Rehoboam's contempt for the kingdom's elder advisors, as well as his arrogance toward the people, precipitates the secession of ten of the kingdom's twelve tribes—thus confirming the prophecy of Ahijah the Shilonite that Solomon's kingdom shall be divided upon his death and that Jeroboam, Solomon's nemesis, will reign over ten of the twelve tribes. As Jeroboam is anointed king of Israel in the north, Rehoboam reigns over only two tribes: Judah and Benjamin in the south. Since Jerusalem was the center of priesthood and of religious worship, Jeroboam institutes different religious practices in the Kingdom of Israel to establish that subjects of the Northern Kingdom should not look to Jerusalem for spiritual sustenance. Jeroboam's new practices, however, are clearly idolatrous. Consequently, Ahijah the Shilonite prophesizes that Jeroboam's son, Abijah (Aviya), shall die and that "the Lord will strike Israel until it sways like a reed in water. He will uproot Israel from this good land that He gave to their fathers, and will scatter them beyond the Euphrates, because they have provoked the Lord by the sacred posts that they have made for themselves" (1 Kings 14:15). Meanwhile, the reigns of Rehoboam and Jeroboam are marred by civil war between the two Hebrew kingdoms.

The Southern Kingdom of Judah also sinks into idolatry and misbehavior (1 Kings 14:24). Five years after Rehoboam's anointment, Egypt attacks the Kingdom of Judah and pillages the Jerusalem Temple.

Rehoboam's son Abijam (Aviyam) succeeds him and "continue[s] in all the sins that his father before him had committed" (1 Kings 15:3). Abijam's son and successor, Asa, corrects his father's and grandfather's misdeeds (1 Kings 15:11). While the civil war between the kingdoms of Israel and Judah continues, King Asa builds a diplomatic and military alliance with the Kingdom of Aram (today's Syria).

Unlike the Kingdom of Judah, the Kingdom of Israel does not enjoy a period of moral restoration. Jeroboam's successors (Nadab, Baasha, Elah, Zimri, Omri, Ahab) all follow his evil ways, despising the divine commandments. Omri, however, "did worse" than his predecessors, according to the first book of Kings (1 Kings 16:25). Ahab, for his part, marries a woman from the Sidonites, a Canaanite people that worship Ashtoreth as their tutelary goddess as well as their sun-god Baal, from whom their king is named. What is more, after Ahab's marriage to Jezebel he openly practices idolatry, building altars to Baal and prostrating himself before the idol of Baal. Indeed, "Ahab did more to vex the Lord, the God of Israel, than all the kings of Israel who preceded him" (1 Kings 16:33).

In biblical times, the main opposition to the kings' misuse of their power came from the prophets. Having crossed a limit by marrying an idolatrous woman and adopting her cult, Ahab arouses the personal ire and public outcry of Elijah (Eliahu) the prophet. Elijah predicts that the Kingdom of Israel shall suffer from drought, and his prediction materializes. Rightly seeing the prophets of Israel as her fiercest opponents, Ahab's foreign wife Jezebel first persecutes and then executes them. Instead of admitting that the kingdom's troubles are the result of his own misdeeds, Ahab blames Elijah (and Jezebel tries to kill him). Elijah is an irritant to Ahab precisely because he has an excellent point: Israel has to decide whether or not the nation believes in God; there is no halfway position. "How long will you keep hopping between two opinions?" Elijah asks the people on Mount Carmel. "If the Lord is God, follow Him; and if Baal, follow him!" (1 Kings 18:21).

While the people are impressed by Elijah's straightforward argument, King Ahab is not. He persists in his ways, and disaster ensues. A coalition of thirty-two warlords led by King Ben-hadad of Aram besieges—and nearly destroys—the Kingdom of Israel. In the subsequent diplomatic negotiations, Ahab's indecisiveness and lack of resolve are fully exposed. First, King Ben-hadad makes demands, which Ahab accepts without even negotiating. Then, realizing that he is dealing with a weak leader, Ben-hadad insists on new conditions for stopping the war against Israel. At this point, Ahab realizes he is being extorted and asks the "elders of the land" for advice (1 Kings 20:7). While their answer is clear—do not give in—Ahab continues to demonstrate the very behavior Elijah denounced him for on Mount Carmel: oscillating between two incompatible positions. On the one hand, Ahab rejects Ben-hadad's second, abusive demands. On the other hand, he announces this rejection in conciliatory and apologetic terms, adding that he is still willing to accept the original demands and conditions. Ahab's eagerness to compromise emboldens Ben-hadad's confidence and bellicosity. Realizing he is dealing with a coward, Ben-hadad decides to resume war.

Yet there is a reversal: Ahab's forces defeat the enemy, creating a de facto peace. Vanquished, Ben-hadad now asks for Ahab's mercy. Instead of recognizing Ben-hadad as an enemy vanquished thanks to divine intervention, however, Ahab calls him "my brother" and signs a peace agreement with him. An unidentified prophet sternly condemns this act, warning the king, "Because you have set free the man whom I doomed, your life shall be forfeit for his life and your people for his people" (1 Kings 20:42).

This sentence, however, is suspended for three years, because of Ahab's partial repentance (1 Kings 21:29). Emboldened by the respite,

Ahab decides to renew the war against the King of Aram after "remembering" that Aram controls Ramoth and that Ramoth "is ours" (1 Kings 22:3). This time, Ahab prepares for war carefully. He works to build a coalition with the Kingdom of Judah, explaining to King Jehoshaphat of Judah that the four hundred prophets he has now gathered for counsel all say that God approves of this venture. Even though Jehoshaphat initially agrees to join forces with Israel, in his opinion the complete unanimity among the four hundred prophets is suspect, too good to be true. Jehoshaphat asks if there isn't a minority opinion among the prophets of Israel. Ahab admits there is one opponent in his rubber-stamp parliament: Micaiah (Mikhayahu) the prophet. "I hate him," Ahab confesses candidly (1 Kings 22:8). To make sure he is not being dragged into a doomed adventure, Jehoshaphat insists on hearing the lonely opposition leader. Micaiah is frank indeed: he declares that Ahab's four hundred prophets are lying and that Israel is like a sheep without a shepherd (1 Kings 22:17). Ahab throws Micaiah into jail and decides, together with Jehoshaphat, to ignore him. Micaiah, of course, turns out to be right. Ahab is killed in battle, and his blood-stained chariot is licked by dogs before being washed up in a pool used by harlots.

Ahab's son Ahazya briefly reigns over further decay and trouble. Moab rebels against Israel, and King Ahazia suffers from illness. Praying to God for his recovery does not occur to him; instead he instructs his advisors to ask Baal-zebub (Baal-zevuv), a god from a foreign pantheon, whether his is a curable disease. Elijah the prophet then meets and scolds Ahazia's advisors thus: "Is there no God in Israel that you go to inquire of Baal-zebub, the god of Ekron? Assuredly, thus said the Lord: You shall not rise from the bed you are lying on, but you shall die" (2 Kings 1:3–4). Ahazia ends up dying tragically, just as Elijah had prophesized. Since Ahazia is childless, his brother Joram (Yoram) succeeds him. The kingdoms of Israel and Judah conclude a military alliance against King Hazael of Aram, which again fails to deliver victory.

Appeasement and Resistance

To Elisha, a prophet who appears in the second book of Kings, the cause of military defeat is clear: like the kings of Israel, the kings of Judah have drifted away from the Sinai covenant, and thus the military alliance between two wrongdoers unsurprisingly brings disaster upon both. Elisha calls for a revolt by anointing Jehu (Yehu) as the tenth king of the Northern Kingdom of Israel, with the explicit mandate of eradicating Ahab's legacy and killing his descendants. Aware of the coming danger, Joram asks Jehu if the clash can be avoided; is peace possible? Jehu's straightforward reply leaves no room for negotiation: "How can all be well as long as your mother Jezebel carries on her countless harlotries and sorceries?" (2 Kings 9:22).

Jehu kills both Joram and Ahaziah. He also fulfills his mission of eradicating Ahab's legacy by killing his wife Jezebel as well as his seventy sons. Jehu then extends his mandate to Ahaziah's family, slaying his forty-two brothers. From there he strategizes to obliterate the cult of Baal in Israel. He deceives the Baal worshipers by pretending that he wishes to extend the cult practices Ahab initiated; all the Baal worshipers gather in one place, assuming their cult is about to be adopted as the kingdom's official religion. Jehu has them all massacred at once and burns down their places of worship. Jehu's zeal, however, is more military than religious. He does not remove the golden calves Jeroboam built for worship in the towns of Bethel and Dan (2 Kings 10:31). Because idolatry is not eradicated, "the Lord began to reduce Israel; and Hazael harassed them throughout the territory of Israel" (2 Kings 10:32).

After Jehu dies, power struggles and political intrigues ensue. In the Kingdom of Judah, Ahaziah's widow Athaliah seizes power and ruthlessly eliminates her enemies. Jehoiada the priest overthrows and kills her to install King Jehoash in her stead. For his part, Jehoash undertakes a policy of moral regeneration in the Kingdom of Judah.

He eliminates the worship of Baal. He also puts the Temple's finances in order, by forbidding the priests to take the Temple's money for themselves and initially instructing them to allocate the funds for repairs and proper upkeep.

Jehoash's foreign policy, however, is one of appeasement. When King Hazael of Aram tries to besiege Jerusalem, King Jehoash gives him the Temple's treasures, and this works: Hazael does relinquish the conquest. However, Yehoash's interference with the Temple's finances and subsequent use of the Temple's resources for foreign policy purposes creates enemies who eventually murder him.

His son Amaziah succeeds him (2 Kings 14:1). Even when he eliminates his father's murderers, Amaziah spares their descendants out of respect for the Torah's injunction not to kill children for the crime of their parents. Amaziah also scores military victories, which contrast with the setbacks and humiliations encountered by the Kingdom of Israel, where Jehu's revolution is not followed by the moral restorations undertaken by Jehoash and Amaziah in Judah. Jehu's son Jehoahaz (Yehoahaz) replaces his father, but only to do evil (2 Kings 13:2). Hazael, the king of Aram, conquers and subdues Israel (2 Kings 13:3).

The two books of Kings state more than once that the Kingdom of Judah lived by higher moral and religious standards than the Kingdom of Israel. Thus Israel suffers from foreign domination and exile. While foreign occupation first occurs under King Jehoahaz, deportation and exile begin under King Hoshea (2 Kings 17:23). The king of Assyria (Ashur) deports the Hebrews to Babylon and colonizes their land with his own subjects.

The new king of Judah, Hezekiah, is faithful to the legacy of King David (2 Kings 18:5–7). Hezekiah's first military and foreign policy acts are to fight against the mighty king of Assyria (by now the master of Israel) in the north and to expel the Philistines in the south. But while his military campaign against the Philistines is successful, the one against the king of Assyria is not. The mighty conqueror who

succeeded in subjugating Israel manages to also subdue the forti-
fied cities of Judah. Capitulating, Hezekiah is forced to pay huge war
reparations financed by the Temple's treasury. This, though, does not
quite satiate his conquerer's thirst.

The king of Assyria prepares both militarily and psychologically for
his planned capture of Jerusalem. He tries to convince King Hezekiah
that he stands no chance of overcoming the mighty king of Assyria:
Hezekiah should be realistic. He publicly questions the sanity of Hezekiah's faith when power and strength are objectively on Assyria's side
(2 Kings 18:19–20). Then he tries to convince the people of Judah to
face reality (2 Kings 18:29–33). Hezekiah, however, refuses to budge —
and he eventually achieves victory.

Hezekiah's son Manasseh (Menashe) brings ruin upon Judah (2 Kings
21:2). The new king introduces idolatrous and pagan rites throughout
the Judean kingdom, including in the Jerusalem Temple. Manasseh's
grandson Josiah (Yoshiyahu) tries to rectify his grandfather's (and
father's) legacy by eradicating idolatrous practices and foreign cults,
shuttering the brothels operating next to the Temple, and destroying
alien places of worship (2 Kings 23:7). The Hebrews have become
so remote from the practice of their own religion that Josiah has to
summon them to keep Passover (2 Kings 23:21). Even though "there
was no king like him before who turned back to the Lord with all his
heart and soul and might, in full accord with the Teaching of Moses"
(2 Kings 23:25), God's pledge to wipe out Jerusalem is irrevocable (2
Kings 23:26–27). Josiah's only consolation is to die before the destruction of his kingdom: "Your eyes shall not see all the disaster which I
will bring upon this place" (2 Kings 22:20). Josiah's death, however, is
tragic: Pharoah Neco (Paronekho), the king of Egypt, kills him in battle.

After killing Josiah, Pharoah Neco subdues the Kingdom of Judah
to his rule. He nominates the new king of Judah (and even changes his
name from Eliakim to Jehoiakim) and levies a tax from the defeated
kingdom. With the balance of power between Egypt and Babylon

tilting toward the latter, Jehoiakim switches allegiance to Babylon's King Nebuchadnezzar. The Kingdom of Judah effectively becomes a Babylonian colony. When Jehoiakim tries to revolt, his army and regime are crushed (2 Kings 24:2).

The demise of Judah is gradual, however. It is only under the reign of Jehoiakim's son Jehoiachin that the king and his people are expelled from their land and exiled to Babylon. Nebuchadnezzar nominates Mattaniah (renamed Zedekiah) to reign over his new Judean colony; Zedekiah, however, rebels against Nebuchadnezzar. The result is Judah's final and tragic *coup de grâce*: Nebuchadnezzar burns down the Temple and Jerusalem as a whole, exiles the Jews from their land, and puts an end to the Kingdom of Judah. Zedekiah, the last king of Judah, is publicly humiliated before being savagely killed. In his stead, Nebuchadnezzar nominates a governor, Gedaliah (Gedalyahu), to administer what is left of the former Judean kingdom. But Gedaliah is himself murdered, and with his death the last remnant of Jewish sovereignty vanishes.

Jeremiah: Prophet of Political Realism?

The prophet Jeremiah (Yirmeyahu) witnesses Judah's decline, defeat, and exile. His prophecy begins under King Amon, after the demise of Judah has been proclaimed, and ends under King Zedekiah, with the destruction of the First Temple and the Babylonian exile.

From the outset, Jeremiah's message is meant to be universal, for he is ordained to be "a prophet concerning the nations" (Jer. 1:5). Echoing the book of Judges (Judg. 10:14), Jeremiah sarcastically enjoins Israel to take responsibility for the nation's betrayal of the Sinai covenant: "And where are those gods you made for yourself? Let them arise and save you, if they can, in your hour of calamity" (Jer. 2:28). Israel needs to repent not only for the sake of the nation, but also for the sake of humanity. Indeed, God will never annul the alliance with Israel, and humanity will recognize God only through Israel. In other words, for the world to have faith, Israel must be faithful (Jer. 4:1–2).

The cause of the coming danger and doom is clear: Israel is going to be punished for forsaking the Sinai covenant. But Jeremiah expresses a more specific complaint about the hypocrisy, vanity, and sophism of the people's self-appointed leaders: "From the smallest to the greatest, they are all greedy for gain; priest and prophet alike, they all act falsely. They offer healing offhand for the wounds of My people, saying 'all is well, all is well' when nothing is well" (Jer. 6:13–14). The people's wicked rulers try to conceal their moral bankruptcy by falsely promising peace, but the peace they pledge is currently unreachable because of the people's immorality and unfaithfulness to the Sinai covenant. This is why "we hoped for good fortune, but no happiness came; for a time of relief—instead there is terror!" (Jer. 8:15).

Jeremiah is incensed by Israel's unfaithfulness to its own legacy and identity. Why is the nation so eager to forgo its heritage and its mission? "Can the Cushite [African] change his skin, or the leopard his spots?" (Jer. 13:23). Why, for instance, does Israel desecrate the Sabbath, which is both a blessing and a cornerstone of Jewish faith and identity? (Jer. 17:24–27). Jeremiah is reviled, derided, and targeted (Pashhur the High Priest harasses him) for speaking the truth. Falsehood has become so widespread that truth is offensive. Jeremiah's prophecy is both bleak and accusatory: Judah's destruction and exile to Babylon is inevitable, because Judah's sins are unforgivable (Jer. 21:14). When King Zedekiah of Judah inquires about his chances of overcoming Nebuchadnezzar, Jeremiah replies that Judah is doomed (Jer. 21:5).

Echoing the book of Deuteronomy (Deut. 29:22–24), Jeremiah explains that if Israel has any doubts about the reasons for its demise, the rest of the world does not. The nations understand that the people of God is being smitten and scattered because of its unfaithfulness to the Sinai covenant, and they shall remind Israel of this unfaithfulness (Jer. 22:8–9). Jeremiah also confirms Deuteronomy's promise that the scattered people of Israel will be despised and derided by the nations (Jer. 24:9) and that those who repent will eventually come back to the Promised Land (Jer. 24:6–7).

Jeremiah's call to capitulate to the Babylonian king Nebuchadnezzar and accept his rule (Jer. 27:6–11) runs counter to the other prophets' appeals for struggle and resistance. Is Jeremiah a realist or a doomsayer? Does he care for his people's interests, or is he a traitor? What makes him a better judge of the international reality than others?

Jeremiah asserts that resistance to Babylon is pointless. Yes, in general the Jews should fight for their freedom, but currently they are unworthy of that freedom. Because the Jews did not obey the commandment of freeing their slaves after seven years, they themselves will be enslaved by Babylon and get a taste of their own medicine (Jer. 34:8–20). The Jews are powerful when God is on their side and powerless when God wishes to make them pay for their misdeeds. Since God has decided to punish Judah, Jeremiah declares, rebelling against Babylon would be tantamount to rebelling against God. It would be militarily disastrous and religiously blasphemous.

Not only does Jeremiah advocate surrender to Nebuchadnezzar, he also enjoins the Jewish Diaspora of Babylon to settle there and not try to return to the Land of Israel. While bowing to foreign rule both in Jerusalem and in Babylon seems defeatist and unpatriotic, Jeremiah explains that Israel's current servitude is part of a divine decree; therefore, it should be accepted until the decree is repealed (Jer. 29:10). Eventually, however, "I will bring them in from the northland, gather them from the ends of the earth. . . . He who scattered Israel will gather them" (Jer. 31:7–9).

The people do not listen to Jeremiah, his prophecy materializes, and Nebuchadnezzar conquers Jerusalem in the ninth year of Zedekiah's reign. Jerusalem is destroyed, and all of King Zedekiah's sons are murdered in front of him. Nebuchadnezzar burns down the Jerusalem

Temple and deports the Jews to Babylon. But this ordeal is temporary: "I will make an end to all the nations among which I have banished you, but I will not make an end of you! I will not leave you unpunished, but I will chastise you in measure" (Jer. 46:28). Hence must the exiled Jews remain resilient and hopeful.

Conclusion

King Saul was not merciless with Amalek, Israel's historical nemesis. His reign ended in disgrace. Under the reigns of David and Solomon, the peace enjoyed by the Kingdom of Israel was based on power and deterrence. After Solomon's death, the kingdom was divided between Israel in the north and Judah in the south. The two kingdoms had to resort to diplomacy for survival, and both oscillated between assertiveness and appeasement. In the biblical narrative, both strategies are legitimate so long as they are carried out by a king faithful to the Sinai covenant.

The books of Kings describe the Kingdom of Judah as living by higher moral and religious standards than the Kingdom of Israel, and therefore as enjoying a higher degree of independence. Yet eventually, the mightier Kingdom of Babylon would conquer and defeat both Jewish kingdoms. To Jeremiah the prophet, there was no doubt that the historical disaster to come was the inevitable result of the Jews' violation of the Sinai covenant.

Meanwhile, the nation on the brink of defeat faced a dilemma: would capitulation be an act of realism or of betrayal? In Jeremiah's view, realism, paradoxically, was an act of faith: kowtowing to reality meant accepting a divine decree. The people, however, did not listen to Jeremiah. Jerusalem was destroyed, and Israel exiled. Yet precisely because the Jews perceived their defeat as temporary, they remained resilient.

3. The Writings

There is a certain people, scattered and dispersed among the other peoples in all the provinces of your realm, whose laws are different from those of any other people.

ESTHER 3:8

Between Mercy and Revenge

The book of Ruth offers an optimistic glimpse into Israel's relations with the nations. A Jewish couple — Elimelech and Naomi — and their two sons leave the famine-stricken Kingdom of Judah for the Kingdom of Moab. The two sons marry Moabite women. All three men (Elimelech and his sons) die unexpectedly, leaving three childless widows. Naomi decides to head back home, but one of her daughters-in-law, Ruth, insists on following her both physically and spiritually: "Wherever you go, I will go. . . . Your people shall be my people, and your God my God" (Ruth 1:16).

The intermarriage with Moabite women as well as Ruth's conversion to Judaism are incompatible with Jewish law (Deut. 23:4). Moabites and Ammonites are forbidden to become Jewish through conversion, because they both tried to curse Israel through Balaam and attempted to doom Jewish survival through intermarriage. Still, after Ruth settles in the Kingdom of Judah, she marries Boaz the Judean. According to the Babylonian Talmud, Tractate *Yevamot* 76b, the prohibition on conversion and marriage only applies to Moabite and Ammonite males, not to females.

The relationship between Boaz the Judean and Ruth the Moabite is one of gentleness, tolerance, and compassion. Boaz is charitable to Ruth, letting her take food from his field although he knows she is a descendant from Israel's sworn enemies. Ruth herself is surprised by Boaz's generosity. Asked about it, Boaz answers that he admires and respects Ruth for having left her parents, her home, and her country to join another people without even knowing what to expect. Boaz treats Ruth with love because she decided to "take refuge under the wings of the God of Israel" (Ruth 2:12). Despite her Moabite background, Ruth is declared to have become like Israel's matriarchs Rachel and Leah (Ruth 4:11), and because Boaz redeemed Ruth, their great-grandson will be King David. Boaz himself is a descendant of Perez (Peretz), who was born from the redeeming of Tamar by her father-in-law Judah.

The book of Esther, by contrast, seems to convey the opposite message. Ruth's story is one of reconciliation between Israel and its ancient nemesis; Esther's story is one of confrontation with Israel's eternal foes. Both books describe a marriage between Jews and non-Jews, but in reverse circumstances. Ruth marries Boaz after embracing the Jewish faith. Esther marries King Ahasuerus (Ahashverosh) after hiding her Jewish identity.

From the moment King Ahasuerus selects Esther to become the new queen of Persia, her uncle Mordecai (Mordechai) makes good use of his new connection with the center of power. Wandering around the palace, Mordecai learns of a plot to murder the king and duly reports it via his newly appointed niece. As a result, Mordecai becomes known overnight as someone who saved the king.

After secretly conquering the center of power via his niece, Mordecai passively instigates a revolt against that very power. He promotes civil disobedience by refusing to bow to the newly appointed premier, Haman. Asked about the reason for his insubordination, Mordecai reveals what he had asked Esther to hide: he is Jewish and therefore bows only to God.

But why would Mordecai want to foment a Jewish revolt against the powerful and seemingly benevolent Persian government? Because that government has changed and can no longer be trusted. This change cannot be tolerated, since the very existence of the stateless and dispersed Jews is in the hands of their powerful ruler. The reader learns about this change in the third chapter of the book of Esther. Haman's promotion is a clear sign that the Jews are in danger. Haman is an Agagite, a descendant of King Agag, who ruled over the Amalekites, who come from Amalek, the archenemy of Israel. Amalek is also the irreconcilable enemy of Israel—there can be no compromise with him—because he is "undeterred by fear of God" (Deut. 25:18). Hence the Torah enjoins Israel to "blot out the memory of Amalek" (Deut. 25:19). Mordecai is merely fulfilling his duty through a sophisticated strategy.

Haman's reaction to Mordecai's insubordination proves that Mordecai was right. Haman is not content with punishing Mordecai; he wants to kill the Jews—all of them. This demonic hatred is precisely what Amalek is about. Amalek wants to erase the Jews from the face of the earth because the Jews are the witnesses of God and the depositories of the Bible's message to humanity. Mordecai's defiance is simply an excuse Haman deploys in his quest to eradicate a "certain people" whose laws "are different from those of any other people" (Esther 3:8). Haman convinces Ahasuerus to commit genocide against the Jewish people. The king signs the decree, and the instructions are clear: "To destroy, massacre, and exterminate all the Jews, young and old, children and women, on a single day" (Esther 3:13).

Luckily, Mordecai has foreseen the impending disaster and has a plan to stop the annihilation of his people. He asks Esther to use her influence over the king to persuade him to cancel the decree. There is a problem, however. The law states that whoever enters the king's inner palace without being summoned shall be put to death—which means that even Queen Esther herself is likely to die if she goes to the king without an invitation. On the other hand, if she doesn't do anything, she will survive but her people will perish. Upon Mordecai's insistence, she decides to risk her life. Mordecai even suggests that the purpose of Esther's marriage to King Ahasuerus was to save the Jewish people: "Who knows, perhaps you have attained to royal position for just such a crisis" (Esther 4:14).

Esther's gamble pays off: the king forgives her for trespassing his private domain and even offers her up to half his kingdom. Then the king, struck by insomnia, asks to be read the Book of Records. The book states, among other things, that Mordecai the Jew saved the king's life, although nothing was done to reward him.

At this point, the fate of the Jews takes a turn. Haman comes to the king to ask for permission to hang the very person the king now wishes to reward: Mordecai. But the king speaks first. Without mentioning Mordecai, the king asks Haman his advice about the best possible reward for a man the king wishes to thank. Wrongly assuming the king has him in mind, Haman suggests dressing the man in the king's clothes and having him ride the king's horse. Liking the idea, the king instructs Haman to grant the reward to Mordecai.

With this *coup de théâtre*, the Jews have won a battle but not the war. Esther hasn't spoken yet, and when the king asks her again for her request, this time in the presence of Haman, Mordecai's plan reaches its climax. The king learns that he has unknowingly ordered the murder of his wife and her people. Haman is hanged instead of Mordecai, and Mordecai assumes Haman's previous position of premier. The king, however, reveals he cannot revoke an order he has signed. The only way to save the Jews from annihilation is to publish another order allowing them to initiate a preemptive strike against their enemies.

The king's new order immediately changes the way the empire's subjects perceive and treat the Jews. The formerly reviled and vulnerable minority is now feared and respected by the Persians—to the point that many of them decide to convert to Judaism (Esther 8:17). Most crucially, thanks to the king's new order, the Jews are able to preempt their enemies with an early strike. Their strength is both physical and psychological. The Jews are outnumbered, and yet they are feared: "No one could withstand them, for the fear of them had fallen upon all the peoples" (Esther 9:2). Local governors switch allegiance from Haman's followers to Mordecai's once the Jews start gaining the upper hand. In this war, the Jews are merciless: all of Haman's descendants and followers are killed. Esther orders the hanging of Haman's ten sons. The Jews are now in power, but that power is not considered an end in itself; Mordecai uses it for "the good of his people" and "for the welfare of all his kindred" (Esther 10:3).

God is nominally absent from the book of Esther. Indeed, the very name "Esther" echoes the Hebrew word *astir*, used in Deuteronomy when God warns, "I will abandon them and hide [*astir* in Hebrew] My countenance from them" (Deut. 31:17). Despite the nominal absence of God, however, the book of Esther enjoys a special status in Rabbinic literature. The Babylonian Talmud (Tractate *Shabbat* 88a) claims that the Torah was accepted twice by the Jewish people: once at Mount Sinai and once in the time of Esther. The Jerusalem Talmud states, "The Book of Esther and the Torah will never be abolished" (Tractate *Megillah* 1:5).

Legacy of the Court Jew

The book of Daniel relates historical events already mentioned in the second book of Kings: Nebuchadnezzar's destruction of the First Temple and the Kingdom of Judah, and the Jews' exile to Babylon. Daniel, one of four Judean captives selected by Nebuchadnezzar to serve in his court, becomes an advisor to the Babylonian king. His wisdom is greatly appreciated by his new master, even as Daniel makes a point of reminding himself and his gentile entourage that he is Jewish, starting with his refusal to eat nonkosher food.

Like Joseph, Daniel is a court Jew who knows how to interpret dreams and becomes the king's favorite advisor; also like Joseph, when he is asked to interpret dreams, Daniel brings God into the king's godless world. When Pharaoh tells Joseph he has heard of his interpretive ability, Joseph answers, "Not I! God will see to Pharaoh's welfare" (Gen. 41:16). Likewise, Daniel declares to Nebuchadnezzar, "There is a God in heaven who reveals mysteries" (Dan. 2:28). After Daniel successfully explains the king's dream, the latter declares, "Your God must be the God of gods, and the Lord of kings" (Dan. 2:47). Thanks to his skills, Daniel is appointed governor of Babylon, just as Joseph had become viceroy of Egypt.

Despite Nebuchadnezzar's recognition that "your God must be the God of gods, and the Lord of kings," he still worships man-made gods and orders his subjects to follow suit. The Jews refuse to bow to the king's god, just as Mordecai refused to bow to Haman. When threatened with cruel death, the Jews remain adamant. Their faithfulness to God is proved by their answer to the king: We believe that God will save us from you; but even if God does not, we still believe in God and put our faith before our lives. Furious, the king of Babylon orders the three leaders of the Jewish rebellion, Hananiah (or Shadrach), Mishael (or Meshach), and Azariah (or Abed-nego), to be thrown into a furnace. Because they come out intact, the king once again concedes: "Blessed be the God of Shadrach, Meshach, and Abed-nego, who sent His angel to save His servants who, trusting in Him, flouted the king's decree at the risk of their lives rather than serve or worship any god but their own God" (Dan. 3:28).

By proclaiming the existence of God and risking their lives for their faith—with miraculous results—Daniel, Hananiah, Mishael, and Azariah have changed the king's thinking. He now recognizes there is a force above him. Instead of the Jews bowing to his god, the king bows to the God of the Jews. He also forbids his subjects to speak against "the God of Shadrach, Meshach, and Abed-nego."

And yet, the king's conversion is not wholehearted. He has another dream, which Daniel interprets thus: The king's demise is near; it will be cruel and abrupt (Dan. 4:22). If the king wants to avoid this dreadful fate, he must repent by giving charity and being merciful to the poor (the text does not tell us whether the king followed Daniel's advice). The terrifying dream becomes true, as the king loses his throne in humiliation and in pain. This very pain, however, serves its purpose. Now that he has nothing to lose, the king wholeheartedly proclaims what he was thus far reluctantly willing to admit: "So now I, Nebuchadnezzar, praise, exalt, and glorify the King of Heaven, all of whose works are just and whose ways are right, and who is able to humble those who behave arrogantly" (Dan. 4:34).

While Nebuchadnezzar has come to fully recognize and internalize the supremacy of God, it seems that he did not share his rejection of idolatry with his son and successor, Belshazzar. King Belshazzar throws a party in which his concubines drink wine from the golden cups stolen from the Jerusalem Temple while "praising the gods of gold" (Dan. 5:4). A mysterious sign spoils the decadent party: a writing on the wall, which the king does not understand, but whose meaning he guesses and fears.

Belshazzar's clinging to idolatry is confirmed by his comment to Daniel: "I have heard about you that you have the spirit of the gods in you" (Dan. 5:14). In turn, the latter explains the meaning of the mysterious writing on the wall: God decided to make your father great, but that made him too proud, so God decided to put him down in order for him to become humble and realize who made him great in the first place. But you, Belshazzar, haven't learned anything from your father's experience, and you are guilty of pride. Indeed, you praise the "gods of gold." And so, the meaning of the mysterious sign

("Mene Mene Tekel Upharsin") is the following: God has decided to bring your kingdom to an end.

With Belshazzar's demise, Daniel becomes one of three governors to answer to the new king, Darius. Daniel's skills attract the favor of the king and the jealousy of his peers, who try to undermine him. Daniel, however, derives his strength from his candor. Because he is honest, his enemies cannot find good reason to accuse him of wrongdoing before the king. The only thing Daniel can be "accused" of is that he is Jewish. Thus the governors and ministers convince the king to issue an edict forbidding his subjects to revere any deity other than the king himself; then Daniel is "caught" praying to God, so reported to the king, and condemned to death. The death sentence is being thrown into the lions' den.

Like King Ahasuerus in the book of Esther, King Darius is bound by the edict he was maneuvered into signing. And like Ahasuerus, he wishes he did not have to implement his own edict. For Darius, as opposed to Belshazzar, fears God. He tells Daniel, "Your God, whom you serve so regularly, will deliver you" (Dan. 6:17). Darius fasts all night, putting his trust in God. In the morning, he discovers that Daniel has emerged unscathed from the lions' den, and he decides to give Daniel's accusers a taste of their own medicine by throwing them (together with their families) to the lions. Daniel prevails not only because he survived the lions, but also—indeed mostly—because Darius sends the following declaration to his subjects: "I have hereby given an order that throughout my royal domain men must tremble in fear before the God of Daniel, for He is the living God who endures forever; His kingdom is indestructible, and His dominion is to the end of time" (Dan. 6:27).

After fulfilling his mission, Daniel sets out his vision. He sees four kingdoms rising and falling, and eventually adopting faith in God. The fourth kingdom will be different; it will stretch its power and impose its rule over other nations. It will reach the height of its might and then crumble. From this empire's demise will emerge nations that shall recognize the God of Israel. While the book of Daniel does not specify these four empires, Rashi, a medieval French rabbi known for his comprehensive interpretation of the Bible and Talmud, identifies them as Babylon, Persia, Greece, and Rome.

Daniel thinks about the meaning of history, and he prays to bring Israel's wanderings and suffering to an end. Though the text does not say so explicitly, the reader is left with a feeling that the Jews have paid a price for their inequities, that they have fulfilled their mission in exile, and that the time has come for them to return to their forsaken land.

The Return to Zion

The new king of Persia, Cyrus, allows the Jews to return to their land and to rebuild their temple. The Jews' return, however, is met by local opposition. The people who now inhabit the Land of Israel have no objection per se to the return of some Jews, but they object to the restoration of the Jewish kingdom. By saying "Let us build with you, since we too worship your God" (Ezra 4:2), the land's new inhabitants mean that they too claim property over the land and that the rebuilt kingdom should not be exclusively Jewish. Yet the Jews are determined to rebuild their country.

Faced with such determination, the land's inhabitants try to undermine the rebuilding of the Jerusalem Temple and the larger Jewish kingdom through terror and propaganda: "The people of the land undermined the resolve of the people of Judah, and made them afraid to build. They bribed ministers in order to thwart their plans" (Ezra 4:4–5). The local leaders send a smear letter to the new Persian king, Artaxerxes, accusing the Jews of building their country in order to rebel against Persia and spread trouble throughout the empire. Since the Jews rebelled in the past, the letter states, they will rebel again in the future. The strategy succeeds: King Artaxerxes orders a halt to the rebuilding work on the Temple. Hence the paradox of Persia's attitude toward the Jews: the king is caught between his formal commitment to the Jews and the unrest that this commitment produces within the empire. Eventually, the Jews decide to bypass the limitations imposed by the local Persian administration and proceed with rebuilding their Temple. The Jews' opponents duly report this supposedly unauthorized construction to Darius, who has now assumed the Persian throne. Darius confronts the Jews, and they reply that the previous king, Cyrus, had authorized the construction. Challenged by the Jews to search his archives, King Darius does so, finds Cyrus's decision, relents, and allows the Jews to pursue the building of their Temple.

The construction of the Second Temple symbolizes the end of the Babylonian exile, but it does not mark the full restoration of Jewish sovereignty. On balance, the newly reborn Jewish kingdom is in effect a vassal of the Persian Empire. After all, it is the king of Persia who sanctions the rebuilding of the Jerusalem Temple.

Conclusion

The Writings offer a glimpse into Jewish diplomacy in exile. Esther and Mordecai conquer the center of power and save their people from annihilation thanks to a combination of courage, ruthlessness, and a well-conceived strategy. Because Jews were at the mercy of foreign rulers in exile, their lives were imperiled whenever those rulers were advised by the Jews' sworn enemies. Under regimes that were not based on the rule of law, the Jews had to build political power discreetly and use it with daring when danger came.

The book of Daniel describes a different policy: one of persuasion and trust. Daniel's unwavering devotion to his faith and his people while advising the king of Babylon has a strong impact on how the king perceives and treats the Jews.

In a way, the books of Esther and of Daniel offer two different approaches to Jewish diplomacy in exile. The former is about "hard power," the latter about "soft power." Esther doesn't rely on miracles; Daniel does.

Daniel also offers a historical vision of the rise and decline of empires. The Jews' misfortunes are not permanent, because neither are their mighty rulers—a lesson confirmed by the book of Ezra. Ezra and Nehemiah oversee the Jews' return to Zion. The king of Persia approves the rebuilding of the Jerusalem Temple, but the land's inhabitants maneuver to make its reconstruction illegal, because they also feel entitled to the land. Despite a decree issued by the world's greatest power, the Jews need to battle yet again for their contested rights. Interestingly, a similar scenario shall repeat itself some twenty-five hundred years later with the British Empire's publication of the Balfour Declaration.

PART 2. Jewish Diplomacy from Antiquity to Modernity

4. From Kingdom to Serfdom

When the Samaritans had obtained permission from Alexander to destroy the Temple in Jerusalem, the High Priest Simon the Just, arrayed in his pontifical garments and followed by a number of distinguished Jews, went out to meet the conqueror and joined him at Antipatris, on the northern border. At the sight of Simon, Alexander fell prostrate at his feet and explained to his astonished companions that the image of the Jewish High Priest was always with him in battle, fighting for him and leading him to victory.

BABYLONIAN TALMUD, Tractate *Yoma* 69a

Judea or Palestine?

Biblical narrative and historiography are distinct fields but not mutually exclusive ones, due to the historical value of some of the Bible's passages. In Jewish history, facts and narratives are often intertwined. The various and contentious names of the Land of Israel are a case in point.

With the Israelites' conquest of the land of Canaan in the thirteenth century BCE, the Philistines became the fiercest enemies of the conquering nation. Although the Philistines eventually vanished like most ancient people, their name had many reincarnations thanks to the Latin language. In 135 CE, after the Romans crushed the Bar Kokhba revolt,[1] what used to be the Kingdom of Judah became the province of Judea under Roman rule. The Latin name Iudæa, meaning Judea, was derived from the Hebrew name Yehuda (Judah). The Romans, however, renamed Judea "Palæstina" to humiliate the defeated Jews. The Romans' choice of the word "Palæstina" reflected their knowledge that the Philistines were the Jews' historical enemies and that the land of the Philistines was called "Philistia."

In the nineteenth century, British writers would often refer to the Arabs of Palestine as Philistines. The Arabic word for Palestine is Filasṭīn (Arabic has no "P"), which derives from the Latin Palæstina. Most Latin-derived languages adopted a version of the word Palæstina (most commonly, Palestine). In Norwegian, by contrast, the country never ceased to be called Jødeland (the Jews' land).[2]

Military and Diplomatic Alliances of the Israelite Kingdoms

King David, who reigned around 1000 BCE, was the first Israelite leader to successfully subdue the Philistines. By combining military victories with diplomatic alliances and taking advantage of Egypt's declining power, he significantly expanded Israel's borders.

King Solomon, who reigned around 970 BCE, chose to relinquish some of his father's territorial conquests in the north because of their financial cost. Solomon withdrew from Damascus and transferred some territories to King Hiram of Tyre, who became a strong ally. Together with King Hiram, King Solomon ran a commercial fleet that traveled between the Gulf of Aqaba and eastern Africa. He sealed a de facto alliance with his southern neighbor, Egypt, by marrying Pharaoh's daughter. His legendary polygamy was also a useful tool for diplomatic alliances.[3]

After the split of Solomon's kingdom and the Assyrian invasion of northern Israel in 850 BCE, the Kingdom of Judah tried to preserve

---

Map 1. The kingdom of David and Solomon, 1000–925 BCE. Reproduced by arrangement with Taylor & Francis from Martin Gilbert, *Atlas Jewish History*, 2nd ed. (1993), published by William Morrow and Company, Inc. © Martin Gilbert.

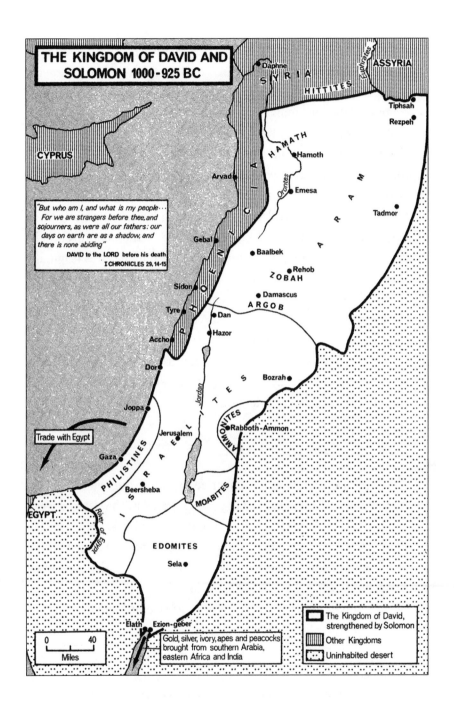

THE KINGDOM OF DAVID AND SOLOMON 1000-925 BC

ASSYRIA

Daphne

SYRIA

HITTITES

Euphrates

Tiphsah

Rezpeh

HAMATH

CYPRUS

Hamoth

Orontes

Arvad

Emesa

A R A M

Tadmor

"But who am I, and what is my people...
For we are strangers before thee, and
sojourners, as were all our fathers: our
days on earth are as a shadow, and
there is none abiding"
DAVID to the LORD before his death
I CHRONICLES 29, 14-15

Gebal

Baalbek

Z O B A H

Rehob

P H O E N I C I A

Sidon

Damascus

Tyre

A R G O B

Dan

Accho

Hazor

Dor

J E B U S I T E S

Jordan

Bozrah

Joppa

A M M O N I T E S

Trade with Egypt

Jerusalem

Rabboth-Ammon

Gaza

P H I L I S T I N E S

I S R A E L

Beersheba

MOABITES

EGYPT

River of Egypt

E D O M I T E S

Sela

0   40
Miles

Elath   Ezion-geber

Gold, silver, ivory, apes and peacocks
brought from southern Arabia,
eastern Africa and India

☐ The Kingdom of David,
   strengthened by Solomon

▨ Other Kingdoms

⋰ Uninhabited desert

its independence through diplomatic alliances, including with the declining Kingdom of Egypt.

The Babylonian Empire first overcame its Assyrian rival and then conquered the Kingdom of Judah, burning down the Jerusalem Temple in 586–587 BCE. In 539 BCE Babylon was itself defeated by the Persian king Cyrus, who allowed the Jews of his empire to resettle their forsaken country and rebuild their Temple. The Jews' return under Cyrus was partial and gradual. The first wave of Jewish return in 538 BCE was opposed by the land's subsequent inhabitants, among them Samaritans, Edomites, and Arabs, but Jewish settlements eventually prospered. The total population of the "New Judea" was originally small, about sixty thousand, but it kept growing. The Jews progressively settled the Galilee, Transjordan, and the coastal plain.

The Jews' fortunes changed with Alexander's eastern conquests in 332 BCE. Alexander the Great may have been revered by Jewish tradition (traditionally, "Alexander" has been the only non-Jewish name that Jewish parents may choose for their newborn sons), but Greek rule also brought political unrest.

Diplomacy under Foreign Empires

The Greeks were conquerors who tried to impose their culture. Some Jews embraced hellenization, but others rejected it. The clash between "hellenizers" and traditional Jews climaxed with King Antiochus Epiphanes. In 175 BCE, determined to accelerate the hellenization of his empire and counting on the cooperation of hellenized Jews, Antiochus replaced Jerusalem's orthodox High Priest with a hellenizer called Jason. Jason renamed Jerusalem "Antiochus" and built a gym-

---

Map 2. The destruction of Jewish independence, 722–586 BCE. Reproduced by arrangement with Taylor & Francis from Martin Gilbert, *Atlas Jewish History*, 2nd ed. (1993), published by William Morrow and Company, Inc. © Martin Gilbert.

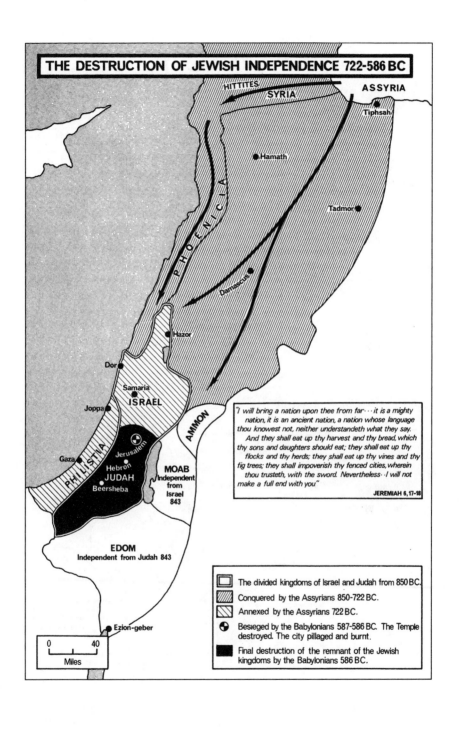

THE DESTRUCTION OF JEWISH INDEPENDENCE 722-586 BC

HITTITES
SYRIA
ASSYRIA
Tiphsah
Hamath
Tadmor
PHOENICIA
Damascus
Hazor
Dor
Samaria
ISRAEL
Joppa
AMMON

"I will bring a nation upon thee from far··· it is a mighty
nation, it is an ancient nation, a nation whose language
thou knowest not, neither understandeth what they say.
And they shall eat up thy harvest and thy bread, which
thy sons and daughters should eat; they shall eat up thy
flocks and thy herds; they shall eat up thy vines and thy
fig trees; they shall impoverish thy fenced cities, wherein
thou trusteth, with the sword. Nevertheless··· I will not
make a full end with you"

JEREMIAH 6, 17-18

Gaza
PHILISTIA
Jerusalem
Hebron
JUDAH
Beersheba

MOAB
Independent
from
Israel
843

EDOM
Independent from Judah 843

Ezion-geber

0   40
Miles

☐ The divided kingdoms of Israel and Judah from 850 BC.

▨ Conquered by the Assyrians 850-722 BC.

▨ Annexed by the Assyrians 722 BC.

✪ Besieged by the Babylonians 587-586 BC. The Temple
destroyed. The city pillaged and burnt.

■ Final destruction of the remnant of the Jewish
kingdoms by the Babylonians 586 BC.

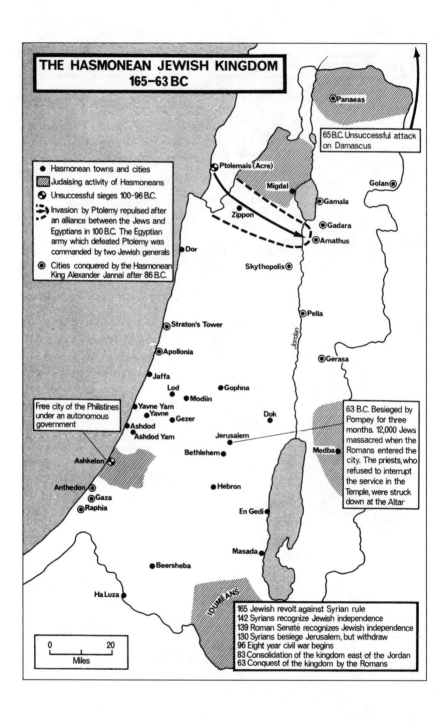

THE HASMONEAN JEWISH KINGDOM
165–63 BC

⊙Panaeas

65 B.C. Unsuccessful attack on Damascus

● Hasmonean towns and cities

▨ Judaising activity of Hasmoneans

✛ Unsuccessful sieges 100-96 B.C.

⇢ Invasion by Ptolemy repulsed after an alliance between the Jews and Egyptians in 100 B.C. The Egyptian army which defeated Ptolemy was commanded by two Jewish generals

⊙ Cities conquered by the Hasmonean King Alexander Jannai after 86 B.C.

Ptolemais (Acre)

Migdal

Golan⊙

⊙Gamala

Zippon

⊙Gadara

⊙Amathus

●Dor

Skythopolis⊙

⊙Pella

⊙Straton's Tower

Jordan

⊙Apollonia

⊙Gerasa

●Jaffa

Lod ●Gophna

●Modiin

Free city of the Philistines under an autonomous government

●Yavne Yam
●Yavne ●Gezer

Dok●

⊙Ashdod

⊙Ashdod Yam

Jerusalem●

Bethlehem●

Medba⊙

63 B.C. Besieged by Pompey for three months. 12,000 Jews massacred when the Romans entered the city. The priests, who refused to interrupt the service in the Temple, were struck down at the Altar

Ashkelon⊙

●Hebron

Anthedon⊙

⊙Gaza

⊙Raphia

En Gedi●

Masada●

●Beersheba

Ha Luza●

IDUMEANS

165 Jewish revolt against Syrian rule
142 Syrians recognize Jewish independence
139 Roman Senate recognizes Jewish independence
130 Syrians besiege Jerusalem, but withdraw
96 Eight year civil war begins
83 Consolidation of the kingdom east of the Jordan
63 Conquest of the kingdom by the Romans

0   20
Miles

nasium next to the Temple; subsequently a huge acropolis was built in Jerusalem to physically dominate the Temple. Jason's successor, Menelaus, took the hellenization of the Jews even further. In 167 BCE he introduced a statue of Zeus, Greek god of the sky and thunder and king of all other gods, into the Temple—a provocation that would be the final blow triggering the revolt of the Maccabees.

The Jewish guerilla war against Greece lasted for more than two years (between 167 and 164 BCE) and culminated with the expulsion of the Greeks and their Jewish supporters from Jerusalem. Eventually, in 142 BCE, Greece formally recognized the full independence of Judea. After 440 years of subjugation to foreign empires, the Jewish state had recovered its independence.

The successful revolt of the Maccabees was followed by the establishment of the Hasmonean dynasty. The Hasmoneans, who ruled Judea between 140 and 37 BCE, led a nationalist counterrevolution. Yohanan Hyrcanus, who ruled Judea between 134 and 104 BCE, implemented a policy of territorial conquests and forced conversions.

His successor, Alexander Jannaeus, continued this policy. His nationalism, however, was opposed by the Pharisees, for whom religious observance was more important than territorial expansion. By the time Jannaeus died in 76 BCE, the Hasmonean kingdom had mostly recovered the political independence and territorial integrity that had been lost with the breakup of Solomon's kingdom.

Yet the renewed grandeur of the Jewish state was threatened from within and without. While political and religious disagreements between the Hasmoneans and the Pharisees were a source of internal instability, the ascending Roman Empire—which had formerly lent its support to the Hasmonean kings in their effort to subdue Greek

---

Map 3. The Hasmonean Jewish kingdom, 165–63 BCE. Reproduced by arrangement with Taylor & Francis from Martin Gilbert, *Atlas Jewish History*, 2nd ed. (1993), published by William Morrow and Company, Inc. © Martin Gilbert.

rule—could not tolerate a strong and nationalistic state on the eastern shore of the Mediterranean.

Judea's Queen Salome Alexandra, who began her reign in 76 BCE, unsuccessfully tried to restore political unity at home. After her death in 67 BCE, Antipater the Idumaean took charge of the kingdom's foreign affairs and adopted an accommodating policy toward Rome. According to the Roman Jewish historian Flavius Josephus, Antipater's family had converted to Judaism during the forced conversions of the Hasmoneans. Antipater claimed to want to avoid conflict, but more likely he wanted to preserve the rule of his family and cronies. His pro-Roman policies were opposed by non-hellenized Jews. He died of poisoning in 43 BCE. Before his death, however, Antipater had made Judea an ally of the Roman Empire.

Antipater's son, Herod, further consolidated Judea's ties with Rome. Once a Roman ally, Judea now became a vassal state. A tyrant to his fellow Jews, Herod was for Rome a *rex socius et amicus populi Romani* (member king and friend of the Roman people). Still, he wished to re-create Solomon's glory by expanding the Jerusalem Temple. Herod's expanded Temple was magnificent, but this architectural wonder could not mask the fact that Judea had become a Roman province. The Jews still had a country, but they were no longer sovereign.

Yet Judea was wealthy and relatively stable. It enjoyed the benefits of Pax Romana. Why, then, did it rebel in 66 CE? Rome was not only an empire that partially ruled the Jewish polity; it was also the inheritor of Greek culture. Under Hasmonean rule, Judea had been distinctively "un-Greek" in a hellenized world. As the Jews progressively acquiesced to Roman rule, they were increasingly challenged by the supremacy of Greek culture—a culture that did not tolerate Jewish particularism and seclusion. The Greco-Roman concept of *Ecumene* (the "inhabited world" under the Greeks; "civilization" under the Romans) did not only refer to the "civilized world"; it was also an expression of cultural imperialism. Those who did not bow to it were declared enemies of humanity. King Antiochus Epiphanes (who reigned from 175 to 164 BCE) called Judaism "hostile to humanity." King Antiochus Sidetes (who reigned from 138 to 129 BCE) thought the Jews were the only people that could not become part of *Ecumene*.

Denigrating the Jews, their religion, and their national identity became a recurrent theme in Greek writings. And with the establishment of the Hasmonean kingdom, Greek writers only increased their criticism of Jewish culture and historiography. The Greek rhetorician Apollonius Molon, for instance, violently attacked the Jews in his writings. He called the Jews "the most inferior of humans" and described them as primitive and misanthropic cowards.[4] The Greek philosopher, historian, and scientist Posidonius claimed that Moses was Egyptian and that the Jews were a religion but not a nation.[5] While Rome was originally an ally of the Hasmonean kingdom, Greek antisemitism would ultimately have a negative impact on Roman attitudes toward the Jews. Emperor Nero (reigning from 54 to 68 CE), for example, had nothing against the Jews, but his Greek tutor was an antisemite. Most Roman high civil servants in Judea were of Greek background and culture, and they were the ones who convinced Emperor Caligula (who reigned from 37 to 41 CE) to take such hostile measures as erecting a statue of the emperor in the Jerusalem Temple.

Relations between Greeks and Jews became explosive. In 66 CE the Greeks perpetuated a pogrom against the Jews in Caesarea, while Roman soldiers remained passive—triggering a Jewish revolt against both the Greeks and Rome. The revolt turned into a guerilla war that would last four years. In 70 CE Roman forces sacked Jerusalem and burned down the magnificent Temple that Herod had expanded. The Romans also besieged the fortress of Masada in the Judean desert in 72 CE.

Rome's military victory did not end its hostility toward the Jews. Emperor Hadrian (117–138 CE) tried to impose hellenization on Judea. According to some accounts, he outlawed circumcision. Romans were encouraged to settle in the Judean province, fomenting resentment

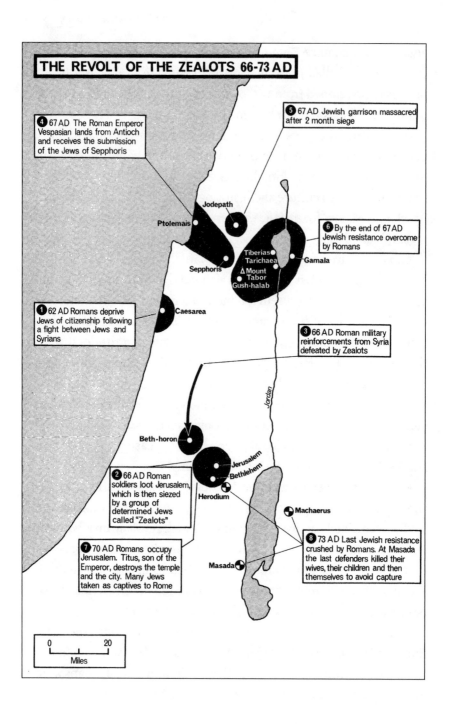

THE REVOLT OF THE ZEALOTS 66-73 AD

5 67 AD Jewish garrison massacred after 2 month siege

4 67 AD The Roman Emperor Vespasian lands from Antioch and receives the submission of the Jews of Sepphoris

Jodepath

Ptolemais

6 By the end of 67 AD Jewish resistance overcome by Romans

Tiberias
Tarichaea
△ Mount Tabor
Gush-halab

Gamala

Sepphoris

Caesarea

1 62 AD Romans deprive Jews of citizenship following a fight between Jews and Syrians

3 66 AD Roman military reinforcements from Syria defeated by Zealots

Jordan

Beth-horon

Jerusalem
Bethlehem

Herodium

2 66 AD Roman soldiers loot Jerusalem, which is then siezed by a group of determined Jews called "Zealots"

Machaerus

8 73 AD Last Jewish resistance crushed by Romans. At Masada the last defenders killed their wives, their children and then themselves to avoid capture

7 70 AD Romans occupy Jerusalem. Titus, son of the Emperor, destroys the temple and the city. Many Jews taken as captives to Rome

Masada

0   20
Miles

among Jews. Based on Jeremiah's prophecy, many Jews believed that the construction of the Third Temple was approaching: the Second Temple had been destroyed in 70 CE, and the third would therefore be built in 140 CE (Jeremiah's prophecy was about the construction of the Second Temple, but the seventy-year period between temples had become a popular belief). The combination of political resentment and messianic beliefs produced a new Jewish revolt in 132, under the leadership of Simon Bar Kokhba. Rome's reaction was merciless and devastating. By 135, more than half a million Jews had been killed, and more were exiled. The Jewish kingdom had effectively ceased to exist. From here on, it would take another 1,813 years to reestablish Jewish sovereignty, in 1948, in the Land of Israel.

Yet there were expressions of Jewish statehood far from the Promised Land. At the beginning of the sixth century, the leader of the Jewish Diaspora in Babylon (today's Iraq), Mar Zutra II, formed an independent state that would rule for approximately seven years from the city of Mahuza (known today as Al-Mada'in in Arabic). At the beginning of the eighth century, the king of the Khazars, Bulan, converted to Judaism after inquiring about the three Abrahamic religions, and so between 700 and 1016, a Khazar Jewish kingdom existed in what is today central Asia. There was also a Jewish kingdom for about three hundred years near Lake Tana in Ethiopia, between 1320 and 1624 (or 1627).[6] Known as the Kingdom of Semien, and sometimes referred to as the Kingdom of Beta Israel, it was established by Ethiopian Jews who refused to convert to Christianity.

Exiled throughout the Roman Empire and beyond, the Jews became guests in Christian and Muslim lands. For Christianity, the Jews were living proof of the cancellation of the Sinai covenant and its replace-

---

Map 4. The revolt of the Zealots, 66–73 CE. Reproduced by arrangement with Taylor & Francis from Martin Gilbert, *Atlas Jewish History*, 2nd ed. (1993), published by William Morrow and Company, Inc. © Martin Gilbert.

ment by a new one (the New Testament). The Jews' survival was tolerated as long as their misery proved the veracity of the Christian faith. For Islam, which claims to have succeeded both Judaism and Christianity, the Jews were guilty of not accepting Muhammad's prophecy. Since they had refused to join Dar al-Islam (the house of Islam), they belonged to Dar al-Harab (the territory of War) and were therefore a legitimate target of jihad. In 627 Muhammad massacred the Jews of Medina (in the Arabian Peninsula), beheading men and enslaving women and children. In Muslim lands, those Jews who refused to convert yet bowed to Islamic rule were tolerated as dhimmis, that is, second-class citizens. They had to pay a special tax, they were not allowed to ride horses, and their houses had to be lower than those of Muslims. The Muslim sovereign could also revoke their dhimmi status at any time.

With the conquest of the Land of Israel by Muslim armies in 635, the Jews became dhimmis in their own land.

The land itself suffered from Muslim rule, especially because of the Arabs' introduction of goats. Because they graze at ground level, goats turned whole forests and cultivated areas into bare limestone — witnessed in modern Israel, for example, by the presence of ancient, half-ruined terraces.[7]

Conclusion

The Jews' return to the Land of Israel did not occur for the first time in the late nineteenth century. It took place in the sixth century BCE, and then it was also opposed by the land's new inhabitants (such as the Samaritans, the Edomites, and the Arabs).

Map 5. The Jews of Palestine, 636 CE–1880 CE. Reproduced by arrangement with Taylor & Francis from Martin Gilbert, *Atlas Jewish History*, 2nd ed. (1993) by Martin, Gilbert, published by William Morrow and Company, Inc. © Martin Gilbert.

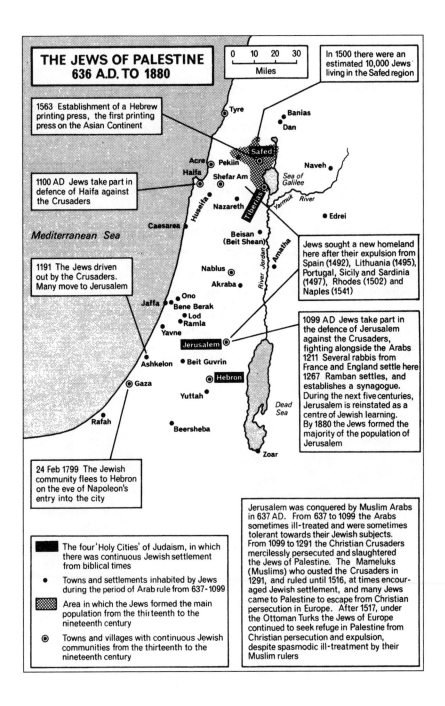

THE JEWS OF PALESTINE 636 A.D. TO 1880

0 10 20 30
Miles

In 1500 there were an estimated 10,000 Jews living in the Safed region

1563 Establishment of a Hebrew printing press, the first printing press on the Asian Continent

1100 AD Jews take part in defence of Haifa against the Crusaders

1191 The Jews driven out by the Crusaders. Many move to Jerusalem

Mediterranean Sea

Tyre

Banias
Dan

Acre Pekiin
Halfa
Shefar Am

Safed

Naveh

Sea of Galilee

Huseifa

Nazareth

Tiberias

Yarmuk River

Edrei

Caesarea

Beisan (Beit Shean)

Amatha

Nablus
Akraba

River Jordan

Jews sought a new homeland here after their expulsion from Spain (1492), Lithuania (1495), Portugal, Sicily and Sardinia (1497), Rhodes (1502) and Naples (1541)

Ono
Jaffa Bene Berak
Lod
Ramla
Yavne

Jerusalem

Ashkelon Beit Guvrin

Gaza

Hebron

Yuttah

Dead Sea

Rafah

Beersheba

Zoar

1099 AD Jews take part in the defence of Jerusalem against the Crusaders, fighting alongside the Arabs
1211 Several rabbis from France and England settle here
1267 Ramban settles, and establishes a synagogue. During the next five centuries, Jerusalem is reinstated as a centre of Jewish learning. By 1880 the Jews formed the majority of the population of Jerusalem

24 Feb 1799 The Jewish community flees to Hebron on the eve of Napoleon's entry into the city

The four 'Holy Cities' of Judaism, in which there was continuous Jewish settlement from biblical times

Towns and settlements inhabited by Jews during the period of Arab rule from 637–1099

Area in which the Jews formed the main population from the thirteenth to the nineteenth century

Towns and villages with continuous Jewish communities from the thirteenth to the nineteenth century

Jerusalem was conquered by Muslim Arabs in 637 AD. From 637 to 1099 the Arabs sometimes ill-treated and were sometimes tolerant towards their Jewish subjects. From 1099 to 1291 the Christian Crusaders mercilessly persecuted and slaughtered the Jews of Palestine. The Mameluks (Muslims) who ousted the Crusaders in 1291, and ruled until 1516, at times encouraged Jewish settlement, and many Jews came to Palestine to escape from Christian persecution in Europe. After 1517, under the Ottoman Turks the Jews of Europe continued to seek refuge in Palestine from Christian persecution and expulsion, despite spasmodic ill-treatment by their Muslim rulers

The clash between secular and traditionalist Jews is not new either, as it existed under Greek rule in the second century BCE: Jason and Menelaus were "hellenized" Jewish priests, but the Maccabees fought the Greeks; Herod turned Judea into a Roman ally, but Bar Kokhba and his followers rebelled against Roman rule. The Hasmonean dynasty restored and even expanded the Jewish kingdom, but Jewish particularism was challenged by Greek culture and crushed by Roman imperialism. Eventually, the Jews lost their sovereignty and became reviled hosts in the two civilizations that, paradoxically, had their spiritual roots in Judaism: Christianity and Islam.

Still, a few expressions of Jewish statehood existed far from the Promised Land: a seven-year rule by the leader of the Jewish Diaspora in Babylon (today's Iraq) in the sixth century, a Khazar Jewish kingdom in what is today central Asia for some three hundred years in the eighth to eleventh centuries, and an Ethiopian Jewish kingdom for about three hundred years in the fourteenth through seventeenth centuries.

5. Between Powerlessness and Empowerment

Yes, I am a Jew; and when the ancestors of the right honorable gentleman were brutal savages in an unknown
island, mine were priests in the Temple of Solomon!

BENJAMIN DISRAELI

Jewish Vulnerability in Europe

In Christian countries Jews were not only considered foreigners; their
very survival constituted a living challenge to the church's dogma.
If Jesus was the Messiah, why were Jews clinging to Judaism? Jews
were also accused of killing Jesus, and so they became the victims of
persecutions, defamations, and massacres. Thousands of Jews were
killed during the Crusades in the eleventh century, both in Europe
and in the Land of Israel. In 1144 the Jewish community of Norwich,
England, was accused of murdering a Christian boy to use his blood
for the baking of matzah—an accusation that took hold and came to
be known as "blood libel." In 1290 King Edward I expelled the Jews
from England. During the first half of the fourteenth century Jews
were accused of spreading the Black Plague throughout Europe. In the
fifteenth century Spanish Jews were forced to convert to Christianity.

Even after their conversions, however, Jews were accused of not
adhering to Christianity in good faith and of preserving a double
identity. In the 1440s many riots targeted Conversos (converted Jews)
in Spain. In the 1480s a policy of inquisition was implemented to spot

Jews whose conversion to Christianity was "insincere" and to kill them. The exact number of Jews murdered in the Inquisition is not known, but when it was over, Jews were still living in Spain. Having failed to solve its "Jewish problem" through conversions and the Inquisition, Spain eventually decided to expel the remainder in 1492.

As long as Europe was exclusively Catholic, there was no escape from theological damnation and political persecution. The Reformation in the sixteenth century brought some hope. Within the Christian world, the Protestants had become a religious minority, too. Early Protestant scholars were Hebraists with a good knowledge of Jewish texts. Yet Martin Luther's writings about the Jews were as hostile as they were violent. In his 1543 treatise *On the Jews and Their Lies*, Luther called for synagogues and Jewish schools and homes to be set on fire and for Jewish property to be confiscated. He denounced Jews as "poisonous worms" and wrote that Christians "are at fault for not slaying them." Luther not only incited against Jews; he expelled them from Saxony in 1537. The Jews' hopes for the Reformation were therefore short-lived.

By the end of the sixteenth century, however, the church's authority had to compete with the growing power of the state. This gradual power shift enabled many Jews to climb the social ladder, and even to become powerful, in cities, regions, and countries such as Venice, Tuscany, Frankfurt, Holland, and France. The predominant status of the state was institutionalized by the Treaty of Westphalia in 1648, which officially put an end to the Thirty Years' War—a protracted conflict between Catholics and Protestants.

Jewish life became even more precarious in post-Westphalian Europe. During the war, prominent Jewish financiers had helped European monarchs fund their armies and military operations. In many cases, money had been raised by mortgaging lands. In Poland and the Ukraine, peasants accused Jews of taking away land for their own enrichment. Public resentment turned into a series of pogroms that killed tens of thousands of Jews in 1648.

False Promises: Messianism and the Enlightenment

Some Jews interpreted the blood libels in England, the Inquisition and expulsion from Spain, the disappointment with the Reformation, and the massacres in post-Westphalian Europe in messianic terms. Could it be that those calamities were the birth pangs of the Messiah? After all, many Jewish texts and traditions taught that the coming of the Messiah would be preceded by cataclysmic historical events.

The prominent twelfth-century Jewish scholar and scientist Moses Maimonides warned against such messianic speculations, but the phenomenon of false messiahs did not abate. The list included David Reubeni in Venice in 1523, Solomon Molcho in Rome in 1530, and Sabbatai Zevi in Turkey from 1648. After the 1648 massacres, Sabbatai Zevi, in his hometown of Smyrna (in today's Turkey), started claiming he was the Messiah. In 1665 Zevi proclaimed himself Messiah in Gaza. The Turkish authorities arrested him in 1666, after he declared that he would grab the Turkish crown for himself. The sultan gave him the choice between death and conversion to Islam; Zevi chose the latter.

The Sabbatai Zevi fraud was soon forgotten, but the trauma of the 1648 massacres remained. Following the massacres, many Jews from Eastern Europe had fled westward. A new immigration opportunity for them arose in England, where Jews had not lived openly since the expulsion of English Jews in 1290. The year 1648 had constituted a turning point in European history, as it marked both the end of the Thirty Years' War and the outbreak of the Second English Civil War. In 1649 King Charles I was executed, and the military leader Oliver Cromwell had proclaimed a republic known as the Commonwealth of England. Well-versed in the Hebrew Bible, Cromwell and his followers would quote it to justify their rebellion against the king (Cromwell was particularly fond of the books of Isaiah and Amos). They believed in the Second Coming (i.e., Jesus's return) and in the ingathering of the Jews. Thus the new regime in England was better disposed toward the Jews.

The case for Jewish immigration to England was made by Menashe Ben-Israel, a Portuguese Jewish scholar who traveled to England and met with Cromwell in 1655. Cromwell was sympathetic to Ben-Israel's requests, but no official decision was made to announce that Jews could immigrate to England. On the other hand, the meeting between Cromwell and Ben-Israel revealed that there was no legal restriction to Jewish immigration, since the expulsion order of 1290 was against individuals and did not legally ban Jews from living in England. Jewish émigrés from Eastern Europe entered the British Isles, and progressively English Jews — most of them of Sephardic origin who had until then pretended to be Christian — started to practice their religion openly. By the late seventeenth century, British Jews were mostly free and almost equal subjects. So were Jews who settled in British colonies overseas, such as the Dutch settlement of Nieuw (New) Amsterdam, which England conquered (and renamed New York) in 1664. By the early eighteenth century, the Jewish subjects of the British colonies in North America were the world's freest Jews.

This freedom became greater still after the American colonies declared their independence from Britain in 1776 and then adopted a Constitution in 1787 and a Bill of Rights in 1791. The American Constitution gave the Jews what they had been denied in Europe: separation of church and state, liberty of conscience, and the end (officially at least) of social segregation. Unlike in Western Europe, the Jewish devotion to family life, hard work, and religious observance was valued by the American ethos.

Hence the major difference between the American and European Enlightenments, as far as Jews were concerned: in America, the Enlightenment had delivered its promises; in Europe, those promises were never fully kept. The French Revolution, for example, was more than ambivalent toward the Jews. Stanislas de Clermont-Tonnerre, a conservative member of the new French National Assembly, typically expressed this ambivalence during a debate in September 1789 on the status of the Jews in a French democracy. "The Jews," he said, "cannot be a nation within a nation," and therefore, they must "be denied everything as a nation but be granted everything as individuals."[1] In other words, the Jews' entry ticket into France's emerging democracy required them to abandon their self-identification as a nation. They were asked to become French nationals of the Jewish faith. Meanwhile, most French revolutionaries, shaped by the philosophy of "Radical Enlightenment," despised religion. The writings of Voltaire, Denis Diderot, and Baron d'Holbach were full of antisemitic slurs. Jews, in other words, were accepted into the republic on the condition of restricting their identity to a religion that was derided and despised. Eventually France emancipated its Jews and granted them full citizenship in September 1791, but the ambiguity remained.

Napoléon Bonaparte tried to lift this ambiguity by convoking a Sanhedrin and officially declaring his empire's Jews "French citizens of the Mosaic faith." Before he became emperor, however, Napoléon seemed to be favorable to the restoration of a Jewish state in the Land of Israel, and indeed many Jews saw Napoléon as a savior, if not a Messiah. When Napoléon's expedition to the Middle East was launched in 1798, some Jews believed that he would restore Jewish sovereignty and even rebuild the Jerusalem Temple. On February 17 of that year, Thomas Corbet, a rebel Irish soldier who had joined Bonaparte's army in Egypt, addressed a letter to Paul Barras, the main leader of France's "Directoire" regime, asking the French government to promote the establishment of a Jewish state after Napoléon's anticipated Middle East victory.[2] On May 22, 1799, the official French newspaper *Le Moniteur Universel* published the announcement: "Bonaparte has issued a statement calling upon Asian and African Jews to gather around his flag and restore the Jerusalem kingdom."[3] Whether Bonaparte actually called upon Jews to join him and rebuild their country is a question historians continue to debate. Still, historical documents do suggest that Napoléon was sympathetic to the idea.

Once he became emperor, however, Napoléon demanded the Jews' full allegiance to the French nation. And even after declaring their full allegiance to France, Jews were still considered an alien nation by their fellow citizens. Worse, Jews became the scapegoats of both anti-clerical revolutionaries and Catholic monarchists: the former blamed the Jews for sowing the seeds of religious obscurantism and superstition in Western culture; the latter accused the Jews of being the instigators of a revolution from which they had obviously benefited.

Emergence of Jewish Power in the Anglo-Saxon World

With the final defeat of Napoleonic France in 1815, Britain became the world's greatest power. In the process, some British Jews reached the height of political and economic clout. Though converted to Anglicanism as a child, the Jewish-born Benjamin Disraeli served as prime minister of Great Britain for seven years (in 1868 and again between 1874 and 1880) at the apex of British power. In 1876 Disraeli proclaimed Queen Victoria "Empress of India."

A master of diplomacy, Disraeli outmaneuvered the German chancellor Otto von Bismarck at the Congress of Berlin in July 1878 by forcing Russia, Germany's ally, to downscale its claims against the Ottoman Empire. Asked who was the winner of the Congress of Berlin, Bismarck replied (referring to Disraeli), "Der alter Jude, das ist der Mann!" ("The old Jew, he is the man!")[4]

Though baptized, Disraeli proudly claimed his Jewish ancestry. His 1830 journey to the Middle East took him to Jerusalem and left a strong impression on him. In Disraeli's 1833 novel *Alroy*, a Jewish hero who reconquered the Holy Land from the Babylonians voiced these unambiguous sentiments: "You ask me what I wish? My answer is: Jerusalem—all we have forfeited, all we have yearned after, all for which we have fought—our beauteous country, our holy creed, our simple manners. . . . Yet again I will build thee, and thou shalt be built,

O . . . Israel!"[5] Disraeli's 1847 novel *Tancred* was no less explicit: "The vineyards of Israel have ceased to exist, but the eternal law enjoins the Children of Israel to celebrate the vintage. A race that persists in celebrating their vintage although they have no fruit to gather, will regain their vineyards."[6] Disraeli's books were Zionist manifestos *avant la lettre*.

What is more, Disraeli seriously considered the possibility of restoring a Jewish state in the Land of Israel. He shared his vision with Foreign Secretary Edward Stanley: land would be bought from the bankrupt Turks with the help of the Rothschilds, and Jews would establish settlements throughout the country. (Stanley did not follow up on the matter.)[7] Disraeli also castigated Christians for persecuting a people to which they owed so much. In *Coningsby* (1844), he wrote that the Jew is "the pariah of that ungrateful Europe that owes him the best part of its laws, a fine portion of its literature, all its religion."[8] When a fellow parliamentarian referred to Disraeli as a Jew and questioned his Britishness, Disraeli reportedly replied, "Yes, I am a Jew; and when the ancestors of the right honorable gentleman were brutal savages in an unknown island, mine were priests in the Temple of Solomon!"[9]

Another powerful British Jew was Lionel de Rothschild (1808–79). A close friend of Disraeli, Rothschild financed the British government's involvement in the Crimean War (1853–56) and its purchase of shares in the Suez Canal (in 1875). Disraeli ruled the world's superpower; Rothschild ran the world's largest financial empire. Unmatched in power and influence in Britain, Rothschild managed to turn the otherwise hostile Lord Randolph Churchill (Winston's father) and Lord Balfour (who issued the Balfour Declaration in 1917) into philosemites.

Lord Palmerston, who served as Britain's foreign secretary and prime minister in the mid-nineteenth century, was a proto-Zionist. His wife's father-in-law, Lord Shaftesbury, was a Christian Zionist who had called for resettling the Jews in Palestine. In 1838 Palmerston appointed Britain's first vice-consul in Jerusalem and asked him to grant protection to the Jews. In 1840 he instructed Britain's ambassador to Constantinople to ask the Ottomans to let Jews resettle Palestine. That same year, after Damascus's Jewish community was accused of murdering a Christian monk to use his blood for ritual purposes (the Damascus Affair), Palmerston was instrumental in convincing the Ottoman authorities to free the Jewish detainees and end the blood libel.

The outcome of the Damascus Affair would reveal the potency of Jewish diplomacy. Precisely because European nations were competing for influence in the Middle East, consular officials in Damascus tried to transform the case's outcome to their advantage. The Rothschilds got involved (James in France, Nathaniel in Britain, Solomon in Austria), as did Adolphe Crémieux (a Jewish member of the French parliament) and the British philanthropist Sir Moses Montefiore. Sephardic and Ashkenazic Jews also drew together to pressure the Ottoman authorities — an unprecedented cross-border solidarity. Sir Moses Montefiore had traveled to Alexandria and met the sultan as a Jewish emissary. The sultan promised Montefiore that from now on, Ottoman Jews would enjoy the same rights and freedoms as his other subjects. Montefiore described this declaration as "the Magna Carta of the Jews in the Turkish dominions."[10]

In Germany, by contrast, Jews were not nearly as accepted, as free, and as powerful as they were in Britain. Many German Jews felt the need to reform, or even to abandon, Judaism in order to be fully accepted in German society. Moreover, since Protestant nations (Britain, Prussia, the United States) were on the rise after the Napoleonic Wars, wasn't this a sign that the Jews would gain from their own reformation? In 1818 the first Reform temple (the "Israelite Temple," or *Israelitischer Tempel* in German) opened in Hamburg.

Yet German Reform Jews did not gain hoped-for acceptance among the gentiles. In 1822 the Prussian government introduced a law excluding the Jews from academic careers. Hence did Heinrich Heine convert to Protestantism, a move he famously described as "the ticket of admission into European culture" (though he never got a job as a professor). In a way, German Jews had good reasons to envy their British brethren.

Even conversions did not grant German Jews a "ticket of admission" into German culture. Germans always considered them Jews, and some had to leave Germany because of their radical ideas. Heine became an émigré in Paris; Karl Marx—who maligned Jews and Judaism as responsible for the "evils" of capitalism and Protestant culture—in London.[11] In the Middle Ages, Catholics had reviled Jews for rejecting Christianity. In the nineteenth century, secularists blamed Jews for being at the origins of Christianity.

There was nonetheless a thriving Jewish life in Germany from the mid-nineteenth century to the early twentieth century. After 1848 German Jews enjoyed relative equality and freedom. In the 1860s the states of Baden and Württemberg granted Jews equality before the law. When Bismarck established the German empire in 1871, he granted civic equality to the Jews throughout the newly unified Germany. By the early twentieth century, Jews were integrated and mostly accepted in German culture and public life, though they rarely made it to the top echelons of the army and government.

Meanwhile, Russian Jews enjoyed none of the rights granted to their Western brethren. They were confined to the Pale of Settlement, an area stretching from the Baltic to the Black Sea. As their brethren increasingly enjoyed freedom and sometimes wealth in England, France, and Germany in the early and mid-nineteenth century, their situation kept deteriorating. They were barred from most professions and forcibly enrolled in the military (though they could not become officers), while their religious freedom was curtailed and their culture undermined. In czarist Russia, Jews were persecuted, humiliated, and defamed. In 1903 the czarist regime published *The Protocols of the Elders of Zion*, an antisemitic fabricated text supposedly revealing a secret Jewish plot for world domination. While the Russian state deprived the Jews of basic freedoms, reduced them to poverty, and excluded them from society, its propaganda machine described them as a fantastically powerful sect bent on taking over the world.

Jews were also physically unsecure, exposed to pogroms that authorities not only failed to prevent but often encouraged. In 1871 a pogrom targeting Jews took place in Odessa. After the murder of Czar Alexander II in 1881, pogroms were initiated against Jews by the government itself. Jews had to run for their lives and started emigrating. From 1881 onward, tens of thousands of Jews fled Russia yearly. In 1905–6 alone, a "prime" year of pogroms, some two hundred thousand Jews left Russia. The most sought-after destination was the United States, to which over two million Jews eventually emigrated.

This massive Jewish immigration from Russia had a profound impact on American Jewry. At the beginning of the nineteenth century there were only a few thousand Jews in the United States. They were fairly well integrated into American society, even if prejudice against them persisted. Most of them were German Jews, immigrants themselves, who did their best to fit in with the American ethos of the period. They established Reform congregations that were more or less modeled on Christian churches. They largely abandoned the concepts of Jewish peoplehood and the return to Zion; for them, Judaism was only a religion, and they were American patriots now. Russian Jews, by contrast, were mostly Orthodox, spoke Yiddish, and were socially distinct from the general population. American Jews of German background looked down on their Russian coreligionists, fearing that the newcomers would give Jews a bad name. To their dismay, Russian Jews kept immigrating, in large numbers. The Jewish population of the United States grew from 250,000 in 1880 to 4.5 million in 1920.

Conclusion

The persecution of European Jews in the Middle Ages culminated in the Inquisition and the mass expulsion from Spain in 1492. It was only when Jews emigrated to England in the second half of the seventeenth century, and later on to the English colonies of North America, that they started to enjoy freedom, wealth, and even power.

In post-revolutionary France, the Jews were nominally free, but only at the price of assimilation. In Germany, even assimilation never gave the Jews a full "entry ticket" into German society. In Russia, state antisemitism and pogroms produced waves of Jewish migration—mostly to the United States.

The emergence of Jewish power in Britain, and to a lesser extent in France, enabled European Jews to successfully exert international pressure on the Ottoman Empire in 1840 regarding the Damascus Affair. The Damascus Affair laid the ground for a European Jewish lobby that overcame the abuse and threats of the Ottoman sultan. By the mid-nineteenth century, European Jews were no longer powerless.

6. The Zionist Controversy

> The Jews who wish for a state will have it. We shall live
> at last as free men on our own soil and die peacefully in
> our own homes. The world will be freed by our liberty,
> enriched by our wealth, magnified by our greatness.
>
> THEODOR HERZL, *Der Judenstaat*

Understanding the Emergence of Modern Zionism

Russia's anti-Jewish pogroms did not only induce mass emigration to
the United States. They also revived the idea of a Jewish state, where
Jews would be sovereign and, therefore, no longer at the mercy of
other nations.

The return to Zion and the restoration of the Jewish kingdom had
always been a central tenet of Judaism since the final destruction
of Jewish sovereignty by the Romans in 135 CE. In their three daily
prayers, Jews asked God to gather the scattered people and to rebuild
the Jerusalem Temple. Jews broke a glass at the end of every wedding
to remind the joyous couple of the destruction of Jerusalem and, thus,
to temper their joy. Then, too, the Passover ceremony ended with the
words "Next year in Jerusalem!" Precisely because they prayed for it,
Jews considered the return to Zion to be beyond their control: God
would decide when to bring the Jews back to their land, and only the
Messiah would restore the Jewish kingdom. The Jews yearned for their
old glory, but passively and religiously. The embarrassing "Sabbatai

Zevi" flop in the seventeenth century (see chapter 5) had made Jews suspicious of self-proclaimed Messiahs.

This mixture of religiously sanctioned passivity and historically justified suspicion was challenged in the nineteenth century by such dramatic events as the Damascus blood libel of 1840 and the Russian pogroms from 1881 onward. Even Orthodox rabbis started wondering out loud if human action was not called for in order to rescue endangered Jews. In 1836 German rabbi Zvi Hirsch Kalischer asked the Rothschilds to buy the historical Land of Israel from the Ottomans (the Rothschilds did not oblige). In 1840 Serbian rabbi Judah Alkalai claimed that the time for Jews to resettle their land had arrived. He set an example by doing so himself.

Secular Jewish thinkers also started promoting the idea of a Jewish national renaissance. Prominent among them was the German socialist author Moses Hess, whose 1862 book *Rome and Jerusalem* called for Jews to embrace nationalism in order to avoid both the assimilationist path of secularism and the seclusion imposed by religion. Furthermore, some non-Jews (mostly in the English-speaking world) advocated the idea of a Jewish national renaissance. British novelist George Eliot, for one, ended her 1876 novel *Daniel Deronda* with an emotional call for Israel's rebirth.

As for Russia's Jews, until the pogroms of 1881 and 1882, many had believed that either liberalism or socialism would eventually set them free. But, as Israeli historian Benny Morris succinctly put it, "The events of 1881–82 were a stunning slap in the face to both the liberals and the revolutionaries."[1] In 1882 the Russian Jewish physician Leon Pinsker published his pamphlet *Auto-Emancipation*, urging the Jews to fight for their self-determination and national independence. This pamphlet was significant because Pinsker had originally advocated full Jewish assimilation to solve the "Jewish problem." Pinsker's call for action was followed by the creation, in 1890, of the Society for the Support of Jewish Farmers and Artisans in Syria and Palestine. The czarist regime gave its blessing: any move that could rid Russia of its Jews was welcome. Russian Jews started emigrating to the Ottoman-ruled Land of Israel in 1882, soon establishing agricultural settlements such as Rishon Le-Zion, Rosh Pina, Zikhron Ya'akov, and Petah Tik-vah (the last had actually been established, but then abandoned, by Jerusalem Jews in 1878).

While the idea of restoring Jewish sovereignty by way of human action started taking shape among Russian Jews, as well as among romantic British philosemites, by the end of the nineteenth century, it was actually translated into a political movement in France. In principle, the French Third Republic was supposed to be an enlightened and secular regime with no prejudice toward Jews or other minorities. Since the days of the Revolution and of Bonaparte, Jews had been asked to empty Judaism of its national component in order to fully espouse the French national ideal. Alfred Dreyfus, an Alsatian Jew who had risen to the rank of officer in the French army, had done just that; he had assimilated, and yet in 1894 he was falsely accused of treason because he was Jewish. He would eventually be acquitted, but not without years of political struggles that tore French society to the core. When Theodor Herzl, the Paris correspondent of the Austrian newspaper *Neue Freie Presse* (New free press), heard the crowds shout, "Mort aux Juifs!" (Death to the Jews!) on the streets of Paris after Dreyfus's conviction and degradation, he became convinced that emancipation had been a scam. The Enlightenment had not kept its promises to the Jews. No matter how far the Jews went in abandoning their national identity, they were still considered a foreign nation, even in Europe's most liberal and secular country. And if the Jews were still considered a nation, then they had no other choice but to rebuild their own nation-state.

Herzl decided to make this idea a reality by writing a book, *Der Judenstaat* (*The Jewish State*); by conveying an international gathering, the First Zionist Congress; and by establishing a political movement with funding and elected institutions. Thus it was that modern Zionism as an organized political movement was born.

So was the controversy around it. To most Orthodox Jews who clung to the messianic dogma, Herzl was rebelling against God's will by forcing a historical process that had to be decreed from above. To assimilated Western Jews, Herzl was reviving an old demon by proclaiming loud and clear that Jews were a nation.

Yet to Herzl, European Jews failed to see and understand the nature of modern antisemitism. Yes, Jews were indeed free in France, but the principles of the French Revolution had not permeated French society—and, indeed, those principles (such as equality of all citizens and the separation of church and state) were reviled by many, especially traditionalist Catholics who resented the republic's anti-clericalism. Many Alsatian Jews had moved to France in the aftermath of the Franco-Prussian War and the loss of Alsace-Lorraine in 1871, and so did Russian Jews after 1881. Meanwhile, Jewish emigration brought back to life old anti-Jewish prejudices, whose main loudspeaker was the French journalist and politician Édouard Drumont. Drumont's best-selling book *La France juive* (Jewish France) in 1886 combined classical Christian antisemitism (the Jews are deicide people) with modern racism (the Jews are an inferior race) and Catholic hostility to capitalism (the Jews control global finance and steal our money). In 1892 Drumont founded his own newspaper, *La libre parole* (The free talk), a socialist newspaper full of conspiracy theories about the alleged secret plans of "Jewish capitalism." The Dreyfus Affair, which erupted in 1894, was not accidental. Anti-Jewish defamation and conspiracy theories were far from being alien to late nineteenth-century French political culture. And this was precisely Herzl's point: the promises of the Enlightenment could no longer be trusted, and thus the Jews had to draw practical conclusions from this historical disappointment.

Herzl himself had grown up in a deeply antisemitic Germanic culture. In the German *völkisch* (populist) ideology of the nineteenth century, the Jew was the ultimate enemy of authentic German values and culture. German ultranationalist historian and politician Heinrich von Treitscke famously coined the expression "Die Juden sind unser Unglück" (The Jews are our misfortune), which the Nazi publication *Der Stürmer* would later adopt as its motto. In an 1862 essay, von Treitscke wrote that the eastern German soil was "magic" because it had been "fertilized" by "noble German blood." Jews, he claimed, were not only alien to German culture, but also an obstacle to German power. German orientalist Paul de Lagarde blamed the Jews for having invented the vile religion of Christianity, which was incompatible with Germanic values. He called for Christianity's replacement with a German national religion and for Germany's Jews to be expelled (he suggested Madagascar as a possible destination, an idea the Nazis weighed in June 1940 but eventually shelved in January 1942 with the beginning of the Final Solution). In 1887 he wrote in the essay "Jews and Indo-Germanics" that he couldn't think of a reason not to "crush these vermin." Jews were "pests and parasites" that should be destroyed "as speedily and thoroughly as possible." The German composer Richard Wagner wrote in his 1880 article "Religion und Kunst" ("Religion and Art") that the Jews were the enemies of humanity and that Germany had been defeated, culturally, by Judaism. The German philosopher and economist Eugen Dühring wrote in his 1881 book *Die Judenfrage als Racen, Sitten und Kulturefrage* (The Jewish question as a racial, moral, and cultural question) that Jews had to be removed from Germany. He further called for the "removal of the Jewish race from modern peoplehood" (Ausscheidung der Judenrace aus dem modernen Völkerleben) and for the "extermination of the Jewish people" (Vernichtung des Judenvolkes).[2]

The very word "antisemitism" was popularized by the German publicist and agitator Wilhelm Marr in his 1880 pamphlet *Der Weg zum Siege des Germanenthums über das Judenthum* (The way to victory of the German spirit over the Jewish spirit). Marr came up with the word

Antisemitismus (antisemitism) because he sought, in his own words, "a new, nonreligious connotation to the term 'anti-Jewish.'"[3] Marr warned his readers that "someday the Jews will use the law and the state to attain a feudal domination over us. We Germans will become their slaves."[4] The pamphlet was so popular that shortly after its publication, a League of Antisemites (Antisemiten-Liga) was founded, with the declared purpose of fighting Jewish influence over German culture and expelling Jews from Germany. In 1882 the First Anti-Jewish Congress was held in Dresden, Germany. It became common for candidates to run for Reichstag seats as proud antisemites.

Precisely because Theodor Herzl was all too aware of the deeply rooted antisemitism of German culture, he had held high hopes for the fate of the Jews in the supposedly tolerant, enlightened, and secular French Republic. But witnessing the public degradation of Alfred Dreyfus in the court of the École militaire (France's military academy) in January 1895 shattered his illusions. In February 1896 Herzl published *Der Judenstaat*, the Zionist manifesto.

Paradoxically, even though little was new in the idea he promoted, Herzl changed the course of Jewish history. What was in fact revolutionary in Herzl's book was that it came from an assimilated Western Jew. As Chaim Weizmann was to explain, "The very fact that this Westerner [Herzl] came to us unencumbered by our own preconceptions has its appeal. . . . What had emerged from *Der Judenstaat* was less a concept than a historic personality. . . . What has given greatness to his name is Herzl's rôle [sic] as a man of action, as the founder of the Zionist Congress, and as an example of daring and devotion."[5]

In August 1897 Herzl convened the First Zionist Congress in Basel, Switzerland. It comprised Zionist delegates from sixteen countries, and Herzl brought correspondents from twenty-six newspapers. Delegates were asked to wear tuxedoes and top hats. When Herzl entered the conference hall, delegates exclaimed the Hebrew expression *Yechi Hamelekh!* (Long live the King!). Herzl explicitly told delegates of his purpose—to establish a Jewish state—and he spelled out that vision. Among Herzl's young and early admirers were Chaim Weizmann and David Grün (later known as David Ben-Gurion).

But Herzl had many enemies. Both Orthodox rabbis and assimilated Western Jews staunchly opposed the idea of a Jewish state—the former because they believed in waiting for divine intervention; the latter because they believed that the era of Jewish nationhood was over and that Judaism was by now only a religion. Herzl also soon came to realize that for his project to materialize, he needed the support of the great powers.

Zionism Enters the World of Diplomacy

Though a mere journalist, Herzl was able to meet world leaders whose support he sought. He generally did not request and obtain those meetings as the Paris correspondent of the *Neue Freie Presse*, but as the president of the Zionist Congress. Herzl met with the German emperor, the pope, the grand vizier of the Ottoman Empire, the British colonial secretary, and the Russian interior and finance ministers. Wilhelm, the German emperor, was all too happy to get rid of Germany's Jews, as he explicitly told Herzl. But realpolitik got in the way: Germany was trying to build an alliance with the Ottoman Empire, and a German endorsement of the Zionist project would derail such an alliance. The Turks would never agree to the national renaissance of despised dhimmis (i.e., non-Muslim, second-class citizens, such as Jews, living in Muslim lands). In addition, the sultan had no intention of bringing more trouble into his dysfunctional empire by allowing a mass migration of Jews, which would inevitably create friction with the Arabs. The sultan also suspected the Russian Jewish immigrants of being dangerous revolutionaries. Jewish immigration under Ottoman rule was officially illegal but was frequently overcome by bribing Ottoman officials (baksheesh). Typically, Jews entered as tourists or pilgrims and illegally stayed on in the "Sanjak" (district) of Jerusalem or of Beirut (see map 6).

Meanwhile, Herzl's diplomacy was proving disappointing. Weizmann complained that "Herzl had seen the Sultan. He had seen the Kaiser. He had seen the British Foreign Secretary. He was about to see this or that important man. And the practical effect was nothing. We could not help becoming skeptical about these nebulous negotiations."[6] All the while, pogroms in Russia were raging.

Herzl figured that only imperialist Britain, with its philosemites and Christian Zionists, might be of any help. In 1902 he testified in front of the royal inquiry commission on foreign immigration to Great Britain. In London he met with Lord Rothschild (who subsequently abandoned his hostility to the Zionist project), with Joseph Chamberlain (the secretary of state for the colonies), and with the Marquess of Lansdowne (the secretary of state for foreign affairs). Both Chamberlain and Lansdowne were sympathetic, but Britain did not control Palestine. In 1903 they suggested that Herzl establish the Jewish national home in Uganda. Herzl was willing to consider the plan, even as a temporary solution, but the Sixth Zionist Congress rejected it after heated debates.

Jewish and Arab Nationalisms

Herzl died in 1904 at the young age of forty-four, seven years after convening the First Zionist Congress. By the time of his death, Zionism was an established political movement, with institutions, funding, and the sympathy of the world's largest empire, Great Britain. This was no mean achievement. Yet most Jewish leaders continued to reject the very idea. Orthodox rabbis considered it a religious heresy, assimilated Jews saw it as a dangerous challenge to their social status, and most French and German Jews thought that antisemitism was abating and therefore there was no need for a solution to the Jewish

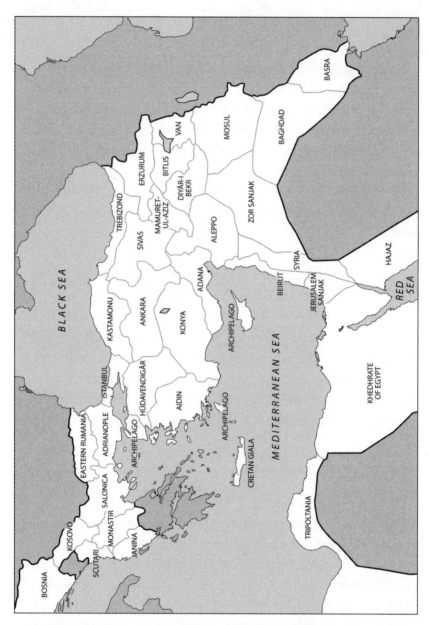

Map 6. The Middle East before World War I: the Ottoman Empire. Cartography by Bill Nelson.

question. In 1906 Alfred Dreyfus was fully exonerated; that same year, the *dreyfusard* (i.e., pro-Dreyfus) left won a majority in the French elections. Hadn't the antisemites lost for good? As for German Jews, no amount of antisemitism could unravel their total identification with German culture. The Jewish German philosopher Hermann Cohen became the apostle of the alleged affinity between Judaism and German culture. An expert on the eighteenth-century German philosopher Immanuel Kant, Cohen held that German culture and philosophy were the ultimate expression of biblical values (in effect, the very opposite position of that of the German antisemites, who claimed that Judaism was the ultimate enemy of the German ethos). Hence was Cohen a fierce opponent of Zionism: if the Jewish spirit had found the ideal home in Germany, why rewind the wheels of history away from such a wonderful achievement?

Objectively, German Jews had good reasons to feel like the elite of a country that was at the forefront of science, industry, and culture. Eight German Jews won the Nobel Prize (two in medicine, four in chemistry, and two in physics) before World War I. Felix Mendelssohn and Gustav Mahler, both Jews who had converted to Christianity, were the pride of "German music." Walter Rathenau (whose father founded the electrical giant AEG) played a key role at the War Ministry during World War I and briefly served as foreign minister under the Weimar Republic. Who needed the fantasies of Dr. Herzl? Yet, as Chaim Weizmann was to write of Rathenau, "He plunged at once into eloquent argument against Zionism. . . . The gist of what he had to say was that he was a Jew, but felt entirely German and was devoting all his energy to the building of German industry and the redeeming of Germany's political position. . . . Not many months were to pass before he fell at the hands of Nazi assassins."[7]

No such abandonment of Zionism occurred among Russian Jews in the early years of the twentieth century. Quite the contrary: the devastating Kishinev pogrom of April 1903 and Odessa pogrom of

October 1905 triggered a second wave of Jewish immigration to the Land of Israel (known as the Second Aliyah). Jewish nationalism was taking shape.

So was, around the same time, Arab nationalism. The 1908 revolution of the Young Turks in the Ottoman Empire (which replaced the absolute monarchy with a constitutional one), with its forced "Turkification" (i.e., the imposition of Turkish language and culture on the empire's non-Turkish subjects) and anti-Arab policies, spurred Arab nationalism. In November 1909 the secret Society of the Young Arab Nation (known as al-Fatat) was founded in Paris.[8]

The reaction to Zionism was a key factor in the emergence of a Palestinian Arab nationalism. "Two important phenomena, of the same nature but opposed, are emerging at this moment in Asiatic Turkey," the Arab nationalist Najib Azouri wrote in his 1905 book *Le réveil de la nation arabe* (The awakening of the Arab nation). "They are the awakening of the Arab nation and the latent effort of the Jews to reconstitute on a very large scale the ancient kingdom of Israel. These movements are destined to fight each other continually until one of them wins."[9] As summarized by Israeli historian and one-time foreign minister Shlomo Ben-Ami, "Palestine was not even considered a distinct province in the Ottoman empire. . . . The prevailing concept was more that of the 'Arab nation' than that of, say, the 'Palestinian' or the 'Iraqi' and 'Syrian' nation and state. But Palestinian nationalism would emerge and crystallize in the first two decades of the century as a defensive response to the Zionist arrival."[10]

Conclusion

Anti-Jewish pogroms in late nineteenth-century Russia revived the idea of Jewish national sovereignty. Yet it was the Dreyfus Affair in France that triggered the establishment of a political movement dedicated to Jewish statehood, because this political drama convinced the journalist Theodor Herzl that emancipation had been a sham and that the time had come to translate the age-old dream of return to Zion into reality. What was revolutionary about Herzl was less the idea he promoted than the fact that it was promoted by a Western Jew who established a political movement to turn vision into reality. Herzl met the opposition both of ultra-Orthodox Jews, for whom Zionism was heretical, and of assimilated Jews, for whom Zionism unnecessarily revived the idea of Jewish nationhood. Even though Germany was a hotbed of antisemitism, it was also a great power in which Jews enjoyed affluence and influence, and German Jews felt at home there.

From the moment Herzl convened the First Zionist Congress in 1897, Zionist leaders became de facto diplomats. Gathering the support of world powers to establish a Jewish state turned out to be an uphill and difficult battle. Germany was happy to get rid of its Jews, but it feared alienating its Turkish ally. Britain had some influential pro-Zionist writers and politicians, but it did not control the Middle East. Its 1903 Uganda proposal created a dilemma for the Zionist movement, but the Sixth Zionist Congress ultimately rejected the proposal, and immigration to the Land of Israel continued. This immigration, which originated mostly from Russia and would increase after pogroms there, contributed to the emergence of a Palestinian Arab nationalism that progressively took shape as a reaction to Zionism.

1. Zionist Diplomacy in the Post–World War I International System

CHAIM WEIZMANN: "Would you trade London for
Saskatchewan?"
ARTHUR BALFOUR: "Of course not. London is the
capital of my country."
CHAIM WEIZMANN: "Well, Jerusalem was the capital
of my country when London was a marsh."

The Debate over Zionism's International Orientation

The First World War profoundly reshaped the international system, as well as the fate of the Jews. By the end of the war, Britain—having ousted the Turks—ruled over the Land of Israel, and it issued the 1917 Balfour Declaration, its public commitment to establishing "a national home for the Jewish people" there. Britain would bring the order and civility that the Ottomans lacked.

The international reality, however, made it difficult and soon nearly impossible for the Zionist movement to advance its agenda. Britain had likely underestimated the Arabs' fierce opposition to Jewish immigration and land purchase. Moreover, key British officials in Palestine did not endorse or implement the Balfour Declaration. The discrepancy between the declaration and its actual impact (or, rather, lack thereof) was thus summarized by Chaim Weizmann: "I soon discovered that the Balfour Declaration, which had made such a stir in the outside world, had never reached many of [General Edmund] Allenby's officers, even those of high rank. They knew nothing about it. . . . Russians, Jews, Bolsheviks were different words for the same thing in the minds of most of the British officers in Palestine in those days, and even when they were not entirely ignorant of developments, they saw little reason to put themselves out for the Jews—Declaration or no Declaration."[1]

Meanwhile, in Britain itself, some prominent public figures were fiercely criticizing the Balfour Declaration. Historian Arnold Toynbee, who influenced British policy in his capacity as director of studies at Chatham House, for one, believed that the Balfour Declaration had caused irreversible damage to British interests in the Arab world. Many senior Foreign Office civil servants shared this view.

Indeed, Britain could not ignore the Arab subjects of its empire. When the Ottoman Empire joined Germany and the Austro-Hungarian Empire in the First World War, the sultan declared a jihad against Britain. To help dismantle the Ottoman Empire, the British promised the Arabs under Ottoman rule that Britain would grant them independence after the war.

During the First World War, Jews fought as French, German, British, and Austrian soldiers. To most Jews in Eastern Europe (or *Ostjuden* in German), supporting Germany in the war was self-evident. German was the official language of the Zionist Congress. A German victory was deemed preferable: Russia was the Jews' worst enemy, and Germany was a beacon of civilization. As for the German Jews, they were diehard patriots despite the widespread antisemitism that prevailed in their country.

Among *Ostjuden*, Chaim Weizmann, who after Herzl's death would replace him as the de facto chief diplomat of the Zionist movement, saw things differently. Born in Belarus (then part of the Russian Empire) in 1874 to a traditional Jewish family, Weizmann had studied chemistry in Germany and Switzerland, obtained his PhD at age twenty-five, moved to Britain in 1904 to lecture at the University of Manchester, and in 1910 became a British subject. He was of the opinion that only Britain would be of any help in advancing the Zionist project. The outbreak of World War I and the German-Turkish alliance confirmed the wisdom of Weizmann's diplomatic choice.

While in Britain, Weizmann became familiar, and often friendly, with British political leaders, and he rallied many of them to the Zionist cause. Among them was Herbert Samuel, the first Jew to serve as a British cabinet minister (in 1909). Another friend was Arthur Balfour, who served as prime minister between 1902 and 1905 and as foreign secretary between 1916 and 1919. Weizmann was instrumental in turning Balfour into an ardent Zionist. When Balfour complained to Weizmann about the World Zionist Congress's rejection of the Uganda proposal in 1903, Weizmann rhetorically asked Balfour if he would trade London for Saskatchewan. "Of course not," Balfour said. "London is the capital of my country"—to which Weizmann replied, "Jerusalem was the capital of my country when London was a marsh."

Weizmann's wit and persuasiveness were legendary. He inspired awe despite his powerlessness. Abba Eban would later write of Weizmann, "He could dominate a room by the mere act of entering it. The word 'dignity' sprang to the lips of everyone meeting him for the first time."[2]

When, in 1917, British troops started their advance against the Ottomans from the eastern shores of the Mediterranean, the prospect of British rule over Palestine became real. At the time Britain had few qualms about advancing the "national home for the Jewish people," since the Arabs had been mostly useless in the war against the Turks, and their "great revolt" had turned out to be a flop. But for Britain to officially endorse the Zionist project in Palestine, a government decision was needed. And, ironically, the strongest opposition to Zionism in the British government came from a Jew: Edwin Samuel Montagu (the second British Jew to enter the cabinet), who feared that Zionism would undermine the social status and political equality enjoyed by British Jews. Montagu managed to dilute the first legal document to recognize the Jews' right to establish a "national home" by removing from the Balfour Declaration Jewish self-rule and unlimited immigration. Nonetheless, the November 1917 declaration was one of Weizmann's greatest diplomatic achievements.

Weizmann, already an Anglophile, would remain forever indebted to Britain. Even in the 1930s, as British governments started forgoing their commitments to the Jews while appeasing the Arabs, Weizmann chose to avoid open confrontation with Britain. After all, as opposed to many Zionist leaders, he had realized early on that the pro-Ottoman German Empire would be of no help to the Zionist cause and that, with the outbreak of World War I and the German-Turkish alliance, the Zionist movement could only gain from a diplomatic alliance with Britain. Yet in the 1930s, Britain's strategic interests and geopolitical calculations had changed. Other Zionists increasingly criticized Weizmann for not reassessing his nearly dogmatic pro-British policy.

Among Weizmann's challengers in this regard was Vladimir (Ze'ev) Jabotinsky. Himself an *Ostjude* (he was born in 1880 in Odessa, a liberal city by Russian standards), Jabotinsky had also advocated a pro-British policy with the outbreak of the First World War. He had even convinced Britain to establish a Jewish army to fight alongside the British against the Turks. In 1917 the British government established three Jewish battalions known as the Jewish Legion. Jabotinsky served as an officer, and his battalion contributed to the conquest of what would become British Palestine.[3]

Once Palestine was in British hands, however, Jabotinsky realized that Britain was in no hurry to establish "a national home for the Jewish people." He openly complained to the British authorities about British army officers' cold, if not hostile, attitude toward Zionism. Discharged from the British army in 1919, Jabotinsky was elected to the first Assembly of Representatives in Palestine (established by the

British authorities) a year later and to the World Zionist Organization (WZO) Executive Council in 1921. By now he disagreed with the WZO over its conciliatory attitude toward Britain. In 1920 the British arrested and imprisoned him for hiding weapons and secretly training Jewish soldiers in Palestine to fight against both the Arabs and the British. Although he was pardoned and freed from a British jail after a couple of months, the British government never forgave him for his insubordination. Authorities considered him an agitator and blamed him for encouraging unrest. After the 1929 wave of violence in Palestine, Jabotinsky was barred from re-entering Palestine. He would live in Europe for the rest of his days.

In May 1939 the House of Commons approved the "White Paper," which drastically curtailed Jewish immigration and Jewish land purchases. Jabotinsky called for an armed Jewish revolt against Britain—which did not immediately materialize because of the outbreak of the Second World War in September 1939 and Jabotinsky's own premature death in August 1940.

Ideologically Jabotinsky's sympathies lay with Britain and the Western democracies. As opposed to most Zionist leaders at the time, he was not a socialist but a classical liberal, and as such he opposed a diplomatic alignment with the Soviet Union. Yet he also realized that from the mid-1930s onward, Jewish statehood no longer served British interests.

By contrast, to dogmatic Marxists—and there were many of those among the early Zionist settlers—conflicts could only be social and economic. Hence were Jewish and Arab "workers" on the same side of history's barricades. As the feud between Arabs and Jews escalated under British rule, most Socialist Zionists reassessed the conflict as a national one—but they also thought the Arabs would eventually see the light, thanks to the economic benefits brought by Jewish settlement, agriculture, and industry.

For his part, Jabotinsky thought the material benefits theory was wishful thinking. In his 1923 article "The Iron Wall" he asserted that Arab nationalism was authentic, and as such Palestine's Arabs would not trade their national pride and aspirations for economic benefits. Therefore, the Zionists had two choices: abandon their project altogether or pursue it behind an allegorical "iron wall" of deterrence and determination. Only once the Jewish state had become powerful and indestructible might the Arabs acquiesce to a reality they understandably abhorred.

Jabotinsky had no monopoly over political realism, of course. In fact, David Ben-Gurion was no less of an "iron wall" disciple than Jabotinsky himself. As former Israeli foreign minister Shlomo Ben-Ami wrote of Ben-Gurion, "[He] accepted for all practical purposes Jabotinsky's iron-wall strategy. The Jewish State could only emerge, and force the Arabs to accept it, if it erected around it an impregnable wall of Jewish might and deterrence."[4]

Ben-Gurion was born in Russian Poland (or "Congress Poland") in 1886. A politically active Zionist from a young age, he immigrated by himself to the Land of Israel at age twenty. Shortly after his arrival, he was elected to the central committee of Po'alei Zion, a Marxist Zionist party. He worked as a farmer on a collective farm (kibbutz) and joined an armed force of Jewish watchmen. In 1912 (when the Land of Israel was ruled by the Turks) he temporarily moved to Istanbul to study law, in 1917 he fought in the Jewish Legion, and in 1919 he was elected head of the new Ahdut Ha-Avoda party. By the 1920s he emerged as a dominant political figure. In 1935 he was elected chairman of the executive committee of the Jewish Agency, the de facto "Zionist government" during the British Mandate. It was in this capacity that Ben-Gurion would declare Israel's independence in May 1948 and became Israel's first prime minister.

Ben-Gurion's decisiveness and pragmatism would turn out to be valuable assets both for himself and for the country he came to lead.

Between Ideology and Realpolitik

Great Britain proved an unreliable ally for the Zionist movement. For a start, Britain cut off over two-thirds of the Palestine Mandate from Jewish immigration by creating "Transjordan" (the territory east of the Jordan River) in 1922. Britain was more invested in compensating Emir Faisal and his brother Abdullah, whom they had promised a "Great Arab Kingdom." Then, during the war, Britain made promises to the Arabs and to the Jews, whose support was needed to fight the Ottomans, but once the Ottomans were defeated, Britain became evasive toward the Jews. As the conflict between Jews and Arabs escalated, Britain could not afford to alienate a vast and oil-rich Arab world that stood between the Mediterranean and Britain's empire in India. By contrast, alienating the small Jewish community of Palestine was politically affordable.

British rule in Palestine was mired in conflict from day one. To the Arabs, the Balfour Declaration was an illegitimate document that infringed upon their rights. To the Jews, the British tendency to downplay the Balfour Declaration and to delay its implementation was a breach of a written commitment and contrary to the Jews' right to self-determination. The Jewish population of Palestine increased at the beginning of the British Mandate, both because the Palestinian Jews whom the Ottomans had expelled during World War I returned from their Egyptian exile and because some of the Russian Jews who had fled the Bolshevik revolution in 1917 chose Palestine as their destination. The new British regime was "welcomed" in 1920 by Arab riots and attacks again Jewish settlements.

Britain mishandled the nascent Arab-Jewish conflict in Palestine from the very beginning. It alienated the Jews when it tried to appease the Arabs, and vice versa. This might have been inevitable, but poor judgment and flawed decisions often made things worse. One of the British government's early faux pas was to appoint Herbert Samuel as

its first high commissioner in Palestine. The intention was undoubtedly good: the Jews of Palestine complained that the British authorities did not protect them from Arab violence, and so appointing a
Jew as high commissioner would surely reassure them. But precisely
because Samuel was Jewish, he went out of his way to convince the
Arabs of his complete lack of pro-Jewish bias. When he pardoned
Jabotinsky in 1920, Samuel also pardoned the Arab rioters who had
initiated the violence. Samuel's gravest mistake, however, was his 1921
appointment of Hadj Amin al-Husseini—who was already known to
be deeply antisemitic and passionately anti-British—as "Great Mufti
of Jerusalem." (Samuel likely picked him under the influence of Ernest
Richmond, the assistant civil secretary to the Government of Palestine
between 1920 and 1924. Richmond, an anti-Zionist, would resign from
his post in protest against what he considered to be the pro-Zionist
policy of the British government.)

Shortly after his appointment, al-Husseini started instigating riots
and violence against the Jewish population. To appease him, Samuel
ordered a temporary suspension of Jewish immigration—infuriating
the Jews. It was thanks to Winston Churchill that Jewish immigration
to Palestine became unrestricted again in 1922.

Yet, despite the fact that Churchill lifted restriction on Jewish
immigration to Palestine, Jews did not immigrate en masse. In the
1920s living conditions were harsh in Palestine. Europe, by contrast,
was recovering from the Great War; until the 1929 financial crisis,
the Old Continent was relatively stable and prosperous. Hence the
tragic paradox: at the very time the gates of Palestine were relatively
open to Jewish immigration, only a small number of Jews did immigrate. In the mid-1920s, Chaim Weizmann cried out, "Jews, where are
you?"[5] After the 1929 financial crisis, economic turmoil in Europe, and
the Nazis' rise to power in Germany, more and more Jews asked for
immigration permits to Palestine, but by then British authorities were
again restricting Jewish immigration (following the 1929 Arab wave

of violence initiated by al-Husseini in which 133 Jews were murdered in Jerusalem, Hebron, and Safed). While condemning the violence, the British high commissioner Sir John Chancellor wrote to his government that the Balfour Declaration had been "a colossal blunder."[6]

Another Arab revolt erupted in 1936, and the British government was anxious not to alienate Arab leaders whose support was thought to be crucial in the looming war with Nazi Germany. During the 1936–39 Arab revolt, the mufti benefited from generous funds provided by both Hitler and Mussolini.[7] Indeed, the two European dictators were equally involved in the civil wars that simultaneously took place in Palestine and Spain.

In May 1939 the British government published a "White Paper" that limited Jewish immigration to 75,000 a year for the next five years; after that, any further Jewish immigration would need the approval of the Arab leadership of Palestine. Palestine would also be granted independence "within ten years." According to the White Paper, Palestine was then home to 450,000 Jews, which represented a third of the Mandate's population. The implementation of the White Paper, therefore, would lead to an independent Palestine with a two-thirds Arab majority. The idea of partition was dropped, dismissed by the White Paper as "impracticable." A one-third Jewish minority in an Arab state would not have come close to a Jewish "national home," let alone a Jewish state. Indeed, the White Paper explicitly stated that "His Majesty's Government... now declare[s] unequivocally that it is not part of their policy that Palestine should become a Jewish State."

The publication of the 1939 White Paper had been preceded by Hitler's unopposed invasion of Czechoslovakia. Czechs and Jews alike were never to forget British prime minister Neville Chamberlain's words upon Hitler's occupation of Prague: why should England, Chamberlain rhetorically asked, risk war for "a far-away country of which we know very little and whose language we don't understand?" Adding insult to injury, Chamberlain told Czech diplomat Jan Masaryk about the Czech president, "Mr. Masaryk, you happen to believe in Dr. Beneš, I happen to trust Herr Hitler." As Chaim Weizmann was to reflect on those dark hours, "We could not tell what the future held in store for us; we only knew that we had little to expect in the way of sympathy or action from the Western democracies."[8] (Ten years later, in 1948, Israel would win its war of independence thanks to Czech military supplies. Jan Masaryk, a strong supporter of Zionism, said in 1945 that he might have joined the Haganah and fought for Israel's independence had he been younger.[9])

Ironically, the White Paper concurred with Jabotinsky's 1923 prediction in "The Iron Wall": "It has been the hope of British Governments ever since the Balfour Declaration was issued that in time the Arab population, recognizing the advantages to be derived from Jewish settlement and development in Palestine, would become reconciled to the further growth of the Jewish National Home. This hope has not been fulfilled."[10] Jabotinsky had opted for the "iron wall" strategy; the British government chose to abandon the Zionist project. Indeed, Jabotinsky and his followers broke away from the Haganah, the military wing of the *Yishuv*, to form their own military force, the Irgun. An open war between Britain and the Irgun had begun.

Ben-Gurion also strongly opposed the White Paper, but once World War II erupted Britain found itself fighting the Jews' worst enemy: Nazi Germany. Hence was the *Yishuv* faced with a Cornelian dilemma, which Ben-Gurion famously summarized thus: "We must fight the White Paper as if there were no war and fight together with Britain as if there were no White Paper." Less famous, but no less cogent, was Ben-Gurion's rhetorical question "Who is going to stop the Nazis from sweeping into Palestine, the members of the Zionist Executive or the British generals in the Western Desert?"[11] The British government knew that the Jews would have no choice but to rally against Nazi Germany, despite the White Paper, as Prime Minister Neville Chamberlain explained cynically: "When war comes, the Jews will have to support us because the enemy is Hitler. The Arabs will have a choice. Support of Hitler is a viable option for them. Therefore, we must support the hostile Arabs and distance ourselves from the cooperative Jews."[12] The British Committee of Imperial Defense was no less explicit when it stated in January 1939, "We assume that, immediately on the outbreak of war, the necessary measures would be taken. . . in order to bring about a completed appeasement of Arab opinion in Palestine and in neighboring countries."[13]

Though a socialist, Ben-Gurion was no dogmatic Marxist. He had no doubt that the conflict between Jews and Arabs in Palestine was national and that the alleged "proletarian" solidarity between Arab and Jewish workers against capitalism was nonsense. As for the search for international allies, Ben-Gurion's approach was pragmatic. He saw the Soviet Union as an unreconcilable, historic enemy of the Jewish people; denounced it as a "regime which destroyed, shattered and uprooted all of human dignity, all of workers' rights, all of human freedom, and is sustained by terror and a secret police"; and avowed that "the Stalinist regime in its essence and its historical aspirations of imperialism and Russian chauvinism *par excellence*, cannot be reconciled with the existence of a Jewish people having the right of self-determination."[14]

For the *Yishuv's* diehard Marxists, by contrast, their common struggle with their Soviet "brothers" was self-evident; and since Communist Russia was leading the global struggle against "imperialism," including the British in Palestine, colluding with the Soviets made complete sense. The radical fringes of Palestine's socialists were never willing to face the fact that the Soviet regime was fundamentally both anti-Zionistic and antisemitic.

Zionism and Marxism were conceptually incompatible, at least on paper. Zionism offered a national solution to the "Jewish problem," while for Marxism this "problem" would only be solved with the end of capitalism. With the proletarian revolution, nationalities would become irrelevant, and the Jews would be no exception. Zionism, by contrast, maintained that the Jews were a nation entitled to self-determination like any other nation. This incompatibility was both understood and denounced by Communist Russian leader Vladimir Lenin, who declared, "Whoever directly or indirectly puts forward the slogan of a Jewish 'national culture' is (whatever his good intentions may be) an enemy of the proletariat, a supporter of the *old* and of the *caste* position of the Jews, an accomplice of the rabbis and the bourgeoisie."[15] The Soviet regime translated its doctrine into policy by shutting down synagogues, banning the learning of Hebrew, and denouncing "Zionist activities" as a betrayal of the revolution. The Cheka, the military arm of the Bolshevik party, closed down Zionist offices and arrested Zionist activists. The official Soviet stance on Zionism was that "under the mask of democracy, [Zionism] seeks to corrupt the Jewish youth and to throw them into the arms of the counter-revolutionary bourgeoisie in the interests of Anglo-French capitalism. To restore the Palestine state, these representatives of the Jewish bourgeoisie rely on reactionary forces [including] such rapacious imperialists as Raymond Poincaré, Lloyd George, and the Pope."[16]

Even though Russian Jews were persecuted by the repressive Soviet regime, they were accused in the West of being the instigators of Bolshevism. Indeed, there were many Communist leaders of Jewish descent (such as Leon Trotsky). Once Stalin effectively took control of the Soviet state after Lenin's death in 1924, however, the persecution of Jews and of Zionist activists redoubled. The most doctrinaire Marxist Zionists in British Palestine were either ignorant of or blind to Stalin's antisemitism and anti-Zionism. They insisted on aligning with the Soviet Union against "British imperialism."

"Biltmore, Shmiltmore"

On May 11, 1942, six hundred delegates from the World Zionist Congress (including Chaim Weizmann and David Ben-Gurion) convened in New York's Biltmore Hotel and issued a declaration on the political aims of Zionism.[17] What became known as the "Biltmore Program" demanded that "Palestine be established as a Jewish Commonwealth" and that all restrictions to Jewish immigration be lifted. The program did not use the word "state," but unlike the Balfour Declaration (which agreed to a Jewish national home "in Palestine"), the Biltmore Program designated "Palestine" as a whole as the future "Jewish Commonwealth."

The Biltmore Program was adopted less than four months after the Wannsee Conference, which formalized the Nazi policy of the final extermination of European Jews. As the Zionist leadership was vainly demanding from Britain unrestricted Jewish immigration and Jewish national sovereignty, it helplessly heard reports on the ongoing genocide in Europe. The mass murder of Jews had already begun in German-occupied Europe. On January 30, 1939, Hitler had declared to the Reichstag, "If the international Jewish financiers in and outside Europe should succeed in plunging the nations once more into a world war, then the result will not be the Bolshevization of the earth, and thus the victory of Jewry, but the annihilation of the Jewish race in Europe!"

How could "Jewish financiers" (i.e., capitalists) wish to promote "Bolshevization" (i.e., Communism)? And how could Soviet Jews possibly be the agents of a regime that enslaved them and destroyed their cultural heritage? These contradictions typically characterized Hitler's irrational hatred of the Jews. He was convinced that the Jews ruled the world and were out to destroy Germany. Hence his threat to annihilate European Jews if a new war (which, in Hitler's mind, only Jews could trigger) were to erupt. It is also telling that the Wannsee Conference was convened after the prospect of a German victory became doomed: in December 1941 Germany lost the Battle of Moscow and declared war on the United States. If the odds were turning against Germany, Hitler believed, it could only be because of the Jews. Eliminate them and Germany would have the upper hand again. Moreover, Hitler believed that the *Germans*, not the Jews, were *the* chosen people. Since, in Hitler's view, both nations were vying for world domination, one of the two (the Jews, of course) had to be eliminated: "The struggle for world domination will be fought entirely between us, between Germans and Jews. . . . There cannot be two Chosen People. We are God's People!"[18] The belief that Jews run the world and manipulate the great powers to prostrate Germany was ingrained among Nazis. A German officer explained Germany's defeat in May 1945 thus: "It is the second time that the Jews win, but next time we'll get them."[19]

In the prewar years, the Zionist leadership encouraged Jewish immigration to Palestine and fought the 1939 White Paper. But few predicted the Holocaust. Jabotinsky, for one, was adamant that the catastrophe was coming and that the Jews had to get out of Europe. In 1936 he conceived an "evacuation plan" to Palestine for the Jews of Poland, Hungary, and Romania. He met with Polish foreign minister Józef Beck, with Hungarian leader Miklós Horthy, and Romanian prime minister Gheorghe Tătărescu to promote his plan. All three leaders were sympathetic, but local Jewish leaders were skeptical and even hostile. For its part, the British government made it clear that it would not allow such massive immigration to Palestine, and Chaim Weizmann, then chairman of the World Zionist Organization, dismissed Jabotinsky's plan as unrealistic. Addressing the Jews of Warsaw in August 1938, one year before the German invasion of Poland, Jabotinsky told them to run for their lives while they still could:

> For three years I have been imploring you, Jews of Poland, the glory of world Jewry. I have been ceaselessly warning you that the catastrophe is coming closer. My hair has turned white and I have aged in these years, because my heart is bleeding because you, dear brothers and sisters, do not see the volcano which will soon begin to spurt out the fire of destruction. I see a terrifying

sight. The time is short in which one can still be saved. . . . Listen
to my remarks at this twelfth hour. For God's sake: may each one
save his life while there is still time. And time is short.[20]

On September 2, 1939, the day after the German invasion of Poland,
Jabotinsky met with British colonel John Patterson (who had co-
commanded with him the Jewish Legion during World War I) to
discuss the formation of a British-commanded Jewish army. In the
summer of 1940, Jabotinsky toured the United States to make the
case for a Jewish army fighting alongside the Allies. Addressing the
Manhattan Center on June 19, 1940 (the day after Churchill's "finest
hour" speech and de Gaulle's call for resistance after the appointment of Philippe Pétain as France's premier), Jabotinsky reminded
his audience of "the principle which is the secret of our Jewish people's survival through all these centuries of torture: No Surrender!"[21]
Jabotinsky died a few weeks later (on August 4) from a heart attack.
In his eulogy, Chaim Weizmann recalled the disagreement between
Jabotinsky and the World Zionist Organization over the question
of urgency. "In his opinion," said Weizmann of Jabotinsky, "we had
only limited time in which our program could be realized. This may
and may not be so."[22] Within four years, the Nazis had exterminated
six million Jews.

The Zionist dilemma vis-à-vis Britain remained. The British were
fighting Germany but were also preventing Jewish immigration to
Palestine (while in the United States, the Roosevelt administration
was suppressing immigration far below the limits set by American
law). When World War II broke out, Chaim Weizmann announced
that Palestine's Jews would in fact "stand by Great Britain and will
fight on the side of the democracies."[23]

Palestine Jews also helped the Free French in Lebanon and Syria.
Between September 1940 and June 1941, the Levant radio of the Free
French operated in Haifa from the home of a sympathetic Palestin-

ian Jew by the name of David Hacohen.[24] Moshe Dayan lost an eye during one of the military operations in which Jewish commandos from Palestine helped the Free French fight Vichy forces. Maurice Fischer, a Belgian Jew who had emigrated to Palestine in 1930, joined de Gaulle's Free French Forces in Beirut in 1940 and was decorated for his prowess (later, he would become Israel's first ambassador to Paris). Indeed, de Gaulle would later confess to French journalist Jean-Jacques Servan-Schreiber, "I remember Palestine in 1941. Those Jewish youngsters were wonderful. They fought on our side, while the Arabs — we must admit — supported the other side."[25]

Yet Palestinian Jews were hardly given the opportunity to fight collectively for the Allies. Given the deep animosity between Britain and the Zionist movement ever since the publication of the 1939 White Paper, the British establishment regarded with suspicion the idea of a battalion composed of Palestinian Jews. Nonetheless, Chaim Weizmann (whose son Michael was killed in 1942 as a Royal Air Force pilot) promoted it, and Churchill approved of it, mainly to free up British manpower in Palestine for the European front. By the fall of 1940, Churchill had decided to proceed with the establishment of a Jewish army, but the British High Command blocked the idea, and Churchill obliged.[26] Nonetheless, in 1942, Churchill ordered the creation of the SOE (Subversive Operations Executive), a secret Jewish guerilla force in Palestine meant to fight the Germans, should they invade Palestine. Overseen by Abba (Aubrey) Eban, the SOE was never called to action. Only toward the end of the war, in September 1944, did the British government establish a Jewish Brigade composed of about five thousand Palestinian Jews. The brigade fought in Italy, and Jewish soldiers wearing a Star of David insignia on their uniforms arrested German soldiers. By that time, Menachem Begin had declared, in February 1944, a "revolt" against the British Empire.

Menachem Begin arrived in Palestine in May 1942 as a Polish soldier. In December 1942, after being granted a leave of absence by his commander, he joined the Irgun, the underground paramilitary Zionist organization that had split from the Haganah (military arm of the Jewish Agency) in 1931. Begin became leader of the Irgun in 1944. He declared the recommencement of the Jewish revolt against Britain once the Allied victory against Nazi Germany was assured, since Britain had continued to curtail, and even to prevent, Jewish immigration to Palestine, despite the Holocaust. His sabotage operations against the mandatory authorities in Palestine enraged the British government and embarrassed the Jewish Agency, which still believed the Zionists could not afford to alienate Great Britain.

In fact, at the beginning of the war, Britain and the Irgun *had* fought together against the Nazis and their Arab allies In May 1941 the British government had sent David Raziel, then commander-in-chief of the Irgun, to Iraq to help the British army defeat the pro-Nazi rebellion of Rashid Ali al-Gaylani. The Luftwaffe (German air force) killed Raziel and a British officer during the operation. It is precisely because the Irgun fought alongside Britain until 1944 that the Lehi (Hebrew acronym for "Fighters for the Freedom of Israel") was established as a split organization in September 1940. One of the founders and leaders of Lehi, Avraham Stern, was so determined to fight Britain regardless of the military situation in Europe that he contacted Nazi diplomats to offer Jewish participation in the German war effort in return for German support for Jewish immigration to Palestine. In the last months of 1940, Stern sent a Lehi militant named Naftali Lubenchik to meet with the German diplomat Werner Otto von Hentig in Beirut to propose a new alliance, a "community of interests between the intentions of the new order in Germany" and the Jewish people.[27] Stern had ideological sympathies for militarism and fascism but completely misunderstood the Nazi ideology. The Nazis did not only want to remove Jews from Europe; they wanted to erase the Jews from the face of the earth. Hitler himself had expressed his opposition to Jewish immigration to

Palestine, which, he claimed, was "suffering the cruelest maltreatment for the benefit of Jewish interlopers."[28] The German government did not bother to reply to Stern's delusional offer.

Lehi's folly and clumsiness (its attempts to rob banks generally ended in lethal fiascos) caused much harm to the Zionist cause. On November 6, 1944, Lehi members assassinated Lord Moyne, a personal friend of Winston Churchill who had served in the war cabinet after Churchill became prime minister in May 1940. At the time of his assassination, Moyne was resident minister in Cairo, and his tasks had included the struggle against Rommel's Afrika Korps in North Africa. That Lehi considered Moyne an enemy despite his struggle against Nazism in the Middle East and North Africa indicated that Stern's followers had not abandoned their illusions about Nazi Germany and their blind hatred of Britain. Targeting Moyne, of all British officials, was dismayingly ironic to boot, since Moyne, as opposed to most British civil and military officials in the Middle East, had just come out as supporting the establishment of a Jewish state within a partitioned Palestine.[29] Two days before Moyne's assassination, Churchill had met with Weizmann and told him that "our Zionist cause is going well. Moyne is now on our side."[30] Churchill also spoke of partition and said he was in favor of including the Negev in the territory of the Jewish state.[31]

Moyne's assassination dealt a fatal and long-term blow to Zionism. It angered and alienated the otherwise pro-Zionist Winston Churchill, it ruined the chances of establishing a Jewish state while Churchill was still in power, and it nearly ignited a civil war within the *Yishuv*. As Chaim Weizmann was to lament, "The harm done to our cause by the assassination of Lord Moyne . . . was . . . in providing our enemies with a convenient excuse, and in helping to justify their course before the bar of public opinion."[32]

Shortly after the announcement of Lord Moyne's death, Secretary of State for the Colonies Oliver Stanley told Chaim Weizmann that "unless the Jews [can] rid themselves of this murderous tail, people like [Churchill] who [have] done so much for [you] in the past [will] feel relieved of any responsibility in the future."[33] Churchill himself issued a grave warning: "If our dreams for Zionism are to end in the smoke of assassins' pistols and our labours for its future to produce only a new set of gangsters worthy of Nazi Germany, many like myself will have to reconsider the position we have maintained so consistently and so long in the past. If there is to be any hope of a peaceful and successful future for Zionism, these wicked activities must cease, and those responsible for them must be destroyed root and branch."[34] Churchill, therefore, expected and demanded "the wholehearted cooperation of the entire Jewish community."[35]

The political leadership of the *Yishuv* complied and started cracking down on Jewish terrorists. It was the beginning of the "Hunting Season," or *saison* (from the French "la saison de chasse"). By this time, once there was no doubt about the Allies' victory, the Irgun had also turned its guns against Britain. Thus the Jewish Agency hunted down both Irgun and Lehi militants, and had it not been for Menachem Begin's call for restraint, the *saison* could have degenerated into civil war.

Despite the cooperation of the Jewish Agency, however, the murder of Lord Moyne deepened British Foreign Office hostility toward Zionism. While Churchill retained his Zionist sympathies, proposals for the partition of Palestine, which had been scheduled for discussion in the British cabinet, were shelved indefinitely. According to British historian Bernard Wasserstein, a Jewish state in a partitioned Palestine might have materialized toward the end of World War II had it not been for the assassination of Lord Moyne.[36]

Other reasons underlay Britain's decision to stick to the 1939 White Paper. Churchill, a longtime friend of the Jews, had lost the British general election of July 1945. The new prime minister, Clement Attlee, and his foreign secretary, Ernest Bevin, steadfastly maintained the White Paper policy, motivated by a cold calculation: Britain had been bled and impoverished by six years of war, and thus the Middle East oil fields it controlled were more precious than ever. It therefore could not afford to alienate the Arab world.

The British government's decision to stick to the White Paper despite its victory in World War II and the revelations of the Holocaust convinced Jewish Agency executive committee chairman David Ben-Gurion to also conduct operations against Britain. On October 1, 1945, he ordered Haganah commander Moshe Sneh to target the British military. The Haganah and the Irgun made a joint decision to bomb the King David Hotel, the then headquarters of the British armed forces in Palestine, but the Haganah asked Begin to push off the bombing, as Chaim Weizmann (then wzo president) had heard of the plan and threatened to reveal it to British authorities. The Haganah itself backed down, and Weizmann did not inform the authorities, but the Irgun carried out the operation on July 22, 1946. In addition, the Irgun began a practice of hanging and flogging British officers in retaliation for the hanging and flogging of Irgun fighters. The situation of British forces in Palestine became untenable. In February 1947 the British government announced that it was referring the question of Palestine to the United Nations.

While Britain had abandoned the idea of partition in 1937 (see chapter 8), it re-emerged at the United Nations ten years later. In the meantime, one-third of the Jewish people had perished in the Holocaust, and the need for statehood had become urgent. Ben-Gurion realized that claiming all of Mandatory Palestine was not a realistic option, and he considered partition a lesser evil. When reminded about the 1942 Biltmore Program, Ben-Gurion replied, "Biltmore, shmiltmore. We must have a Jewish state."[37]

Conclusion

World War I reshaped the international system, and Great Britain replaced the Ottoman Empire as the ruler of the Land of Israel. The 1917 Balfour Declaration proclaiming Britain's public commitment to establishing a Jewish national home constituted a diplomatic achievement, but its content was vague, and many senior British diplomats thought it unnecessarily alienated the Arab world and therefore undermined British interests. Britain tried to please both Jews and Arabs but ended up losing the confidence of both communities. With the looming threat of war with Germany and the Arab revolt in Palestine (1936–39), Britain adopted a policy of appeasement and reneged on its commitment to Zionism. Chamberlain calculated that since the Arabs had a choice whether to support Hitler and the Jews did not, Britain "must support the hostile Arabs and distance ourselves from the cooperative Jews."

The Second World War and the Holocaust created an acute dilemma for Zionist leaders, because Britain was fighting both Nazi Germany and Jewish statehood. Ben-Gurion summarized it thus: "We must fight the White Paper as if there were no war and fight together with Britain as if there were no White Paper." This dilemma split the Jewish underground: the Irgun declared war on Britain in 1944, the Haganah did not target the British military until 1945, and Lehi viewed the war against Britain as so imperative it even justified an alliance with Nazi Germany. At the same time, the Jews of Palestine fought with the Allies against the Third Reich.

Despite the Holocaust and Jewish support during the war, Britain maintained its strict restrictions on Jewish immigration and its opposition to a Jewish state. Hence, once the outcome of World War II was assured, the tension between Zionism and Britain turned into an open conflict. As Britain started losing control of its Palestine Mandate, the United Nations was asked to propose a solution to the Palestine conflict. In the wake of the Holocaust, the need for Jewish statehood in the Land of Israel had become urgent, and Ben-Gurion concluded that partition was now the only realistic pathway to statehood. He therefore came to endorse partition.

8. The British Mandate and Its Dilemmas

We Arabs, especially the educated among us, look with the
deepest sympathy on the Zionist movement. Our deputation here in Paris is fully acquainted with the proposals submitted by the Zionist Organization to the Peace Conference,
and we regard them as moderate and proper. We will do our
best, in so far as we are concerned, to help them through;
we will wish the Jews a most hearty welcome home.

FAISAL I BIN HUSSEIN BIN ALI AL-HASHEMI

The Middle East's New Borders

The founders of the Zionist movement had an ideal: to establish a
Jewish nation-state in the biblical Land of Israel. Most early Zionists
also wanted the Jewish state to be a socialist model of equality. They
soon came to realize, however, that it is easier to have ideals as an
author than as a diplomat and that the encounter between ideals
and the reality of world politics can be painful. As Abba Eban wrote,
"Writers who have described the ideal society have usually contrived
to situate their Utopias on desert islands or on the peaks of inacces-
sible mountains, thus avoiding the two conditions that make Utopia
impossible: boundaries and neighbors. . . . It is not surprising that
Plato's *Republic*, having no neighbors, had no need for a foreign policy."[1]

Theodor Herzl experienced the dilemmas of diplomacy in 1903,
shortly before his death. In 1897 he had gathered the First Zionist

Congress in Basel, Switzerland, to launch the political movement toward the establishment of a Jewish state. Six years later, in 1903, British colonial secretary Joseph Chamberlain offered the Zionist movement the opportunity to establish a Jewish state in Uganda. At the time, the Ottoman Empire was still ruling the Middle East, and so Britain was in no position to accept or reject the Zionist movement's plan to settle in Palestine. Chamberlain's offer produced a Cornelian dilemma for at least part of the Zionist leadership. Zionism aspired to restore Jewish sovereignty in Zion, not in Africa. On the other hand, Jews were being killed by pogroms in Russia, and they urgently needed a safe haven. Herzl did not want to establish a Jewish state in Uganda, but since he also thought the Jews needed a "night shelter," he was willing to consider Chamberlain's offer as a temporary solution.

Herzl brought the proposal up for debate at the Sixth Zionist Congress in 1903. Debate among the delegates was heated and passionate. Chaim Weizmann, who took part, would later write that "it was all very well to talk of Uganda as an auxiliary and a temporary measure, but the deflection of our energies to a purely relief effort would mean, whatever Herzl's intentions were, the practical dismantling of the Zionist Organization in so far as it had to do with Zion."[2] Surprisingly, the religious Zionists of the Mizrachi movement were mostly in favor of the Uganda proposal.[3] Nonetheless, Herzl was fiercely criticized for being willing to even consider the Uganda plan and for bringing it up for discussion. One member of the Zionist Congress shouted at Herzl (in French), "Monsieur le Président, vous êtes un traître!" ("Mr. President, you are a traitor!")[4]

Herzl's de facto successor was Chaim Weizmann, who had made the case for Zionism among world leaders and was instrumental in obtaining the Balfour Declaration from Great Britain in 1917. The Balfour Declaration stated that "His Majesty's government views with favour the establishment in Palestine of a national home for the Jewish people." Yet Britain had many contradictory interests in the Middle

East, and its commitment to the Balfour Declaration could not be taken for granted. France's interests were relevant in the post–World War I Middle East, as Britain and France fought over the spoils of the crumbling Ottoman Empire. Though officially a secular republic, France claimed responsibility for Middle East Christians. British prime minister Lloyd George's attitude to the Holy Land and to France were summarized by his predecessor Herbert Henry Asquith: "Lloyd George . . . does not care a damn for the Jews or their past or their future, but thinks it will be an outrage to let the holy places pass into the possession or under the protectorate of 'agnostic and atheistic' France."[5]

In fact, the British government had published the Balfour Declaration partly to preempt and counter French claims to Palestine.[6] Another reason was the belief that by pleasing "world Jewry," Britain would more likely convince America to join the war and Russia not to capitulate. Indeed, Lord Balfour said so himself: "The vast majority of Jews in Russia and America, as indeed all over the world, now appear to be favorable to Zionism. If we could make a declaration favorable to such an ideal, we should be able to carry on extremely useful propaganda both in Russia and America."[7]

Not all Arab leaders were categorically opposed to the Balfour Declaration. In March 1918 the Arabic newspaper *Al-Kibla* called for cooperation with "the Jews and their settlement movement in Palestine."[8] In June 1918 Chaim Weizmann met with Emir Faisal, son of the Saudi king Hussein Ben-Ali, and seven months later, in January 1919, Weizmann and Faisal signed an agreement in which Faisal recognized the Balfour Declaration and the Jews' right to settle in Palestine and in which Weizmann declared that all Muslim holy sites would remain under Muslim control.

Faisal was a descendant of the Hashemite dynasty. For a short time, in 1920, he crowned himself "king of Greater Syria," a new entity established on the ruins of the Ottoman Empire. He had opposed the

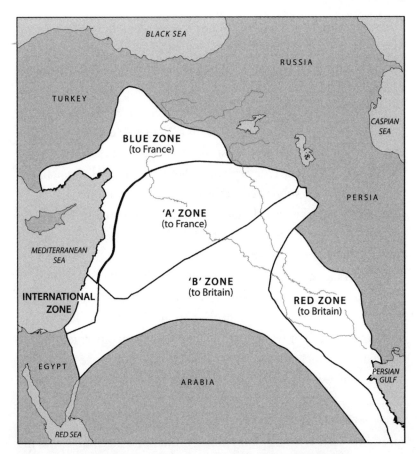

Map 7. The 1916 Sykes-Picot Agreement. Cartography by Bill Nelson.

1916 Sykes-Picot Agreement between Britain and France, in which the two great powers had carved up the Middle East between them, for the very reason that Faisal wanted to establish and rule his own large Arab state.

Now, the agreement between Faisal and Weizmann stipulated that if the Greater Syria kingdom were to be preserved, then Faisal would agree to Jewish self-rule in what he called "southern Syria" and Britain called "Palestine." Faisal added a handwritten note to the agreement stipulating that it would only be valid if his demands toward Britain were met. Otherwise, he maintained, the agreement would become null and void. Britain could not commit to a Greater Syria because of its agreement with France; the Sykes-Picot Agreement had granted France both Syria and Lebanon.

In March 1919 Faisal wrote to Prof. Felix Frankfurter, who had participated in the Paris Peace Conference as a Zionist delegate: "We Arabs, especially the educated among us, look with the deepest sympathy on the Zionist movement. Our deputation here in Paris is fully acquainted with the proposals submitted by the Zionist Organization to the Peace Conference, and we regard them as moderate and proper. We will do our best, in so far as we are concerned, to help them through; we will wish the Jews a most hearty welcome home."[9]

When France conquered Syria in July 1920, it expelled Faisal and put an end to his dream of a Greater Syria. Faisal then asked the British to compensate both him and his brother Abdullah. After all, the two had been promised their own kingdom after the dismemberment of the Ottoman Empire. In response, in August 1921 Britain made Faisal king of Iraq (Iraq was still a British Mandate at the time; it would become an independent country in 1932). As for Abdullah, he had not given up on Syria—he thought there was still a chance to challenge French rule there—but Winston Churchill, who did not want trouble with his French allies, dissuaded him from doing so. During the Cairo Conference of March 1921, Churchill (now the newly appointed colonial secretary) offered Abdullah two-thirds of the Palestine Mandate—essentially the territory east of the Jordan River. Hence was Transjordan created with the stroke of a pen. Churchill and Abdullah agreed that the clauses of the Balfour Declaration pertaining to the Jews' rights to immigrate and to settle the land would not apply to Transjordan. Abdullah would rule over the newly delineated territory and relinquish his claims over Syria.

In July 1922, a year after the 1921 partition of the putative Palestine, the Council of the League of Nations discussed the ratification of the

Palestine Mandate. Its larger body, the League of Nations, had been established after World War I to preserve world peace (it would be replaced by the United Nations after the Second World War) and was then composed of all European countries except Germany and Russia; the British Empire (Canada, India, Australia, etc.); China, Japan, Iran, and most Latin American countries. (The United States did not join the League of Nations.) The League's Council, which served as its executive body, however, was solely composed of the United Kingdom, France, Italy, and Japan. There was no guarantee that the Council would ratify the British Mandate on Palestine. Tensions and uncertainties were not unlike those to surround the United Nations' deliberations regarding the fledgling State of Israel twenty-five years later. Finally, on July 24, 1922, the Council officially approved the Middle East mandates — a landmark decision that granted international legitimacy to the Balfour Declaration.

On the one hand, the League of Nations' endorsement of the Palestine Mandate — including the Balfour Declaration — was binding in international law, because this endorsement came from the Council, the League's executive body. On the other hand, half of the Council was composed of the two countries — Britain and France — that had decided back in 1916 (with the Sykes-Picot Agreement) that the Middle East would be theirs at the end of the war. The Middle East's new borders had been arbitrarily drawn by Britain and France along with U.S. president Woodrow Wilson, who had been involved in drawing the Middle East's borders since the 1919 peace conference in Versailles. As Lord Balfour was to recall, "These three all-powerful, all-ignorant men [Lloyd George of England, Georges Clémenceau of France, and Wilson of America] [were] sitting there and carving up continents."[10]

The Ottoman Empire was composed of provinces (vilayets), themselves subdivided into administrative divisions (sanjaks). Prior to the League of Nations' establishment of British Palestine in 1922, there had been a "Sanjak of Jerusalem," a "Sanjak of Nablus [Sichem]," and

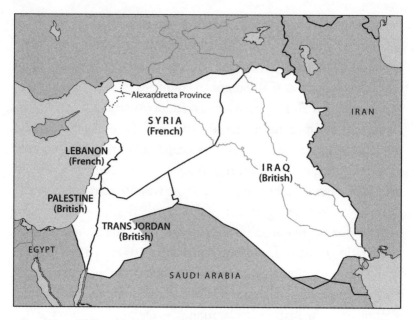

Map 8. The Middle East after World War I: the League of Nations Mandates. Cartography by Bill Nelson.

a "Sanjak of Acre." The newly established British Palestine contained those sanjaks as well as the southern parts of the Vilayets of Syria and Beirut.

To the Zionist leadership, the deal between Churchill and Abdullah unduly removed 77 percent of the original mandate from Jewish immigration and land purchase. Yet nothing could be done; borders were determined by the great powers. When, in 1925, Vladimir Jabotinsky established, from his Parisian exile, his alternative "Union of Revisionist Zionists" that called for the establishment of a Jewish state on both sides of the river Jordan (i.e., both the Palestine Mandate and the Kingdom of Jordan), he was indulging in wishful thinking; Transjordan had been created as a British protectorate to settle the dispute between Abdullah and France, and Britain was not going to revive this dispute to please the Revisionists.

For their part, the Arabs opposed the Balfour Declaration's inclusion within the British Mandate on Palestine, but British leaders largely perceived that opposition as unreasonable and greedy. Lloyd George wrote that the Arabs "have already won independence in Iraq, Arabia, Syria, and Trans-Jordania [*sic*], although most of the Arab races fought throughout the war for the Turkish oppressors. . . . The Palestinian Arabs [in particular] fought for Turkish rule."[11] Yet Britain remained ambivalent and unsure about her endgame in Palestine. As a British diplomat would later admit about the Palestine Mandate, "We never solved the fuzziness of our commitments. Decision makers were torn. Some of them felt guilt about how we treated Jews. . . . Others felt guilt about how we treated the Arabs."[12]

The 1937 Partition Plan and Its Impact on Zionist Diplomacy

The Zionist movement's disappointment over the de facto partition of 1921 paled in comparison with the bad omens the 1930s had in store. The Arab revolt that erupted in Palestine in 1936 convinced the British to limit Jewish immigration and land purchases—a policy that culminated with the 1939 White Paper, which strictly restricted Jewish immigration and land purchases by Jews. As Chaim Weizmann was to summarize British responses to Arab violence in the 1930s, "The Colonial Office which, having been unable to guarantee the security of the Jewish community in Palestine, having ignored our repeated warnings concerning the activities of the Mufti and of his friends of the Arab Executive, having made no attempt to correct the indifference or hostility of British officials in Palestine, now proposed to make us pay the price of its failure."[13]

Indeed, British policy in Palestine was part of its larger diplomacy of appeasement. In the 1930s, Britain tried to appease Fascist Italy and Nazi Germany: it let Mussolini get away with his conquest of Abyssinia (today's Ethiopia), and it looked the other way as Hitler invaded Austria. The British Foreign Office also tried to appease Hadj Amin al-Husseini (who threatened to join forces with Germany and Italy) by publishing the 1939 White Paper. In Palestine, appeasing the Arabs meant rescinding any prospect of Jewish statehood. Yet the 1936 Arab revolt in Palestine erupted precisely because Britain was perceived as weak and indecisive in the wake of Italian and German aggressions. Indeed, as Chaim Weizmann wrote about this unfolding of events, "England's indecisiveness towards Mussolini, who was sending his warships through the Suez Canal, tended to give the Arabs the impression that with the democracies force alone won concessions."[14]

As Nazi Germany was persecuting Jews and challenging the Treaty of Versailles, Socialist Zionists were confident that the Soviet Union would valiantly oppose Hitler. Since, for Hitler, both the Jews and Soviet communism were the enemies of Nazi Germany, many in the *Yishuv* (the Jewish community of British Palestine) hoped that the Soviet Union would keep Germany in check. But the 1939 Ribbentrop-Molotov Pact, in which the Soviet Union and Nazi Germany agreed to share Poland without fighting each other, shattered those illusions; three million Polish Jews were now trapped under two antisemitic dictatorships.

With the collapse of the Versailles treaty in the 1930s, the Wilsonian vision of the end of all wars thanks to agreed-upon rules enforced by the League of Nations became increasingly discredited. Italy's conquest of Abyssinia in 1935, the remilitarization of the Rhineland in 1936, and the German occupation of Austria and Czechoslovakia in 1938 revealed the flimsiness of the Versailles order and the Western democracies' lack of resolve. Liberals who hoped that the Versailles order would hold had their ideals shattered by recurrent international crises. As for Marxists, their faith in the moral irreproachability of the Soviet Union was exposed as hollow when Stalin signed the pact with Hitler in August 1939. Zionist leaders too were not immune from this global disillusionment.

David Ben-Gurion was a Marxist, at least in his younger days. According to Marxist theory, nationalism is an artificial ideology invented by the bourgeoisie to better rule over workers. In a socialist world, so the theory went, there will no longer be nationalist conflicts. If true conflicts are only between social classes, there could not be a nationalist conflict between Jews and Arabs, but only a social conflict between Jewish and Arab workers on the one hand and British imperialists on the other. Ben-Gurion might have bought into this theory when he was young, but he grew out of it. The 1929 riots convinced him that the conflict between Jews and Arabs was indeed national. As he declared in November 1929, "An Arab from the Land of Israel doesn't need and doesn't have to be a Zionist. He cannot agree for the Jews to become the majority."[15] Ben-Gurion still thought, however, that Zionism could buy Arab goodwill by bringing economic development to a backward land.

Ben-Gurion's perception of the conflict between Zionism and the Arabs slowly began to change. The violent opposition to Zionism led by the Jerusalem mufti Hadj Amin al-Husseini had convinced him that establishing a Jewish state with Arab agreement was impossible. The Arab revolt of 1936–39 confirmed his conclusions. In 1937 Ben-Gurion asked Musa al-Alami, a Palestinian leader who was considered a moderate, if the Arab population would abandon violence in exchange for economic aid; al-Alami replied that he'd rather starve than forgo independence. Ben-Gurion was now certain that no agreement with the Arabs would be reached until Jewish power became unassailable.[16]

In addition, Ben-Gurion started having serious doubts about the intentions and reliability of the British authorities. The British had tried to dissuade al-Husseini from maintaining ties with Hitler with appeasement — meeting al-Husseini's demands to end Jewish immigration and Jewish land purchases with the 1939 White Paper — but in the end al-Husseini had only deepened his ties with Hitler. And al-Husseini was not the only Arab leader who aligned with Hitler despite Chamberlain's concessions. In Iraq (a former British Mandate that, despite formal independence in 1932, remained faithful to Great Britain), the revolt of Rashid Ali al-Gaylani was also pro-German. As Abba Eban succinctly put it, "Britain had achieved an acrobatic success in alienating the Jews without winning the hearts of the Arabs."[17]

In terms of international alliances and support, Zionism's last hope seemed to be the Soviet Union. Ben-Gurion's Mapai party was the dominant political force of the *Yishuv*, and it had pro-Soviet sympathies. This last hope fell apart with the signature of the Ribbentrop-Molotov Pact between the Soviet Union and Nazi Germany in 1939. Zionist diplomacy had learned the rules of realpolitik the hard way.

Ben-Gurion's embrace of realism was put to test in 1937 with the partition proposal of the Peel Commission. In 1936, when widespread Arab violence broke out to protest Jewish immigration and land purchases, the British government finally accepted that that the claims of Arabs and Jews were incompatible and it was losing control of its Mandate. As a result, the British government decided to appoint a commission of inquiry, headed by William Peel. The subsequent Peel Commission report, submitted in July 1937, suggested the partition of British Palestine between an Arab state, a Jewish state, and a shrunken British Mandate between Jerusalem and Jaffa.

The Peel Commission's recommendations divided the political leadership of the *Yishuv* and produced an acute dilemma of realpolitik versus ideology. In the end, however, the executive committee of the Jewish Agency (chaired by David Ben-Gurion since 1935) announced its willingness to accept the recommendations. The Arab leadership, on the other hand, flatly rejected the recommendations. In response, British authorities initially adopted the recommendations but eventually abandoned them, so they became moot.

Map 9. The 1937 Peel partition plan. Cartography by Bill Nelson.

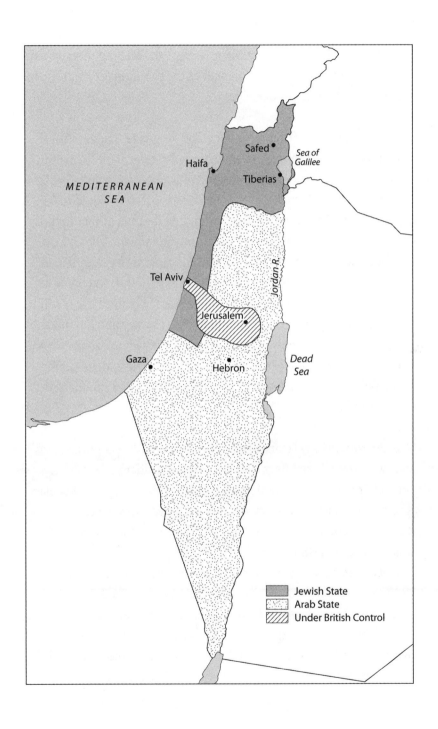

MEDITERRANEAN
SEA

Safed
Haifa
Tiberias
Sea of
Galilee

Tel Aviv

Jerusalem

Jordan R.

Gaza
Hebron

Dead
Sea

Jewish State
Arab State
Under British Control

Professor Sir Reginald Coupland, one of the leading members of the Peel Commission and the pioneer of the partition idea, explained the thinking behind his decision:

> [Arabs and Jews] differ in religion and language. Their cultural and social life, their ways of thought and conduct, are as incompatible as their national aspirations. Arabs and Jews could possibly learn to live and work together in Palestine if they would make a genuine effort to reconcile their national ideals and build up in time a joint or dual nationality. But this they cannot do. . . . Peace and order and good government can only be maintained in a unitary Palestine for any length of time by a rigorous system of suppression. The answer to the question which of them will in the end govern all Palestine surely must be neither. But while neither race can justly rule all Palestine we see no reason why each should not rule part of it. There is little value in maintaining the political unity of Palestine at the cost of perpetual hatred, strife and bloodshed.[18]

The territory the Peel Commission attributed to the potential Jewish state was so small that most Zionist leaders considered the offer unacceptable. On the other hand, the debate over the Peel plan took place four years after the Nazis had assumed power in Germany. A clear danger was looming for the Jews of Europe, and Jewish statehood was more urgent than ever.

Thus the Zionist debate over the Peel plan was—not unlike the 1903 Uganda controversy—heated and passionate. In the end, Ben-Gurion decided to respond favorably to the plan, hoping that the Jewish state would later be able to expand its borders. Yet Ben-Gurion's acceptance turned out to be irrelevant, since al-Husseini flatly rejected it and the British government eventually shelved it, because (in line with its appeasement policy) endorsing it would have alienated al-Husseini and other Arab leaders.

Despite the recommendation of Lord Peel, the British government now tried to revert to the idea of an Arab state with a Jewish minority. Flatly rejecting the idea, Chaim Weizmann complained to the permanent under-secretary for the colonies Sir John Shuckburgh that the British government was not only not promoting the Peel Commission report but instead proposing all kinds of ideas whose ultimate goal was "the liquidation of the National Home and the virtual handing of the country to the clique of so-called Arab leaders who organized the disturbances of last year and from their hiding places are now running the terrorist campaign."[19] Preferring partition, even an unfavorable one, to the status of minority, Weizmann made his point sternly to Shuckburgh: "Jews are not going to Palestine to become in their ancient home 'Arabs of the Mosaic Faith' or to exchange their German or Polish ghetto for an Arab one. Whoever knows what Arab government looks like, what 'minority status' signifies nowadays, and what a Jewish ghetto in an Arab state means—there are quite a number of precedents—will be able to form his own conclusions as to what would be in store for us if we accepted the position allotted to us in these 'solutions.'"[20]

The mainstream Zionist leadership's formal acceptance of partition solved a moral dilemma but also created an illusion. As Abba Eban would later write, "It was impossible for us to avoid struggling for Jewish statehood and equally impossible for them to grant us what we asked.... It was only when the Zionist leadership agreed to the principle of partition that a moral crisis became transmuted into a classic issue of territorial distribution."[21] Yet, for the Arabs, the principle of partition did not transmute the conflict with Zionism into a mere issue of territorial distribution. They rejected partition precisely because they did not agree to any Jewish sovereignty within Palestine. The Zionists may have felt that their acceptance of partition had strengthened their case, but that acceptance did not diminish the Arab rejection of Zionism.

In August 1939, as the news of the just-signed Ribbentrop-Molotov Pact broke to the Zionist Congress in Geneva, Chaim Weizmann poignantly expressed the feeling of imminent disaster: "There is darkness all around us and we cannot see through the clouds. If, as I hope, we are spared in life and our work continues, who knows, a new light may shine upon us from the thick, black gloom. . . . The remnant shall work on, fight on, live on until the dawn of better days. Toward that dawn I greet you. May we meet again in peace."[22]

Mosaic of Foreign Policy Worldviews

The controversy around the Peel proposal revealed the political and ideological divide of the *Yishuv*. The prevailing political ideas were based on eclectic sources such as Jewish tradition, Marxism, and continental European nationalism. The politics were dominated by a rivalry between the Labor Movement and the Revisionist Right. The center was divided and unorganized. Smaller parties or groups such as Communists, Orthodox Jews, and academics tried—unsuccessfully—to challenge the quasi-monopoly of Socialist Zionism.

The Zionist Left was the *Yishuv*'s dominant political force. Its main component was Mapai (Workers Party of the Land of Israel), but it also included Ahdut Ha-Avoda (Unity of Labor), Left Po'alei Zion (Left Workers of Zion), and Ha-Shomer Ha-Tza'ir (the Young Guard), which later came to be known as Mapam (United Workers Party). At the far left of the political spectrum was the Palestine Communist Party (PCP).

The Revisionist Right consisted of the Revisionist Party, the New Zionist Organization (NZO), the Irgun (Irgun Zvai Leumi, or National Military Organization), and Lehi (Lohamei Herut Yisrael, or Fighters for the Freedom of Israel).

The center was composed of the Civil Right, which was close to European conservatism, the more liberal Aliya Hadasha (New Immigration), and Ha-Oved Ha-Tzioni (the Zionist Worker). The Civil Right also included small political organizations of merchants, farmers, and Sephardic notables.

The religious parties were divided into two factions: the national-religious (Mizrachi and Ha-Po'el Ha-Mizrachi) and the ultra-Orthodox (Agudat Israel and Po'alei Agudat Israel). Other voices were the Canaanites and Semites, and Ihud (Union), the main intellectual groups and voluntary associations that did not belong to any of the above categories.

For their part, inasmuch as the *Yishuv*'s socialist leaders were compelled to make diplomatic decisions, they had little interest in international affairs. Israel's founding fathers wanted to create an egalitarian, even utopian society. They were disciples of Marx, not of Clausewitz, and Marxist socialism and nationalism were not compatible, at least in theory. Leaders had hoped to solve this contradiction by advocating proletarian solidarity between Jewish and Arab workers, but the 1929 pogrom and the 1936 Arab revolt confirmed beyond doubt that the struggle between Arabs and Jews was national and not social and would have a lasting impact on Socialist Zionism. In the mid-1930s, most Socialist Zionists abandoned their utopian view of international relations (as theorized by Dov Ber Borochov, Nachman Syrkin, and Aharon David Gordon) and embraced political realism.

Ben-Gurion's attitudes toward the Soviet Union and the Arab world were not influenced by socialism. When he asserted that the Soviets were supporting the Arabs because of the weakness of the *Yishuv*, he was displaying pure realpolitik. He had ambivalently accepted the 1937 partition plan, based in part on a cold assessment of the *Yishuv*'s weakness and his recalibration of the plan as a step toward the realization of Zionism's territorial aspirations: "Once we become a mighty force following the establishment of the State, we will annul partition and continue to expand in the entire Land of Israel."[23] He also stated, "We must insist on our rights to the full [land], and be ready to accept a territorial compromise."[24]

Not all Socialist Zionists endorsed Ben-Gurion's realism. The Kibbutz Ha-Me'uhad movement tended to dismiss diplomacy and territorial compromise (it would eventually split from Mapai in 1944). The Kibbutz Ha-Me'uhad movement, which provided the core of the officers of the War of Independence—such as Yitzhak Rabin and Yigal Allon—was vehemently opposed to the idea of partition. One of its leaders, Yitzhak Tabenkin, had never accepted the separation of Transjordan from Mandatory Palestine in 1922. Another Kibbutz Ha-Me'uhad leader, Yitzhak Ben-Aharon, claimed, "If we could once again organize a revolt such as that of Bar-Kochba, I would recommend doing so."[25] Yigal Allon would later advocate the conquest of all of Mandatory Palestine during Israel's War of Independence. Shortly before his death he confessed that he had told Ben-Gurion, "The map on the basis of which the armistice agreements were signed at the end of the war will be the direct cause of many future wars."[26]

Ha-Shomer Ha-Tza'ir also opposed partition, but for different reasons. It never departed from its socialist principles, and thus continued to advocate a common class struggle between Arabs and Jews against the British. It dismissed the very concept of a sovereign state as a tool invented by the bourgeoisie to maintain its rule. As for Left Po'alei Zion, its influence declined in the wake of the Arab revolt and the pro-Arab stance of the Soviet Union. And the Communist Party, being anti-Zionist, demanded the cancellation of the Balfour Declaration, supported the Arab revolt, and opposed Jewish immigration.

The Revisionist Right, led by Jabotinsky, was ambivalently realistic. Jabotinsky was acutely aware of the constraints of reality. According to Israeli scholar Sasson Sofer, "Jabotinsky did not reject the partition outright . . . and there is a great deal of evidence to indicate that he was prepared to accept the plan, with certain territorial changes."[27]

Indeed, when Menachem Begin (a disciple and admirer of Jabotinsky) said during the Third World Congress of Betar in September 1938 that the Jews should drive out the British just like the Irish did, Jabotinsky's reply was that of a realist, not of an exalted romantic: "No strategist anywhere in the world would say that in our situation we can do what [Giuseppe] Garibaldi and [Éamond] De Valera did. That is idle chatter. Our position is a far cry from that of the Italians or the Irish, and if you think there is no other way than that proposed by Mr. Begin and you have arms—go ahead and commit suicide."[28] According to Chaim Weizmann, however, Jabotinsky "lacked realism" and "was immensely optimistic, seeing too much and expecting too much."[29]

On the far right, Lehi had an even more ambivalent approach to reality. Lehi's leader, Avraham Stern, went so far as to attempt to reach an agreement with the Axis powers (see chapter 7). Israel Eldad, one of Lehi's ideologues, explained that Zionism is "an expression of the national will to change the face of reality"[30] and that "romanticism, which does not take facts into account,"[31] will win the battle of history.

Between the Socialists and the Revisionists stood a frail liberal movement with weak ideological commitments but strong economic interests. The Civil Right represented farmers and house owners, Sephardic notables and central European liberals, artisans and merchants— social groups that had little in common but were united in their aversion to socialism. Dismissing both the pro-Soviet orientation of the Left and the messianism of the Right, the Civil Right political leader Yitzhak Gruenbaum, a conservative and a political realist, reluctantly accepted the 1937 partition plan on his assessment that the *Yishuv* could not achieve more in the difficult context of the late 1930s. He also reminded his audiences that nations generally expand their territory after achieving independence: "We are not relinquishing anything; a nation never abandons its aspirations. ... Our task is to undertake this generation's mission and lead the Zionist enterprise to a safe haven in these stormy times."[32]

As for religious Jewry, the populace was split between the ultra-Orthodoxy of Agudat Israel and the religious nationalism of Mizrachi. Agudat Israel's attitude toward Zionism ranged between hostility and indifference. Mizrachi's political outlook was influenced by the teachings of Rabbi Avraham Isaac Kook, who presented a sort of religious Hegelianism: Zionism was a transitory stage in which it was necessary to take part until its secular aspect would be replaced by its religious Jewish character. This compromise was a necessary prelude to redemption. There could be no territorial compromise, however, since the land was given by God.

Intellectuals and artists within the *Yishuv* also advanced disparate views. The poet Yonatan Ratosh, the leading figure of Canaanism (an ideology that wanted to replace Jewish nationalism with a nativist link to the pre-biblical land of Canaan), advocated a secular nationalism detached from Judaism. Ratosh rejected partition, as he perceived the British, the Arabs, and even the Jews as the enemies of his "Canaanite revolution." After Israel's independence, Ratosh would support the Arabs in the wars they launched against Israel, claiming that the time had come for a victory over Judaism and Zionism. Journalist and writer Uri Avineri, who started out on the fringes of the Revisionists and the Irgun, was attracted to Canaanism at an early stage before founding his own "Semitic Revolution" movement. He believed that both Arab and Jewish nationalisms were about to wane and that the time had come to merge them into a "Semitic National Movement"; therefore, he rejected partition too.

Martin Buber and Yehuda Magnes, the two leading figures of the Ihud movement who represented the academic elite from the Hebrew University, had an ambivalent, if not contradictory, approach to Zionism. Both were very critical of Ben-Gurion and thought that Jews should keep their distance from nationalism. They opposed the establishment of a Jewish state and advocated a binational Jewish-Arab confederation. The American-born Magnes objected to the use of violence in international relations; he had endorsed pacifism during the First World War. Buber, for his part, was a German-born idealist. In theory, he was prepared to support the establishment of a Jewish state, but not to accept the injustices that would ensue—which is why he opposed it in practice. He believed that Jewish and Arab nationalisms were compatible and even complementary. He was also an internationalist, seeing in the state an interim stage prior to the establishment of a community of nations.

From this ideological mosaic, Mapai and the Revisionists emerged as the *Yishuv's* two dominant political forces. The *Yishuv* had no liberal tradition capable of competing with socialism and nationalism. The Civil Right was weak both ideologically and socially and would eventually become a minority within the union it formed with the nationalistic Right.

Conclusion

Britain's 1917 Balfour Declaration "favour[ing] the establishment in Palestine of a national home for the Jewish people" was ambiguous and vague. Was the Jewish "national home" supposed to become a state? And where exactly "in Palestine" was it to apply?

Britain was soon caught by its contradictory commitments: it had promised a "national home" to the Zionists, hoping to attract the sympathy of American and Russian Jews at a critical moment of World War I; but it had also promised kingdoms to Arab leaders who had fought against the Turks during the war. In 1922 the League of Nations Council endorsed the partition of the Middle East between Britain and France, as well as Britain's commitment to the Zionist movement. This international legitimation of the Balfour Declaration, however, had no effect on the Arabs' opposition to Zionism. Tensions between Arabs and Jews in British Palestine climaxed with the 1929 pogrom and the 1936 "great revolt."

Asked in 1937 how to solve the Palestine quagmire, the Peel Commission suggested partition. The 1937 partition plan created a harsh dilemma for the Zionist leadership, because the proposed Jewish state was minuscule and did not include Jerusalem. Yet establishing a safe haven for the Jews after four years of Nazi rule in Germany had become urgent. As in 1903 with the Uganda proposal, the Zionist movement had to make a hard policy choice. This choice, as well as the mounting conflict between Jews and Arabs, shaped the political divide of the *Yishuv*. Ideologues from right and left stuck to their principles regardless of what reality had to offer. By contrast, Ben-Gurion was acutely aware of the constraints of reality. He ambivalently accepted the 1937 partition plan, based in part on a cold assessment of the *Yishuv*'s weakness and his recalibration of the plan as a step toward the realization of Zionism's territorial aspirations. From the dilemmas of the British Mandate emerged a realistic and resolute Jewish leadership that would lead the *Yishuv* toward independence.

PART 3.   The Rebirth of Israel and the Arab-Israeli Conflict

9. Israel and the Middle East at the Beginning of the Cold War

> We hereby declare the establishment of a Jewish state in
> the land of Israel, to be called: The State of Israel.
>
> ISRAEL'S DECLARATION OF INDEPENDENCE

Navigating a New International System

Israel was born at the beginning of the Cold War. As a young and small state, it had to navigate in an international system that was new, challenging, and unprecedented.

In the 1920s the Zionist movement had to steer among the conflicting colonial interests of Britain and France. The Second World War had reshaped the international system and the balance of powers in the Middle East. After the collapse of France in June 1940 and its capitulation to Germany, Britain managed to resist Germany alone until the Soviet Union and the United States joined the war; but it was exhausted and nearly bankrupt after six years of war. In addition, British colonies around the world were demanding their independence. The British Empire was showing clear signs of disintegration.

The United States and the Soviet Union emerged as the world's two dominant, and rival, powers. As soon as Nazi Germany was defeated, the two former allies became implacable enemies. In the new international context of the Cold War, Zionism tried to gather international support for the establishment of a Jewish state. And once the State of

Israel became independent, its diplomacy had to face the conflicting interests of the superpowers, as well as a hostile Middle East.

With the unexpected defeat of Winston Churchill in the 1945 elections, Britain was no longer led by a pro-Zionist prime minister. Churchill's successor, Clement Attlee, appointed Ernest Bevin as foreign secretary, and Bevin, opposed to the establishment of a Jewish state, did everything he could to prevent Holocaust refugees from entering British Palestine. There was now an open war between Britain and the Zionist movement.

Because the Zionists were fighting the British, they found a natural ally in France, Britain's historical colonial rival. The old colonial rivalry between Britain and France had turned bitter after the collapse of France in June 1940 when the Free French, led by Charles de Gaulle, accused Britain of trying to take over Syria and Lebanon. The two formerly French mandates had become fully independent in 1946, and de Gaulle suspected that Britain had encouraged Arab nationalists in both countries. When Britain got into trouble with its Palestine Mandate, France eagerly volunteered to help the Zionists give "la perfide Albion" a taste of its own medicine.

Another unexpected ally of the Zionist movement at the time was the Soviet Union. Stalin wanted to break up the British Empire in the Middle East and establish a Soviet presence there. For him, establishing a Jewish state was a first step toward driving the British out of the Middle East. Thus Stalin voted in favor of the 1947 UN partition plan, recognized Israel as soon as it declared independence, and approved the sale of Czech weapons to Israel during its war of independence.

The 1947 UN Partition Plan and the 1949 Armistice Agreements

Britain's position in Palestine became untenable after the war. Britain had fought Nazi Germany for six years, and it had fought alone between June 1940 and June 1941. Its economy was exhausted. In 1947 and 1948

Britain was enduring food rationing, fuel shortage, and foreign currency depletion. Maintaining one hundred thousand troops in Palestine was not sustainable. Palestine had been strategically important as part of British bases "on the way to India," but the Indian subcontinent became independent in August 1947.

In January 1946 a joint British-American committee, the Anglo-American Committee of Inquiry, was established to attempt to solve the Jewish-Arab conflict in Palestine in light of renewed Jewish demands for increased immigration following the Holocaust. The British government refused to accept an influx of Jewish immigrants, for fear of alienating the Arab population. It would only meet the U.S. demand for admission of one hundred thousand new Jewish immigrants if America provided troops to handle a possible Arab revolt. The U.S. government refused to make such commitment, and the matter was dropped.

As Britain became increasingly isolated and criticized for its policy in Palestine, it decided to ask the United Nations (UN) for advice. The UN had inherited the League of Nations, the international organization that had originally granted Britain its Mandate in Palestine. In response, the UN established a United Nations Special Committee on Palestine (UNSCOP), composed of eleven countries (Australia, Canada, Czechoslovakia, Guatemala, India, Iran, the Netherlands, Peru, Sweden, Uruguay, and Yugoslavia), which eventually recommended the partition of the British Mandate between an Arab state and a Jewish state. Chaim Weizmann quipped that UNSCOP constituted an improvement upon the Anglo-American Committee (which had twelve members) because it was composed of "one gentile less" ("Ein goy weniger" in the original Yiddish).

UNSCOP members were hardly Middle East experts. When they visited British Palestine in 1947, they came to learn. The Indian member of the delegation, Sir Abdul Rahman (a Muslim), said during the visit, "All, right, we have seen a Jewish kibbutz; I assume that we shall be seeing an Arab kibbutz tomorrow."[1]

As UNSCOP members were deliberating, the *Exodus* ship arrived at Haifa port. On board were forty-five hundred Holocaust survivors, whom Bevin ordered back to Germany. The scene of British soldiers using rifle butts, hose pipes, and tear gas against survivors of death camps made a strong impression on the UNSCOP delegation. UNSCOP even met secretly with Menachem Begin, to Britain's fury (Begin had just ordered the hanging of two British sergeants).

After the *Exodus* episode, UNSCOP members were no longer willing to consider the maintenance of the British Mandate. Still, they determined they would not initiate a partition proposal; they would only react to the idea if it were proposed by one of the sides. Since the Arabs opposed partition, this meant that the Jews had to submit the idea if they wanted it. Ben-Gurion did just that in a meeting he initiated with UNSCOP, and along with the idea he submitted a draft map.[2]

The principle of partition started taking root among UNSCOP members. As Henri Vigier, the French political advisor to UNSCOP, told Moshe Sharett (who headed the Jewish Agency's political department and would become Israel's first foreign minister), "You will have to choose between complete independence in a limited area or limited sovereignty in a larger area."[3]

Like the Peel Commission ten years before, UNSCOP decided to reenact the Judgment of Solomon. It had four choices: (1) a continuation of the British Mandate; (2) an Arab state in all of Palestine; (3) a Jewish state in all of Palestine; (4) a partition of Palestine into a Jewish and an Arab state. On September 1, 1947, UNSCOP submitted its first report at the Palais des Nations in Geneva. Sweden, Canada, Czechoslovakia, Guatemala, Uruguay, Peru, and the Netherlands favored partition. Yugoslavia, India, and Iran favored a form of federation, with Jewish immigration ultimately to be determined by the Arab majority. Australia abstained from the UNSCOP vote.

On the face of it, this first report favored the Jews. It attributed 55 percent of the British Mandate to a Jewish state and 45 percent to an Arab state. Still, more than half of the proposed Jewish state was composed of the arid—albeit still valuable—Negev desert, while the Arab state was mostly granted arable lands. And in reality the partition plan made little geographical sense. It suggested two intertwined ministates with bizarre borders and proposed that Jerusalem (together with its surroundings) become an international territory under UN rule (*corpus separatum*). UNSCOP members had fiercely debated the status of Jerusalem. The Peruvian representative, Arturo García Salazar, had advocated for internationalizing the city; he was also his country's ambassador to the Vatican and was likely influenced by the pope. Other UNSCOP members had proposed the city's partition between the Arab and Jewish states, with a special status for the holy sites. In the end, a majority recommended the internationalization model.

The Arab League and Palestinian leader Hadj Amin al-Husseini flatly rejected the proposal. The Zionist leadership reluctantly accepted it. As Abba Eban explained, "We knew that a Jewish state in part of Palestine was our maximal prospect."[4] Ben-Gurion thought that partition was a lesser evil, and an inevitable one: "I was in favor of the principle of the Peel Report in 1937 and would even now accept a Jewish State in an adequate part of the country rather than a British Mandate with a White Paper in all of the country."[5]

The Arab states not only rejected the idea of partition; they also rejected any solution that would recognize and protect Jewish national rights in Palestine in any shape or form. Since the Arabs already had a few sovereign states (and were expected to acquire more after decolonization), and since a third of the Jewish people had just been murdered in Europe, the Arab position seemed completely unreasonable and unfair to most UN members. Thus the Arabs' flat rejection of any compromise actually helped the Zionist cause. As Abba Eban explained, "It should have been obvious to them that any idea of disregarding the existence of a Jewish nationhood was now internationally unacceptable. By the extremism of their demands, the Arabs strengthened the impression that Jews would need powerful safeguards not only to defend their national existence, but even to protect their very lives."[6]

Once Ben-Gurion knew that the UN would recommend partition, he was convinced that war with the Arab world was inevitable. Hence his obsession with achieving what German sociologist Max Weber called the "legitimate monopoly of violence." As Ben-Gurion learned of UNSCOP's recommendation in September 1947, he declared, "We must get rid of the dissident armies. . . . There cannot be any progress unless underground forces are eliminated. . . . We must eliminate the Etzel [Irgun]. . . . We must finish with the Stern group as well."[7] The confrontation between Ben-Gurion and the Irgun would nearly turn into a civil war.

Like the 1937 partition plan of the Peel Commission, the 1947 UN partition plan was controversial among *Yishuv* leaders because it traded territorial integrity for immediate sovereignty. Peretz Bernstein, one of the leaders of the *Yishuv*'s liberal party, described the 1947 plan as "a nightmare," to which Ben-Gurion replied, "This is the only time that I've wanted a nightmare to come true."[8]

The Jewish Agency actively lobbied countries around the world to vote in favor of partition. On November 29, 1947, the UN General Assembly approved UNSCOP's proposal in a dramatic vote that was broadcast live on the radio. In British Palestine and around the world, Jews anxiously wrote down the ayes and nays as well as the abstentions as they were being counted one by one by the president of the General Assembly. Thirty-three countries voted in favor of the plan (Australia, Belgium, Bolivia, Brazil, Byelorussia, Canada, Costa Rica, Czechoslovakia, Denmark, Dominican Republic, Ecuador, France, Guatemala, Haiti, Iceland, Liberia, Luxemburg, Netherlands, New Zealand, Nicaragua, Norway, Panama, Paraguay, Peru, Philippines, Poland, South Africa, Sweden, Ukraine, United States, Uruguay, USSR, Venezuela); thirteen voted against (Afghanistan, Cuba, Egypt, Greece, India, Iran, Iraq, Lebanon, Pakistan, Saudi Arabia, Syria, Turkey, Yemen); and ten abstained (Argentina, Chile, China, Columbia, El Salvador, Ethiopia, Honduras, Mexico, United Kingdom, Yugoslavia). The vote was celebrated in the *Yishuv* and denounced in the Arab world, although in truth it bore little legal significance. There was nothing binding in the General Assembly vote of November 29, 1947. It merely expressed support for a recommendation that had become moot the moment it was rejected by the Arab League.

The widespread idea the UN "created" the State of Israel in November 1947 is, therefore, a myth. The Syrian representative at the UN was correct when he declared after the November 29 vote, "The recommendations of the General Assembly are not imperative on those to whom they are addressed. I fail to find in this Charter any text which implies, directly or indirectly, that the General Assembly has the authority to enforce its recommendations by military force. The General Assembly only gives advice and the parties to whom advice is addressed accept it when it is rightful and just and when it does not impair their fundamental rights."[9]

Moreover, the UN did not act to implement its partition resolution. The UN knew full well that the Arab League opposed the resolution and was preparing for war to prevent its implementation.

In September 1947 the Arab League established an Arab Liberation Army. It was led by Fawzi al-Qawuqji, who had been in charge of broadcasting Nazi propaganda in the Arab world during the Second World War.[10] Al-Husseini's chief bomb-maker, Fawzi al-Kutub, had learned bomb construction in an SS course in Nazi Germany.[11]

Shortly after the November 29 vote, Arab states went into full gear to downplay its impact and to prevent its implementation. On February 24, 1948, the UN Security Council clarified that only its decisions were binding; the General Assembly's decisions were not. Yet, at the same time, the Security Council did not adopt a resolution that could have turned the General Assembly vote into a binding decision (Britain, which abstained at the General Assembly, would likely have vetoed a binding Security Council vote).

Despite being nonbinding, the UN vote in favor of partition did play a central role in ending the British Mandate. Had the General Assembly rejected UNSCOP's plan, Palestine would have likely continued to live under international tutelage, possibly under a joint American-British administration. The UN could have established a trusteeship to replace the British Mandate. In short, on the one hand, the UN vote had granted international legitimacy to Jewish statehood; but on the other hand, it did not guarantee this statehood. War was inevitable, and only its outcome would determine the fate of the Jewish state.

Ben-Gurion had suggested and accepted partition knowing full well it would not be implemented without the Arab League's consent. In late summer 1947, when Abba Eban and Azzam Pasha, the secretary-general of the Arab League, had met in London, the latter had declared:

> If you win the war, you will get your state. If you do not win the war, then you will not get it. We Arabs once ruled Iran and once ruled Spain. We no longer have Iran or Spain. If you establish your state the Arabs might one day have to accept it, although even that is not certain. But do you really think that we have the option of not trying to prevent you from achieving something that violates our emotion and our interest? It is a question of historic pride. There is no shame in being compelled by force to accept an unjust and unwanted situation. What would be shameful would be to accept this without attempting to prevent it.[12]

Technically, Britain could have ignored the UN's advice, which it had solicited. Article One of the UN Partition Plan stated, "The Mandate for Palestine shall terminate as soon as possible but in any case no later than 1 August 1948." The document was a nonbinding General Assembly resolution that became moot the moment it was rejected by one of the two main parties, and thus its rejection by the Arab League made it inapplicable. Yet Britain was in no mood to exploit legal loopholes to maintain its Mandate. Its position had become intolerable, both because the Irgun was inflicting heavy casualties on the British army and because world opinion was turning against Britain's policy toward the Jews.

Britain announced that it would relinquish the Palestine Mandate on May 15, 1948. Britain was thereby abandoning the territory the League of Nations had allocated to it. From that moment on, there would be a legal void due to the absence of a sovereign.

The Jews had a legal case thanks to the League of Nations mandate and to the United Nations partition plan, but that case would become meaningless if it couldn't withstand the military onslaught of the Arabs.

The 1933 Montevideo Convention on the Rights and Duties of States had codified the declaratory theory of statehood in international law. There were four criteria of statehood: (1) a permanent population; (2) a defined territory; (3) a government; (4) the capacity to enter into relations with other states.[13] The prospective State of Israel met all four criteria except, it could be argued, the second one. A territory had been defined by the partition plan, but this plan was nonbinding, required the consent of both parties, and had been rejected by one of them. The principle of *uti possidetis juris* (the tenet of international law that newly formed sovereign states should have the same borders as their preceding dependent area before their independence) could be claimed by both Arabs and Jews. But for the principle to be claimed, independence had to be declared. The Arabs committed a tactical mistake by failing to do so. Some seventy years later, on January 14, 2018, Palestinian Authority chairman Mahmoud Abbas bemoaned, "When the Partition Resolution was declared, the State of Israel was established, but our state was not. Don't ask me why. I don't know."[14]

The Jewish leadership, by contrast, decided to declare independence right before the end of the British Mandate. The Jewish National Council (JNC), which acted as the political representation of the *Yishuv* under the British Mandate, formed a provisional government on April 12, 1948. One month later, on May 12, the provisional government voted in favor of declaring independence (six members voted in favor, and four against). Israel formally declared independence on May 14, 1948, the day before the British were scheduled to leave Palestine. The risk was high but calculated.

Israel's newly established Foreign Ministry consisted of five people with nearly no experience and expertise in diplomacy. The ministry itself was granted two rooms and a phone line in a decrepit Tel Aviv building. When the phone of the "ministry" rang for the first time, a diligent worker picked up and said, "Foreign Office." The caller was not impressed. "Cut the crap," he said, "and pass me Sharrett [Israel's then foreign minister]."[15] No one in that small team even knew how to write a letter of credence (*lettre de créance*), the document that formally appoints ambassadors to foreign countries. The letter of credence written for the first Israeli ambassador to Czechoslovakia was so improvised and poorly written, the Czech government conveyed its discontent and disbelief. When the first foreign ambassador was appointed to Israel (from the Soviet Union), the Israeli Foreign Ministry duly copied and translated his letter of credence to use for its own ambassadors.[16] The new Foreign Ministry also had to decide what would be the English adjective for the name Israel. Would it be "Israelian," "Israelite," or "Israeli"?[17]

By the time the new State of Israel declared its independence, its military situation was dire and even desperate. Arab forces had managed to cut off the Negev desert from the center of the country, and Jerusalem was isolated from the coast. Most military experts considered that a Jewish state had no chance of survival. Field Marshal Bernard Montgomery told a complacent Ernest Bevin that "the Jews have made a colossal mistake and have lost their cause."[18] In the second week of June 1948, the Arab Legion cut off Jerusalem from the rest of the Jewish population. The Egyptians were within twenty-five miles of

Tel Aviv and had cut off the Negev desert from the rest of the country. The new Israeli army was expecting shipments of Czech arms by early July and was desperate for a ceasefire in the interim. In fact, Israel nearly lost its War of Independence in June 1948. Had it not been for the truce (from mid-June to mid-July 1948), Israel might have lost.

It was during this salutary truce that the dramatic *Altalena* incident took place. Among the various Jewish armed forces that had fought the British, Menachem Begin's Irgun (or Etzel) was considered an outcast by David Ben-Gurion. Ben-Gurion feared that Begin's pledge of loyalty to the new state was insincere and he might try to establish an alternative government. Ben-Gurion had not invited Begin to Israel's Declaration of Independence ceremony on May 14, 1948. Having formally excluded Begin from the pantheon of the "founding fathers," Ben-Gurion now questioned his allegiance to the Israeli government. As the Irgun was in the process of merging with the Israel Defense Forces (IDF), it shipped weapons and fighters from France on a cargo named after Jabotinsky's pen name *Altalena*. Ben-Gurion demanded that all weapons be delivered to the IDF, but the Irgun insisted on transferring some of the weapons to its fighters in Jerusalem. On June 22, claiming that a paramilitary force was challenging the authority of the government, Ben-Gurion ordered the IDF to sink the *Altalena*. Twenty-two Irgun fighters and three IDF soldiers were killed. Menachem Begin nearly lost his life. This tragedy nearly turned into a civil war. Begin claimed that Ben-Gurion wanted to humiliate him and the Irgun. Ben-Gurion claimed that Begin was challenging the authority of the government and had to be forced into submission.

Ben-Gurion would later say that Israeli sovereignty was only established on June 28, 1948, when all armed forces, including the Irgun, pledged allegiance to the IDF. But where did that sovereignty apply? Israel's Declaration of Independence left the question of borders open. The original draft had specified that the new state's borders would be those recommended by the UN partition plan, but when members of the provisional government debated that question, Ben-Gurion had insisted that the final Declaration text not mention the state's borders. Thus the letter that Israel's first ambassador to the United States, Eliahu Eilat (whose last name was Epstein before he joined the foreign office) sent to U.S. president Harry Truman on May 14, 1948, was technically inaccurate: "The State of Israel has been proclaimed as an independent republic within frontiers approved by the General Assembly of the United Nations in its Resolution of November 19, 1947."

Ben-Gurion had reasoned that the Arabs had rejected partition and were about to attack the Jewish state. Borders, therefore, would be determined by war and not by the UN vote from November 1947. If the Jewish state could include the Galilee and Jerusalem in its final borders, Ben-Gurion argued, why waive the option?

History proved him right. Yet Israel's prospects did not look good when it was simultaneously attacked immediately after Israel declared its independence on May 15, 1948, by the armed forces of Egypt, Transjordan, Iraq, Syria, Lebanon, and Saudi Arabia. Israel's military strategy eventually switched from defense to offense, and the IDF managed not only to stop the Arab aggression, but also to progressively turn the tables on the Arab armies.[19]

On September 26 David Ben-Gurion asked the temporary government to approve the conquest of the mountainous heartland attributed by the UN to the Arab state (the area known today as the West Bank), including East Jerusalem, Hebron, Ramallah, Bethlehem, and Jericho. The cabinet turned down the proposal by a small margin of seven to six. The ministers who voted against the proposal feared Britain's direct involvement in the war, since Britain had signed defense treaties with Jordan and Iraq, as well as the demographic burden that such conquest would involve, since the coveted territories were populated by Arabs whose addition to Israel would have doomed a Jewish majority. There was also fear of the possible hostility of Christian countries to Israel's control of Christian sites.[20] Ben-Gurion regretted this vote, which he called a "lamentation for generations."[21]

Israel's first victories panicked the Arab population of the former British Mandate. About 250,000 of them fled their homes for neighboring Arab countries, and about 450,000 took refuge in what would become in 1949 the West Bank and the Gaza Strip. In some cases, such as in the city of Lod (or Lydda), the IDF encouraged their departure.[22]

The war and its aftermath also created a phenomenon of Jewish refugees. Jews had to evacuate both the areas of the former British Mandate conquered by Arab armies and the Arab countries where Jews had lived for centuries. During the two decades that followed the Arab-Israeli war of 1948, nearly nine hundred thousand Jews fled Syria, Lebanon, Egypt, Iraq, Yemen, Libya, Morocco, Algeria, and Tunisia. They lost their property and belongings, which were seized by Arab governments.

The phenomenon of Jewish refugees from Arab countries admittedly happened over a period of two decades, as opposed to the phenomenon of Arab refugees from British Palestine, and not all Jews left because of the threats and violence they experienced in their home countries in the wake of the 1948 Arab-Israeli war. The fact remains, however, that there was a double refugee phenomenon, and not only one.[23]

The Arab states agreed to sign a ceasefire with Israel in 1949 once they realized that they would lose more by continuing the war. Their willingness to sign a ceasefire was influenced by what had become their true motivation. As Israeli historian Benny Morris explains, "The Arab war plan changed in conception and essence from a united effort to conquer parts of the nascent Jewish state and perhaps destroy it, into a multilateral land grab focusing on the Arab areas of the country."[24] The Iraqis wanted to reach Haifa to control the pipeline that connected Mosul to the Mediterranean.[25] Yet as those war goals started fading, the Arab states were willing to end the fighting.

The armistice agreements were signed on the Greek island of Rhodes in February 1949.[26] The UN's special envoy, Dr. Ralph Bunche, negotiated the terms. The Egyptian, Syrian, and Lebanese armies withdrew to the borders that had been theirs since their respective establishment by the League of Nations. Israel inherited the borders of the British Mandate with Egypt, Syria, and Lebanon. Egypt and Jordan had conquered territories that were beyond their borders and had been designated by the UN partition plan as part of the proposed Arab state. Egypt took control of what became the Gaza Strip, and Jordan of a large chunk of the former British Mandate, west of the Jordan River. Since Jordan at the time was known as Transjordan, it decided to call the territory it conquered Cis-Jordan and to annex it. Today, this territory is commonly known as the West Bank (i.e., the west bank of the Jordan River), though in French it is still called Cisjordanie. The international community (except Britain and Pakistan) did not recognize Jordan's annexation of the territories it had conquered from the former British Mandate.

In the 1949 armistice agreements, Israel's de facto borders (the armistice lines delineated in Rhodes) extended beyond the ones recommended by the UN partition plan.

The armistice agreements granted Israel 78 percent of the territory of Mandatory Palestine, as opposed to the 55 percent granted by the UN partition plan. Israel now had international borders with Egypt, Syria, and Lebanon. With Jordan, it had a "temporary ceasefire line," defined as such upon Jordan's insistence. Because Ralph Bunche drew that line on the map with a green marker, this line is also called the "green line" to this day. This green line was not a final border, nor meant to become one.

Thus it was that the borders recommended by UNSCOP never came into being. The UNSCOP plan and the General Assembly vote were

Map 10. The 1947 partition plan and the 1949 armistice agreements. ©2004–2019 The Washington Institute for Near East Policy. All rights reserved.

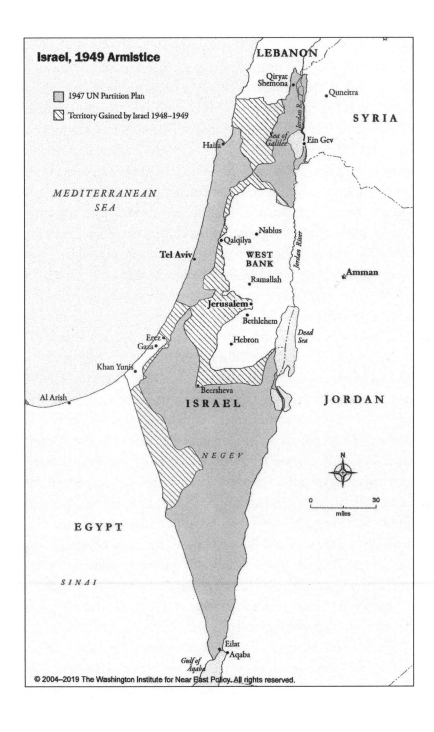

Israel, 1949 Armistice

☐ 1947 UN Partition Plan

◩ Territory Gained by Israel 1948–1949

LEBANON

Qiryat Shemona

•Quneitra

SYRIA

Jordan R.

Sea of Galilee

Haifa•   •Ein Gev

MEDITERRANEAN SEA

•Nablus

•Qalqilya

Tel Aviv•

WEST BANK

Jordan River

•Ramallah

•Amman

Jerusalem•

•Bethlehem

Erez   Dead Sea

Gaza•

•Hebron

Khan Yunis•

Al Arish•

•Beersheva

ISRAEL

JORDAN

NEGEV

N

EGYPT

0   30
miles

SINAI

Eilat•
•Aqaba

Gulf of Aqaba

© 2004–2019 The Washington Institute for Near East Policy. All rights reserved.

recommendations, whereas the 1949 armistice agreements were contractual and therefore arguably more valid in international law.

Nonetheless, the question of Israel's legal border remained ambiguous. Abba Eban thus summarized this ambiguity: "The demarcation lines were not described as permanent, but since they could only be changed by agreement, they were similar in every practical sense to permanent boundaries, which are also subject to change by agreement."[27] When France recognized Israel on January 29, 1949, for example, it specified that its recognition of Israel did not constitute a recognition of its de facto borders (as opposed to the borders recommended by the UN partition plan).[28] The ambiguity of the armistice agreements was potentially explosive regarding Syria. A demilitarized zone with hazy sovereignty was established on the southwestern shore of Lake Tiberias. A belt of ten meters on the northeastern shore was added at the last minute to ensure that no part of the lake would have a Syrian shore.

The armistice agreements did not turn into peace agreements because of unbridgeable gaps between Israeli and Arab expectations and demands. Even though the Arab states had rejected the 1947 partition plan, they now wanted Israel to withdraw to the lines delineated by the UN or at least make significant territorial concessions. Jordan asked for sovereignty over Jaffa, Lydda (Lod), and Ramle. Egypt wanted the Negev.[29] Egypt and Jordan also wanted Israel to take back all the Palestinian Arab refugees. At one point Israel agreed to reinstate one hundred thousand refugees, but the Arab states rejected the offer, insisting on the return of all seven hundred thousand refugees.[30] For Israel, these demands were unacceptable, and so the temporary armistice agreements became de facto a permanent armistice agreement. At some point, Israel offered to integrate the Gaza Strip refugees, provided it was granted control over that territory as well as financial aid for the integration of refugees. Egypt rejected the idea.[31]

The Arab leaders' handling of the refugee issue would continue to be cynical. In the fall of 1956, an Iraqi minister complained to a British journalist about the lack of workforce in Iraq. "Why don't you bring Palestinian refugees?" the journalist asked. "No way!" the minister answered. "That might solve the refugee problem."[32]

Most UN members did not consider the Jerusalem question settled. The UN partition plan had recommended the internationalization of the city. The armistice agreements partitioned Jerusalem between Israeli control in the west and Jordanian control in the east—a de facto situation the international community neither endorsed nor accepted. Israel was not satisfied with the status of Jerusalem: Jews were barred from the Western Wall, and the Mount Scopus Hebrew University campus and Hadassah Hospital were cutoff from Israel. In addition, Jordan had destroyed the synagogues of Jerusalem's Old City (including the landmark Hurva Synagogue) and desecrated the Mount of Olives Jewish cemetery. Yet Israel still preferred its partial and unsatisfactory sovereignty in Jerusalem over the international status recommended by the UN. Jordan preferred the status quo, too.

The UN saw it otherwise. Already in September 1949, the UN General Assembly discussed the internationalization of Jerusalem, and a majority of member states voted in favor of internationalization. This was a diplomatic setback for Israel, but Ben-Gurion responded by moving the Knesset and most government ministries from Tel Aviv to Jerusalem. On the question of Jerusalem, Israel and Jordan would cooperate against the UN's internationalization proposals.[33]

Diplomatic Alliances and Military Conflicts in a Shifting World Order

Since Israel became independent at the beginning of the Cold War, it had to choose which camp to join—that of the United States or the Soviet Union. Many within Ben-Gurion's Mapai party were in favor of aligning with the Soviet Union for ideological reasons. They were overruled by Ben-Gurion, for whom the question of Israel's international alignment was to be determined by interest and not by ideology.[34]

But what was in Israel's best interest? Israel's first foreign minister, Moshe Sharett, thought that Israel should stay neutral in the Cold War and maintain good relations with both sides. After all, both the United States and the Soviet Union had voted in favor of the partition of Palestine, and both had recognized Israel right after its independence. Sharett officially declared Israel's "non-alignment" in the Cold War on December 5, 1949: "Israel's foreign policy is one of non-alignment, which is different from neutrality. . . . Israel shall refrain from identifying with one of the two sides in the Cold War."[35]

A neutral foreign policy made sense in theory, but in practice it did not stand the test of reality. In the international system of the early Cold War, small countries could hardly afford to remain neutral, as Israel came to realize during the Korean War of 1950–53.

On July 4, 1950, Ben-Gurion announced in the Knesset (Israel's parliament) that Israel would vote in the United Nations General Assembly in favor of a resolution condemning North Korea's aggression against South Korea. The Knesset's most left-wing members (from the Mapam and Maki parties) argued that Israel should not take a stance against the Soviet Union (which supported North Korea); Ben-Gurion replied that North Korea had violated international law and the United Nations charter and that Israel could not afford to look the other way and remain neutral.[36] In his view, since Israel was itself threatened of invasion by its neighbors, North Korea could not be allowed to set a precedent. Heated cabinet discussions ensued wherein some cabinet members warned against alienating the Soviet Union.[37] Ben-Gurion even faced a vote of no confidence in the Knesset for abandoning Israel's neutrality principle. Yet the no-confidence vote failed to pass, Israel agreed to back South Korea in 1950, and Israel's neutrality in the Cold War was no more.[38]

Meanwhile there were major changes on the world scene to which Israel's foreign policy needed to adapt. Both the Soviet Union and the United States had recognized Israel in 1948, although for different reasons. Stalin thought that a Jewish state would undermine British influence in the Middle East. Truman agreed because of his personal promise to Chaim Weizmann and because he was personally convinced that the Jews deserved their state, despite State Department reservations. It was unusual for the United States and the Soviet Union to agree on anything at the beginning of the Cold War.

Israel's diplomatic luck did not last, however. Once the Soviet Union had achieved its goal (i.e., British withdrawal from Palestine), it had little reason to support Israel, especially after Israel abandoned its neutrality policy and supported South Korea and the West at the UN. From 1953 onward, Soviet foreign policy in the Middle East became openly pro-Arab (for reasons explained in chapter 15).

This new Soviet policy, however, did not improve Israel's relations with the United States. In fact, the Eisenhower administration (1953–61) was of the opinion that the United States was "losing" the Arab world to the Soviet Union because the Truman administration had been too favorable to Israel. American Middle East policy, therefore, needed to be rectified. Israel fell between the cracks of U.S.-Soviet rivalry over the Arab world.

This rivalry crystalized in 1955. That year, the Soviet Union started supplying weapons to Egypt (via Czechoslovakia), and Great Britain established an anti-Soviet military alliance of Arab and Muslim countries (the Baghdad Pact, also known as Central Treaty Organization, or CENTO). Although the United States was not formally a member of this alliance, which included the United Kingdom, Turkey, Iraq, Iran, and Pakistan, it was involved in its establishment. As the two superpowers competed over the Middle East, Israel became increasingly isolated. Meanwhile, far from containing Soviet influence, the

Baghdad Pact encouraged the anti-Western zeal of Egypt's leader Gamal Abdel Nasser. Convinced that Washington and London were trying to divide the Arab world, Nasser pressed for the overthrow of pro-Western regimes in Baghdad, Amman, and elsewhere. U.S. secretary of state John Foster Dulles argued that the Baghdad Pact was supposed to convince Arab leaders that their true enemy was not Zionism but communism,[39] but this theory was soon to be contradicted by Soviet advances in the Middle East.

The Eisenhower administration thought that by forcing a peace settlement on Israel, Arab hostility toward the United States would end, and with it the incentive to join the Soviet sphere of influence. Dulles wanted Israel to agree to a compromise between the armistice lines of 1949 and the borders recommended by the 1947 partition plan. In August 1955 Dulles declared, "The existing lines . . . were determined by the 1949 Armistice Agreements. They were not designed to be permanent frontiers in every respect."[40] British prime minister Anthony Eden concurred, calling for "a compromise between the boundaries of the 1947 UN Resolution and the 1949 armistice line."[41] Dulles and Eden turned their ideas into a plan, which they code-named "Alpha," that included a land bridge between Egypt and Jordan.

The 1955 alliance between the Soviet Union and Egypt could theoretically have induced the United States to upgrade its ties with Israel. To the Eisenhower administration, however, doing so would have further alienated the Arab world. In those days, Soviet inroads in the Middle East had the effect of driving the United States away from Israel.

Israel's ambassador and American Jewish leaders openly criticized the Eisenhower administration for not assisting Israel despite the Soviet-Egyptian military alliance. Public dismay ran deep, and Albert Einstein volunteered to advocate for Israel in the media. Einstein

Map 11. The 1955 Alpha Plan. Cartography by Bill Nelson.

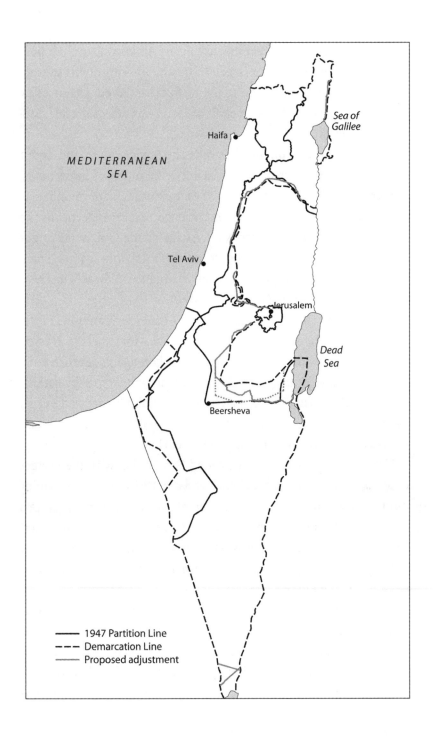

MEDITERRANEAN
SEA

Haifa

Sea of
Galilee

Tel Aviv

Jerusalem

Dead
Sea

Beersheva

——— 1947 Partition Line
- - - Demarcation Line
········ Proposed adjustment

started writing a TV address meant to alert Americans to their government's abandonment of Israel. As he was working on his speech, however, Einstein was taken to the hospital and died within a few days. His unfinished plea on behalf of Israel was one of the last documents he wrote.[42]

The 1955 military alliance between the Soviet Union and Egypt was hardly defensive in nature. It included the supply of heavy tanks, fighter jets, and submarines. Upon the announcement of the alliance, Radio Cairo declared, "We demand revenge, and revenge means the death of Israel."[43] For his part, Nasser, who led the Arab world's fight against Israel, specified that his struggle was not only against Israel, but also against "world Jewry and Jewish finance."[44] Israel's international isolation worried David Ben-Gurion.

Yet at this critical juncture, Israel found an unexpected ally in France. The underlying cause of France's tacit alliance with Israel was Nasser, who actively supported the Algerian rebellion against French rule. Nasser crystallized the Franco-Israeli alliance in July 1956 by nationalizing the Suez Canal, which had been under joint French and British ownership. This was a defiant act of robbery. Yet Nasser felt confident, thanks to his new alliance with the Soviet Union.

Nasser's reckless decision provided Ben-Gurion with the perfect opportunity to convince the French and the British to conduct a joint military operation against Egypt. Israel wanted to destroy Egypt's new military equipment provided by the Soviet Union. France and Britain wanted to get rid of Nasser. In secret negotiations (which excluded the U.S. government), France, Britain, and Israel decided to jointly attack Egypt.

The martial operation, which started on November 20, 1956, was a military success and a diplomatic disaster. Britain and France had not yet internalized that they no longer were world powers. They also miscalculated the U.S. reaction by wrongly assuming that America would back its Western allies in the face of Soviet threats. The Eisenhower administration, however, was of the opinion that anti-Western feelings were pushing the Arab states into the arms of the Soviet Union. Therefore, the last thing the United States needed was to be perceived as colluding with the three *bêtes noires* of the Arab world—France, Britain, and Israel.

The United States joined the Soviet Union in demanding the immediate withdrawal of French, British, and Israeli forces. Shocked and humiliated, France and Britain complied. Ben-Gurion, on the other hand, demanded two guarantees before withdrawing from Sinai: the demilitarization of the peninsula and free passage in the Straits of Tiran. He obtained both. Asked about the purpose of the 1956 war, Ben-Gurion explained, "We are interested first of all in the Straits of Eilat (Tiran) and the Red Sea. Only through them can we secure direct contact with the nations of Asia and East Africa."[45]

The UN dispatched a special force—the United Nations Emergency Force (UNEF)—in Sinai to keep it demilitarized, and Israel received a guarantee from the United States, France, and Britain that any Egyptian attempt to close the Straits of Tiran to Israeli shipping would be considered a *casus belli*—an act of war that granted Israel the right to fight back in self-defense, as recognized by Article 51 of the UN Charter.

Despite the guarantees obtained by Israel, Nasser felt vindicated and even invincible. He had defied the former masters of Egypt (Britain and France) thanks to his Soviet backers and the Eisenhower administration policy. By now he was confident that he had a free hand to attack Israel. Israel, on the other hand, had a guarantee (from the West) that its right to self-defense would be recognized in case of an Egyptian provocation.

Conclusion

As the Zionist movement tried to gather support for a Jewish state after the Second World War, the international system was being fundamentally transformed. Great Britain and France were losing their grip on the Middle East, and their global clout was fading. The United States and the Soviet Union emerged as the world's two dominant powers, but with conflicting agendas. Because Britain was opposed to Jewish statehood, the Zionists benefited from the support of Britain's rivals: the Soviet Union and France. The 1947 UN partition plan was a landmark decision, but not a binding one. The UN General Assembly vote was not in itself binding (as were decisions by the UN Security Council), the partition plan required the consent of both parties, and it became moot the moment it was rejected by the Arab League. The idea that the UN created Israel by a sweeping majority vote is, therefore, a myth.

Ben-Gurion decided not to specify borders in Israel's Declaration of Independence, with the understanding that war would decide future borders. History proved him right. Israel became independent not within the borders recommended by the UN partition plan, but within the armistice lines of the 1949 Rhodes agreement. Those, however, were not internationally recognized borders. Questions of borders, refugees, and the status of Jerusalem became contentious issues between Israel and the Arab states. Furthermore, the international community never recognized the de facto 1949 partition of Jerusalem between Israel and Jordan.

At the beginning of the Cold War, Israel hoped to remain non-aligned, but as Ben-Gurion successfully argued, this policy did not withstand the test of reality. Although Israel took a pro-Western stance during the Korean War (1950–53), the United States kept its distance from Israel under Eisenhower (1953–61), so as not to throw Arab states in the arms of the Soviet Union. In the mid-1950s, Israel's only military and diplomatic ally was France — an alliance motivated by their common enmity toward Egypt's pro-Soviet president Nasser. In 1956 France and Israel (together with Britain) went to war against Egypt, but what began as a military success ended in diplomatic humiliation when the Eisenhower administration took the Soviet side and demanded the withdrawal of Britain, France, and Israel. Israel accepted its withdrawal from Sinai, but only after obtaining guarantees on the demilitarization of the peninsula and the freedom of shipping in the Straits of Tiran. Nasser felt confident that he could attack Israel soon.

10. The Periphery Strategy and Its Aftermath

The mountains are our only friend.

KURDISH PROVERB

Israel's Diplomatic Quagmire in 1958

By the time the Korean War ended in 1953, the Soviet Union's Middle East policy was now openly pro-Arab, while the Eisenhower administration endeavored to thwart Soviet influence in the Middle East and elsewhere. As the two superpowers competed over the Middle East's allegiance, Israel was considered a liability because of its conflict with the Arab world.

Israel's prime minister through most of the 1950s, David Ben-Gurion, hoped to build a strategic alliance with the United States by underlining Israel's reliability against Soviet influence in the Middle East. The Eisenhower administration, however, was not interested. In 1955 it backed, but not formally joined, a Middle East military alliance meant to thwart Soviet influence: the Baghdad Pact, also known as the Central Treaty Organization, composed of the United Kingdom, Turkey, Iraq, Iran, and Pakistan.

In January 1957 the U.S. government announced the "Eisenhower doctrine" guaranteeing American military and economic aid to Middle Eastern countries fighting Soviet influence and aggression. In response, Ben-Gurion declared that Israel fully supported U.S. efforts in the Middle East—but to no avail. That same year, the Soviet Union and

Syria signed a military agreement. Now the Soviets had two allies in the region: Syria on Israel's northern border and Egypt on its southern border.

Concerned by both Soviet progress and American coolness in the region, Ben-Gurion tried his luck with the North Atlantic Treaty Organization (NATO). Recognizing that full membership was unlikely, he asked the Western military alliance to grant Israel a special status: associated state. The United States, Britain, and France were noncommittal. NATO's general secretary Paul-Henri Spaak, though a friend of Israel, advised against the move by arguing that NATO did not need to alienate Arab states and encourage them to join the Soviet bloc.[1]

In 1958 Egypt and Syria merged, becoming the United Arab Republic (UAR), and Israel's only military ally, France, started showing worrying signs of policy reassessment. Charles de Gaulle came back to power that year and immediately downgraded France's military and intelligence cooperation with Israel.[2] Meanwhile, a coup that brought down the Iraqi monarchy opened the door to further Nasserist and Soviet influence in the Middle East. Israel felt increasingly threatened. So did other non-Arab Middle East countries, first and foremost Iran and Turkey.

The Birth and Demise of a Strategic Triangle

For Ben-Gurion, the year 1958 marked a diplomatic dead-end. To break Israel's isolation, he decided to be proactive and think outside the box. This is how he came to conceive the "periphery strategy," together with Reuven Shiloah (head of Mossad, Israel's intelligence agency, between 1949 and 1953) and Isser Harel (head of the Mossad between 1953 and 1963).

The idea was to "bypass" the hostile Arab Middle East by building military ties with the anti-Soviet and non-Arab regimes of the wider Middle East—Iran, Turkey, and Ethiopia—as well as with minorities such as the Kurds of northern Iraq and the Christians of Lebanon and southern Sudan.

Ben-Gurion spelled out his strategy as follows: "Our goal is to create a group of countries, not necessarily a formal and public alliance, that . . . will be able to stand fast against Soviet expansion via Nasser. . . . This group will comprise two non-Arab Muslim states (Persia [Iran] and Turkey), a Christian country (Ethiopia), and Israel."[3] The underlying idea was that "the enemy of my enemy is my friend."

The other nations also saw the tactical advantages of such an alliance with Israel. And so it was that by developing intelligence and military relations with Iran, Turkey, and Ethiopia, Ben-Gurion built in effect a "strategic triangle" around Israel.

There was, however, a built-in contradiction in the "periphery strategy." On the one hand, Israel was developing strategic relations with Iran and Turkey; on the other hand, it was also supporting these two countries' common and sworn enemy, the Kurds. A Foreign Ministry official complained to the Mossad that support for the Kurds was affecting Israel's relations with Turkey.[4] There was no such opposition from Iran to Israel's support for the Kurds, because Iran was first and foremost interested in weakening Iraq via Kurdish secessionism and apparently not concerned that such secessionism would expand to Iran itself.[5] As the shah (the Iranian monarch) said to Mossad director Meir Amit about Israel's support for Iraq's Kurds, "I want the flame alive, [but] I do not want a fire."[6]

ISRAEL AND IRAN

Iran had voted against the partition of Palestine in 1947, both as a member of UNSCOP and at the United Nations General Assembly. But in 1949 Iran had been compelled to negotiate with Israel for unexpected reasons. Some Iranian citizens in British Palestine (most of them Bahais) had fled during the 1948 war and lost their property. As they tried to recover it, they demanded their government's involvement.

The Iranian government sent an official representative to Israel in 1949 to settle the issue.[7] In 1950 Iran recognized Israel de facto though not de jure.

Israel's military exploits and swift victory during the 1956 Suez war had impressed the shah. In January 1957 the shah instructed his intelligence agency, the Savak, to establish secret contacts and cooperation with Israel.[8] Iran also started supplying Israel with oil via the Straits of Tiran, which Israel had reopened during the 1956 Sinai campaign.[9] For Israel, the 1956 war turned Iran into an even more important partner, because the Soviet Union had cut its oil sales to Israel after the war. By 1957 Iran had become Israel's main oil supplier.[10] Following the Pan-Arab nationalists' overthrow of Iraq's Hashemite monarchy in 1958, Iran felt that its now fiercely nationalist and pro-Soviet Arab neighbor had become a threat—and thus Israel could be a valuable ally. As a senior Iranian diplomat candidly admitted in 1959, "Now that Iraq has left the Baghdad Pact and is on practically every front behaving with marked unfriendliness toward Iran, the Iranian government has no particular reason to continue this appeasement [toward Iraq]."[11]

By the end of 1958, the Mossad, Savak, and SNST (Turkey's intelligence) held regular trilateral meetings every six months.[12] El Al was now flying to Tehran, and the shah's personal guards were equipped with Israel's iconic "Uzi" rifle. By the mid-1970s there were about five hundred families of Israeli representatives and businessmen living in Tehran, where a school was set up for Israeli children.[13] The shah, who suffered from lymphoma, was treated by an Israeli doctor, Prof. Moshe Mani.[14] Yet the shah often proved unreliable at times. In 1973, for example, he joined the oil embargo, and in 1975 he signed a reconciliation agreement with Iraq's Saddam Hussein.

Israel and Iran also cooperated to support Iraq's Kurdish rebels. In helping the Kurds of northern Iraq, Israel hoped to challenge the Iraqi army, which had fought against Israel in 1948 and continued to threaten

Israel's eastern front. Kurdish forces trained and advised by the IDF did in fact keep the Iraqi army busy in northern Iraq. Furthermore, Israel's close ties with the Kurds facilitated the *aliyah* of some Iraqi Jews to Israel: Jews from Baghdad and Basra would travel to Kurdistan, and the Kurds would help them enter Iran, where Israeli emissaries awaited them. Hence was Israel disappointed when the Kurds refused to increase hostilities against Saddam Hussein during the 1973 Yom Kippur War (doing so would likely have delayed the transfer of Iraqi divisions to the Golan Heights).

Even more distressing for Israel was Iran's turning from ally to enemy after the 1979 Islamic revolution. This revolution was a major blow to Israel. Besides being a bulwark against Soviet influence in the Middle East, Iran had previously provided Israel with an estimated 60 percent of its oil supplies.[15] The Mossad had considered the option of killing Khomeini in his French residence of Neauphle-le-Château, but one of Israel's Iran "experts" opposed the idea. "Let Khomeini return," he said. "He'll never last. The army and Savak will deal with him and with the mullahs on the streets of Tehran. He represents Iran's past, not its future."[16]

Paradoxically, however, secret relations were maintained between Israel and Iran even after the 1979 revolution. Despite the ayatollahs' fiery rhetoric and the new regime's open hostility to Israel, some analysts thought that a low-key, behind-the-scene relationship could still be sustained, and it turned out, they were right. Israel continued to sell weaponry to Iran post-revolution. Iran was willing to maintain this secret military relation with Israel because of the Iran-Iraq War, which erupted in 1980. When the war broke out, Israeli prime minister Menachem Begin quipped that he wished the best of luck to both sides, yet for Israel, Iraq was more of a military threat. In 1981 (after the release of the U.S. hostages), Israel was reported to have sold ammunitions and spare parts for tanks to Iran[17] at an estimated worth of $75 million.[18] In May 1984 Ariel Sharon would publicly admit the existence of a backdoor military relationship between Israel and Iran.[19] That year Israeli arms sales to Iran reportedly amounted to $500 million.[20]

Israel's backdoor relationship with Iran turned into a public embarrassment with the Iran-Contra scandal. The year 1979 had witnessed not only the Islamic revolution in Iran, but also the Marxist revolution of the Sandinistas in Nicaragua. At first the United States threw its weight behind the Contras, opponents of the new Marxist regime in Nicaragua, but in 1982 the Congress passed the Bolan Amendment, which outlawed U.S. governmental assistance to the Contras. To circumvent the new law, some Reagan administration staffers devised a backdoor channel to transfer money to the Contras: secret and illegal arms sales to Iran via an Iranian embezzler (Manucher Ghorbanifar) and unscrupulous Israeli businessmen. As part of the deal, Iran secured the release of some U.S. hostages held by Hezbollah in Lebanon. This Faustian bargain was approved by Israel's then prime minister Shimon Peres, who apparently thought that helping the mullahs would mollify them and at least partially restore the old alliance between Jerusalem and Tehran.[21] Yet Iranian officials leaked the deal to the Lebanese press in 1986, causing embarrassment in Israel and head rolling in Washington.

With the end of the Iran-Iraq War in 1988 and the blow dealt to Saddam Hussein's army following the 1991 Gulf War, there were no more reasons (if there ever were) for the clandestine relationship between Israel and Iran. In fact, the two countries now became sworn enemies, because of Iran's nuclear program (which is believed to have been launched in the mid-1990s[22]), its support for anti-Israel militias such as Hezbollah in Lebanon, and its direct involvement in terror attacks against Jewish targets (such as the bombing of the Jewish community center in Buenos Aires in 1994).

ISRAEL AND TURKEY

Israel opened a legation to Ankara in 1950—the first Israeli legation in a Muslim country (Turkey had recognized Israel de facto in March 1949). Still, Turkey's relations with Israel remained ambivalent from day one. A Muslim country, Turkey had voted against the partition of Palestine in 1947. At the same time, the Turks never quite forgave the Arabs for breaking up the Ottoman Empire during World War I. Turkish president Ismet Inönü candidly admitted his resentment at the Arabs for fighting against the Turks alongside Britain and France.[23]

Turkey was part of the pro-Western Baghdad Pact signed in 1955 (which included Iraq, Iran, and Pakistan). Following the 1956 Sinai war, Turkey partially met the demands of its Muslim allies to downgrade its relations with Israel. However, the pro-Soviet and Nasser-backed coup in Iraq and the political union between Egypt and Syria in 1958 weakened Turkey's regional standing. Furthermore, Turkey's age-old conflict with Syria (over territory in the Alexandretta/Hatay Province,[24] water resources, and Syria's support for the Kurdish rebels in eastern Turkey) provided yet another incentive for Turkey's rapprochement with Israel.

In short, threatened by Nasserist nationalism (including Nasser's demanded transfer of the Alexandretta Province from Turkey to Syria; see map 8) and by Soviet expansionism, Turkey was interested in upgrading its intelligence cooperation with Israel. What is more, the Turks thought that cooperating with Israel would help activate the pro-Israel lobby in Washington against the Greek and Armenian lobbies, both of which acted against Turkey.[25]

David Ben-Gurion secretly met his Turkish counterpart Adnan Menderes in August 1958. Both leaders agreed to create a united front between Israel, Turkey, Iran, and Ethiopia against Soviet and Nasserist expansionism.[26] Toward this aim, the Mossad, together with its Iranian and Turkish counterparts, established a triangular intelligence agency code-named "Trident" at the end of 1958.[27] Under "Trident," the highest intelligence officers of Israel, Iran, and Turkey met twice a year to share information on the Soviet Union and the Arab states.[28] In 1959 there were even talks of a joint Israeli-Turkish military operation against Syria, but the idea was eventually dropped.[29]

This cooperation between Turkey and Israel did not withstand the test of time, however. In 1961 Yugoslavian leader Josip Broz Tito established the movement of nonaligned countries in Belgrade. Then in 1964 developing countries established the "Group of 77," which turned into a de facto voting bloc at the United Nations General Assembly. Turkey needed the votes of both of these geopolitical blocs at the UN on the issue of Cyprus (an island populated by Greeks and Turks that had become independent in 1960 and was coveted by both Greece and Turkey). Because of the numeric superiority of Arab and Muslim countries, Turkey could not count on diplomatic support at the UN without downgrading its relations with Israel. It did so in the mid-1960s. After the 1967 Six-Day War, and even more so after the 1973 Yom Kippur War, Turkey's foreign policy adopted a pronounced pro-Arab stance in UN votes. However, despite the pressure of the Arab states, Turkey never severed its relations with Israel.

The 1979 Iranian revolution added a shared enemy for both Israel and Turkey. The new Islamic Republic of Iran officially labeled Israel as a "Satan" and, its Shia proselytism in full force, openly challenged Turkey's secular state model. Moreover, the ayatollahs supported the regime of Hafez al-Assad in Syria, a country embroiled in conflict with Turkey. Furthermore, with the end of the Cold War in 1991, both Israel and Turkey became concerned by Iran's increasing influence in the former Soviet republics of the Caucasus and Central Asia (Turkmenistan is ethnically and linguistically Turkic).

Israel and Turkey established full diplomatic relations in 1992, and in 1996 the two countries signed a "Military Training Cooperation Agreement" and a "Defense Industry Cooperation Agreement." Not surprisingly, Syria (harboring territorial conflicts with both Israel and Turkey) strongly condemned the 1996 alignment. Syria's then vice president Abd al Halim Khaddam called it "the worst threat to the Arabs since 1948" and "the most dangerous alliance ever signed since the Second World War."[30]

The Israel and Turkey rapprochement of the 1990s was not only motivated by geopolitical considerations. The Turks continued to see in their close relationship with Israel the best guarantee against U.S. congressional recognition of the Armenian genocide. One Turkish official put it bluntly: "The reason we are so friendly with Israel is that . . . AIPAC [American Israel Public Affairs Committee] . . . is the solution to the Armenian problem."[31]

Yet even with Turkey, relations eventually soured. In 2002 the Justice and Development Party won Turkey's general election. For the first time since the establishment of the secular Turkish Republic in 1923, an Islamic party would head the country. Its leader, Recep Tayyip Erdoğan, changed the course of traditional Turkish policies, both domestically and internationally. In 2003 Erdoğan rejected a U.S. request to use Turkey's territory to invade Iraq from the north—a decision that surprised the United States given Turkey's membership in NATO and turned Erdoğan into a hero in the Muslim world. As a Turkish diplomat admitted candidly to an Israeli audience, "We don't need you anymore. . . . There is no more USSR, no more Arab subversion."[32] Indeed, Erdoğan jailed most of the Turkish army and intelligence officers who had upgraded relations with Israel in the 1990s.

In June 2004 Erdoğan accused Israel of "state terrorism" after the elimination of Hamas leader Sheikh Yassin.[33] In 2005 Turkey normalized its relations with Syria, despite Turkey's adamant refusal to relinquish the Alexandretta Province as Syria had demanded. In 2006 Erdoğan hosted Hamas leader Khaled Mashal in Ankara, and in January 2009 he publicly humiliated Shimon Peres at the Davos Conference by telling him, "When it comes to killing, you know well how to kill."

In October 2009 Erdoğan canceled Israel's participation in the multinational Anatolian Eagle exercise and paid an official visit to Iran.

In short, under Erdoğan, Turkey reversed its perceptions and policies toward Iran and Israel. Right after the 1979 Iranian revolution, and even more so after the Soviet Union's collapse in 1991 and the resulting independence of the former Soviet republics of Central Asia, Turkey had perceived Iran as a regional threat and Israel as an ally. But by June 2010, for example, Turkey voted in the UN Security Council against imposing tougher sanctions on Iran. In November 2009 Erdoğan declared that he would rather meet Sudanese president Omar al-Bashir—who perpetrated genocide in Darfur and South Sudan—than Israeli prime minister Benjamin Netanyahu.[34] In March 2010 the Turkish premier claimed that Rachel's Tomb in Bethlehem was never a Jewish site.[35] In August 2010 Erdoğan appointed a pro-Iranian candidate to run Turkey's spy agency.[36] In February 2013 Erdoğan called Zionism a "crime against humanity,"[37] and in August 2013 he alleged that Israel was responsible for the military coup in Egypt.[38] In October 2013 the head of Turkey's central intelligence agency, Hakim Fidan, revealed the identity of ten Israeli secret agents to Iran—an unprecedented act of intelligence betrayal.[39] Furthermore, most of these outbursts and provocations took place before the *Mavi Marmara* incident of May 2010. This lethal operation, in which the IDF intercepted a Turkish ship that had tried to defy the Gaza blockade, produced a diplomatic crisis and rupture between Israel and Turkey.[40]

Eventually, however, Turkey and Israel overcame some of their differences and reached a reconciliation agreement in June 2016. Turkey's willingness to mend fences has been partially motivated by its energy needs. Turkey produces about 50 percent of its electricity from natural gas—but without any natural gas resources—and natural gas consumption is expected to double within the next two decades. Relying on Russian imports for most of its natural gas is seen as problematic; Turkey wishes to diversify its suppliers.[41] Israel, meanwhile, has been emerging as a major natural gas exporter. In addition, Erdoğan realized that the historical 2005 reconciliation between Turkey and Syria had become pointless, given Syria's civil war and implosion. Turkey could no longer ignore the fact that Israel is the Middle East's most stable and powerful country.

ISRAEL AND ETHIOPIA

Ethiopia was also an important part of Israel's periphery policy, but for different reasons. There was a special historical bond between Israel and Ethiopia, which had a large Jewish community and whose emperor, Haile Selassie, was of the "Solomonic Dynasty." Ethiopia took control of Eritrea in the early 1950s. Eritrea's anti-Ethiopian rebels were mostly Muslim, and since Israel feared a Muslim-ruled new state on the shores of the Red Sea, Israel and Ethiopia (a mostly Christian country) cooperated militarily against Eritrea. Emperor Selassie also saw in Israel a natural ally against his own Marxist rebels, backed by the Soviet Union and the Egyptian president Nasser.

Emperor Selassie's fears were justified: in 1974, a Soviet-backed coup would remove him from power. Ethiopia became a Soviet-aligned socialist republic and, as such, could no longer be counted among Israel's "periphery" allies.

A New Periphery?

Israel's "periphery strategy" progressively lost the allies on which this strategy was built: Ethiopia in 1974, Iran in 1979, and Turkey in 2002. Yet the concept itself of a "periphery" is still relevant, though in a completely different configuration.

Iran has emerged as a challenging regional foe. It constitutes a strategic threat to Israel due to its military nuclear program and its regional proxies (Hezbollah in southern Lebanon, Hamas in the Gaza Strip). This new geopolitical reality has revived Israel's periphery strategy, though admittedly one based on different premises and built with different partners.

Israel has not lost all its allies from the original periphery. In 2015 Israel was reported to import over two-thirds of its oil from Iraqi Kurdistan (via Turkey).[42] In 2011 South Sudan became an independent state. Yet those two allies are of questionable value at best; South Sudan is a failed state, and the Iraqi Kurds are the eternal losers of power politics.

Israel's former periphery allies, Iran and Turkey, have become its foremost regional challengers—though not in comparable ways. Iran pursues a military nuclear program, and it arms Hezbollah. Erdoğan's Turkey conducts a Pan-Islamic foreign policy and openly supports Hamas. Hence have Israeli strategists spoken in recent years of a "new periphery architecture" and of "axes of containment" to handle Israel's new Middle East challenges.[43] This "architecture" contains Azerbaijan (north of Iran) and the Gulf Emirates (Persian Gulf), as well as Greece and Cyprus (Turkey's Mediterranean rivals). The strengthening of ties between Israel, Greece, and Cyprus in recent years is motivated by shared concerns over Erdoğan's foreign policy, along with an emerging partnership between the three countries over natural gas exports to Europe (see chapter 21). In May 2013 Cypriot president Nicos Anastasiades called Israel a "strategic partner."[44]

Another key player in Israel's new periphery architecture is Azerbaijan (a country visited by Israel's prime minister in January 2018). Besides its value as a major oil exporter, Azerbaijan shares with Israel a common enmity toward Iran. A mostly secular Muslim (Shia) country, Azerbaijan resents Iranian proselytism. What Azerbaijan resents the most, however, is Iran's support for Armenia, a country with which Azerbaijan has a territorial dispute. Being a major oil producer, Azerbaijan was never sensitive to threats of oil boycott by Arab states, and therefore it traditionally refrained from adding its voice to the Arab-led anti-Israel coalitions at the UN.

In addition, the Arab states of the Persian Gulf, increasingly concerned by Iran's hegemonic ambitions, nuclear program, and destabilizing policies, have come to see in Israel a tacit and irreplaceable
ally. Israel and the United Arab Emirates (UAE) have conducted joint
military exercises.[45] The UAE hosted an Israeli diplomatic mission
(accredited to the International Renewable Energy Agency) in November 2015, and in December 2017 a large UAE delegation visited Israel.[46]
The Iranian threat has also created an unlikely tacit alliance between
Israel and Saudi Arabia, especially since Muhammad Bin Salman was
appointed crown prince in June 2017. In November 2017 the IDF's
chief of staff declared, "There is complete agreement between us
and Saudi Arabia."[47] In September 2018 it was reported that Saudi
Arabia had purchased the Iron Dome missile defense system from
Israel and that the two countries were negotiating to reach a broad
military agreement.[48]

Conclusion

In the late 1950s Israel initiated a "periphery strategy" meant to create
alliances with the non-Arab and anti-Soviet states of the wider Middle
East. This diplomatic initiative was motivated by three consecutive
trends: the encroachment of Soviet influence and alliance in the Middle
East, the decline of the France-Israel alliance, and the United States'
refusal to treat Israel as an ally.

Israel upgraded its strategic ties with Iran, Turkey, and Ethiopia,
but also with non-state minorities such as the Kurds of northern Iraq,
the Christians of southern Sudan, and the Maronites in Lebanon. This
system of alliances gradually fell apart following the Marxist coup in
Ethiopia in 1974, the Islamic revolution in Iran in 1979, and the election
of Recep Tayyip Erdoğan in Turkey in 2002.

Yet the very concept of periphery strategy has regained some relevance in the past decade due to the threat Iran poses to both Israel

and the Sunni states of Saudi Arabia and the Gulf. While in the 1960s Israel tried to "encircle" the Arab states, today it tries to circumvent both Iran and Turkey. To that end, Israel has developed a new periphery strategy with countries and regions such as Azerbaijan, Saudi Arabia, the Gulf Emirates, Greece, Cyprus, and Iraqi Kurdistan.

Thus, while the periphery policy designed by Ben-Gurion six decades ago eroded over time due to regime changes and policy upheavals, his idea is still relevant as Israel faces new challenges and attracts new allies in the Middle East and beyond.

11. Israel and the Arab States

> O Children of Israel! Remember My favor which I bestowed on you and be faithful to [your] covenant with Me, I will fulfill [My] covenant with you; and of Me, Me alone, should you be afraid.
>
> QUR'AN 2:40

The War of Independence and the Suez Crisis

The 1949 armistice agreements signed between Israel and four Arab countries (Egypt, Syria, Jordan, and Lebanon) after the 1948 war did not turn into peace agreements (see chapter 9). Representatives of Israel and its neighbors held indirect talks through the Palestine Conciliation Commission (which the UN had established in December 1948 to mediate the Arab-Israeli conflict), but the Arab states insisted on major Israeli withdrawals. In early Palestine Conciliation Commission meetings, Egypt announced that it would only consider signing a peace agreement with Israel based on the 1947 partition lines and not on the 1949 armistice lines.[1] When Israeli diplomats and representatives of Palestinian refugees met in Lausanne, Switzerland, between April and September 1949, Israel expressed willingness to accept some one hundred thousand refugees for the sake of family reunifications, but Palestinian representatives were threatened with death by their now-exiled leader Hadj Amin al-Husseini for even considering an agreement with Israel. Still, Israel allowed some of these refugees and their families into the country for humanitarian reasons.[2]

As indirect talks were taking place between Israel and its neighbors, two moderate Arab leaders, with whom Israel might have been able to reach an agreement, were no longer in the picture. Jordan's King Abdullah was murdered on July 20, 1951. In July 1952 a military junta led by the fiercely nationalist Gamal Abdel Nasser overthrew King Farouk of Egypt. The dual elimination ended the secret peace negotiations between Israel and Jordan and between Israel and Egypt.[3]

However, Farouk and Abdullah's earlier insistence on securing territorial gains in the Negev desert (which had been fully under Israeli sovereignty since the 1949 armistice agreements) had made a peace agreement with Israel unlikely in any event. There was also a high level of animosity and suspicion between Farouk and Abdullah. The Jordanian monarch told his Israeli interlocutors about the Gaza Strip, "Take it for yourself or give it to the Devil, but don't give it to Egypt!"[4]

Great Britain was yet another obstacle to a possible peace agreement between Israel and Jordan. In December 1949 Israel and Jordan had agreed on the principles of a peace agreement, but the British ambassador to Amman, Sir Alec Kirkbride, warned Abdullah not to sign a peace agreement with Israel before similar agreements were reached between Israel and other Arab states—especially Egypt. Abdullah backed down.[5]

Yet King Abdullah kept trying to reach an understanding with Israel. When asked about the reason for his persistence, Abdullah told Israeli diplomat Moshe Sasson, "Look, my son, if I don't make peace with you, there will be more wars between us and you will win them all. And so, making peace with you is a vital interest for my people."[6] But in 1951 Abdullah was murdered by Arab nationalists who opposed his conciliatory attitude toward Israel.

After King Farouk's overthrow, there were still attempts to reach an agreement between Israel and Egypt. A 1955 Anglo-American initiative known as Project Alpha called for an expansion of the size of the West Bank, a territorial corridor between Jordan and Egypt in the southern Negev, and the absorption or compensation of Palestinian refugees. But Nasser asked for the entire Negev, and Israel was unwilling to abandon even the southern Negev. The United States and Britain then suggested changes in the Negev that would have created territorial continuity between Egypt and Jordan without cutting off Israel's access to Eilat (a tunnel or a bridge were envisaged), but both Israel and Egypt rejected the Anglo-American proposal.[7] Meanwhile, hostile infiltrations of fedayeen (self-sacrifice fighters) from Jordan and Egypt continued apace between 1948 and 1956, inducing hundreds of Israeli casualties (both civilian and military).

Nasser felt confident enough to defy the United States, Britain, and France thanks to his 1955 military alliance with the Soviet Union—hence his decision to nationalize the Suez Canal in 1956. This maneuver was not as unexpected as it seemed, however. Nasser had tried to undermine King Hussein of Jordan (a U.S. ally) and had established relations with Communist China (an anathema for the United States). In July 1956 the Eisenhower administration had notified Egypt that it was withdrawing its support for the World Bank's funding of the Aswan Dam. Furious at the Americans over the cancellation, shortly after being rebuffed Nasser announced the nationalization of the Suez Canal. Revenues from the canal would then be applied to finance the Aswan Dam.

The nationalization of the Suez Canal meant that Britain and France were being robbed and that their major supplies (including oil) would now depend on the goodwill (or lack thereof) of Egypt. Such prospects made war nearly inevitable. The Eisenhower administration enjoined Nasser to return what he had seized but refrained from threatening to use force. If the United States could let the Soviet Union crush the Hungarian revolt in Budapest in 1956, would it lift a finger against a Soviet ally in the Middle East? The prudent and ambiguous messages coming from Washington convinced Paris and London that they had to act alone.

Like Britain and France, Israel wanted to weaken Nasser—though for different reasons. Nasser was the self-proclaimed leader of the Arab world and of the struggle against Israel. He allowed and sometimes encouraged terrorist attacks from the Gaza Strip to southern Israel, and since 1955 he had enjoyed the military backing of the Soviet Union. Israel, by contrast, was denied similar treatment from the United States.

On October 22 and 23, 1956, Israel's prime minister David Ben-Gurion, IDF chief of staff Moshe Dayan, and director-general of the Ministry of Defense Shimon Peres held a secret meeting in a villa in the Paris suburb of Sèvres attended by French premier Guy Mollet, French foreign minister Christian Pineau, French defense minister Maurice Bourges-Maunoury, and British foreign secretary Selwyn Lloyd. Its purpose was to plan a joint French, British, and Israeli military operation against Egypt. At Sèvres, the three nations designed a stratagem meant to fool the world: Israel would attack Egypt and swiftly move toward the Suez Canal; Britain and France, pretending surprise and indignation, would issue an ultimatum calling for both Egyptians and Israelis to remove their forces from the canal; Egypt would expectedly refuse, at which point Britain and France would intervene to remove Egyptian forces.

This coalition went against U.S. interests. Since the policy of the Eisenhower administration was to avoid losing more Arab countries to the Soviet Union, the administration did not wish to be identified with the *bêtes noires* of the Arab world in the midst of a geopolitical contest with the Soviet Union.

The short war was a military success, and as a result, Israel managed to reopen the Straits of Tiran. For a decade after the Suez conflagration, Israeli shipping would pass freely through the Straits of Tiran without a single clash with Egypt. Israel also secured Western guarantees recognizing that any additional attempt to close the straits would be considered a *casus belli*, thus allowing Israel to use force in self-defense (in accordance with Article 51 of the UN Charter). In order to thwart further confrontation between Israel and Egypt, a United Nations Emergency Force (UNEF) was deployed in the Sinai Peninsula to maintain its demilitarization. Israel withdrew from the entire Sinai Peninsula, as well as from the Gaza Strip, which Ben-Gurion had described as "a cancer" and "a barrel of gunpowder," and the fedayeen infiltrations from Gaza mostly ceased. Ben-Gurion had also asked a prescient rhetorical question about Gaza back in 1956: "How can we take 350,000 Palestinian Arabs against their own will and against the will of the friendly and hostile nations without exploding our state from within?"[8]

Beyond Israel's diplomatic gains after its 1956 war on Egypt, there were also psychological side effects. As Abba Eban explained, "Israel's sharp reaction to prolonged belligerency had certainly evoked disapproval in many places, but it had also inspired an uneasy respect. . . . The real transformation was in Israel's vision of itself. This had evolved from self-doubt to something like national confidence."[9]

As for the Eisenhower administration, having abandoned its British and French allies in a war against a Soviet client (Egypt) in 1956, and having tacitly acquiesced to the Soviet invasion of Budapest (also in 1956), it now tried to diffuse the impression that it was not opposed to Soviet expansionism. In January 1957 the U.S. government announced the Eisenhower Doctrine, which committed the United States to any Middle East country threatened by communism. Yet this "doctrine" was too little too late.

The Six-Day War and Its Unsettled Consequences

Because Nasser emerged from the 1956 war as an Arab hero who humiliated both Britain and France, and because he felt invincible thanks to Soviet Union backing, he became more confident and increasingly radical. He redoubled his military support for the anti-Western rebels in the Arab world (such as in Algeria and Yemen), and in 1958 he formed the United Arab Republic with Syria. The Soviets now had a strong foothold in the Middle East, and in 1961 the new Kennedy administration started to reassess Eisenhower's Middle East policy.

By now, the Middle East was polarized by the Cold War, with the Soviet Union encouraging Nasser's anti-Western policies, and the United States reassessing its policy toward Israel. This American reassessment occurred at just the right time for Israel, since the alliance with France could no longer be maintained after its underlying cause, the Algerian War, ended in 1962. In 1964 Israeli prime minister Levi Eshkol paid an official visit to the United States. That same year, Nasser created a United Arab Command under Egypt's control as well as the Palestine Liberation Organization (PLO). On July 11, 1965, Nasser declared, "The final account with Israel will be made within five years if we are patient. The Muslims waited seventy years until they expelled the Crusaders from Palestine."[10] Nasser also intensified his verbal attacks on King Hussein of Jordan, calling him "the Hashemite harlot," the "imperialist lackey," and the "treacherous dwarf."

By the mid-1960s, therefore, the Middle East was ripe for a proxy war between the United States and the Soviet Union via their respective protégés. Despite all his inflamed rhetoric, however, Nasser remained prudent. Embroiled by his military involvement in Yemen, he was not ready to fight Israel. Syria's leaders, by contrast, were more gung ho. At the Arab summits of 1964 and 1965, Syria was almost alone in calling for immediate war against Israel. In 1966 a fiercely nationalist government assumed power in Syria. In the early months of 1967, Syrian terrorist units infiltrating Israel conducted attacks against the Jerusalem–Tel Aviv railway as well as in the vicinity of Israel's parliament in Jerusalem. A young Israeli was blown to pieces by mines placed near the Lebanese border, and four Israeli soldiers were killed in the Upper Galilee.[11] Syria also started shelling Israeli villages and kibbutzim in the Galilee. There were no condemnations from the UN

Security Council, where the Soviet Union used its veto to shield its Syrian client. In April 1967, after Syrian attacks on Israeli farmers, Israeli and Syrian armies exchanged fire; dogfights between Israeli and Syrian pilots followed. On April 7 the Israeli Air Force brought down six Russian-made MiGs, humiliating both Syria and the Soviet Union. France, by contrast, congratulated Israel for proving the technological superiority of its Mirage and Mystère fighter jets.[12]

Despite the mounting tension between Israel and Syria, however, war seemed completely unlikely. Abba Eban recalled that "at the beginning of May 1967, there was no premonition of war"[13] and the mood of Israel's military intelligence "was one of complacency."[14] At the same time, Israel's shooting of six MiGs was more than what Moscow could tolerate, because it depreciated the value of pro-Soviet alignment among Third World countries. The Soviet ambassador to Israel warned Israel's foreign minister, "You seem to be celebrating your victory of April 7, but I tell you frankly, before long you will regret your success."[15]

Syrian attacks on Israel redoubled immediately. Israel implored the Soviet Union to restrain its troublemaking ally, but Moscow was in fact interested in an escalation that would prove the superiority of military alliances with the Soviet Union. Moscow tried to mask its duplicity with "arguments" that were grotesque even by the standards of Soviet propaganda. The Soviet ambassador to Israel claimed that Israeli victims of Syrian terror were in fact blowing themselves up and that, in addition, CIA agents disguised as Palestinian infiltrators from Syria were laying mines on Israeli roads to provoke Israel, with the ultimate purposes of weakening the Damascus regime and promoting the U.S. oil industry.[16] The Soviet strategy was counterproductive and became tangled in its own contradictions. It encouraged Syrian provocations to "prove" the military superiority of Soviet-backed Syria, but each Israeli retaliation ended up demonstrating the very opposite.

Hence did Moscow decide to involve its other Middle East ally—Egypt. If Syria alone could not withstand Israeli counterattacks, surely Syria and Egypt, acting together, would keep Israel in its box.

On May 13, 1967, the Kremlin deceived Cairo by falsely claiming that Israel was concentrating troops on its northern border to invade Syria and topple its government. Nasser probably knew this information was false (Israel was successfully repelling the Syrian air force and had everything to lose from invading a Soviet ally). Yet Nasser announced on May 23 his decision to blockade the Straits of Tiran. When Prime Minister Levi Eshkol invited Soviet ambassador Chuvakhin to check for himself that Israeli troops had not concentrated on the Syrian border, Chuvakhin replied that his job was not to question the "facts" emanating from the Kremlin.[17]

What motivations underlay the Kremlin's decision makers in May 1967? There does not seem to be a definite answer to this question. Israeli historian Michael Oren wrote in his book *Six Days of War* that "the Soviets were keen to prevent a battle that was liable to result in Arab defeat and superpower confrontation. Yet, at the same time, they wanted to maintain a heightened level of tension in the area, a reminder of the Arabs' need for Soviet aid." Moreover, Oren argued, "the tendency of Communist decisionmakers to be influenced by their own propaganda on imperialist Zionist perfidy . . . also played a part, magnifying the threat Israel posed to Syria."[18] It also seems that the United States' deepening involvement and increasing losses in the Vietnam War convinced the Soviet Union that President Johnson would not get involved in a conventional war in the Middle East.[19]

There were other reasons for the Soviets to believe that the Middle East was low-hanging fruit. The 1966 coup in Syria had been supported by the Syrian Communist party, turning Syria unto an even stauncher Soviet ally. When, that same year, France quit NATO's military command, the Soviets interpreted the relinquishment as a blow to Western unity. In 1967 Britain pulled out from Yemen, and the first mass demonstrations against the war in Vietnam took place in the United States. To decision makers in the Kremlin, the West looked divided and on the defensive.

On May 16, 1967, Egyptian infantry and armored units started crossing the Suez Canal, thus remilitarizing the Sinai Peninsula. On the morning of May 19, Egypt ordered the UN to remove the United Nations Emergency Force (UNEF) from Sinai. UN secretary-general U Thant complied, thus irresponsibly removing a safety valve that had prevented explosions for a decade. The very day Nasser ordered UNEF out of Sinai, Radio Cairo announced that "Israel's existence has lasted for too long . . . the day of its destruction is approaching."[20]

The Soviet Union was ultimately responsible for the war that broke out in June 1967. It was in response to false Soviet claims that Israel was concentrating forces at its northern border to attack Syria that Nasser concentrated Egyptian forces in Sinai, demanded that UN secretary-general U Thant remove UNEF forces from the peninsula, and announced the closure of the Straits of Tiran. The Soviet embassy in Tel Aviv reported to Moscow that the Israeli government did not have the domestic support and the political authority to wage war[21]— reports that were likely passed on to Cairo. Also, Ben-Gurion's cranky and disloyal attacks on Prime Minister Levi Eshkol were conveying the message that Eshkol would not dare to take military action, likely convincing Soviet leaders that Israel would just swallow the bitter pill of the straits' closure.[22] Meanwhile, Western capitals were displaying hesitation; they paid lip service to Israel's shipping rights, but remained noncommittal. Israel's chief of staff Yitzhak Rabin warned the government that the IDF was unprepared to fight a war with Egypt and that it needed more time to reinforce its southern front.[23]

And yet, when Nasser announced the closure of the Straits of Tiran on May 23, he produced the *casus belli* that justified Israel's right to self-defense. This was not only a matter of legal principle. Since 1957, Israel had developed strong trade ties with east Africa and with Asia, thanks to its access to the Red Sea. Nasser's blockade effectively cut off Israel from Asia and Africa. And the guarantees Israel had obtained in 1957 from the United States, Britain, and France had proved to be mostly worthless with the passing of time, as Israeli foreign minister Abba Eban was to realize after touring Paris, London, and Washington in May 1967. French president Charles de Gaulle cautioned Israel not to launch a preemptive strike ("Don't make war. . . . Do not be the first to shoot!" he warned Eban).[24] When Eban reminded de Gaulle about France's 1957 commitment to Israel's right to self-defense in case of closure of the Straits of Tiran, de Gaulle replied, "That was 1957. It is now 1967."[25] This was, in effect, a repudiation of France's commitment—a commitment made under the defunct Fourth Republic, which de Gaulle despised.

Unlike de Gaulle, British prime minister Harold Wilson was willing to honor Britain's commitment to free shipping in the straits, and he did not give any advice to Israel. As for President Johnson, he fully endorsed Israel's position that Egypt's closure of the straits was an intolerable act of aggression. But Johnson, embroiled as he was in Vietnam, asked for time to convince Congress and public opinion that the United States should enforce free shipping in the Straits of Tiran by all means: "I am well aware of what three past presidents have said, but that will not be worth five cents if the people and the Congress do not support their president now. . . . Without the Congress I am just a six foot four Texan."[26] The American and Israeli governments agreed on the principles, but not on the timetables. Johnson would later confirm that U.S. military experts were confident that Israel would win ("My generals are always right about other people's wars and wrong about our own").[27]

The dithering of Western capitals reinforced Nasser's conviction that no one would come to Israel's help. In fact, Nasser said so himself when he announced the closure of the Straits of Tiran: "In contrast to what happened in 1956, when France and Britain were at its side, Israel is not supported today by any European power."[28] He explained to his cabinet and to his generals that Israel would not fight because it had no allies to count on. In Nasser's opinion, the United States was too deeply and too badly involved in Vietnam to come to Israel's rescue; as for France, it would not commit to Israel's vital interests because Israel's "good old days" with the Fourth Republic were over.[29]

The dithering of Washington and London was confirmed on May 28, 1967. British foreign secretary George Brown declared that "we regard the United Nations as primarily responsible for peace keeping," and U.S. secretary of state Dean Rusk announced that his government was "not planning any military effort in the Middle East."[30] Two days later, on May 30, King Hussein of Jordan placed his army under Egyptian command. On May 31 Israel's prime minister Levi Eshkol expanded his coalition and appointed Moshe Dayan as defense minister. Israel's Mossad chief Meir Amit then met with CIA director Richard Helms and U.S. defense secretary Robert McNamara, reporting on June 3 to his government that the United States was unable (or unwilling) to organize a maritime force to guarantee the freedom of navigation in the Straits of Tiran.

This development was critical, because President Johnson had asked Prime Minister Eshkol to hold his horses and give the United States enough time to reopen the straits either via the UN or an American-led fleet. That latter option, which in any case was never meant to provide a solution to the concentration of Egyptian forces in Sinai, was no longer relevant. McNamara and Helms told Amit that at this point, the U.S. government was neither giving Israel a green light nor holding it back.[31]

With the closing of the Straits of Tiran and the West's feeble reaction, Nasser had achieved a strategic victory and placed Israel in an intolerable position. Israel had lost maritime contact with two-thirds of the world, its workforce was mobilized by the army (thus putting its economy mostly on hold), and it was being asked by its allies to keep on waiting. As such, Nasser's original design might not have been war; humiliating and choking Israel without a fight might well have been good enough for him. This was certainly good enough for the Soviet Union. Eventually, however, Nasser kept concentrating troops in Sinai, recalled Egyptian troops from Yemen, put Jordan's army under his control, and multiplied incendiary calls for Israel's destruction.

On June 4, 1967, the Israeli cabinet instructed the IDF to take action against Egypt for the immediate reopening of the Straits of Tiran. The die was cast. On June 5, at around 7:00 a.m., Israel's French-made Mirage and Mystère fighter jets took off. Within hours, all of Egypt's airfields were bombarded, and most Egyptian airplanes were destroyed on the ground. Israel notified Jordan that its military operation was solely directed at Egypt and that there would be no hostilities against Jordan if it stayed out of the fighting. King Hussein, however, was no longer in control of his own army, having placed it under Egypt's command. Jordanian shelling at Israel consequently extended the war to the eastern front. On June 7 the IDF reopened the Straits of Tiran and conquered Jerusalem's Old City. On June 9 the IDF conquered the Golan Heights in response to Syria's shelling of Israeli kibbutzim in the Upper Galilee. On June 10 the war was over. In six days, the IDF had defeated Egypt, Syria, and Jordan and had conquered the Sinai Peninsula, the West Bank, and the Golan Heights.

When the Israeli government ordered the conquest of the West Bank, Mossad director Meir Amit had asked the following questions: "We must understand what we want in the West Bank. Are we interested in settling in it? Do we want union? Are we interested in some other proposal?"[32] His questions were unanswered then and are unanswered to this day.

The Soviets were aware of the impending war. Between May 25 and May 28, an Egyptian delegation had visited Moscow and explained to Soviet premier Alexei Kosygin that Nasser was ready for war. Kosygin warned Egypt not to be the first to shoot, though he was convinced

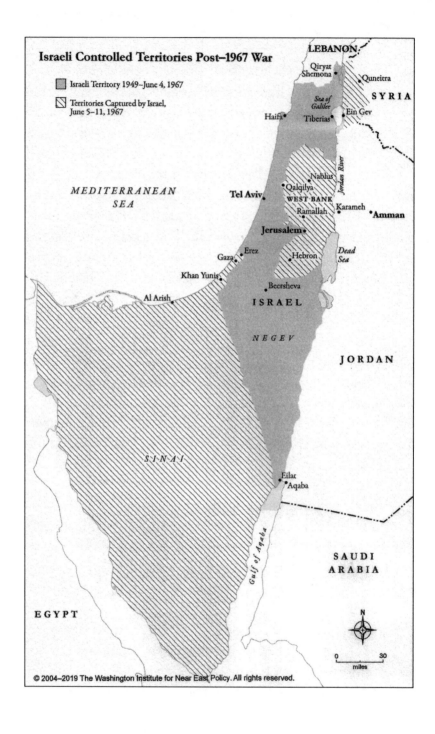

Israeli Controlled Territories Post–1967 War

Israeli Territory 1949–June 4, 1967

Territories Captured by Israel,
June 5–11, 1967

LEBANON

Qiryat
Shemona

Quneitra

SYRIA

Sea of
Galilee

Haifa

Tiberias

Ein Gev

MEDITERRANEAN
SEA

Jordan River

Nablus

Qalqilya

Tel Aviv

WEST BANK

Ramallah

Karameh

Amman

Jerusalem

Gaza

Erez

Hebron

Dead
Sea

Khan Yunis

Beersheva

Al Arish

ISRAEL

NEGEV

JORDAN

SINAI

Eilat
Aqaba

Gulf of Aqaba

SAUDI
ARABIA

N

EGYPT

0   30
miles

© 2004–2019 The Washington Institute for Near East Policy. All rights reserved.

that Egypt would win.[33] Soviet defense minister Andrei Grechko was gung ho, however, and had assured the Egyptians of his support.

While it seems that the Kremlin had provoked a crisis to prove the value of pro-Soviet alignment to skeptical Third World countries, the outcome of the Six-Day War could not have been more humiliating and disastrous for the Soviet Union. As Abba Eban was to characterize it, "The 1967 war is the child of Soviet policy. The Arabs, who were meant to be the beneficiaries of the Kremlin's protection, became its victims. Moscow had provoked the Arabs to make war, but did virtually nothing to help them win it. . . . The Soviet attitude toward the vanquished Arab states had an air of disappointed condescension."[34]

The Six-Day War was a military exploit at the end of which Israel was ecstatic, the Arabs humiliated, and the Soviets furious. On June 19 Israeli foreign minister Abba Eban publicly castigated the Soviet Union at the UN General Assembly. After Soviet prime minster Alexei Kosygin accused Israel of aggression and demanded its complete and unconditional withdrawal from all the territories it had conquered, Eban replied, "You come here in our eyes not as a judge or as a prosecutor, but rather as a legitimate object of international criticism for the part that you have played in the somber events which have brought our region to a point of explosive tension."[35] Before the war, the Soviet Union had blocked the UN Security Council, because it did not want to defuse the crisis it had provoked in the first place.[36] After Israel's victory, the Soviets wanted the Security Council to swiftly impose an immediate, total, and unconditional Israeli withdrawal from all the territories conquered during the war. Yet, as de Gaulle had said to Eban, 1967 was not 1957. After the 1956 war, both the Soviet Union and the United States had agreed that Israel had to pull out of Sinai without delay. The 1967 war, by contrast, had been provoked by the

Map 12. The territorial outcome of the 1967 Six-Day War. © 2004–2019 Washington Institute for Near East Policy. All rights reserved.

Soviet Union, and the United States now considered Israel an ally. In 1967 the United States supported the position that Israel should have secure and recognized borders and that those new borders should be negotiated.

On June 19, 1967, Israel conveyed to Egypt and Syria, via the United States, that it would agree to territorial withdrawals in exchange for peace agreements. Israel also gave assurances that it would negotiate with Jordan. When the Arab League convened in the Sudanese capital of Khartoum in September 1967, however, it rejected negotiations with Israel. As Abba Eban was to quip, the Six-Day War was the first war in history at the end of which the victor sued for peace and the vanquished demanded unconditional surrender. As for the West Bank and the Gaza Strip, the Israeli government discussed the issue at length but never made a clear decision. Prime Minister Eshkol said that any final decision should take into account "security and demography."[37] Menachem Begin opposed the very idea of "autonomy" for the Palestinians because, he claimed, any autonomy would inevitably turn into a state (eventually, however, he would agree to autonomy, by signing the Camp David Agreements in 1978). Both Moshe Dayan and Yigal Allon agreed in principle to the idea of a Palestinian state, though Allon insisted that such a state be surrounded by Israeli territory.[38]

Levi Eshkol had many meetings with local Arab leaders from the West Bank and the Gaza Strip in 1968. In May 1968 the Israeli government reached an agreement with the mayor of Hebron to establish an autonomous civilian authority there—yet as soon as Jordan's King Hussein heard of the plan, he called the mayor of Hebron a traitor. Because King Hussein wanted to retake control of the West Bank, he strongly opposed any type of Palestinian self-rule or government.[39] Thus the autonomy plan fell through. Yet the "Jordanian option" might never have been a realistic one, since both the PLO and Egypt opposed it.

Between June and November 1967, six UN resolutions condemning Israel were rejected, and four UN resolutions demanding a full Israeli withdrawal were defeated.[40] In July 1967 Soviet foreign minister Andrei Gromyko and U.S. ambassador to the UN Arthur Goldberg agreed on a draft resolution that required Israel's withdrawal, without delay, to the lines of June 4, 1967.[41] In effect, Goldberg had subscribed to the Soviet demand of a total and unconditional Israeli withdrawal. This text shocked and disappointed Israel, since the United States had rejected previous draft resolutions making similar demands. Yet this draft, too, soon became moot. Egypt rejected it because it recognized the right of all states in the Middle East to live in peace and security.

UN Security Council Resolution 242 was adopted on November 22, 1967, five months after the war ended. Negotiations over Resolution 242 had begun in mid-October. The British ambassador to the UN, Lord Caradon (also known as Hugh Foot, before being ennobled), had been asked to draft the resolution. On November 6 Israel's foreign minister Abba Eban met with British prime minister Harold Wilson and British foreign minister George Brown at 10 Downing Street. Wilson and Brown made it clear to Eban that the British text would call for Israel's withdrawal from occupied territories without specifying "all the territories" or even "the territories." Brown emphasized that "the omission of the word 'all' and of the word 'the' from the text of 242 was deliberate."[42]

The Security Council's veto-wielding members could not agree on the final wording of the resolution. The final draft was a compromise between the Soviet and American positions. On the one hand, the resolution called for the "withdrawal of Israeli armed forces from territories occupied in the recent conflict." On the other hand, it recognized Israel's right to live "within secure and recognized boundaries free from threats or acts of force." Furthermore, the English version indeed said "from territories" and not "from all the territories" or "from the territories." As Abba Eban emphasized in his remarks at the Security Council on November 22, 1967, "It has been pointed out in the Security Council, and it is stated in the 1949 Agreements, that the armistice demarcation lines have never been regarded as boundaries so that, as the representative of the United States has said, the boundaries between Israel and her neighbors must be mutually worked out and recognized by the parties themselves as part of the peace-making process."[43] Eban also noted with satisfaction that the Soviet demand for an Israel withdrawal to the pre–June 1967 lines had been rejected: "There were proposals, including those submitted by three Powers and then by the Soviet Union, which failed to win the necessary support because they rested in our view on the wrong premise that a solution could be formed on the basis of a return to the situation of 4 June."[44] Resolution 242 avoided any reference to "the June 4 lines" or to "the previous armistice lines." Resolutions that did call for a return to those lines were defeated.[45] President Johnson dismissed Soviet prime minister Kosygin's suggestion, before the passing of the resolution, that "from territories" should be understood as "from all the territories." On the day of the Security Council vote, the Indian and Arab delegations asked Lord Caradon to state off the record that the resolution's intention was to demand an Israeli withdrawal from all the territories. Caradon refused to make such a statement.[46]

The French version of the resolution, however, called for an Israeli withdrawal "des territoires occupés lors du récent conflit" (i.e., from the territories), even though the exact translation of "from territories" into French should have been "de territoires." French ambassador to the UN Armand Bérard asserted, "If we refer to the French text, which is equally authentic with the English, it leaves no room for any ambiguity, since it speaks of withdrawal *des territoires occupés*."[47] Yet, was the French text "equally authentic with the English"? According to Israeli diplomat and international law professor Shabtai Rosenne,[48] the answer to that latter question was no, since the resolution was submitted by the British delegate (Lord Caradon) and worded and reworded in English; furthermore, draft resolutions that added the words "all" and "the" before "territories" had been rejected.[49] Lord Caradon, who supervised the negotiations over the wording of 242, explained that the word "the" was deliberately dropped before "territories" from the resolution in order to gain consensus among Security Council members.[50] British foreign secretary George Brown unequivocally settled the controversy in his memoirs. Resolution 242, he wrote, "does not call for Israeli withdrawal from 'the' territories recently occupied, nor does it use the word 'all.' It would have been impossible to get the resolution through if either of these words had been included, but it does set out the lines on which negotiations for a settlement must take place. Each side must be prepared to give up something: the resolution doesn't attempt to say precisely what, because that is what negotiations for a peace treaty must be about."[51] The resolution's original text is in English, and its other versions (including the French version) were translated from English. French international law expert Charles Rousseau explains that when translations of international treaties produce different interpretations, primacy must be given to the original text ("primauté au texte original").[52]

Resolution 242 dealt with other issues besides borders. It called "for achieving a just settlement of the refugee problem"—a vague formulation open to interpretation: what is "just," and according to whom? Finally, Resolution 242 was not enforceable. It was to be negotiated among the belligerents (or former belligerents) because it was adopted under Chapter VI (and not Chapter VII) of the United Nations Charter.[53] As UN secretary-general Kofi Annan declared on March 19, 1992, "A [Security Council] Resolution not adopted under Chapter VII is not binding. . . . Resolution 242 (1967) is not based on Chapter VII of the UN Charter."[54]

On June 19, 1967, the Israeli government announced its willingness to withdraw from the Sinai Peninsula and the Golan Heights in exchange for full peace agreements with Egypt and Syria. Two months later, the Arab League, gathering in Khartoum (Sudan), published its infamous

"Three No's" at the end of the conference: (1) no recognition of Israel; (2) no negotiations with Israel; (3) no peace with Israel.

On the other hand, Israel never adopted a clear policy regarding the West Bank and the Gaza Strip. Three weeks after the Six-Day War, labor minister and former military commander Yigal Allon submitted to the government a plan for Israel's annexation of a third of the West Bank and the return of the rest of the West Bank to Jordanian sovereignty. The Israeli government never officially adopted this "Allon Plan," and King Hussein of Jordan flatly rejected it. Still, Israel started building settlements in the areas of the West Bank meant to be annexed according to the Allon Plan, and Defense Minister Moshe Dayan implemented a de facto power-sharing arrangement between Israel and Jordan in which the latter continued to pay government salaries and to supervise public education in the West Bank (whose Arab inhabitants kept their Jordanian citizenship even after Israel took control of the area in 1967). Yet the many secret contacts and meetings between King Hussein and Israeli leaders on the implementation of the Allon Plan failed to deliver. Israel was proceeding with building in the West Bank, while Hussein insisted on Israel's return of the entire territory. For his part, King Hussein had little reason to show flexibility, because he knew that he was Israel's preferred partner. As U.S. secretary of state Henry Kissinger candidly admitted in a private conversation with the Jordanian monarch, "Israel has two choices: either it can deal with Arafat or it can deal with Your Majesty. If I were an Israeli Prime Minister . . . I would rush into negotiations with Your Majesty because that is the best guarantee against Arafat."[55]

Nonetheless, in time it became apparent that the "Jordanian option" was, in fact, an illusion. Hussein could hardly negotiate on behalf of the Palestinians, especially after the Arab League had decided in 1974 that the PLO was the only legitimate representative of the Palestinians. While the Israeli government officially endorsed Resolution 242, ambiguity thickened over time regarding its plans (or lack thereof) for the West Bank.

The Yom Kippur War and the Peace Agreement with Egypt

There was a psychological gap between Israel and the Arab world. Arab leaders were humiliated, yet they had no intention of surrendering. Soviet military support, oil exports, and numerical superiority at the United Nations were assets that Arab states were determined to use to improve their position and, possibly, to win the next round against Israel. As for Israel's leaders, their stunning victory gave them the mistaken impression that their country had become an unassailable power that could dictate the conditions of peace. But Israel was not the United States after World War II. The Arab states, while defeated on the battlefield, soon had their military capability restored and replenished by the Soviet Union.

Egyptian president Gamal Abdel Nasser thought that with Russian support, he could drive Israel out of Sinai by exhausting its reserve army. Hence did Nasser launch a "War of Attrition" in June 1968. Yet the War of Attrition was causing heavy and humiliating losses to Egypt. Adamant not to end the shelling of Israeli positions, the Soviet Union provided Egypt with new aircraft, Russian pilots, and anti-aircraft missiles. By the summer of 1970, the War of Attrition included dogfights between Israeli and Russian pilots.[56]

Nasser died in September 1970, his War of Attrition having achieved little. The Arab world had lost its champion, but still, Nasser's protégés did not rest. The "Arab Cold War" continued to rage, especially between the pro-Soviet PLO and the pro-U.S. King Hussein of Jordan. The month Nasser died, PLO chief Yasser Arafat tried to take over Jordan, with Soviet Union and Syrian support. The United States and Israel guaranteed Hussein their support, and Hussein fought a merciless war against the PLO, which drove it into Lebanon (a violent repression known as Black September). Inasmuch as Hussein's struggle was against the PLO, it was also against Syria's attempts to appropriate Jordan with Soviet Union backing.

Nasser's successor, Anwar Sadat, tried to obtain an Israeli withdrawal from Sinai through negotiations, but he demanded that Israel commit to a full withdrawal from Sinai as a condition for negotiating—a demand Israel rejected. In February 1971 the UN's special envoy for the Middle East peace process, Gunnar Jarring, proposed a peace framework between Israel and Egypt based on the "land for peace" formula. Sadat wanted an Israeli commitment to withdraw to the pre–June 4, 1967 line. While the Israeli government expressed its readiness to trade territory for peace, it also declared that Israel "will not withdraw to the June 4, 1967 lines." Many have claimed that this sentence caused the failure of the Jarring Mission. Yet it was well known that Israel interpreted Security Council Resolution 242 as leaving room for territorial revisions. Israel did not want to set a precedent that would, in effect, have made future territorial modifications impossible. Sadat, meanwhile, took Israel's response at its word. Neither Jarring nor the Nixon administration made any serious effort to bridge the gap between Egypt and Israel. They simply gave up after Israel's response and Sadat's walkout.

There is no doubt that Israel, at this point, was excessively self-confident. The predominant opinion was that the Arab states could not and would not dare to initiate war. British diplomat Sir Anthony Parsons asked Abba Eban in the early months of 1972 whether Israel was considering the possibility that Sadat might attack Israel without hope of victory but with the ultimate aim of breaking the deadlock. When Eban asked General Zeira, the head of Israel's military intelligence, what he thought of the idea, Zeira dismissed it as very unlikely.[57] Yitzhak Rabin (then Israel's ambassador to the United States) wrote in July 1973 that "the Arabs have little capacity for coordinating their military and political action. To this day, they have not been able to make oil an effective political factor in their struggle against Israel. Renewal of hostilities is always a possibility, but Israel's military strength is sufficient to prevent the other side from gaining any military objective."[58] Ariel Sharon, for his part, assured Israelis that "with our present boundaries we have no security problem."[59] Typical newspaper headlines reporting speeches by politicians or military experts would include statements such as "Arabs Have No Military Capacity / Arabs Flee Whenever There Is War / Our Intelligence Is Never Wrong / Time Is on Our Side / Golda's Boundaries Better Than King Solomon's."[60]

Israeli prime minister Golda Meir thought that it was safe for Israel to play for time. As Henry Kissinger reported in his memoirs, Golda Meir's mindset in March 1972 was upbeat and, as subsequent events were to tragically demonstrate, delusional: "At an appointment with Nixon on March 1, [Golda] proclaimed that 'we never had it so good' and insisted that a stalemate was safe because the Arabs had no military option. Golda's attitude was simple. She considered Israel militarily impregnable; there was strictly speaking no need for any change. But given the congenital inability of Americans to leave well enough alone, she was willing to enter talks though not to commit herself to an outcome."[61]

This complacent mood seems to have been shared by Henry Kissinger himself. When he met with Egyptian emissary Hafiz Ismail in France, in Cairo, and in Washington, Kissinger did not show any willingness to twist Israel's arm. Ismail would later say that Kissinger showed fewer signs of flexibility than even Golda Meir.[62] Kissinger also dismissed Sadat as a "fool" and as a "clown."[63]

As for Egypt, it had never recovered from the Six-Day War's humiliation. Sadat believed that if he could at least partially restore his country's honor and shatter Israel's self-confidence, Israel might be forced to negotiate. In addition, Sadat thought that the U.S. government would have a strong incentive to impose on Israel a withdrawal from Sinai if, as a result of a peace accord between Egypt and Israel, Egypt would switch its Cold War allegiance from the Soviet Union to the United States. As Israeli historian and former foreign minister Shlomo Ben-Ami put it, "The Soviet Union, [Sadat] understood, could offer the Arabs the tools of war, but only the United States could deliver Israel."[64]

Hence did Sadat launch, together with Syria, a surprise attack against Israel on October 6, 1973. And by doing so, Sadat proved Israel's official military doctrine to be flawed. Egypt was neither going to live with the status quo nor negotiate on Israel's terms. It chose the option of war to upset the psychological deadlock.

The "Yom Kippur War" took Israel by surprise. It also contradicted Israel's military doctrine that any attack on Israel would be repelled quickly and decisively. The Bar Lev Line (a chain of fortifications that Israel had built on the eastern bank of the Suez Canal) collapsed within the first few hours of the war. Israel's fighter jets were being brought down by new and highly accurate Soviet anti-aircraft missiles. After the first day of fighting, the Egyptian army crossed the Suez Canal and carried some 70,000 troops and 1,000 tanks into Sinai. In the north, 40,000 Syrian troops and 800 tanks cut deep into the Golan Heights. The IDF suffered heavy losses. By the fourth day of the war, Israel's losses in planes and tanks were so heavy that immediate reinforcement had become vital. On October 10 Israel asked the United States to urgently send a military airlift. Overcoming Pentagon resistance, President Nixon ordered the dispatch of the airlift. Before U.S. planes would take off en route to the Middle East, however, the IDF was retreating from both Sinai and the Golan Heights, and the Israeli government announced it was willing to accept a ceasefire. Sadat rejected the ceasefire idea; his army was doing well, and large amounts of Soviet weaponry were reaching Egypt.

America's airlift to Israel on October 13 was massive and decisive, motivated by Kissinger's concern that "an Israeli defeat by Soviet arms would be a geopolitical disaster for the United States."[65] And Egypt's fortunes in the war started declining on October 16, when General Ariel Sharon crossed the Suez Canal. Disaster was imminent; the IDF was closing in on Ismailia and Suez. As the IDF was about to capture and humiliate Egypt's Third Army, the Soviet Union threatened direct military action against Israel. A ceasefire negotiated between the United States and the Soviet Union went into force on October 26.

In the end, Israel had eventually repelled the Egyptian and Syrian armies, but the Israeli losses were enormous. Precisely 2,838 Israelis had died in a war that Israel's intelligence had dismissed as improbable. The country's self-confidence was shattered.

Thus did Sadat accomplish his double goal of deflating Israel's self-confidence and of restoring Egypt's honor. The psychological balance between Israel and Egypt had been transformed. Sadat's risk had been calculated and rewarded. As Abba Eban would sharply put it, "Sadat's decision for military action in October 1973 refuted the conventional assumption that no state knowingly starts a war unless it has a strong belief in its own victory. Sadat began a war that he knew he could not win, in the knowledge that the war itself would serve his design, irrespective of its result. The October war would unfreeze a deadlock that worked solely in Israel's favor. It would compel the superpowers to address themselves to the Arab-Israeli situation toward which Nixon and Brezhnev were evincing total apathy as late as in the summer of 1972."[66]

At the same time, however, Sadat also realized that Egypt did not have a "military option" against Israel. Egypt had taken Israel by surprise with the most advanced Soviet weaponry. Egyptian chief of staff Saad El Shazly would describe the Soviet Union's October 10 delivery of massive arms supplies to Egypt as "the biggest airlift" in Soviet history.[67] About fifteen thousand tons of military equipment were flown from the Soviet Union to Egypt and to Syria during the war, and yet, at the end of the war, the IDF was on the western shore of the Suez Canal, and it was only due to Soviet threats and U.S. pressure that the IDF did not humiliate the Egyptian Third Army. (For its part, the United States wanted to avoid direct confrontation with the Soviet Union, while also preserving the Egyptians' feeling of having avenged the June 1967 humiliation).[68] As candidly admitted by Egyptian prime minister Mustafa Khalil, "We know that we have no chance of winning a war, and we also know that you have the atomic bomb. . . . Egypt has no military solution, and we must seek another solution."[69]

In fact, Sadat himself would recognize that he came to opt for diplomacy after having tried all other options. Asked in 1978 why he chose peace negotiations with Israel, he answered bluntly, "Because you had my land. I tried every way to recover it without the hazard of making peace: I tried UN action, four-power, three-power, two-power pressure. I tried war, armistice, international condemnation. I reached the answer that only by peace could I recover my land."[70]

Sadat sent messages to Israel via Romanian despot Nicolai Ceaușescu, who explained to Abba Eban in Bucharest in November 1973 that the Egyptian president was serious about reaching a peace agreement with Israel. When Eban reported his conversation with Ceaușescu to Golda Meir, she reacted dismissively.[71]

Yet Sadat's underlying strategy was to trade Egypt's pro-Soviet allegiance for the Sinai Peninsula. Kissinger, a man of realpolitik, clearly understood Sadat's strategy and was more than willing to cooperate. As Kissinger would later explain, "Sooner or later, we were convinced, either Egypt or some other state would recognize that reliance on Soviet support and radical rhetoric guaranteed the frustration of its aspirations. At that point, it might be willing to eliminate the Soviet military presence—'expel' was the word I used in a much criticized briefing on June 26, 1970—and to consider attainable goals. *Then* would come the moment for a major American initiative, if necessary urging new approaches on our Israeli friends."[72]

Already in January 1974, Kissinger was convinced that Sadat had made a dramatic policy shift and was ready to end Egypt's alliance with the Soviet Union.[73] Yet Sadat needed to know that America could deliver. The "down payment" he asked for was a second dis-engagement agreement with Israel (the first one had been signed in January 1974) that would entail a significant Israeli withdrawal from the Sinai Peninsula. Israeli prime minister Yitzhak Rabin was willing to go along (he favored ending the Soviet presence in Egypt), but not to pay the territorial price. Israel already had a ceasefire agreement with Egypt, so why agree to a significant pullout for nothing tangible in return? Kissinger, however, was adamant. He twisted Rabin's arm to pull out from about 20 percent of the Sinai Peninsula in 1975. Finally, in September 1975, Rabin agreed to sign the "Sinai 2" accord with Egypt.

Rabin's Sinai withdrawal was the result of U.S. president Ford's pressure and even threats. Ford had warned Rabin that an Israeli refusal to meet U.S. demands would lead to "a reassessment of the United States policy in the region, including our relations with Israel."[74] Hence had Kissinger demonstrated to Sadat that America could indeed deliver and that it made sense for Egypt to abandon its Soviet patron. As for Israel, it gained diplomatically from widening the gap between Egypt and the staunchly pro-Soviet Syria.

Other Arab leaders did not follow Sadat's example. Syrian leader Hafez al-Assad and PLO chief Yasser Arafat remained faithful to their Soviet ally. Arafat had good reasons to believe that sticking to his pro-Soviet strategy would eventually pay off. While the Yom Kippur War had ended in Arab military defeat, it came at an enormous price for Israel. Over 2,800 Israelis had died, and more than 7,000 were wounded. Hostages had been taken. The material cost was very high as well—the IDF lost more than a thousand tanks and about one hundred aircraft. Israelis were shocked and angered. Their leadership had been taken by surprise, and the first days of the war had been

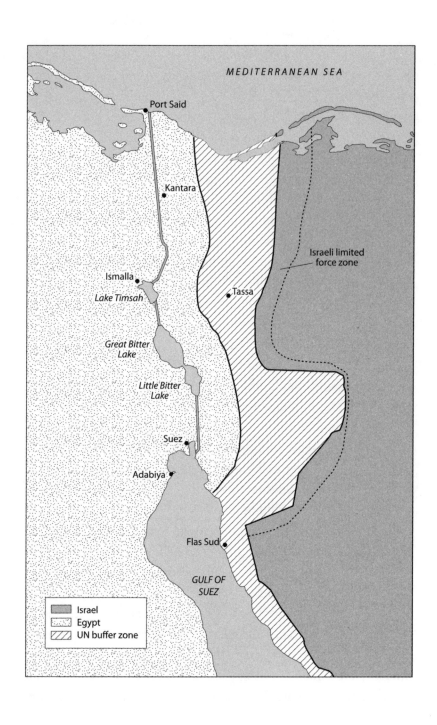

MEDITERRANEAN SEA

Port Said

Kantara

Israeli limited
force zone

Ismalla
Lake Timsah

Tassa

Great Bitter
Lake

Little Bitter
Lake

Suez

Adabiya

Flas Sud

GULF OF
SUEZ

Israel
Egypt
UN buffer zone

both life-threatening and humiliating. Technically, Israel had won. Psychologically, it was shattered.

Furthermore, the Yom Kippur War had erupted nine months after the signing of the Paris Peace Accords of January 1973, which officially ended the Vietnam War. Despite its overwhelming military superiority, the United States had suffered a diplomatic setback and a psychological blow. If a superpower like the United States could be persuaded to end the fighting, it was not far-fetched to conclude that Israel (itself militarily dependent on the United States) could be coerced into major concessions. Moreover, the Paris Peace Accords proved to be a temporary truce, at the end of which the Communists conquered and subdued South Vietnam.

The lessons of Vietnam left a strong impression on Yasser Arafat, who visited Northern Vietnam many times and developed a close friendship with Communist Vietnamese general Võ Nguyên Giáp. Indeed, the PLO upheld the Communist Vietnamese victory against the United States as a model of successful guerilla and psychological warfare against a more powerful military enemy.[75] PLO leaders would openly declare that their aim was to turn Amman (the capital of Jordan) into the "Palestinian Hanoi," and Tel Aviv into the "Israeli Saigon."[76] Arafat was to declare many years later, in 1997, that "in 1974 this movement [the PLO] received the banner of the revolution from the Vietnamese revolution."[77]

Arafat obviously understood that the Yom Kippur War had proved beyond doubt that there was no military option against Israel. But, as opposed to Sadat, who decided to abandon the Soviet Union for the United States and recover the Sinai via a peace agreement, Arafat decided to implement a Trojan horse strategy. The PLO's "Phased Plan," adopted in June 1974, called for the establishment of a Palestinian state

---

Map 13. The 1975 redeployment agreement between Israel and Egypt. Cartography by Bill Nelson.

in the West Bank and in Gaza in order to create a military presence within Israel as a first step toward the "liberation of all of Palestine." The very same year, the Arab League recognized the PLO as the sole representative of the Palestinians.

The Arab League's decision challenged both Israel and Jordan. Four years after driving the PLO out of Jordan (in September 1970), King Hussein was now officially competing with Arafat over the West Bank. This inter-Arab struggle was not unrelated to the Cold War: the United States backed Jordan, and the Soviet Union supported the PLO. But by failing to engage Jordan more forcefully, Israel indirectly facilitated the PLO's advance. Yitzhak Rabin's first government (1974–77) depended on the National Religious Party, which rejected the idea of relinquishing even parts of the West Bank. Hence did Rabin set the Palestinian issue aside, out of domestic political concerns. Yet the Palestinians themselves were divided. In a meeting between Palestinian notables and President Anwar Sadat in Jerusalem in November 1977, some expressed support for the PLO, others for Jordan.[78]

Nor was the Arab-Israel conflict disconnected from U.S. politics. With the swearing in of President Jimmy Carter in January 1977, the United States adopted a new and different approach to the Middle East. Carter wanted Israel to negotiate with the PLO and to withdraw to the 1949 armistice lines, as Rabin realized, to his horror, after his first meeting with Carter. Rabin refused to deal with the PLO and to even consider a full withdrawal to the pre–June 1967 lines, as he reported to the Knesset after meeting with Carter: "I cannot say that there is a similarity of views between the U.S. and Israel as we would have liked to see. Israel saw and sees in secure borders such lines that cannot be based on those that existed on June 4, 1967."[79]

As opposed to Henry Kissinger, who saw the Cold War as a zero-sum game, Carter was not a man of realpolitik. Carter believed in engaging the Soviet Union, and he thought that the Middle East was a good place to start. Hence did Carter suggest an international conference for the Middle East with both U.S. and Soviet Union participation.

Carter's initiative came as a surprise to Egyptian president Anwar Sadat, whose unwritten understanding with Henry Kissinger had been that the severing of Egypt's alliance with the Soviet Union would be rewarded by an Israeli withdrawal from the Sinai Peninsula. Sadat, who felt betrayed by Carter's overture to the Soviet Union, reportedly exclaimed, "We kicked the Russians out the door and now Mr. Carter is bringing them back in through the window!"[80]

Meanwhile, there was a political upheaval in Israel too. In 1977 the Labor Party lost its first election since Israel's independence in 1948, and the Likud party, led by Menachem Begin, formed a government. Not only was Sadat wary of Carter's policy, but he did not know what to expect from Menachem Begin, who was described by most journalists at the time as an intransigent nationalist. Sadat decided to probe Begin's personality and intentions via secret meetings between Egypt's deputy prime minister Hassan Tuhami and Moshe Dayan (Begin's newly appointed foreign minister) in Romania and Morocco.[81] The role of Romania's dictator Nicolae Ceauşescu was so critical in the early contacts between Israel and Egypt that Jimmy Carter would later praise Ceauşescu as "the architect of Saddat's visit to Jerusalem."[82]

Morocco's king Hassan II also played an important role in those secret contacts between Egypt and Israel. Having Moshe Dayan travel to Morocco incognito required creativity; Dayan went through passport control in the Rabat airport without his legendary eye patch and with a fedora hat on.

The secret early meetings convinced Sadat that Begin was willing to trade Sinai for peace and that he could be trusted. On November 9, 1977, he shocked the Egyptian parliament by announcing that he would be willing to travel to Israel for the sake of peace.

There was something dramatic, unprecedented, and emotional about the images of Sadat landing at Ben-Gurion Airport and addressing the Knesset. In his speech to the Knesset, Sadat said that he had not come to sign a separate peace with Israel and abandon the Palestinians to their own fate (though that was precisely what he ended up doing). Sadat's main objective was to recoup the territory his country had lost to Israel in June 1967. Menachem Begin was an ideologue for whom the Land of Israel was nonnegotiable, but he did not consider the Sinai Peninsula to be part of the Jewish territorial heritage.[83] Hence was an agreement eventually reached between Begin and Sadat, admittedly with enormous pressure from Jimmy Carter, as well as economic incentives (both Israel and Egypt were given generous U.S. military aid as part of their peace agreement). Begin had originally sworn not to dismantle Israeli settlements in Sinai, but he ended up agreeing to it after Ariel Sharon said it was a price worth paying for a full peace agreement. Sadat had originally pledged that he would not sign a separate peace with Israel, yet he eventually did so after realizing that linking peace with Israel to the fate of the West Bank would lead to a dead end. The peace agreement also enabled Israel to cut $600 million in its annual military budget.[84] Moreover, as Menachem Begin would emphasize, "We signed a peace treaty . . . with the largest and most powerful of our neighbors. The population of all our neighbors is barely half that of Egypt."[85] With Egypt formally at peace with Israel, Israel's other neighbors had lost their most powerful military ally.

Clearly, the Israel-Egypt agreement was one of realpolitik, made possible by mutual interests and by American pressures and incentives. Egypt had regained the entire Sinai Peninsula, and it was relieved from the economic burden of the conflict with Israel; it would also benefit from U.S. economic aid. The United States removed Egypt from the Soviet Union's Middle East sphere of influence. As for Carter, the peace agreement between Israel and Egypt was a personal achievement that contrasted with his serial international humiliations (in 1979 alone the Soviet Union invaded Afghanistan, Iran became an anti-American Islamic republic, and Communists overtook Nicaragua).

In addition to their peace agreement, Israel and Egypt signed a "framework for peace in the Middle East" that had the declared purposes of addressing the Palestinian issue and solving the Arab-Israeli conflict. The "framework" agreement recognized the "legitimate right of the Palestinian people and their just requirements." It called for elections in the West Bank and the Gaza Strip, for the establishment of a Palestinian government, and for the dissolution of Israel's military government. As Abba Eban commented on Menachem Begin's acquiescence to the "framework" agreement, "Anyone who wanted an undivided Land of Israel under exclusive Israeli rule should not have signed the Camp David Accord at all."[86] Henry Kissinger presciently wrote, "Paradoxically, the Begin government, against its preferences and ideology, was really proposing what all other nations were certain to read as an embryo Palestinian state and, to compound the irony, within the 1967 border, since none other was under discussion. Once there was an elected, self-governing authority on the West Bank, an irreversible political fact would be created on the territory over which its authority was supposed to run. However limited, this authority would soon turn into the nucleus of something like a Palestinian state, probably under PLO control."[87]

And yet, Begin relinquished Sinai not only to reach an agreement with Egypt, but also to solidify Israel's presence in the West Bank. As for Sadat, there is evidence that he favored a return of the West Bank to Jordan, and not a PLO-ruled state there. Sadat would call Arafat and the PLO "pygmies and hired killers," and he admitted in private to "have excluded the PLO."[88]

In any case, the "framework" agreement did not materialize. Arafat would later claim that the Russians and the Syrians had told him not to accept the Camp David Agreements, "when there were only 5,000 settlers in the West Bank and the Palestinians could have vetoed there being any more."[89] Arafat also said at one point, "Do you know who was the first one to offer me a Palestinian state? It was Begin. But back then I couldn't [accept]: there was huge pressure on us from the Syrians."[90] In 1981 Anwar Sadat was assassinated, Menachem Begin re-elected, and Ronald Reagan sworn into office.

Conclusion

The first Arab-Israeli war of 1948 left many issues unresolved, among them Israel's borders, the question of refugees, and the status of Jerusalem. Gamal Abdel Nasser, who overthrew the Egyptian monarchy in 1952, aligned Egypt with the Soviet Union in 1955. By supporting the Algerian rebels and by nationalizing the Suez Canal in 1956, Nasser produced a de facto alliance between Israel and France—an alliance that culminated in the 1956 Suez War. As a result of that war, Israel's right of passage in the Straits of Tiran was guaranteed by the West. Yet this guarantee proved hollow when put to the test a decade later: France was now ruled by de Gaulle, and the war in Algeria that had cemented the Israeli-French alliance was over; the United Sates was embroiled in Vietnam; and the United Kingdom was aligned with the United States.

Western setbacks and divisions and the U.S. quagmire in Vietnam convinced the Soviet Union that the Middle East was a low-hanging fruit and Israel was on its own. Yet the Soviets miscalculated by encouraging a war that its allies lost in June 1967. Israel's performance was impressive, and its swift victory confirmed its strategic value to the United States. The Arab-Israeli conflict became polarized by the Cold War; the United States was now fully supportive of Israel, while Egypt, Syria, and Iraq had Soviet Union support. The Soviet Union and its Arab allies had been humiliated, but neither intended to capitulate. Still, despite Soviet support and rearmament, Israel seemed impregnable.

Egypt's new leader, Anwar Sadat, took a calculated risk by launching a new war against Israel in October 1973, knowing that he could not win it outright but strategizing that he could in fact shake Israel's self-confidence and partially restore Egypt's honor. More significantly, Sadat came to realize that he would not recuperate the Sinai via war, and therefore his country's alliance with the Soviet Union had become pointless.

The 1979 peace agreement between Israel and Egypt was thus the outcome of realpolitik. Egypt regained Sinai after switching alliances from the Soviet Union to the United States, Israel partially neutralized its most powerful enemy, and both Israel and Egypt benefited economically from the new arrangement. The PLO, by contrast, adopted a "phased strategy" (inspired by the 1973 agreement signed between North Vietnam and the United States, as well as by the way North Vietnam had fought the war)—a strategy that would shape the conflict between Israel and the Palestinians in the years to come.

12. Israel and the Palestinians

They [the Jews] were behind the French Revolution, the Communist revolution and most of the revolutions. . . . With their money
they formed secret societies, such as Freemasons, Rotary Clubs,
the Lions and others in different parts of the world for the purpose of sabotaging societies and achieving Zionist interests. . . .
They were behind World War I, when they were able to destroy
the Islamic Caliphate, making financial gains and controlling
resources. They obtained the Balfour Declaration, formed the
League of Nations through which they could rule the world. They
were behind World War II, through which they made huge financial gains by trading in armaments and paved the way for the establishment of their state. It was they who instigated the replacement
of the League of Nations with the United Nations and the Security
Council to enable them to rule the world through them. There
is no war going on anywhere, without having their finger in it.

THE HAMAS CHARTER, Article 22

The Lebanon War and the First Intifada

Menachem Begin was elected to a second term as prime minister
in 1981. He gave the defense portfolio to Ariel Sharon, who started
floating the idea of building a "triangle of peace" around Israel, with
Egypt in the south, Jordan in the east, and Lebanon in the north.[1] By

Sharon's plan, Lebanon would be rid of the PLO, and the Christians would retake control of their half-Christian, half-Muslim country.

Lebanon's Christians (also known as Maronites) and the Zionists had long had a special relationship. In the 1930s Maronite patriarch Antoine Pierre Arida had praised the "brave Israelites" facing, together with Middle Eastern Christians, what he called "the sea of savage Muslims."[2] Maronite and Zionist leaders met regularly in the 1930s. Arida testified in favor of the Zionist movement to the United Nations Special Committee on Palestine in 1947. Yet the Christians never fully controlled Lebanon; indeed, successive civil wars and outside intrusions from Syria and the PLO sidelined the Christians and devastated a country once hailed as "the Switzerland of the Middle East." Israeli leaders did not hide their hopes of seeing the Maronites take full control of Lebanon and sign a peace agreement with Israel. In 1954 Ben-Gurion spoke of helping the Maronites retake control of their country. In 1955 Moshe Dayan suggested that Israel invade Lebanon to help impose a Christian government there.[3]

Israel's stake in Lebanon was related to the PLO's presence in this country. After the "Black September" of 1970, PLO forces were expelled from Jordan to Lebanon. By the mid-1970s, the PLO had become a state-within-a-state in Lebanon, with its own army, taxation system, police, judiciary, schools, and health care. In 1975, following clashes between PLO forces and the Maronites, the Lebanese civil war erupted. This civil war was related to the Arab-Israeli conflict and to the Cold War: Israel and the United States supported the Maronites, while Syria and the Soviet Union backed the PLO. In 1976 Syria invaded Lebanon to boost the PLO in the Lebanese civil war and take control of the country. Once reinforced, the PLO intensified its shelling of northern Israel. From 1977 onward, the PLO shelled northern Israel on a regular basis. When Israel sporadically intervened in Lebanon (such as in March 1978 with Operation Litani), it did so not only to push back the PLO, but also to help the Christians retake control of their hijacked country.

In March 1976 the Maronite Phalange Party asked for Israel's help. Prime Minister Yitzhak Rabin eventually agreed to sell weapons to the Maronites, led by Bachir Gemayel. Israel's defense establishment was divided. The IDF's intelligence branch was suspicious of the Maronites and skeptical of their commitments; the Mossad was in favor of an alliance.

Menachem Begin favored the Mossad's approach and implemented it upon becoming prime minister in 1977. In June 1982 Israel's defense minister Ariel Sharon convinced the government to launch an attack against the PLO in Lebanon after an assassination attempt on Israel's ambassador in Britain, Shlomo Argov (even though the assassination attempt had been carried out by the Abu Nidal terror group, which did not belong to the PLO).

Sharon had told the Israeli government that the purpose of the war was only to drive the PLO out of southern Lebanon. But Sharon misled his government, and foremost Begin, by instructing the IDF to reach Beirut and by actively assisting the Maronites in the Lebanese civil war. Sharon had also misled U.S. secretary of state Alexander Haig, who had tacitly acquiesced to Israel's intrusion into Lebanon based on the understanding that there would be no confrontation with Syria.[4] Later Begin would candidly admit that he was "kept informed either before or after action had been taken."[5]

By 1982 Israel had expelled Arafat to Tunis, but Sharon's hope to transfer political power to Lebanon's Christians soon collapsed. The Christian and anti-PLO Bachir Gemayel was elected president of Lebanon in August 1982 but assassinated three weeks later. The Christians took revenge by massacring Palestinians in the Sabra and Shatila refugee camps in Beirut. This episode incited outrage in Israel and around the world. An Israeli commission of inquiry determined that

Sharon should have been aware of the Christians' revengeful mood. He was forced to resign.

As for Begin, he felt manipulated by Sharon and was haunted by the death of Israeli soldiers in Lebanon. With the passing of his beloved wife, Aliza, he sunk into depression and eventually resigned in August 1983.

Reality had confounded Sharon's "grand design." The Lebanon War was costly and counterproductive. Lebanon's Christians, far from taking control of the country, were further marginalized. IDF officer Amos Gilead would later say of Israel's Lebanese adventure that the Israeli government had "linked up with a non-existent partner . . . a gang of lowly charlatans . . . that deceived us into thinking it was possible to bring about a 'new order' in the Middle East."[6] While the Syrian army suffered devastating losses (the IDF wiped out its air defense system), it remained in Lebanon and even strengthened its grip on the country. And while the PLO was expelled to Tunisia, it was replaced by the more fanatical Hezbollah (an Iranian-backed Shia militia).

The 1984 Israeli elections, held in the wake of the Lebanon War, produced a hung parliament. A unity government was established with a rotation system: Labor leader Shimon Peres served as prime minister and Likud leader Yitzhak Shamir as foreign minister between 1984 and 1986; they then switched roles between 1986 and 1988. Yitzhak Rabin held the defense portfolio during the entire duration of the unity government.

Despite their formal unity, Peres and Shamir agreed on little—especially regarding the Arab-Israeli conflict. Yet negotiations on Palestinian autonomy were also deadlocked because of the rivalry between King Hussein and Yasser Arafat, as well as by their conflicting geopolitical allegiances. Since the Arab League's 1974 decision recognizing the PLO as the sole legitimate representative of the Palestinians, King Hussein could hardly negotiate the final status of the West Bank with Israel while ignoring the PLO. Yet Israel rejected the PLO's inclusion because it was engaged in terrorism, it refused to recognize Israel, and its 1974 Phased Plan described Palestinian autonomy as a mere step toward continuing the military struggle against Israel. Prime Minister Shimon Peres would justify his government's rejection of the PLO by explaining that "the PLO leaders view the accords as a tactic in their doctrine of phases, not as a strategy in a doctrine of peace."[7]

King Hussein tried unsuccessfully to convince Arafat to accept UN Security Council Resolution 242 and to renounce terrorism. On February 22, 1986, Hussein publicly declared on Jordanian television that he had failed to convince Arafat to accept Resolution 242 and that he now felt entitled to negotiate with Israel without the PLO. Jordan, Hussein said, will be "unable to continue to coordinate politically with the PLO leadership until such time as their words become their bond, characterized by commitment, credibility, and constancy."[8] In March 1986 Hussein closed the PLO's office in Amman.

By the time Hussein gave up on Arafat, Peres and Shamir had switched roles. Peres, now foreign minister, met with Hussein in London to discuss future negotiations over the West Bank. In April 1987 Peres and Hussein put in writing their general understanding, which came to be known as the "London Agreement": Israel and Jordan would negotiate the future and final status of the West Bank, those negotiations would be based on Resolution 242, and their opening would be formally inaugurated by an international conference.

When Peres flew back to Israel, he did not inform Shamir of his understanding with Hussein. Rather, Peres asked the U.S. ambassador to Israel, Thomas Pickering, to present the London Agreement as an American initiative.[9] Furious about this manipulation, Shamir demanded to see the London Agreement, but Peres refused to show him the written document for fear that he would leak it to the media. (Shamir did not want an international conference for fear that it would be favorable to the Palestinians, and he did not trust that Peres had only agreed to a symbolic conference with no coercive powers.)

Shamir decided to meet Hussein directly to find out what kind of international conference the Hashemite monarch had in mind. The meeting took place in London on July 18, 1987. Asked by U.S. secretary of state George Shultz how the meeting went, King Hussein replied by succinctly describing his feelings toward Shamir: "I cannot be alone with this man."[10] Shamir, however, eventually accepted the idea of a symbolic international gathering prior to direct negotiations. Yet Hussein, who did not believe that Shamir would make any concessions, decided to disclaim the London Agreement.

This deadlocked situation exploded due to a road accident. On December 9, 1987, an Israeli truck driver accidently killed four Palestinians in the Gaza Strip. The rumor soon spread that the killing had been intentional. Violent protests erupted in the Gaza Strip and the West Bank. The first intifada had started.

Though it was technically sparked by the Gaza Strip incident, the first intifada had deeper causes. The Palestinian economy was partially based on remittances from expats in Europe and the Gulf states. In the 1980s the Iran-Iraq War had forced thousands of Palestinians to leave the Gulf states and return to the West Bank and Gaza without an income. In addition, Soviet Jews (who started immigrating to Israel in large numbers in 1987) took many of the menial jobs hitherto held by Palestinians. Palestinian incomes plummeted, while unemployment soared in the West Bank and in Gaza. In addition, Israel's deterrence was seriously affected by the "Vietnamization" of the Lebanon War and by Israel's many failures in its "security zone" in southern Lebanon. Israel had played the Muslim Brotherhood against the PLO according to the "divide and rule" principle, but after the Iranian revolution of 1979 and the PLO's expulsion from Lebanon in 1982, an increasing number of Palestinians saw the Islamist "resistance" to Israel as an alternative leadership to Arafat's coterie in Tunis.

At the beginning of the first intifada, in December 1987, Hamas was established. A self-described "Islamic Resistance Movement,"

Hamas emerged as the Palestinian branch of the Muslim Brotherhood. Hamas's covenant forbade any compromise with "the Zionists," and it demanded the "liberation" of all of Palestine. The openly antisemitic document (excerpted at the outset of this chapter) referenced *The Protocols of the Elders of Zion*, blamed the Jews for the French and Russian revolutions and the two world wars, and claimed that the Jews had established the UN Security Council in order to rule the world.

The first intifada was a popular uprising with widespread support. As early as January 1988, then defense minister Yitzhak Rabin declared that there could be no military solution to the intifada, but only a political one.[11] King Hussein, not wanting the intifada to spread to his kingdom, announced in July 1988 that Jordan was officially severing ties with the West Bank. Hussein openly declared that he was waiving his claims over the West Bank and that the PLO should take over: "We respect the wish of the PLO, the sole legitimate representative of the Palestinian people, to secede from Jordan as an independent state."[12] In August 1988 Hussein confirmed that Jordan would no longer play a negotiating role on behalf of the Palestinians.[13] Practically, King Hussein's decision meant that his government would no longer pay the salaries of civil servants in the West Bank, that the Jordanian parliament would be dissolved so as to be composed exclusively of East Bankers (as opposed to 50 percent West Bankers until the dissolution), and that West Bankers would eventually lose their Jordanian citizenship. The "Jordanian option," which had been the official policy of Israel's Labor Party, had officially become moot.

Hussein's dramatic decision enabled the PLO to fill a political void and to claim responsibility for the West Bank. On November 14, 1988, Yasser Arafat proclaimed from Algiers the independence of the "State of Palestine." The declaration did not specify the borders of this virtual state. Arafat tried to gain international legitimacy, but the Reagan administration set two conditions before accepting him as a legitimate partner: a renunciation of terrorism and a recognition of UN Security Council Resolution 242. On December 14, 1988, Arafat declared that he recognized "the right of all the parties concerned in the Middle East conflict to exist in peace and security, including the State of Palestine, Israel, and their neighbors." He also announced that he "renounced" terrorism.[14] Despite Israel's strong reservations, the Reagan administration decided to begin a dialogue with the PLO leadership. Claiming that the PLO now met U.S. demands, President Reagan announced that he had "authorized the State Department to enter into a substantive dialogue with PLO representatives."[15]

With the end of the "Jordanian option" and the Reagan administration's legitimization of the PLO, Israel's coalition government felt cornered. Defense Minister Yitzhak Rabin and Foreign Minister Moshe Arens thought that Israel should submit its own plan so as not to be coerced into negotiations with the PLO. Many in the Labor Party (a coalition member in the Likud-led government) started arguing that dialogue with the PLO had become inevitable. Prime Minister Shamir was short of ideas and proposals. In a last attempt to try to sideline the PLO, Arens and Rabin submitted a plan in January 1989 for holding elections in the West Bank and Gaza. According to the plan, locally elected Palestinian officials would then negotiate the final status of the West Bank and the Gaza Strip with Israel. Yet, precisely because the Arens-Rabin plan was truly intended to undermine the PLO leadership, the PLO pressured local Palestinian notables to reject the plan, which they did.[16] Moreover, Shamir had given the plan a cold shoulder because he feared that pro-PLO candidates might do well in such elections, and unofficial contacts between the Labor Party and the PLO had undermined it furthermore (many in the Labor Party thought that negotiations with the PLO had become inevitable and that Labor should quit the Shamir government). Eventually, the Labor Party quit the government in 1990 and left Shamir with a narrow coalition, expanded in June 1990 with the inclusion of the rightist Moledet party. With the Labor Party's departure from Shamir's government, disagreements sharpened between Israel and the United States, led now by the Bush administration. Shamir was willing to consider a vague autonomy model for the Palestinians, but he rejected the full sovereignty U.S. secretary of state James Baker envisioned.

The mounting tension between the Bush administration and the Shamir government was temporarily put on hold by Iraq's invasion of Kuwait in August 1990. Arafat sided with Iraqi dictator Saddam Hussein, thus burning the small amount of political capital he had gathered in Washington and losing the financial support of Saudi Arabia and the Gulf monarchies, who were threatened by Hussein. Exiled in Tunis, diplomatically isolated, and financially bankrupt, Arafat was in dire straits. With the massive immigration of Soviet Jews to Israel, even the Palestinians' demographic prospects seemed doomed.

The Israeli government, by contrast, had met the U.S. demand not to respond to Hussein's firing of Scud missiles during the Gulf War. Still, even while the U.S. government was thankful to Israel for its restraint, it was also eager to pressure Israel into concessions. Prior to the Gulf War, Baker had convinced Arab leaders to join the U.S.-led coalition against Saddam Hussein by committing to tackle the Israeli-Palestinian conflict after the war. Not only was Baker determined to honor his commitment, but the United States was now dominant and unchallenged: Iraq had been defeated, and the Soviet Union was in the midst of a geopolitical collapse. The U.S. government was thus able to pressure Israel as never before, but Israel itself was now more willing to be forthcoming, since Arafat had been blacklisted by the Bush administration.

This new context enabled the convening of the international Madrid Peace Conference in October 1991. The PLO was officially excluded from the "Jordanian-Palestinian delegation," but its influence over the delegation was an open secret. The ambiguity was explained thus by James Baker: "Israel privately understood that any Palestinian delegation would have the tacit acquiescence of the PLO, but a visible PLO role was unacceptable."[17]

Some in the United States, however, thought that the PLO could be sidelined. Such was the opinion of U.S. scholar and diplomat Martin Indyk, whose 1991 article in *Foreign Policy* was titled "Peace without the PLO."[18] In January 1993 King Hassan of Morocco made his case for dismantling the PLO and letting the local Palestinian leadership negotiate with Israel.[19] In any case, Shamir's agreement to take part in the Madrid Conference effectuated the collapse of his coalition and, with it, fresh elections. The Labor Party, led by Yitzhak Rabin, won the 1992 elections.

The Oslo Agreements and the Second Intifada

Originally, Rabin had no intention of dealing with Arafat. There were official negotiations between Israel and the Jordanian-Palestinian delegation in Washington, as had been initiated by the 1991 Madrid Conference, and indeed during his 1992 electoral campaign Rabin had committed to reach an agreement with the delegation within a year after his election, but by March 1993 he realized that commitment could not be honored. Official negotiations between Israel and the Jordanian-Palestinian delegation had reached a dead end.

Just as it was becoming clear that the Washington talks were leading nowhere, Shimon Peres revealed to Rabin that secret back-channel negotiations were taking place between Israeli academics and the PLO in Oslo, and they actually seemed to be delivering. At first dismayed that he had not been informed of these secret negotiations from day one, Rabin eventually decided to give the Oslo back channel a try.

Unofficial contacts with the PLO had been initiated in the late 1980s by Israeli academics such as Yossi Beilin, Yair Hirschfeld, and Ron Pundak, who thought that the Labor Party's leadership was wrong to reject negotiations with the PLO. After his election in 1992, Rabin appointed his longtime political rival Shimon Peres as foreign minister, and Yossi Beilin, a Peres protégé, became deputy foreign minister. Together with his Norwegian counterpart Jan Egeland, Beilin had opened a secret track of negotiations with the PLO in Oslo, keeping this from Rabin, because he feared that Rabin would forbid it. Now, in 1993, the PLO was showing more flexibility than the official Palestinian delegation in Washington. Arafat was eager to be salvaged politically at almost any price, and by his understanding, Oslo would grant him the basis upon which he could build up his power. Thus Peres maneuvered Rabin into opting for the Oslo/PLO option.

The secret Oslo channel eventually produced an agreement. On August 30, 1993, Israel and the PLO signed a Declaration of Principles (DOP) of mutual recognition that included the PLO's commitment to renounce terrorism and to amend its charter.

Arafat's decision to sign the DOP surprised many, though not Palestinian-born U.S. scholar Edward Said, who asserted:

> Arafat rushed to conclude this agreement because he was scared of two things: first the independence of the Occupied Territories under the new leadership made up of those who became polit-ically and publicly prominent during the Washington negotia-tions, like Haidar Abdel Shafi and Hanan Ashrawi. . . . Second, his feeling, along with that of the rest of the leadership, of isolation in Tunis after the disastrous mistakes they made during the Gulf crisis and at the end of the Cold War. As a result, he realized that he had no other alternative but to conclude a secret agreement with Rabin, no matter what kind of concession it would have to include.[20]

Arafat's position had become so precarious that Rabin likely calculated this was the perfect time to coerce him into a deal he might otherwise have rejected. Arafat himself knew his chances of political survival were slim. Joel Singer, an Israeli legal expert who drafted the first agreements between Israel and the PLO, explained that Israel had essentially told Arafat, "You either sign or stay in Tunis."[21] For his part, Edward Said described Arafat as "a great actor and a supreme political animal with only a provisional relationship to the truth"[22] and the Oslo Agreements as a honey trap for the desperate and blunder-prone leader:

> The genius of the DOP (Declaration of Principles) was that Israel caught an isolated, bankrupt, and desperate PLO leader in a dilemma whose resolution could have been easily predicted. Having reviled and ignored him for the twenty years during which he really represented his dispossessed people's national goals, Israel now offered him either an interim settlement that would personally give him limited municipal authority over Gaza and Jericho, with his own police force and the "right" to deliver services to Palestinian residents; or he would face his total marginalization as a result of his catastrophic misjudgments and failures, his alliance with Saddam Hussein being only the latest. He took the former, of course.[23]

As U.S. peace negotiator Dennis Ross put it, "Arafat went to Oslo after the first Gulf War not because he made a choice but because he had no choice.... Oslo was his salvation. As such, it represented less a transformation than a transaction."[24] Israeli historian and former foreign minister Shlomo Ben-Ami concurred: "Oslo was for Arafat more a political maneuver aimed at recovering the control of Palestinian politics and affairs than a peace initiative. He went to Oslo to save the PLO from declining into oblivion."[25]

On May 4, 1994, the Gaza-Jericho Agreement (which formalized PLO rule in those two territories) was signed in Cairo. The signature ceremony produced early warnings of Arafat's deviousness. When Yitzhak Rabin sat down to sign the agreement, he noticed that Arafat had not signed the agreed-upon maps and asked for an explanation. Arafat first demurred and then obliged after Egyptian president Mubarak reportedly shouted at him, "Sign, you dog!"[26] Six days after the signing, Arafat declared in a Johannesburg mosque that the agreement he had just signed with Israel was in fact a modern version of the Hudaybi-yyah Pact signed in the year 628 between the Prophet Muhammad and the Kuraish tribe of Mecca. The Hudaybiyyah Pact was a temporary treaty that Muhammad had signed when he was weak and breached once he got stronger.[27]

Arafat entered the Gaza Strip on July 1, 1994, smuggling in the trunk of his Mercedes notorious terrorists whom Israel had specifically banned from Gaza, such as Mamdouh Nofal (who had planned the 1974 attack on the Ma'alot high school, killing twenty-one Israeli teenagers) and Nihad Jayousi (one of the masterminds of the massacre of Israeli athletes at the 1972 Olympic games in Munich). An incensed Rabin called Arafat to inquire about the smuggling; Arafat denied that he had smuggled the terrorists in, but the Shin Bet (Israel's security agency) had evidence that he did.[28] Arafat had committed to end terrorism, but Hamas initiated major terror attacks within pre-1967 Israel as early as April 1994—killing Israeli civilians in the Israeli cities of Afula on April 6, 1994, in Tel Aviv on October 29, 1994, in Netanya on January 22, 1995, in Ramat Gan on July 24, 1995, and in Jerusalem on August 21, 1995. Hamas and Islamic Jihad were now using the Gaza Strip and Jericho (which Israel had handed to the Palestinian Authority, or PA) as secure bases from which to strike.

Despite the gruesome attacks—which Arafat did not confront Hamas to stop—negotiations between Israel and the PA continued. Neither Israel nor the United States were willing to put negotiations on hold, fearing that doing so might produce more terrorist attacks still.

On September 28, 1995, Israel and the PLO signed the Oslo II Agreements in Washington DC, in the presence of President Bill Clinton as well as representatives of Russia, Egypt, Jordan, Norway, and the European Union. Those agreements, which transferred control and responsibility for the West Bank's Palestinian cities and towns to the Palestinian government, took effect over what was defined as an "interim period," because they were meant to be replaced by a final peace agreement by 1999.

On November 4, 1995, Prime Minister Yitzhak Rabin was assassinated. Despite the shock of the assassination, Rabin's interim successor, Shimon Peres, respected the calendar of the Oslo Agreements. By December 1995, the IDF had withdrawn from the West Bank's main towns—Jenin, Qalqilya, Tulkarm, Nablus, Ramallah, and Bethlehem.

Hit again by major terrorist attacks in February and March 1996 in Jerusalem, Tel Aviv, and Ashkelon, Israelis became increasingly suspicious of a "peace process" that kept producing more victims. Benjamin Netanyahu narrowly won the May 1996 elections, having campaigned on the promise to demand Arafat's compliance to the signed agreement prior to any further negotiations and Israeli concessions. Yet in January 1997, Netanyahu approved the IDF's withdrawal from most of the city of Hebron (under U.S. pressure), and in September 1997 he released Hamas's leader Sheikh Yassin (as "compensation" demanded by King Hussein of Jordan following a botched Israeli attempt to assassinate a senior Hamas official in Jordan). After agreeing (under heavy U.S. pressure) to a further 13.1 percent withdrawal from the West Bank and to the transfer of 14.2 percent of "B areas" (partial Palestinian control) to "A areas" (full Palestinian control) at the October 1998 Wye Plantation summit, Netanyahu lost his majority as well as the snap election held in May 1999—an election won by Ehud Barak.

Israeli historian Avi Shlaim proclaimed that the election of Ehud Barak was "the sunrise after the three dark and terrible years during which Israel had been led by the unreconstructed proponents of the

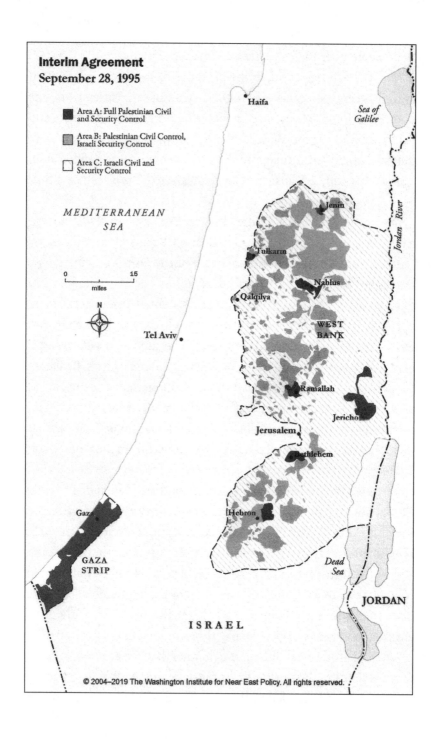

Interim Agreement
September 28, 1995

■ Area A: Full Palestinian Civil and Security Control

▦ Area B: Palestinian Civil Control, Israeli Security Control

□ Area C: Israeli Civil and Security Control

MEDITERRANEAN SEA

0   15
miles

N

Haifa

Sea of Galilee

Jordan River

Jenin

Tulkarm

Nablus

Qalqilya

WEST BANK

Tel Aviv

Ramallah

Jericho

Jerusalem

Bethlehem

Gaza

Hebron

GAZA STRIP

Dead Sea

JORDAN

I S R A E L

© 2004–2019 The Washington Institute for Near East Policy. All rights reserved.

iron wall."[29] In reality, Ehud Barak was himself an iron wall realist who had opposed the 1993 Oslo Agreements (while serving as IDF chief of staff at the time).[30] Barak harshly criticized the Interim Agreement Yitzhak Rabin had submitted to his cabinet in mid-August 1995, and he abstained in the cabinet vote (by that time, Barak had gone into politics, and Rabin had made him a member of his cabinet).[31] As for the alleged "sunrise" Avi Shlaim described, all it did was to shed light on Arafat's deviousness, as well as on the unbridgeable gaps between Israel and the Palestinians.

On the very day he signed the Declaration of Principles with Israel on September 13, 1993, Arafat had declared in a pre-recorded message broadcast by Jordanian television that the accord with Israel was meant to implement the PLO's 1974 Phased Plan.[32] As Arafat left his headquarters in the Jugurtha neighborhood in Tunis, he said the following to Palestinian journalist Abd Al-Bari Atwan: "I want to tell you something that I ask that you not mention or attribute to me until after my death. . . . I am going to Palestine through the Oslo gate, despite my reservations [about this path], in order to bring back to there [i.e., to Palestine] the PLO and the resistance. I promise you that the Jews will leave Palestine like rats abandoning a sinking ship. This will not come true in my lifetime, but it will in your lifetime."[33]

On August 21, 1995, Arafat repeated the comparison between the Oslo Agreements and the treacherous Hudaybiyyah Pact.[34] In March 1996 Arafat declared, "We of the PLO will now concentrate all our efforts on splitting Israel psychologically into two camps. . . . We will make life unbearable for the Jews by psychological warfare and population explosion."[35] In September 1996 Arafat launched a wave of violence in response to the new entrance to an archaeological tunnel in the Old City of Jerusalem that the Israeli government and the Wakf (Islamic

Map 14. The 1995 Interim Agreement. © 2004–2019 Washington Institute for Near East Policy. All rights reserved.

authority in charge of the Temple Mount) had successfully negotiated. Falsely claiming that Israel was plotting the takeover of the Al-Aqsa Mosque, he sent PA forces into battle with the following words: "Our Palestinian people will not stand idly by when their holy sites area being violated. . . . The believers . . . shall fight for Allah and shall kill and be killed."[36] Nabil Shaath, a senior PLO official, had declared in January 1996 (while Shimon Peres was still serving as interim prime minister) that if the Palestinians were unable to impose their demands in the negotiations with Israel, they would use violence again. "But this time" Shaath explained, "this will be done with 30,000 Palestinian soldiers at our disposal and while we control a territory of our own and enjoy freedom and liberty. . . . If we reach a dead end, we will resume the war and struggle exactly as we did forty years ago."[37]

Faisal Husseini, a senior PLO official who served as the Palestinian Authority's minister for Jerusalem affairs, declared in an interview with the Arabic newspaper *Al-Arabi* (published shortly after his death in May 2001) that the Oslo Agreements were a "Trojan horse" aimed at "ambushing the Israelis and cheating them" in order to eventually liberate all of Palestine "from the River to the Sea."[38]

Concerns about Arafat's intentions and strategy were also raised by the fact that he never repealed the Palestinian National Covenant, a document that denied Israel's right to exist in any borders and justified the use of terrorism. Article XXXI-9 of the 1995 Oslo II Agreements stated that "within two months of the date of the inauguration of the Council, the Palestinian National Council will convene and formally approve the necessary changes in regard to the Palestinian Covenant." On September 9, 1993, Yasser Arafat wrote to Yitzhak Rabin that "the PLO undertakes to submit to the Palestinian National Council for formal approval the necessary changes in regard to the Palestinian Covenant," but Arafat never honored this commitment. Since the covenant could only be amended by a two-thirds majority of the Palestinian National Council (PNC), Rabin announced on July 7, 1994, that he would allow all PNC members, including those Israel had banned because of their terrorist record, to enter Gaza for the vote. Yet Arafat pushed off the convening of the PNC indefinitely. After signing Oslo II, he claimed that the covenant did not need to be amended because the PNC had already renounced terrorism and recognized Israel's right to exist.[39]

After Rabin's assassination, his successor, Shimon Peres, pressured Arafat to amend the Palestinian National Covenant. Otherwise, Peres warned, he would likely lose the snap election called for May 29, 1996. On May 4 Arafat wrote to Peres that the covenant had been amended. This was untrue: the PNC had passed a decision stating that the covenant would be amended *in the future* and assigning a legal committee with the task of amending the covenant.[40] PLO spokesman Marwan Kanfani clarified after the vote that "this is not an amendment. This is a license to start a new charter."[41]

Yet no new charter was ever drafted, let alone approved. The "Note for the Record" (an appendix to the January 1997 Hebron Protocol signed by Netanyahu to complete Israel's withdrawal from the city of Hebron) included a clause committing the PLO to "complete the process of revising the Palestinian National Charter." On December 14, 1998, President Clinton attended a gathering in Gaza of hundreds of PNC members who raised their hands to "confirm" that the covenant had been amended—a "confirmation" that was meaningless, since the covenant had never been amended in the first place. Yet there was no record or evidence that two-thirds of PNC members were present (as required by the covenant itself), nor were the number of raised hands counted. Indeed, the Israeli dove Shlomo Ben-Ami (who would later server as Israel's foreign minister) himself admitted that the PLO "failed to devise a new National Covenant, as it was committed to do."[42]

Despite those worrying signs and declarations, Ehud Barak was resolute about reaching a final peace agreement with the PLO. Regardless of Arafat's behavior, he believed it was ultimately in Israel's interest to separate politically from the Palestinians so as to avoid becoming a binational country. To that end, President Clinton convened an Israeli-Palestinian peace conference at Camp David in July 2000. Yet the prospects for this conference were undermined by a dramatic decision made by Barak: one month before the conference, Barak ordered the IDF to unilaterally withdraw from southern Lebanon. PLO leader Marwan Barghouti said of the Israeli withdrawal, "The Israelis left Lebanon under Hezbollah pressure. So why shouldn't this be repeated here?"[43] Arafat declared before his departure to Camp David, "We can see to it that the Hezbollah precedent is replicated in the territories."[44] As for U.S. peace negotiator Dennis Ross, he was to write that "there can be no denying that the success of the Hezbollah model—violence works, negotiations don't—probably had at least some effect on Arafat. . . . It may have convinced him that pressuring the Israelis through violence would produce more for him."[45] Shlomo Ben-Ami, who failed to reach a peace agreement during his stint as foreign minister in 2000, would later write in his memoirs, "It was Israel's withdrawal from Lebanon in June 2000 that served as a major incentive for the Palestinian Intifada. It certainly left a profound mark on Arafat's mind. He felt humiliated and embarrassed that he should negotiate border modifications with Israel when 500 Hezbollah guerillas had forced Israel to withdraw to the international border in Lebanon. 'These are our disciples, we taught them and we financed them.' This was how Arafat referred to Hezbollah in a conversation with me in Nablus on 25 June 2000, where he harshly criticized me for our precipitate pull-out from Lebanon."[46]

The Camp David summit of July 2000 ended up being both the denouement and the coup de grâce of the Oslo Agreements. Ehud Barak would call it "the moment of truth of the Oslo process."[47] Even before Camp David, as Israelis and Palestinians were conducting secret preparatory negotiations in Stockholm, Arafat was preparing for war.[48]

During the summit, Arafat told President Clinton that Yitzhak Rabin had promised him 90 percent of the West Bank; according to Dennis Ross, "Rabin had never done that, and, in fact, Rabin had envisioned only going between 70 and 80%."[49] On day five of the summit, U.S. secretary of state Madeleine Albright tried to reassure Arafat, "You will get a state," to which Arafat replied, "I already have one. And if Barak doesn't want to recognize it now, I don't care if it is recognized in another twenty years. Our situation is like in South Africa: the entire world is with me."[50]

After a week of discussions, Arafat kept saying no to all the proposals President Clinton submitted to him. When the thorny issue of Jerusalem was raised, Arafat said that "Solomon's Temple was not in Jerusalem, but Nablus."[51] On day twelve, Dennis Ross told CIA director George Tenet that Arafat had so far said no to everything and that "we never hear anything from him except old mythologies and now a new one. Did you know the Temple did not exist in Jerusalem but in Nablus?"[52] On day fourteen, Ross noted that Arafat "had not presented a single idea or single serious comment in two weeks," and Clinton yelled at Arafat that he had "been here fourteen days and said no to everything."[53]

The question of Jerusalem was the most difficult issue to resolve. As it became clear that a Camp David compromise on Jerusalem was not reachable, reports emerged of increased anti-Israel incitement in the PA-controlled territories as well as calls by the Tanzim (the militia Arafat founded in 1995) to target IDF soldiers and Israeli settlers.[54] "You are leading your people and the entire region to a catastrophe. . . . I am very disappointed!" Clinton yelled at Arafat.[55] Ehud Barak told his team, "What we've seen is Palestinian bad faith, and the last days have shed the most worrying light on the past seven years. We are in fact fighting over our holy of holies, over the very heart of Jewish culture. No negotiation can change that."[56]

Toward the end of the summit, Ehud Barak agreed to relinquish 92 percent of the West Bank (91 percent of the West Bank plus a 1 percent swap of territory) as well as the Arab neighborhoods of Jerusalem.

For his part, Arafat refused to even share sovereignty with Israel over the Temple Mount. President Clinton suggested a "horizontal" sharing of sovereignty (Palestinian sovereignty on the upper level, Israeli sovereignty in the Temple Mount's underground), but Arafat rejected this idea as well.[57] Barak's opening offer at Camp David had been 66 percent of the West Bank for a Palestinian state; he ended up accepting 92 percent after two weeks of negotiations.[58] On Jerusalem as well, Arafat thought the Israeli lemon could be further squeezed. Arafat was not the only one to believe that Israel was bluffing about its legendary "red lines" (what Israeli negotiators would describe as the absolute limit of Israel's concessions). Shlomo Ben-Ami candidly admitted that at Camp David, "Clinton had no firm Israeli red lines to work upon, for these kept changing."[59] As Egyptian diplomat Ahmed Aboul Gheit would remark sarcastically to an Israeli colleague at the UN, "Why should we believe you when everybody remembers that you started your voyage into the Palestinian question with Golda Meir denying that a Palestinian people existed at all, and at Camp David you agreed to give away the bulk of the West Bank for an independent Palestinian state and divide Jerusalem? These certainly cannot be the outer limits of your concessions."[60]

It has become conventional wisdom to claim that Rabin's assassination doomed the Oslo process. Yet Arafat himself admitted after the failed Camp David summit of July 2000 that Rabin's successor, Ehud Barak, had gone "beyond my partner Rabin." Upon learning of Barak's concessions at Camp David, Rabin's widow Leah Rabin said that her late husband "would never have accepted this."[61] Shlomo Ben-Ami wrote that Rabin "would have by no means agreed . . . to the kind of compromises that the Barak government was ready to make on Jerusalem and on the other core issues of the conflict."[62] Moreover,

Map Reflecting Actual Proposal at Camp David

- ▓ Proposed Palestinian State
- ☐ Israeli Settlement Blocs Annexed to Israel
- ▨ Israeli Security Border

MEDITERRANEAN SEA

Jenin

Tulkarm   WEST BANK

Nablus

Qalqilya

Tel Aviv

While no map was presented during the final rounds at Camp David, this map illustrates the parameters of what President Clinton proposed and Arafat rejected: Palestinian control over 91% of the West Bank in contiguous territory and an Israeli security presence along 15% of the border with Jordan. This map actually understates the final Camp David proposal because it does not depict the additional territorial swap of 1% that was offered from Israeli territory.

Ramallah

Jericho

Maale Adumim

Jerusalem

ISRAEL

Bethlehem

Jordan River

Hebron

Dead Sea

0   10
miles

© 2004–2019 The Washington Institute for Near East Policy. All rights reserved.

Map 15. The 2000 Camp David proposal. © 2004–2019 Washington Institute for Near East Policy. All rights reserved.

Ben-Ami argued, "by the time Rabin was murdered the peace process was, for all practical purposes, in a state of political coma."[63]

Following the failed Camp David summit, tension was in the air. Yet negotiations continued. To protest Ehud Barak's readiness to (even partially) abandon Israel's sovereignty over the Temple Mount, then-opposition leader Ariel Sharon decided to make a public visit to the compound on September 28, 2000. Although Sharon's visit had been coordinated with the Palestinian Authority, and although Sharon did not enter the mosques, the Friday prayers on September 29 were followed by violence and calls to "protect Al-Aqsa." The second intifada had started. Just like in 1996, Arafat had ignited violence by falsely claiming that Israel was endangering the Al-Aqsa Mosque.

Arafat sought to revive the images of the first intifada and to obtain more concessions from Israel via international pressures. Imad Falouji, the Palestinian minister of post and telecommunications, admitted that "the Palestinian Authority began preparing the present intifada and bracing for it since the return from Camp David at the request of President Yasser Arafat, who envisaged the intifada as a complementary measure to the Palestinian steadfastness in the negotiations, and not as a protest over Sharon's visit to al-Haram al-Sharif."[64] Mamdouh Nofal (whom Arafat had hidden in the trunk of his car while entering Gaza in July 1994) concurred. "The intifada," he said, "was started by a deliberate decision by the highest echelons of the Authority."[65] As for Ehud Barak, he explained that "Sharon's visit, which was coordinated with [Palestinian Authority West Bank security chief] Jibril Rajoub, was directed against me, not the Palestinians, to show that the Likud cared more about Jerusalem than I did. We know, from hard intelligence, that Arafat [after Camp David] intended to unleash a violent confrontation, terrorism. [Sharon's visit and the riots that followed] fell into his hands like an excellent excuse, a pretext."[66] Indeed, three days before Sharon's visit to the Temple Mount, Ehud Barak and his wife had hosted Arafat for dinner in their private home. The atmosphere was reportedly courteous and warm, and Sharon's upcoming visit was known to all.

If Sharon's visit to the Temple Mount served as an excuse for the ensuing unrest, the second intifada became widespread and violent with the broadcast by French TV channel France 2 of images allegedly showing Israeli soldiers killing a Palestinian child in Gaza on September 30, 2000. The images were dramatic: a father and his child (Mohammed Al Dura) hiding behind a concrete cylinder, desperately trying to protect themselves from shootings between Israeli soldiers and Palestinian gunmen. France 2's veteran Middle East correspondent, Charles Enderlin—who was not present at the event filmed by his Palestinian cameraman, Talal Abu Rahma—asserted in his commentary that Mohammed Al Dura had died as a result of the shooting and that both he and his father had been "the target of shooting coming from the Israeli position" (in French: "la cible de tirs venus de la position israélienne"). Abu Rahma's images and Enderlin's commentary conveyed the message that the IDF had killed the child, possibly intentionally. Eventually, the IDF contested that the child had been killed by Israeli bullets, and in 2013 the Israeli government published a report accusing France 2 of making unproven accusations and of misleading its viewers.[67] Yet the France 2 report had an immense and immediate impact on the second intifada. Shortly after its airing, two Israeli reservists who had inadvertently driven into Ramallah were arrested by the Palestinian police and then lynched by a mob. The torturers jubilantly held up their bloody hands to a crowd of onlookers. Shortly afterward, Palestinians vandalized and destroyed Joseph's tomb in Nablus (Shechem). Negotiations between Israel and the Palestinians continued nevertheless. There were more than fifty meetings between Israeli and Palestinian negotiators after the collapse of the Camp David summit.

On December 22, 2000, the Israeli and Palestinian negotiating teams met at Bolling Air Force Base near Washington DC. Shlomo Ben-Ami (now acting as foreign minister) agreed to grant exclusive Palestinian sovereignty over the Temple Mount, provided that the future Palestinian state recognized the historical and religious importance of the site to the Jewish people and refrained from excavating in the Temple's underground so as not to desecrate Temple remains. The Palestinian team rejected the formula out of hand. "If you reject even that," Ben-Ami said, "then I must say with a broken heart that there can be no deal." Palestinian negotiator Yasser Abed-Rabbo dismissively replied that he had no interest in Israel's self-perceived rights.[68]

The next day, December 23, President Clinton read aloud to both delegations an American proposal for ending the conflict. The Clinton Parameters, as this proposal became known, stipulated that a Palestinian state was to be established on 94 or 96 percent of the West Bank (and all of the Gaza Strip), with a 1 or 3 percent land swap from within Israel proper to "compensate" the Palestinian state (i.e., in the medium range, a Palestinian state would have been established on 97 percent of the West Bank). There would also be a "safe passage," without Israeli interference, between the West Bank and the Gaza Strip. Jerusalem would be divided between the two states, with Israeli sovereignty over the Western Wall and a corridor in the Armenian Quarter, and Palestinian sovereignty over the Muslim and Christian Quarters. The Palestinians would have sovereignty over the Temple Mount, with a symbolic Israeli link to the Holy of Holies in the depths of the Mount. The right of return of Palestinian refugees would only be applied to the Palestinian state, but Israel would recognize the suffering of the 1948 refugees, and a multibillion-dollar fund would be established to finance the compensation and resettlement of Palestinian refugees. The Palestinian state would be demilitarized, and Israel would eventually abandon its sovereignty over the Jordan Valley. This agreement,

Map 16. The 2000 Clinton Parameters. © 2004–2019 Washington Institute for Near East Policy. All rights reserved.

Map Reflecting Clinton Ideas

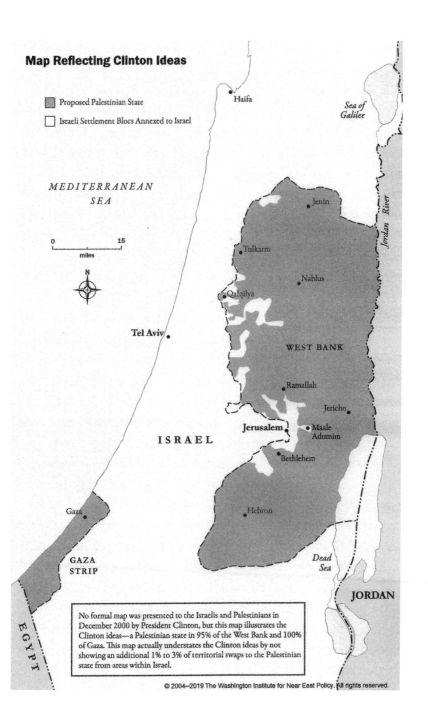

Proposed Palestinian State

Israeli Settlement Blocs Annexed to Israel

Haifa

Sea of Galilee

MEDITERRANEAN SEA

0   15
miles

N

Jenin

Tulkarm

Nablus

Qalqilya

Tel Aviv

WEST BANK

Ramallah

Jericho

Jerusalem   Maale Adumim

ISRAEL

Bethlehem

Jordan River

Gaza

Hebron

GAZA STRIP

Dead Sea

JORDAN

EGYPT

No formal map was presented to the Israelis and Palestinians in December 2000 by President Clinton, but this map illustrates the Clinton ideas—a Palestinian state in 95% of the West Bank and 100% of Gaza. This map actually understates the Clinton ideas by not showing an additional 1% to 3% of territorial swaps to the Palestinian state from areas within Israel.

© 2004–2019 The Washington Institute for Near East Policy. All rights reserved.

based on all these nonnegotiable parameters, would put an end to the conflict and to all claims.

Both Israelis and Palestinians were given four days to give an answer, which had to be either a "yes" or a "no." On December 27 the Israeli government voted in favor of answering yes. The positive answer was transmitted to the U.S. government. As Dennis Ross wrote, "Barak's government had now formally accepted ideas that would effectively divide East Jerusalem, end the IDF's presence in the Jordan Valley, and produce a Palestinian state in roughly 97 percent of the West Bank and 100 percent of Gaza."[69] Though the deadline for giving an answer was December 29, Arafat asked for a delay, and he obtained one. On January 1 Barak, sensing that Arafat would reject the Clinton Parameters, declared to his close advisors that Israel had "to get ready for a unilateral separation [from the Palestinians]."[70] On January 2, eighteen days before the end of Clinton's presidency, Arafat met with Clinton in Washington. "He effectively rejected the President's ideas," Dennis Ross recounted. "His reservations were deal-killers, involving his actual rejection of the Western Wall part of the formula, . . . his rejection of the most basic elements of the Israeli security needs, and his dismissal of our refugee formula."[71]

"How many times did Arafat have to tell us no before we heard no?" Ross would later say. "How many times could excuses be made for him? Those who argue that we just ran out of time ignore the many opportunities Arafat had refused. They ignore that within the Clinton ideas practically on the table at the end of September, Arafat either let the intifada begin or, as some argue, actually gave orders for it."[72]

Arafat's strategy paid off in the short term. Though he had rejected Barak's peace proposal at Camp David without making a counteroffer, the images of the new intifada (some of them staged) conveyed the message that at the end of the day, Palestinian demands had to be met for the violence to abate. French president Jacques Chirac epitomized the success of Arafat's strategy. "Israel may have made an effort at

Camp David," Chirac told Barak, but "you will not convince anyone that the Palestinians are the aggressors."[73]

Final negotiations took place in January 2001 during Israel's election campaign (Barak had called a snap election), despite ongoing Palestinian terrorist attacks and Palestinian negotiator Rabbo's declaration that "Barak is a war criminal who must be put on trial."[74] On January 11, both sides' negotiating teams met at the Erez crossing between Israel and Gaza. The Palestinians clarified that they would not agree to Israeli sovereignty over the Western Wall, but only on part of it. The Palestinians would have full and exclusive sovereignty on the Temple Mount. Any Israeli annexation in the West Bank had to be compensated by a Palestinian annexation of the same size in Israel. The Palestinian "right" of return had to be specifically mentioned and recognized, and the "end of the conflict" would only be considered after Israel freed all Palestinian prisoners.[75]

The Israeli and Palestinian teams met for a last time in Taba (near Eilat) on January 21, 2001. Bill Clinton was no longer president of the United States (George W. Bush had been sworn in the day before), and Ehud Barak had another two weeks to go. All polls predicted that Barak would lose his job after the snap election called for February 6. What, then, was the purpose of those negotiations? Dennis Ross answered this question candidly: "The real purpose was not to reach an agreement, but on the Israeli side to try to constrain what Sharon could do and on the Palestinian side to try to get the Bush administration to buy into the Clinton ideas."[76] To Israeli negotiator Gilead Sher, the purpose was "to lock the incoming Republican administration into a framework based on the Clinton parameters."[77] Justice minister Yossi Beilin, one of the main architects of the Oslo Agreements, agreed to an ambiguously worded acceptance of the Palestinian "right of return" which would have brought some two hundred thousand Palestinian refugees within Israel proper.[78]

Once again, Israel's foreign minister Shlomo Ben-Ami agreed to abandon Israel's sovereignty on the Temple Mount, provided that the Palestinians recognized the site's holiness to the Jews and ceased their excavations there. The Palestinians rejected the request. "At the deepest level," Ben-Ami concluded, "they are not prepared to recognize that we have any right to this land."[79]

In effect, at Taba, the Palestinians tried to treat the Clinton Parameters as negotiable—which they were not. "The boss doesn't want an agreement," admitted a Palestinian negotiator on January 24.[80] Four days later, Arafat alleged at the Davos Conference, "Israel conducts a fascist war against our people. Israel conducts a barbaric and cruel war against the Palestinians, especially against Palestinian children. . . . Israel occupies, destroys, and bombards the Palestinians with uranium bombs."[81]

In private, senior U.S. officials judged Arafat severely. President Clinton called Arafat "a liar who screwed up the whole thing and deceived us." Dennis Ross warned the new secretary of state, Colin Powell, "Don't believe a word from Arafat. He's a con man."[82]

Israeli dove and tireless peace negotiator Shlomo Ben-Ami admitted, *post factum*, that Oslo had been doomed from day one precisely because Arafat had agreed to the Oslo terms solely to save his political life: "Arafat's 'cheap price' for a settlement turned out to be, however, a tactical plot aimed at sidelining the local leadership and gaining a foothold in the occupied territories from which he could move to the next stage in his wider strategy. . . . The eventual collapse of the Oslo process into an all-out Israeli-Palestinian war, for which successive Israeli governments need of course to assume their share of the blame, was therefore not exactly an unexpected accident; rather it was a failure written into the genetic code of Oslo."[83]

At Camp David, some members of the Palestinian delegations had admitted in private their bewilderment at what they called "Arafat's personal obsession" with Jerusalem.[84] Yet this obsession was not Arafat's alone. Rather, he inherited the stratagem of making Jerusalem a focal point of the nascent Palestinian nationalism from his role model Hadj Amin al-Husseini, the first to employ the Temple Mount as a symbol to mobilize the Muslim world in his struggle against Zionism. Al-Husseini's claim that Jews were threatening the Al-Aqsa Mosque had ignited the 1929 pogrom in which Arab mobs murdered dozens of Jews throughout British Palestine. In 1931 al-Husseini convened a Pan-Islamic conference in Jerusalem at which he distributed doctored pictures of Jews with machine guns directed at the Dome of the Rock.

Jerusalem, however, is never mentioned in the Qur'an, and Muslims direct their prayers toward Mecca. Muhammad eliminated pagan sites of worship and determined that the Kaaba in Mecca was the only whole Muslim site. Islamic scholar Taqi al-Din Ibn Taymiyya wrote in the fourteenth century that sacred Muslim sites are only to be found in the Arabian Peninsula.[85] In the past there was no consensus among Muslim scholars regarding the exact place where Muhammad tied his horse when he came to Jerusalem. Only at the end of the nineteenth century did some Muslim clerics begin claiming that Muhammad had tied his horse to the Western Wall. This happened at precisely the same time Jews tried to purchase ownership rights over the Western Wall and asked Ottoman authorities to repair the floor for them to pray there.[86] In February 2001 the Jerusalem mufti issued a fatwa declaring that the Western Wall is in fact part of the Al-Aqsa Mosque.[87]

Denying the existence of the Jerusalem Temples, while at the same time accusing the Jews of plotting to *rebuild* the Temple, became a widespread Palestinian myth. Yet this myth is not consistent with Muslim tradition. The original Arabic name of Jerusalem is Bayt al-Maqdis, a transliteration of the Hebrew *Beit ha-Mikdash* (Temple). The Muslim Brotherhood battalions that fought in Jerusalem in 1948 were named Al-Jihad al-Maqdis (literally "the Jihad of Jerusalem/the Temple"). The Islamic State's branch in Sinai (which operated from 2011 to 2014) was called Ansar Bayt al-Maqdis (the Defenders of Jerusalem/of the Temple). In the sixteenth century Ottoman sultan Suleiman the Magnificent ordered his architect to build a praying plaza for Jews in front of the Western (Wailing) Wall.[88] A tourist guidebook published in 1924 by the Supreme Muslim Council says that the Temple Mount is where King Solomon's Temple once stood.[89] Araf al-Araf, a Palestinian historian who was close to Hadj Amin al-Husseini, wrote in his 1951 book *Tariah Al-Quds* that the Temple Mount "was bought by David to build the Temple, but it is Solomon who built it in 1007 BCE."[90] In his 1961 book *A Detailed History of Jerusalem*, al-Araf writes that "the Western Wall is the outside wall of the Temple erected by Herod."[91]

Arafat, however, had no interest in facts, and he would not get past his mythology. Neither was he devoid of contradictions. He cherished his image of a secular national movement leader but, at the same time, frequently evoked the religious themes he had learned in his early years as a member of the Muslim Brotherhood in Cairo.

Arafat dismissed the concessions Israel made at Taba in January 2001. The terror war he had launched in September 2000 continued with terrorist attacks by suicide bombers and snipers against Israeli civilians. Horrified, Israelis elected Ariel Sharon as their new prime minister in the February 2001 snap election.

Israel, of course, was not faultless during the Oslo process. It continued expansion of settlements during negotiations. Although settlement construction did not technically constitute a breach of the Oslo Agreements, the Palestinians perceived the settlements as attempts to grant Israel territorial gains.

Nor was America faultless. Successive U.S. administrations made the mistake of letting both sides get away with their respective violations of the Oslo Agreements for fear of ending "the peace process." As Dennis Ross admitted, "By never holding either side accountable, by never being prepared to disrupt the process and put it on hold, we contributed to an environment in which commitments were rarely taken seriously by either side, knowing there would never be any consequences."[92]

Yet Ross only diagnosed part of the problem. Fundamentally, it was easier to sign a vague "declaration of principles" in 1993 than to reach a compromise on the core issues in 2000. And Israel had wrongly assumed that the conflict was about 1967, while for the Palestinians the real issue was 1948. As Shlomo Ben-Ami put it, "Constructive ambiguity facilitated an agreement in Oslo at the price of creating potentially irreconcilable misconceptions with regard to the final settlement. Moreover, the Israeli negotiators came to solve the problems created by the 1967 war and were surprised to discover that the intractable issues of 1948, first and foremost that of the refugees' right of return, were now high on the Palestinian agenda."[93]

Disengagement and Stalemate

Ariel Sharon easily won the February 2001 snap election called by Ehud Barak at the height of the second intifada. The tide started turning against Arafat. In the United States, the new Bush administration (sworn in January 20, 2001) was far less forgiving of Arafat's deviousness. Former U.S. secretary of state Condoleezza Rice wrote that President Bush "was disgusted with Yasser Arafat, whom he saw, accurately, as a terrorist and a crook."[94] The 9/11 terrorist attacks were an embarrassment to Arafat, the man who had introduced airplane hijacking in the repertoire of terrorism. In January 2002 the IDF caught Arafat red-handed trying to smuggle into Gaza a vessel (the *Karine A*) loaded with fifty tons of Iranian ammunitions and explosives, including sixty-two Katyusha rockets capable of hitting almost any Israeli city from Gaza. Though the evidence was irrefutable, Arafat denied that he had purchased the weapons from Iran. He even claimed that the Mossad had arranged the order and shipping to embarrass the PA. At this point, President Bush wrote Arafat off.

Meanwhile, Palestinian terrorist attacks kept killing Israeli civilians. In March 2002 alone, 126 Israelis were murdered. On March 27 a Palestinian suicide bomber killed 29 and injured 140 celebrants at a Passover seder in the Park Hotel in Netanya. Two days later, Israel launched Operation Defensive Shield to retake control of the PA territories the terrorists were using as safe havens. Yet Arafat was not targeted; Ariel Sharon had promised President Bush that Israel would not kill the Palestinian leader.[95]

In mid-2002 the Israeli government started building a wall, mostly along the "green line" (the 1949 armistice line separating between Israel and the West Bank), as a physical obstacle to suicide bombers. There was something symbolic in the fact that Israel started building a physical wall eight decades after Jabotinsky had advocated an allegorical one in his 1923 article "The Iron Wall."

The delineation of the security fence Israel approved in 2003 was supposed to incorporate 17 percent of the West Bank. In April 2006, following Israel High Court of Justice rulings that the government change the delineation of the fence so as to facilitate the Palestinians' access to their fields, the de facto annexation of the West Bank was reduced from 17 to 8 percent. As of today, the fence incorporates under 5 percent of the West Bank.[96]

Operation Defensive Shield, together with the construction of the security fence, progressively reduced the intensity of terror attacks perpetuated by Hamas and the PLO. Arafat, who had mistakenly assumed that Israelis lacked stamina for a protracted guerilla war, moved Israeli voters to the right. Horrified by Arafat's rejection of the Camp David and Taba peace proposals, and even more so by his decision to go to war, most Israelis chose to fight back. They voted twice (in 2001 and 2003) for Ariel Sharon, a septuagenarian whose career (until then) had never recovered from the botched Lebanon War. The fact that Arafat rescued Sharon from his political demise ranks high on the list of Israeli history's ironies.

Indeed, Arafat dealt the Israeli left a fatal blow from which as of this writing it has yet to recover. When Shlomo Ben-Ami told Palestinian negotiator Saeb Erekat on the last day of the July 2000 Camp David summit that "this is the defeat of the peace camp in Israel for many years to come," he likely did not imagine how long those "many years" would last.[97]

In January 2003 Ariel Sharon was reelected with a comfortable majority. The wide public support he enjoyed was overshadowed by police investigations liable to lead to his indictment and, therefore, resignation. In addition, the October 2003 publication of the "Geneva Initiative," a virtual peace agreement written by Israeli and Palestinian politicians such as Yossi Beilin and Yasser Abed Rabbo (two former negotiators who were no longer in office), produced an international momentum meant to create the impression that an agreement was possible and that it depended on Israel's goodwill. The Geneva Initiative proposed an Israeli withdrawal to the 1949 armistice lines and land swaps between the State of Israel and the State of Palestine to compensate the latter for Israel's annexation of settlements adjacent to the green line, a solution to the refugee issue based on the 2000 Clinton Parameters, and a partition of Jerusalem between Israel and Palestine.

Ariel Sharon felt he was being cornered. Thirty years exactly after his brilliant crossing of the Suez Canal, Sharon decided once again to surprise his enemies from the rear. In December 2003, at the Herzliya Conference, he announced his decision to unilaterally "separate/disengage" from the Palestinians. A few month later, Sharon admitted that "so many plans were around . . . from the Saudis, from Geneva, from the Arab League, and I saw we could not resist those pressures without a plan of our own."[98]

Behind Sharon's unilateralism was his conviction that an agreement with the Palestinians was impossible and the status quo untenable. In his view, the only way out of this catch-22 predicament was to unilaterally withdraw from the Gaza Strip and from most of the West Bank—not in order to achieve an impossible peace, but to preserve Israel's Jewish majority.[99] In truth, Ehud Barak himself had thought along the same lines after the failure of Camp David, telling his negotiating team that "we need to start the preparations for our unilateral separation plan."[100] In this plan, eventually endorsed by Sharon himself, Israel would unilaterally delineate its borders; it would build the "iron wall" around the Jewish state and leave most of the Palestinians outside of it. Those borders would not be internationally recognized, but they would be tacitly endorsed, at least by the United States. Sharon even insisted on obtaining a written commitment from President Bush to that effect. On April 14, 2004, Bush wrote to Sharon, "In light of new realities on the ground, including already existing major Israeli population centers, it is unrealistic to expect that the outcome of final status negotiations will be a full and complete return to the armistice lines of 1949."[101]

In the summer of 2005, Sharon went ahead: Israel dismantled sixteen settlements in the Gaza Strip and four in northern Samaria. About 8,500 Jews were removed from the Gaza Strip and 680 from northern Samaria.

Ariel Sharon addressed the UN General Assembly shortly after the completion of Israel's unilateral withdrawal from the Gaza Strip and northern Samaria in September 2005. He said that he saw the achievement of peace with the Palestinians as his historic mission in the coming years. Three months later, Sharon suffered a minor stroke. Undeterred, Sharon maintained his work schedule. In January 2006 he suffered a major stroke that would put him in a coma for eight years until his death in 2014.

His successor, Ehud Olmert, won the March 2006 elections on a platform that explicitly called for further unilateral withdrawals from the West Bank (in Olmert's campaign, disengagement from most of the West Bank was labeled "realignment"). Yet Olmert's three-year

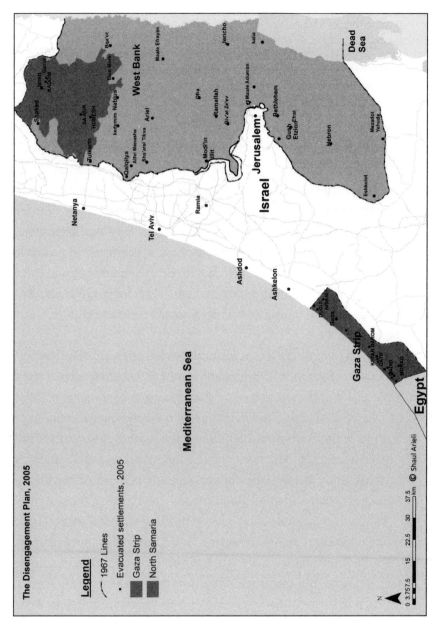

Map 17. The 2005 disengagement plan. Map courtesy Shaul Arieli.

tenure began and ended with wars that were at least partially caused by Israel's unilateral withdrawals. Israel's unilateral withdrawal from southern Lebanon in 2000 had left a void filled by Hezbollah, which provoked the Second Lebanon War in the summer of 2006 after trespassing Israel's border, killing three Israeli soldiers, and abducting two more.

When Ehud Olmert was elected Israel's prime minister in March 2006, he had good reasons to be skeptical about negotiations with the Palestinians. On January 24, 2006, literally the day before the Palestinian elections, Olmert (then serving as interim prime minister after Sharon's stroke) had addressed the annual Herzliya Conference, declaring, "In the elections tomorrow . . . [the Palestinians] will have to decide: whether to take their fate in their hands, or to again leave the keys in the hands of the extremists."[102] His message to the Palestinians was clear, and so was their answer: Hamas won the next day's elections.

Olmert was comforted in his unilateralist approach. Yet Hezbollah's assumption of full control of southern Lebanon after Israel's unilateral withdrawal there and the ensuing Second Lebanon War had discredited unilateralism in the eyes of many Israelis. In 2007 the Bush administration persuaded Olmert to abandon unilateralism and engage in negotiations with the Palestinian Authority. Negotiations between Israel and the Palestinians were formally renewed with the November 2007 Annapolis Conference.

In May 2008 Olmert had a private meeting with U.S. secretary of state Condoleezza Rice in Jerusalem. "Israel needs to get an agreement with the Palestinians before you leave office," he told her.[103] Olmert said he wanted to negotiate directly with PA chairman Mahmoud Abbas, and he spelled out his endgame: 94 percent of the West Bank with land swaps, two capitals in Jerusalem with a joint city council, about five thousand Palestinian refugees returned to Israel, and an international custodianship for Jerusalem's holy sites. Abbas rejected

Olmert's framework because the "right of return" was not included. "I can't tell four million Palestinians that only five thousand of them can go home," he told Condoleezza Rice.[104]

The "Annapolis process" culminated in the Olmert proposal of September 2008. Olmert offered Abbas a Palestinian state over nearly all of the West Bank and the Gaza Strip. Israel would annex 6.3 percent of the West Bank and would compensate the Palestinian state with territories equivalent in size within pre-1967 Israel.[105] Israel would also evacuate all its settlements in the West Bank with the exception of the heavily populated Etzion Bloc, Ma'ale Adumim, and Ariel. A tunnel would connect the West Bank to Gaza. Jerusalem would be divided between the two states, with Israel retaining the Jewish neighborhoods of Jerusalem and an international trusteeship overseeing the Temple Mount. Palestinian refugees and their descendants would be admitted to the Palestinian state, and five thousand to Israel, based on family reunifications. An international fund would compensate both Palestinian refugees and Jewish refugees from Arab lands. Olmert did not insist on an Israeli presence in the Jordan Valley; he was willing to accept international troops there.[106]

After receiving Olmert's proposal in September 2008, Abbas said he would think about it and convey his answer. He never did. Olmert was admittedly a lame duck at this point. He had announced in July 2008 that he would not vie for the party leadership due to corruption charges, and he stepped down shortly after submitting his peace proposal to Abbas. Yet Abbas could have pocketed the offer and negotiated on its basis with Olmert's successor.

Condoleezza Rice wrote that "to have an Israeli prime minister on record offering those remarkable elements and a Palestinian president accepting them would have pushed the peace process to a new level. Abbas refused."[107] Abbas explicitly told Rice that he could agree to Israel's acceptance of "only" 25,000 Palestinian refugees over a period of five years; he had proposed to Rice that Israel take in 100,000 Pal-

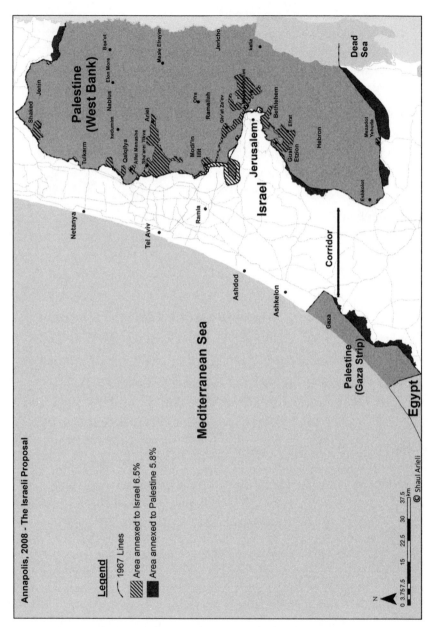

Map 18. The 2008 Olmert proposal. Map courtesy Shaul Arieli.

estinian refugees over a period of ten years.[108] According to Olmert, Abbas had said to him, "I need something symbolic on the refugees. I don't want to change the nature of the State of Israel."[109] Olmert also wrote that President Bush was willing to offer U.S. citizenship to 100,000 Palestinian refugees.[110] "In the end," Condoleezza Rice concluded, "the Palestinians walked away from the negotiations."[111]

Benjamin Netanyahu succeeded Ehud Olmert in March 2009. Under pressure from the Obama administration, Netanyahu publicly agreed to a Palestinian state in his June 2009 "Bar-Ilan Speech," and his government approved, in November 2009, a ten-month freeze on settlement construction. Back-channel negotiations took place in London between Yitzhak Molcho and Hussein Agha, the respective confidants of Netanyahu and Abbas. Dennis Ross served as an intermediary and facilitator on behalf of the United States. By early 2013, Netanyahu had reportedly agreed to negotiate on the basis of "the 1967 lines," and he had shown some surprising flexibility on the question of refugees.[112] In June 2013 Netanyahu reportedly told U.S. secretary of state John Kerry that he would agree to acknowledge the 1967 lines as the basis for negotiations.[113]

Kerry decided to abandon the London backdoor channel despite its ostensible progress on many core issues. Instead, in July 2013, he set a nine-month time limit to reach a final agreement between Israel and the Palestinians.

In February 2014 the U.S. State Department issued an internal document stating that a peace agreement between Israel and the Palestinians "will need to be based on a shared commitment to fulfilling the vision of two states for two peoples, with full equal rights and no discrimination against any member of any ethnic or religious community." On borders, the document stated that "the new secure and recognized international borders between Israel and Palestine will be negotiated based on the 1967 lines with mutually-agreed swaps whose size and location will be negotiated, so that Palestine will have viable territory corresponding in size to the territory controlled by Egypt and Jordan before June 4, 1967, with territorial contiguity in the West Bank." On Jerusalem: any solution "must correspond to the deep historic, religious, cultural and emotional ties of both peoples to the city's holy sites, which must be protected." On refugees: "The establishment of an independent Palestinian state will provide a national homeland for all Palestinians, including the refugees, and thereby bring an end to the historic Palestinian refugee issue and the assertion of any claims against Israel arising from it." The document also included a reference to "an international effort to deal with the property claims" of Jews expelled from Arab countries. Palestine was to be a demilitarized state, but with an effective internal security force. Benjamin Netanyahu expressed his openness to this document during his discussions with John Kerry.[114] Abbas rejected the document during a meeting with John Kerry in Paris in February 2014.[115]

On March 16, 2014, President Obama met with Mahmoud Abbas in Washington. Presenting the document to Abbas, Obama added that both Israel and Palestine would have "their internationally recognized capitals in Jerusalem, with East Jerusalem serving as the Palestinian capital." Abbas simply did not respond.[116] National Security Advisor Susan Rice, who had modified the U.S. proposal to make it more acceptable to the Palestinians, was furious. "You have to be complete idiots to reject this offer," she told Palestinian negotiator Saeb Erekat.[117]

Despite Abbas's rejection of the February 2014 U.S. proposal, the Obama administration was mostly frustrated with Netanyahu because of his policy of continued settlement construction. In December 2016, at the end of his second term, Obama decided not to veto UN Security Council Resolution 2334, which constituted a setback for Israel.

Resolution 242 had left the question of final borders flexible. Israel was expected to withdraw "from territories" to "secure and recognized boundaries." Israel's final border was negotiable, and 242 implicitly recognized future changes to the 1949 armistice lines.

By contrast, Article 3 of the new resolution passed in 2016 stated that the Security Council "will not recognize any changes to the 4 June 1967 lines, including with regard to Jerusalem, other than those agreed by the parties through negotiations." As for possible changes "agreed by the parties through negotiations," they were moot, since the Palestinians had rejected them in previous negotiations.

The implicit recognition by 242 of changes to the armistice lines of 1949 had been made explicit by President George W. Bush's letter to Prime Minister Ariel Sharon on April 14, 2004. The aforementioned letter stated that "in light of new realities on the ground, including already existing major Israeli populations centers, it is unrealistic to expect that the outcome of final status negotiations will be a full and complete return to the armistice lines of 1949." In July 2010 President Obama declined to publicly confirm the U.S. government's commitment to this letter. On May 19, 2011, he declared that "the borders of Israel and Palestine should be based on the 1967 lines with mutually agreed swaps." This statement left no room for Israeli territorial annexations beyond the 1949 lines (since in a swap, annexations are mutual and net territorial gains nil). By not vetoing Resolution 2334, Obama had made it virtually impossible for Israel to change the 1949 lines to its advantage in future negotiations.

Since Camp David 2000, the Palestinian strategy appeared to amount to say no to peace offers, play for time, and expect more favorable peace offers and/or UN decisions in the future. Over the ensuing years, this strategy proved mostly successful, except that more Israeli settlements continued to be built as the Palestinians stonewalled.

The swearing in of Donald Trump in January 2017 was a game-changer, since the new administration was less sympathetic to Palestinian demands and negotiating tactics. Realizing that an upcoming U.S. peace proposal was going to be much less advantageous to the Palestinians than the ones they had previously rejected, PA chairman Mahmoud Abbas declared on January 14, 2018, that the Palestinians

were the descendants of the Canaanites[118] (i.e., that they had lived
in the land continuously for millennia). He said that Britain should
apologize for the Balfour Declaration and that by 1653 Oliver Cromwell
had already planned to massively transfer Jews to the Middle East for
the purpose of serving British commercial interests. He described
nineteenth-century Jews as mere pawns and objects of the European
powers, but with no actual desire to immigrate to the holy land. Abbas's
point was to deny Israel's very legitimacy as he was coming under
pressure to accept it. He also declared that the Oslo Agreements were
no longer relevant, which indicated that the PLO's recognition of Israel
may no longer be valid.

Thus it has been that the two-state solution first proposed in 1937
has worked in theory but failed in practice. While it made sense on
paper, it has not worked out in the real world.

Some Israelis on both sides of the political spectrum advocate
the annexation of the West Bank. This would accomplish political
equality between Jews and Arabs, but a full annexation would involve
granting Israeli citizenship to some 2.5 million Palestinians, thereby
more than doubling Israel's Arab population and turning Israel into
a binational state.

Others propose annexing only Area C (the area not yet transferred
to Palestinian sovereignty by the Oslo Agreements). Such annexation
would create some thirty Palestinian enclaves (currently Areas A and
B) inside what would become sovereign Israeli territory. There is no
territorial continuity between those enclaves, and one of them, Jericho, is remote and isolated. Connecting the enclaves would require
building roads that would cut through sovereign Israeli territory.

Still others advocate a unilateral withdrawal to the security fence.
However, the precedent of the 2005 withdrawal from Gaza has undermined the credibility of such a policy. A unilateral withdrawal to the
security fence would leave about 95 percent of the West Bank in Israel's
hands, a de facto annexation of the three settlement blocks (which

could turn into a de jure annexation). Such a scenario would admittedly remove the specter of a binational state, but it would produce an unmanageable danger to Israel's security, with hostile forces threatening Israel's population centers and international airport. Moreover, Israel would likely be dragged into military operations in the West Bank (as has been the case in Gaza since the 2005 withdrawal). Once again Israel's international image and standing would be at stake. Just as Israel's 2009 military operation in Gaza and the subsequent UN-sponsored Goldstone Report made clear, military operations, with their unavoidable civilian casualties, put Israel on the defensive against accusations of war crimes.

In January 2020 the Trump administration submitted its long-awaited "deal of the century" to solve the Israeli-Palestinian conflict. The plan proposed significant land swaps between Israel and a future demilitarized Palestinian state (Israel would annex most of Area C in the West Bank, and the Palestinian state would annex territories of a nearly similar size in pre-1967 Israel). A tunnel would connect the two parts of the Palestinian state (in the West Bank and Gaza), and the Palestinian economy would be boosted by a $50 billion investment. Israel accepted the U.S. plan, and the Palestinian Authority flatly rejected it.

An agreement between Israel and the Palestinians is not in the cards at the time of this writing. Israel, therefore, has a choice of bad options. Yet prudence and patience have proved to be a wise policy choice in the Arab-Israeli conflict. Israel's first foreign minister, Moshe Sharett, commonly considered a dove (especially in comparison with his nemesis David Ben-Gurion), was nonetheless a pragmatic statesman who did not believe in a full resolution of the Arab-Israeli conflict. He believed in what he called "conflict reduction" (what we would call today "conflict management").[119]

Back in 1999, the Israeli historian Benny Morris wrote, "So far the Zionists have been the winners in this conflict."[120] This statement is even more valid two decades later, as Israel is a success story surrounded by failed states. It is both telling and ironic that Israeli dove and former peace negotiator Shlomo Ben-Ami wrote the following about the Arab-Israeli conflict: "At the end of the day, it was Israel's 'bad behavior,' Jabotinsky's iron-wall philosophy, and Ben-Gurion's doctrine of offensive defense, backed by the ultimate nuclear deterrence, which changed the Arabs' attitude to the Jewish state."[121] Though Israel has been unable, so far, to reach a historical compromise with the Palestinians, it has also become a major power coveted by Arab states that fear Iran's nuclear ambitions.

From a historical perspective, one could argue that Israel's iron-wall strategy has been vindicated. Yet this strategy has yet to produce what Jabotinsky had hoped and envisioned back in 1923 — that is, to eventually achieve peace between Israel and the Palestinians.

Conclusion

Israel's involvement in the Lebanese civil war culminated in the botched 1982 Lebanon War. The PLO was expelled from Lebanon, only to be replaced by the Iran-backed Hezbollah militia. As for Lebanon's Christians, far from regaining control of their country, they were further marginalized. The "Jordanian option" (i.e., negotiating the final status of the West Bank between Israel and Jordan) collapsed in 1988, and as a result, the United States engaged in a dialogue with the PLO, to Israel's dismay. The collapse of the Soviet Union and Arafat's miscalculations in the 1991 Gulf War marginalized the PLO and threatened its very relevance. Israel extracted concessions from Arafat, and Arafat signed the Oslo Agreements precisely because he had no better choice. When the time came for decisions and compromise, however, Arafat dithered, maneuvered, and eventually reverted to violence. By launching the second intifada, Arafat unintentionally brought back to power his ultimate nemesis, Ariel Sharon. After mostly defeating the intifada, Sharon adopted a unilateralist strategy that stemmed from two conclusions: (a) a peace agreement with the PLO was beyond reach; and (b) the status quo was demographically unsustainable.

Yet the 2005 unilateral withdrawal from Gaza made things worse for Israelis and Palestinians alike. And today, in light of the Gaza experiment, the idea of unilaterally withdrawing from most of the West Bank has become a nonstarter, especially as Iran and radical Islam have been progressively filling the void left by imploding Arab states. On the other hand, full annexation would turn Israel into a binational (or nearly binational) state. The Israeli-Palestinian conflict remains unresolved.

PART 4. Israel on the World Scene

13. The European Paradox

I have never quite understood why the Jews don't have a sovereign state with schools and universities where they can talk and debate freely. For only then shall we know what they have to say.

JEAN-JACQUES ROUSSEAU, *Émile*

The First Tier: Britain, France, Germany

BRITAIN

From the mid-1930s onward, relations between the *Yishuv* and the British government deteriorated. Arab leaders had pressured Britain not to implement the Balfour Declaration. Arab opposition turned into a widespread wave of violence in 1936, as Hitler's Germany was undoing the post–World War I Versailles Treaty. Right after he seized power in 1933, Hitler pulled Germany out of the League of Nations, and he started rearming. In 1936 he remilitarized the Ruhr (a buffer zone in western Germany that had been demilitarized by the Versailles Treaty). In 1938 Hitler annexed Austria and invaded Czechoslovakia. It became clear to all that war was coming and that England would have to fight Germany again.

As the war loomed, Britain tried to secure the support of its rebellious Middle East allies—hence its policy of appeasement. This policy proved ineffective, as Arab leaders in the British Empire sided with Nazi Germany anyway. Hadj Amin al-Husseini, the Jerusalem mufti, admired Adolph Hitler and collaborated with him before and during World War II. In Iraq, Rashid Ali al-Gaylani briefly overthrew the pro-British regime of Abd al-Ilah in 1941, assisted by al-Husseini and hundreds of Palestinians exiles, all of them backed by Hitler.[1] After Nazi Germany defeated France in June 1940, a popular song on the streets of Damascus went, "No more Monsieur, no more Mister, Allah's in heaven and Hitler's on earth."[2] Many Arabs hoped that Nazi Germany would rid them of British and French colonialism. And at the height of Britain and Germany's struggle in the Middle East (epitomized by the 1942 battle of El Alamein between the British officer Field Marshal Bernard Montgomery and his German opponent General Erwin Rommel), the British could hardly afford to alienate the Arabs. Neither did they want to. A deeply ingrained romance with the Arab world—symbolized by Lawrence of Arabia—heavily influenced British foreign policy tradition.

Winston Churchill was sympathetic to the Jews and to Zionism, but he lost the 1945 general elections. Britain's new Labour government, led by Clement Attlee, turned out to be a great disappointment to the *Yishuv*; the Jewish proto-government of Palestine was dominated by Laborites who had expected sympathy from their British counterparts. As Abba Eban was to quip, "It became a Zionist truism that our friends were former ministers, while incumbent ministers were our former friends."[3] Attlee's foreign minister Ernest Bevin had once described communism as a "Jewish plot" against Britain.[4] Bevin's hostility toward the Jews even confounded his own supporters, one of whom recorded his bewilderment thus: "There is no doubt to my mind that Ernest detests Jews. . . . He says they [the Jews] taught Hitler the technique of terror and were even now paralleling the Nazis in Palestine. They were preachers of violence and war. 'What could you expect when people are brought up from the cradle on the Old Testament?'"[5]

Even after the horrors of the Holocaust became known, and Jewish survivors were desperately trying to reach the shores of the Promised Land, Bevin refused to let them in. "It had been our hope," Weizmann wrote of Britain's postwar policy, "that when at last there was no longer the ignominious need to appease the Nazis and Arab leaders, there would be a relaxation of the anti-immigration rulings for Palestine. Nothing of the sort happened."[6]

On the one hand, Bevin referred the Palestine conflict to the UN. But on the other hand, he disapproved of the UN's partition solution. The British Foreign Office thought that establishing a Jewish state would negatively affect British influence in the Middle East as well as Britain's interests in the Arab world. Already the Arabs resented Britain for the 1917 Balfour Declaration, and Britain could not afford to further alienate emerging Arab states whose oil reserves were vital to the British economy. More than geopolitical calculations seemed to be at play, however. Abba Eban wrote that in the working meetings between Bevin and the Jewish Agency, "Not for a single moment did he show us any human respect, let alone diplomatic deference."[7]

The Labour government's opposition to Zionism surprised and disappointed many because back in April 1944, the Labour Party had issued a report stating, "There is surely neither hope nor meaning in a Jewish National Home unless we are prepared to let the Jews, if they wish, enter this tiny land in such numbers as to become a majority. There was a strong case for this before the war, and there is an irresistible case for it now, after the unspeakable atrocities of the cold-blooded, calculated German-Nazi plan to kill all the Jews of Europe."[8]

But from the time Ernest Bevin became foreign secretary in 1945, Britain and the Zionist movement were on a collision course. And after Israel's independence, that collision deteriorated into military conflict. On January 7, 1949, Israeli fighters shot down five Royal Air Force (RAF) planes carrying out reconnaissance flights over Israel. Britain was reminded the hard way that its mandate in Palestine was over, yet it still refused to recognize Israel. Winston Churchill would castigate Bevin about this stubbornness with his legendary rhetorical skills:

I am quite sure that the Right Honorable Gentleman will have to recognize the Israeli government and that this cannot be long delayed. . . . There are half a dozen countries today in Europe which are recognized today whose territorial frontiers are not finally settled. . . . Whether the Right Honorable Gentleman likes it or not, and whether we like it or not, the coming into being of a Jewish state in Palestine is an event in world history to be viewed in the perspective not of a generation or a century, but in the perspective of a thousand, two thousand or even three thousand years.[9]

Britain eventually recognized Israel de jure in April 1950, but its Middle East policy consisted of trying to contain Soviet influence. Hence its decision, in 1955, to establish the Baghdad Pact and to promote the Alpha Plan (see chapter 9). However, these diplomatic initiatives did not impress Nasser, who became a Soviet ally in 1955 and nationalized the Suez Canal a year later.

Following the nationalization, Britain went to war with Egypt. Yet Britain had not foreseen that the United States would so strongly condemn the attempt to regain control of the Suez Canal by force. The 1956 humiliation convinced Britain to avoid further clashes with the United States and to strengthen the Atlantic alliance. When the United States started reassessing its Middle East foreign policy under the Kennedy administration (1961–63), Britain went along. Moreover, Britain came to be impressed by Israel's military strength and its willingness to use it against Egypt, a Soviet ally, in 1956.[10]

When, in 1964, Harold Wilson formed Britain's first Labour government since Attlee and Bevin, Israel's prime minister Levi Eshkol was invited to Downing Street and treated with deference. The underlying reason for this meeting was far from innocent: Britain asked Israel to help it fight anti-British forces in the Middle East. On board, Israel backed Yemen's pro-British (and anti-Nasserist) fighters between

1964 and 1967, in coordination with Britain.[11] The Israeli Air Force (IAF) parachuted military equipment to pro-British forces in Yemen, which handled the logistics on the ground.[12] Hence did Nasser's anti-British activities in Yemen produce a rapprochement between Britain and Israel.

Cooperation between the two countries expanded to Oman. Impressed by Israel's efficiency in Yemen and by its stunning military victory in June 1967, the British asked Israel to create a clandestine route of oil import from Oman to Europe via Eilat.[13] During the 1967 UN Security Council negotiations over Resolution 242, Britain supported the position that Israel should not be coerced into an unconditional and total withdrawal to the 1949 armistice lines.

Britain's Middle East policy, however, remained influenced by its oil interests and the Arabist tradition of the Foreign Office, which kept relations with Israel at a low profile and did not allow members of the royal family to pay an official visit to Israel. Many years after Israel's independence, Foreign Office officials would continue to complain about the Balfour Declaration and its supposedly devastating effects on Britain's standing in the Arab world. "Our dealings with many of the Arab countries are soured by our historical responsibility for Israel's creation," said a Foreign Office document in 1985.[14]

Margaret Thatcher, Britain's prime minister between 1979 and 1990, was well disposed toward the Jews and toward Israel. Her Finchley constituency had a strong Jewish population, and her daughter Carol had volunteered on a kibbutz (Thatcher would subsequently quip that she would forever be thankful to Israel for vaccinating her daughter from socialism). Yet the European Economic Community (EEC) passed the 1980 Venice Declaration, which called upon Israel to negotiate with the PLO, on Thatcher's watch and with her full support. Just like British and American foreign policy decision makers in the 1950s, Thatcher thought that only a full resolution of the Arab-Israeli conflict would thwart further Soviet influence in the Middle East.[15] She strongly condemned Israel's bombing of Iraq's nuclear reactor in 1981, even though Iraq was a Soviet ally. Moreover, despite Israeli and American requests, the Thatcher government refused to sell oil to Israel for fear of retaliation from the Arab states. Indeed, Israel's ambassador to the United Kingdom, Shlomo Argov, expressed the opinion that under Margaret Thatcher relations between Israel and Britain had reached their lowest point since the days of Clement Attlee and Ernest Bevin.[16] These tense relations further deteriorated with the 1982 Falklands War, during which Britain complained to Israel about its selling military hardware (including Gabriel anti-ship missiles) to Argentina. Thatcher also strongly condemned Israel's 1982 invasion of Lebanon, which was intended to stop PLO terrorists from shelling Israel's northern towns. Bizarrely, she compared it to Argentina's invasion of the Falklands (as if missiles had ever rained from the Falklands on Argentina).[17] Further, Thatcher's government sold tanks to Jordan and military aircraft to Saudi Arabia, but it imposed a military embargo on Israel.

On the other hand, Margaret Thatcher was the first British head of government to pay an official visit to Israel in 1986. She also steadfastly opposed Saddam Hussein's "linkage" proposal (i.e., linking Iraq's withdrawal from Kuwait to Israel's withdrawal from the West Bank and Gaza) after his 1990 invasion of Kuwait.[18]

In more recent years, Israel has become a partisan issue in British politics. The Conservative governments of David Cameron (2010–16) and Theresa May (2016–19) were staunch supporters of Israel, seeing it as an ally in the fight against terrorism. By contrast, the Labour Party under Jeremy Corbyn (2015–20) turned anti-Israel and pro-Hamas and Hezbollah (back in 2009, Corbyn had described Hamas and Hezbollah as "friends").[19] Britain's former chief rabbi Lord Jonathan Sachs accused Corbyn of being an antisemite.[20]

At the same time, however, economic relations between Britain and Israel have flourished. Although the BDS (Boycott, Divestment, Sanctions) movement against Israel has many UK supporters, it has had an insignificant impact on trade relations between the two countries. In 2017 trade between Britain and Israel increased by 26 percent, and 32 Israeli companies established a permanent presence in Britain, adding to the nearly 340 Israeli high-tech companies operating there.[21] Israeli technology is sought after by the UK, whose main banks are protected by Israeli cybersecurity technologies. Israel and the UK are founding members of D7, a network of the world's most digitized countries. Defense cooperation between Israel and Britain has been upgraded in recent years. In 2017 British air chief marshal Sir Stuart Peach paid an official visit to Israel, and a joint exercise between the Royal Air Force and the Israeli Air Force took place in Cyprus. In June 2018 Prince William (second in the line of succession to the British throne) became the first member of the British royal family to pay an official visit to Israel.

FRANCE

In 1947 France had supported the partition of Palestine mostly because Britain was against it. During World War II, Charles de Gaulle had accused Britain of undermining French sovereignty in Syria and Lebanon (both territories the British and Free French forces had conquered from the Vichy regime in 1941). Syria and Lebanon became fully independent in 1946, and a year later, when France was presented with the prospect of ending the British Mandate in Palestine, it eagerly volunteered to help.

At the same time, however, France had to be prudent: it could not ignore and alienate its Muslim subjects in North Africa. Arab countries were strongly pressuring France not to support the creation of a Jewish state. Yet French president Vincent Auriol and French premier Paul Ramadier supported the partition of Palestine and an independent Jewish state. Both were members of the French Socialist Party (SFIO), which had close ties with Israel's socialist Mapai party.[22] The personal plea of Léon Blum (the first Jew who served as France's premier in

1936) for France's vote in favor of partition was also decisive.[23] The first Israeli passports were printed in Hebrew and in French (English being the language of the reviled Ernest Bevin).

With the eruption of the Algerian War in 1954, France and Israel became tacit allies because Egyptian president Gamal Abdel Nasser, who led the Arab struggle against Israel, also supported the Algerian nationalists against France. This common enmity eventually turned into a military alliance between France and Israel, culminating in the 1956 war fought jointly against Egypt.

Besides common interests, there were also personal bonds between French and Israeli politicians and generals. Marie-Pierre Kœnig, who served as France's defense minister in 1954–55, had heroically led the Free French Forces in the Battle of Bir Hakeim (1942) in North Africa together with a battalion of Palestinian Jews. Kœning had allowed the Jewish soldiers to fly their Star of David flag, thus defying British orders. As for French premier Guy Mollet, who headed the French government during the Suez campaign, he was fully supportive of Israel. The Quai d'Orsay (France's foreign ministry) and other French ministries opposed Mollet's policy and often tried to ignore his instructions,[24] but the pro-Israel foreign minister Christian Pineau eventually imposed his will on the recalcitrant ministry, and France lifted its military embargo on Israel in February 1956.[25] This decision was followed by France's delivery of dozens of Mystère fighter jets and AMX-13 tanks. Military cooperation between the two countries even extended to nuclear technology.[26]

Yet Ben-Gurion knew that the underlying cause of France's military alliance with Israel was the Algerian War and that this war would not last forever. In fact, cracks in the Franco-Israeli alliance started appearing even before the end of the war in 1962. As soon as Charles de Gaulle returned to power in 1958, he downgraded France's relations with Israel. He thought that the Fourth Republic (France's political regime between 1946 and 1958) had irresponsibly dragged France into a foolish military adventure with Israel. De Gaulle spelled out his ambiguous attitude toward Israel in his memoirs:

> Although France did not formally take part in the creation of this state [Israel], which was the outcome of a joint British, American, and Soviet decision, it had warmly approved of it. I myself had sympathized with the noble idea of allowing Jews to fulfill their right to self-determination in a land they had owned nineteen centuries ago and which had witnessed their fabulous history. From a humanitarian point of view, the Jews were entitled to a national home as a reparation for the sufferings they had endured throughout the ages and which had reached their gruesome apex under Hitler's Germany. While Israel's existence is justified, however, its attitude toward the Arabs should be prudent. . . . It is on their lands and against their will that Israel was established. Israel wounds their pride and affronts their religion.[27]

It is not clear what de Gaulle meant by a joint "British, American, and Soviet decision" to establish Israel. France had supported the Balfour Declaration in February 1918.[28] It had established, together with Britain, the Middle East's mandates after World War I. The British government had consistently tried to prevent the establishment of a Jewish state since 1939, and Britain had abstained from the UN's 1947 partition plan. As for the United States, Roosevelt and the State Department were opposed to a Jewish state. Had it not been for Harry Truman's personal decision, the United States would not have approved the UN partition plan.

De Gaulle did not only rewrite the history of France's attitude toward Zionism. He also told Ben-Gurion, in 1960, that his government would oppose any Israeli territorial expansion. Furthermore, he ended what he called "abusive practices of military collaboration established since the Suez expedition between Tel Aviv and Paris, which introduced

Israelis to all levels of French intelligence and of the French army," as well as France's assistance to "a uranium enrichment plant [in Israel] which might, someday, produce nuclear bombs."[29]

Sure enough, when the Algerian War ended in 1962, the Franco-Israel alliance lost its raison d'être. De Gaulle was eager to repair France's image and economic interests in the Arab world, something that could not be achieved without downgrading relations with Israel. While he knew that French public opinion at the time was mostly favorable to Israel, his priority was to restore France's ties with the Arab world nonetheless. Indeed, he said so explicitly to British prime minister Harold Wilson: why, he asked rhetorically, ruin relations with the Arab world just because French public opinion had some "superficial sympathy" with Israel?[30]

There was no official rupture until the Six-Day War, however. In 1966 France was still Israel's main military supplier. Yet the June 1967 war provided de Gaulle with the perfect opportunity to demonstrate to the Arab world that France's Middle East policy had changed course.

In June 1967 de Gaulle reneged on France's 1957 commitment to recognize Israel's right to self-defense in case of an Egyptian closure of the Straits of Tiran ("That was 1957. It is now 1967," he told Abba Eban).[31] He warned Israel not to "be the first to shoot."[32] Technically Israel was the first to shoot even though Nasser had initiated the dynamic of war. De Gaulle never forgave Israel for not heeding his injunction. "Monsieur Eban," de Gaulle would later relay, "sat there. I told him not to make war—and we [royal plural] were not obeyed."[33]

In response to the Six-Day War, de Gaulle imposed a French military embargo that primarily affected Israel. He also proclaimed, in his press conference of November 27, 1967, that at the time of Israel's establishment, "some had feared that the Jews, who had been scattered but had never ceased to be what they had always been, that is, an elitist, self-assured and domineering people, might, once gathered in the site of their former greatness, turn into a burning and conquering ambition the moving wishes they had expressed for nineteen centuries: next year in Jerusalem!"[34] This statement shocked France's Jewish community, which was de facto singled out as "the Jews" together with Israel. Both Jews and non-Jews wondered how a "domineering" people could have ended up in concentration camps and gas chambers during the Holocaust.[35]

In his infamous statement, de Gaulle also admitted his ultimate motive for ending the Franco-Israel alliance: "Once the Algerian affair was resolved, we restored with Middle East Arabs a policy of friendship and of cooperation that had been France's policy for centuries."[36] De Gaulle voiced another reason for ending France's alliance with Israel: the United States had replaced France as Israel's main ally, and France now disapproved of American foreign policy. De Gaulle explained, illogically, that he did "not see how an agreement can emerge as long as [the United States] fights this odious war [in Vietnam]. . . . Without the Vietnamese tragedy, the conflict between Israel and the Arabs would not have turned that way."[37] Central among the tenets of de Gaulle's foreign policy was to challenge America and reduce French dependence on U.S. power. Hence he decided to turn France into a nuclear power (France detonated its first nuclear bomb in 1960) and to withdraw France from NATO's military command in 1966.

As the alliance between America and Israel deepened in the 1960s, so did de Gaulle's criticism of Israel. Yet acquiring nuclear weapons and withdrawing from NATO's military power did not suffice to restore France's standing as a great power, a status lost in the humiliating 1956 Suez crisis. When Abba Eban informed President Johnson, in May 1967, that de Gaulle wanted a coordinated action by "the four Great Powers," Johnson asked with his trademark wit, "Who the hell are the other two?"[38]

De Gaulle perceived Israel's 1967 victory as a challenge not only to his warnings ("Ne faites pas la guerre!"), but also to his judgment. Thus, ironically, while Israel won the Six-Day War with French military jets, the victory marked the end of the nations' historical alliance. De Gaulle's foreign minister, Maurice Couve de Murville, admitted that since the Six-Day War, France no longer had a Middle East policy, but only "an Arab policy."[39]

De Gaulle resigned in 1969, but his conservative successors preserved his foreign policy legacy. President Valéry Giscard d'Estaing (1974–81) toured the Middle East in March 1980 and pointedly skipped Israel. The image of Giscard d'Estaing contemplating Israel from Jordan through binoculars was worth a thousand words. Under the socialist François Mitterrand (1981–95), France's Gaullist "Arab policy" (la politique arabe de la France) was partially reassessed. Mitterrand was the first French head of state who paid an official visit to Israel (in 1982). He was a philosemite despite his complex and sometimes shady past (he had joined the Resistance after working in a low-level position for the Vichy government; and he remained a friend of former Vichy official René Bousquet, who was indicted for his role in the deportation of French Jews).

His successor, Jacques Chirac (1995–2007) was dogmatically Gaullist when it came to foreign policy. As France's prime minister, Chirac had played a key role in selling a nuclear plant to Saddam Hussein in 1976. Once president, Chirac visited Israel in October 1996 as part of a Middle East tour, and in the Old City of Jerusalem, he humiliated Israel's security forces, demanding that they get out of his way. The images of Chirac yelling at Israeli soldiers made him immensely popular among the Palestinians and in the Arab world.

Chirac's policy ended up sabotaging U.S. peacemaking efforts, because Arafat knew he could count on France to blame Israel for the failure of the peace process. As expected, in October 2000, after the outbreak of the second intifada, U.S. secretary of state Madeleine Albright summoned Israeli prime minister Ehud Barak and Palestinian Authority chairman Yasser Arafat to the U.S. embassy in Paris to conclude a ceasefire. Chirac, however, advised Arafat to demand an international presence in the West Bank and the Gaza Strip, specifically an international inquiry commission[40]—something Barak had adamantly rejected and had not been included in the agreement brokered by the United States.[41] Arafat made the ultimatum, it was not met, and Arafat did not sign the agreed-upon cease-fire agreement.

Relations between France and Israel improved after Chirac, as his successors (Nicolas Sarkozy, François Hollande, and Emmanuel Macron) had a friendly and more balanced attitude toward Israel. In June 2008 Nicolas Sarkozy (2007–12) declared at the Knesset, "France is the friend of Israel and shall always be on its side whenever its security and existence are threatened." In November 2013 François Hollande (2012–17) said, also at the Knesset, that Israel could count on France's friendship. In July 2017 Emmanuel Macron (2017–) condemned anti-Zionism as a disguised form of antisemitism. All three leaders have expressed their steadfast opposition to Iran's nuclear program.

GERMANY

In the early years of Israel's independence, Germans were not allowed to enter Israel, and Israelis were not allowed to travel to Germany. Israeli passports bore a stamp stating that they were valid for all countries except for Germany. The Holocaust was an open wound, and Germany was completely banned.

Officially, Israeli diplomats were not even allowed to talk to their German counterparts.[42] Behind this official stance, however, contacts took place between Israel and West Germany for the express purpose of reaching a reparation agreement. Signed in 1952, that agreement required West Germany to pay financial reparations to Israel for the integration of Jewish refugees and Holocaust survivors.

This agreement was very controversial in Israel at the time. Prime Minister David Ben-Gurion said that the Israeli economy could not sustain the cost of mass immigration without it; opposition leader Menachem Begin claimed that the Israeli government was in effect absolving Germany of its guilt for money. In Israel, demonstrations against the agreement turned violent.

For German chancellor Konrad Adenauer, the 1952 reparation agreement with Israel was part of Germany's *Wiedergutmachung* (doing good again) policy. Yet when Israeli officials insisted on signing the agreement without photographs and handshakes, Adenauer grumbled about Israel's "biblical unforgiveness."[43]

Relations between Israel and Germany bore the painful scars of history. Those scars reopened with the 1960 trial of Adolph Eichmann in Israel and also by reports that German scientists were advising the Egyptian government on missile development. In the late 1950s and early 1960s, Israel's Mossad was actively trying to dissuade and prevent German scientists from helping Egypt build its rocket industry by eliminating German scientists working for Egypt. On September 11, 1962, for example, the German scientist Heinz Krug, who topped the Mossad's "wanted" list of German scientists working with Egypt, disappeared and never reappeared. Krug had been shot by a former Nazi officer, Otto Skorzeny, whom the Mossad had recruited to target other Nazis,[44] expressly to intimidate other German scientists who were also helping Egypt build rockets. Israel's intimidation campaign was successful, as most German scientists eventually left Egypt.

The Mossad's effort to scare German scientists out of Egypt thwarted the capture of Joseph Mengele, infamously known for his cruel "medical" experiments on Auschwitz inmates. In July 1962 Mengele was within the Mossad's grip. Yet Mossad's director at the time, Isser Harel, ordered that attempts to capture Mengele be dropped to focus instead on the German scientists building missiles for Egypt.[45] Harel's successor, Meir Amit, implicitly justified the strategic decision to let go of Mengele when he declared that Israel's intelligence should "stop chasing after ghosts from the past and devote all our manpower and resources to threats against the security of the state."[46]

Relations between Israel and West Germany also took on a military dimension in the late 1950s. As Israel's relation with France was starting to show signs of decline, and Israel did not yet have a strategic relationship with the United States, Israel needed military allies and weaponry. Meanwhile, Reinhard Gehlen, chief of Germany's Federal Intelligence Service (Bundesnachichtendienst, or BND), was impressed by Israel's swift military victory against Egypt in 1956 and thought that Israel could become a valuable partner.[47] In 1957 Gehlen reached out to Israel's Mossad, and Isser Harel eventually gave his approval to a mutually beneficial intelligence operation. German defense minister Franz-Josef Strauss and Israel deputy defense minister Shimon Peres drew up a secret military agreement through which Germany would supply tanks and helicopters to Israel.[48] In 1958 Chancellor Konrad Adenauer approved the deal on condition of strict secrecy (Germany feared Arab economic reprisals), and the operation commenced.

The secret military relationship was broken when newspapers revealed the deal in October 1964. Under heavy pressure from the Arab world—Arab states threatened to recognize East Germany—West Germany rescinded its arms supplies to Israel in 1965.

Israel's elimination of Heinz Krug in 1962 and the cessation of German arms supplies to Israel in 1965 had the effect of undermining Germany's effort to regain respectability. As Abba Eban explained, Germany "was assailed for insensitivity to the memory of the Jewish tragedy, for disregard of its relations with the Arabs, and for a total lack of backbone as exemplified by the arms conspiracy and by the hasty and craven retreat."[49]

Negotiations over the establishment of full diplomatic relations were handled by Abba Eban (serving as deputy prime minister) and Kurt Birrenbach (a confidante of the German chancellor). The two countries established full diplomatic relations in 1965.

Once full diplomatic relations were established, West Germany turned out to be one of Israel's strongest supports within the EEC and

NATO. Israel and Germany also established advanced military ties. In the early 1970s, when Germany developed (together with Britain and Italy) the Tornado fighter aircraft, Israel's aircraft industry was selected to develop the new aircraft's electronic warfare system — and the Mossad was entrusted with keeping this cooperation secret.[50]

In recent years, Israel has purchased German-made submarines that are crucial to Israel's deterrence vis-à-vis Iran. Furthermore, successive German governments have consistently promoted Holocaust education as well as educational and cultural exchange programs between young Germans and young Israelis. Berlin, which has a reborn Jewish life as well as a significant community of Israeli expats, displays both the symbols of a tragic past and the images of a thriving present: the memorial of the murdered Jews of Europe (inaugurated in 2005), and the enormous *hanukkiah* lit every year in front of the Brandenburg Gate.

Israel's Complicated Relations in Europe

SPAIN

Spain and Israel established diplomatic relations only in 1986, the year Spain joined the EEC. The historical scars of the 1492 expulsion of Spanish Jewry and of the ensuing Inquisition never waned from collective Jewish memory. In addition, Francisco Franco (Spain's military dictator from 1939 to 1975) had sided with the Axis powers during World War II, even though Spain did not formally take part in the war against the Allies. There are conflicting accounts of Franco's policy toward the Jews during the Holocaust: he granted refuge to some Jews but was also suspected of having handed lists of Jews over to the Germans. For those reasons, Israel considered Spain "untouchable." There were only two countries from which Israel did not ask recognition upon its independence: Germany and Spain. In May 1949 Israel voted at the

UN against lifting diplomatic sanctions on Spain, despite the pressure of many Latin American countries that sympathized with Franco.[51]

Yet if Israel could sign a reparation agreement with Germany in 1952 and maintain diplomatic relations with the Soviet Union despite its mistreatment of Jews, why not establish diplomatic relations with Franco's Spain? Such was the argument of the "pragmatists" at Israel's Foreign Ministry. Franco, however, was not interested in diplomatic relations with Israel. Spain's ties with the Arab world were complex. Spain had won the Reconquista (the war against the Arabs between the early eighth century and the late fifteenth century), and the surname of the legendary Spanish hero Santiago (Saint James) was "the Moor-slayer" (Matamoros). At the same time, Franco had close ties with North African Arabs, some of whom served in his security guard. Arab votes at the UN were critical to Spain when it came to defending its colonies in Gibraltar, northern Morocco, Western Sahara, and the Canary Islands. Spanish foreign minister Fernando María Castiella candidly admitted that not having diplomatic relations with Israel served Spain's interests in the Arab world.[52]

Although Spain's transition to democracy after Franco's death in 1975 was not immediate, the electoral victory of the Socialist party (PSOE) in 1982 facilitated the establishment of diplomatic relations with Israel. Spanish prime minister Felipe Gonzáles was a member of the Socialist International, like his counterpart Shimon Peres (who would become Israel's prime minister in 1984). Spain joined the EEC in January 1986 and therefore became a member of an organization that had a free trade agreement with Israel. Not having diplomatic relations with an EEC partner was awkward, and so Israel and Spain established full diplomatic relations in 1986.

In October 2015 Spain passed a law that enables descendants of Jews who were expelled from Spain in 1492 to claim Spanish citizenship. The law also states that the 1492 expulsion and the Inquisition were "historical mistakes."

ITALY

Italian Jews became fully emancipated following Italy's unification in 1871, and many of them reached senior government positions. Italy had two Jewish prime ministers in the early twentieth century: Alessandro Fortis (1905–6) and Luigi Luzzatti (1910–11). Sidney Sonnino, Italy's foreign minister during and after World War I, turned out to be a kind of Italian Disraeli who put all his weight behind the Zionist project during the 1919 Paris Peace Conference (Sonnino had a Jewish father, and he felt a connection to the Jewish people). It was partly thanks to Sonnino that the Balfour Declaration was incorporated into the British Mandate on Palestine.

Sonnino died shortly after returning from the Paris Peace Conference, and in 1922 Mussolini formed a government that eventually turned Italy into a police state that aligned with Nazi Germany. Still, the Italian state did not directly take part in the Holocaust. In 1942 the Italian military commander in Croatia refused to deliver Jews to the Germans, and in January 1943 the Italians did not cooperate with the Nazis in rounding up the Jews in the Italian-occupied French zone. Deportations of Italian Jews to Nazi death camps began in September 1943, after the Germans invaded northern Italy and Italy capitulated to the Allies.

In recent years, Italian premiers have prided themselves on their friendship with Israel. Both Silvio Berlusconi and Matteo Renzi lavished Israel with praise in their addresses to the Knesset (in February 2010 and July 2015, respectively). Behind this warmth, however, the reality can at times be grimmer. In February 2018 the Italian news magazine *L'Espresso* revealed that Yasser Arafat had helped Premier Berlusconi during his trial for illegally funding Bettino Craxi's Italian Socialist Party. Arafat falsely testified that €5 million was destined not to the Italian Socialist Party but to the PLO; Berlusconi had paid him a kickback for lying to the prosecutors. *L'Espresso* further revealed that successive Italian governments had reached a secret arrangement with Arafat to protect Italy from Palestinian terrorist attacks: Palestinian terrorists would not carry out attacks in Italy in exchange for free movement throughout the country. Because of the mutual nonaggression pact, Italian authorities allowed the escape of the Palestinian terrorists behind the 1985 hijacking of the Italian liner *Achille Lauro*, in which wheelchair-bound American Jewish passenger Leon Klinghoffer was murdered and thrown overboard. Italian premier Giulio Andreotti had enabled the hijacking's mastermind Muhammad Zaidan (also known as Abu Abbas) to escape U.S. extradition and flee from Italy to Tunisia (via Bulgaria).[53]

In recent years, Israel and Italy have developed a close partnership for the export of natural gas to Europe. In November 2018 Israel signed a memorandum of understanding with Cyprus, Greece, and Italy for construction of the world's longest natural gas pipeline, meant to connect Israel to Italy via Cyprus and Greece. In January 2019 the Eastern Mediterranean Gas Forum was established between Israel, Egypt, Greece, Cyprus, Italy, Jordan, and the Palestinian Authority.

GREECE

Greece was the only European country that voted in 1947 against the UN partition plan for Palestine. For forty-two years after Israel's independence, Greece refused to recognize Israel de jure and to establish full diplomatic relations.

A central reason was Greek fear of Arab reprisals. There was an ancient, large, and wealthy Greek diaspora in Egypt, and Egyptian leaders threatened to expel or loot this community if Greece established full diplomatic relations with Israel. After four years of German occupation (1940–44) and six years of civil war (1945–51), a weakened Greece was sensitive to those pressures. (The Egyptians eventually confiscated most of the assets of the Greek diaspora anyway.) When Cyprus declared independence in 1960, Greece lobbied for UN recognition of its claims on the island. With Cyprus populated by Greeks and Turks, both Greece and Turkey had sovereignty claims, and in that diplomatic struggle Greece was easily blackmailed by the Arab and Muslim states, whose natural sympathy was for Turkey (a Muslim country). During the 1982 Lebanon War, Greece's prime minister Andreas Papandreou accused Israel of committing "crimes against humanity" and drew a parallel between Israel and Nazi Germany: "We have seen what Nazism did to the Jews and now the Jews are doing the same to the Palestinians."[54] Under Papandreou, the PLO's "embassy" in Athens became one of its strong international footholds.

Only after Papandreou's electoral defeat in 1990 and the formation of a center-right government did Greece establish full diplomatic relations with Israel, in 1991. In recent years, relations between Israel and Greece have warmed considerably, due to the deterioration of relations between Israel and Turkey (see chapter 10) and the common geopolitical interests created by Israel's emergence as a natural gas exporter (see chapter 21).

SWEDEN

Sweden has had an uneasy "Jewish past" and tense relations with Israel. Sweden did not allow Jewish immigration after Hitler's rise to power (though it did accept Jewish refugees after the German occupation of Norway in 1940). During the war, Sweden was officially neutral, but it let Germany use its territory, and it sold Germany raw materials. Jews were legally barred from being government ministers in Sweden until 1951.[55] In 1948 Lehi militants assassinated Count Folke Bernadotte (a Swedish royal who, acting on the behalf of the UN, had suggested reducing Israel's territory and curtailing Jewish immigration), leaving the Swedes resentful and unforgiving.

Sweden's relations with Israel were influenced by Swedish prime minister Olof Palme (1969–76 and 1982–86), who praised Cuban and

Cambodian revolutionaries and was a steadfast apologist for the PLO. After the Yom Kippur War, Sweden's support for the PLO became outspoken. On December 4, 1975, Sweden was the only Western country to vote at the UN Security Council in favor of inviting the PLO for an audience at the council (Israel called back its ambassador to Stockholm to protest the vote). On November 28, 1986, Sweden's ambassador at the UN declared that his country did not recognize any change made to the UN partition plan of 1947,[56] thus repudiating Israel's de facto borders since the 1949 Rhodes agreements. Sweden was also the first EU country to recognize the State of Palestine in 2014.

The rhetoric of Swedish officials, institutions, and media on Israel has generally been harsher than in the rest of Europe. In 2004 the Swedish History Museum displayed the installation art piece that depicted Palestinian suicide bomber Hanadi Jaradat as Snow White. In August 2009 the Swedish tabloid newspaper *Aftonbladet* published an article by freelance writer Donald Boström alleging that the IDF harvests the organs of Palestinians who die in custody. In the aftermath of the murderous November 2015 Paris attacks, Swedish foreign minister Margot Wallström said that "to counteract the radicalization we must go back to the situation such as the one in the Middle East of which not the least the Palestinians see that, for us, there is no future: we must either accept a desperate situation or resort to violence" — thereby implying that those attacks' ultimate cause was Palestinian frustration.[57]

Sweden's Muslim population, which has been growing significantly in recent years thanks to Sweden's generous immigration policy, has had an impact not only on the country's Middle East policy, but also on the life of Swedish Jews. Harassment of Jews in the city of Malmö became so frequent and intense that in 2010 the Simon Wiesenthal Center issued a warning advising Jews to take "extreme caution when visiting southern Sweden."

THE VATICAN

The pope was on the list of world leaders whose support Herzl tried to gather. Herzl met with Pope Pius X on February 25, 1904, with the aim of convincing him to support Jewish statehood in the Holy Land. Dismissing Herzl's request, Pius explained why the Catholic Church could not endorse Zionism: "Even though the land of Jerusalem was not always holy, it was sanctified by Jesus Christ. . . . The Jews did not recognize our lord and, therefore, we cannot recognize the Jewish people. . . . The religion of Israel was the basis of our religion, but it was replaced by the New Testament and we cannot grant it recognition."[58]

Once Israel became a reality, the Vatican not only refrained from recognizing the Jewish state, but also tried to depict the new State of Israel as unrelated to the historic Jewish people. The Vatican's daily newspaper *L'Osservatore Romano* observed on May 29, 1948, that "Zionism is not the Israel of the Bible but of the Balfour Declaration, of the 20th century, of the modern secular state."[59]

This theory, however, could not in itself justify the Vatican's refusal to recognize Israel. The Vatican would henceforth explain this refusal with three arguments: (1) the Israeli leadership was mostly socialist and of Russian descent, and therefore Israel was likely to become an ally of Soviet communism; (2) Israel partially controlled Jerusalem (its western neighborhoods), which was supposed to become an international city according to the UN partition plan; and (3) Arab Palestinian refugees should be allowed to return to their homes prior to recognition of Israel. Further, the Vatican presented the Soviet Union's immediate recognition of Israel in 1948 and its supply of weaponry to the new state (see chapter 15) as evidence that Israel was an agent of bolshevism. After the 1949 armistice agreements and the de facto partition of Jerusalem between Israel and Jordan, the Vatican continued to call for the city's internationalization according to the UN partition plan. Indeed, the pope tried—unsuccessfully—to convince

French foreign minister Robert Schuman (a devout Catholic) not to recognize Israel without guarantees on the status of the Christian holy places.[60] The Vatican also tried to convince Catholic countries to vote against Israel's admission to the UN in May 1949 or at least to make Israel's admission conditional on the internationalization of Jerusalem.

The Vatican was in fact instrumental in building a coalition of Catholic states that voted, on December 9, 1949, in favor of a UN General Assembly resolution that called for the internationalization of Jerusalem. In response, Ben-Gurion transferred the Israeli government and the Knesset from Tel Aviv to Jerusalem.

By 1952 the Vatican stopped calling for the internationalization of Jerusalem, realizing after three years of fruitless diplomatic efforts that the post-1949 status quo was here to stay.

Relations between Israel and the Vatican improved under Pope John XXIII (1958–63), who convened the Second Vatican Council. The council's deliberations eventually produced the 1965 declaration known as *Nostra Aetate*, which absolved Jews of the collective responsibility for killing Jesus. Significantly, *Nostra Aetate* also stated, albeit non-explicitly, that God does not revoke divine promises — the implication being that the Holy Land is still promised to the Jews.

Despite the PLO's central role in the Lebanese civil war (1975–90), which posed a threat to Lebanon's Christians, contacts were established between the PLO and the Vatican. Cardinal Paolo Bertoli met with Yasser Arafat in Beirut in November 1975. In June 1976 the Vatican voted in favor of the final declaration of the UN's "Habitat Conference" in Vancouver, which drew a parallel between Zionism and racism.[61]

A turning point in the Vatican's policy toward Israel was the election of Pope John Paul II in 1978. John Paul II grew up in Poland as Karol Józef Wojtyła, where he had witnessed the Holocaust and lost many of his Jewish friends. Right after World War II, a Catholic couple solicited his advice on what to do about two Jewish children they had hidden during the war. The children's parents had died in Auschwitz, and

their Catholic adoptive parents wanted to know if they should baptize
them and raise them as Christians. "No way. Do not baptize them,"
Priest Wojtyła told them. "They were handed to you as Jews and they
must remain Jewish. You must raise them as Jews."[62] John Paul II was
the first pope to pay an official visit to the Great Synagogue of Rome,
in 1986. There, he called the Jews the "elder brothers" of the church.

Despite John Paul II's more favorable attitude toward the Jews, however, his Middle East policy was not devoid of paradoxes. For example,
John Paul II met Arafat at the Vatican on September 15, 1982, the day
after the assassination of Lebanon's Christian president-elect Bachir
Gemayel, thereby dismaying both Israelis and Lebanese Christians.

In 1986 the pope announced in private conversations that he had
decided to establish diplomatic relations with Israel. The outbreak
of the first intifada in December 1987, however, convinced him to
push off his decision. With the Madrid Peace Conference of October
1991, John Paul II decided to renew discussions with Israel for the
establishment of diplomatic relations. U.S. president George H. W.
Bush encouraged him to officially recognize Israel. In December 1993
Israel and the Vatican signed an agreement that dealt mostly with the
church's property rights in Israel. Full diplomatic relations between
the two countries were established in June 1994.

Israel and the European Union

Today's European Union (EU) was preceded by the European Coal
and Steel Community (ECSC, established in 1951) and by the European
Economic Community (EEC, established in 1957). In 1964 the EEC and
Israel signed a trade agreement that cut tariffs on Israeli exports.
In May 1975 this trade agreement was significantly expanded into a
free-trade zone for industrial products between the EEC and Israel:
European tariffs on Israeli agricultural exports were cut by 85 per-

cent, and capital investments as well as cooperation in research and development were encouraged.

The 1975 agreement was a major diplomatic and economic achievement for Israel's foreign minister Yigal Allon. As explained by veteran Israeli diplomat Gideon Rafael, "Allon recognized the damage caused to Israel by the erosion of its European relations. He devoted considerable personal efforts to stemming the tide. Unlike Prime Minister Rabin, who since the Yom Kippur War had written off Europe as a significant factor in world affairs, Allon realized that Israel's position in Europe had a direct bearing on its economic and political fortunes."[63]

The agreement was signed despite political tensions between Israel and the EEC. Those relations had been strained by the oil embargo, which made European governments more supportive of Arab demands and more critical of Israel. During the 1973 Yom Kippur War, the nine EEC governments had rejected an official U.S. request to allow an American airlift en route to Israel to land on European territory. When Israel and Egypt signed the Camp David Agreements, France criticized the 1978 agreements for not including the PLO—and convinced its EEC partners to adopt a common resolution calling upon Israel and the United States to add the PLO to future peace negotiations. The EEC eventually adopted such a resolution in 1980, in Venice (the Venice Declaration), which openly advocated inclusion of the PLO in future negotiations.

France had leveraged the oil embargo imposed by the Arab states after the 1973 Yom Kippur War to convince its EEC partners to sign the declaration. Before the 1973 oil embargo, European countries sympathetic to Israel (such as Holland and West Germany) were unwilling to add their voices to France's Middle East policies. After 1973, when Arab oil exporters threatened not to sell oil to countries supportive of Israel, France's Middle East policy could count on EEC acquiescence and support.

The fact that the EEC and Israel signed a free trade agreement in 1975 can seem paradoxical in light of the political gap that widened with the oil embargo. Yet by then EEC members had secured their oil supplies, and their statements on the Middle East were consistently critical of Israel. Signing a free trade agreement was beneficial to both the EEC and to Israel, and since the agreement did not apply to the disputed territories of the West Bank, Gaza, East Jerusalem, Sinai, and the Golan Heights, the Arab world did not view it as a "provocation."

It took precisely another twenty years, until 1995, for the EU to update and further upgrade its 1975 free trade agreement with Israel. The 1993 Oslo Agreement convinced the EU to be forthcoming toward Israel. And thanks to the 1995 agreement, Israel became the first non-European country to join the prestigious Framework Programme for research and development in 1996.[64]

Although the Oslo Agreements had originally been brokered by Norway (a European country, though not an EU member), negotiations between Israel and the PLO were coordinated by the United States after the signature ceremony of the Declaration of Principles in September 1993. While the EU insisted on playing a role in the Israeli-Palestinian negotiations, its diplomatic credibility had been seriously affected by its failure in handling the Yugoslavian civil war. Yitzhak Rabin wondered aloud why the EU thought it could be so helpful in the Middle East when it was so helpless in Europe itself: "The Europeans are volunteering to participate in peace processes all over the world, and when there is trouble at their doorstep, where are they?"[65]

While for many years political differences did not significantly affect the deepening of economic ties between Israel and the EEC or EU, in more recent years the EU has been challenging the decoupling of political disagreements and economic cooperation. Since the Amsterdam Treaty of 1997 (which came into force in 1999), the EU has had a High Representative for Foreign Affairs and Security Policy (whose powers and role were finalized with the Lisbon Treaty of 2009). Even though EU members still conduct their own foreign policies, and they remain divided on many foreign policy issues, they are at least trying to adopt a common policy on major international issues, and the High Representative is supposed to represent and defend that policy.

In recent years, the EU has largely been speaking in a unified voice on the question of Israeli settlements. There is a clear tendency to ensure that trade and scientific agreements between Israel and the EU do not apply beyond the armistice lines of 1949. In 2013 the Horizon 2020 agreement on research and development between Israel and the EU was only signed after Israel agreed to exclude from the agreement Israeli companies that operate beyond the green line. In November 2015 the European Commission instructed member states to label Israeli products manufactured or produced outside of the green line (those products can still be sold in Europe, but they cannot benefit from the EU-Israel trade agreement). Israel has an economic interest in maintaining its trade relations with the EU (Israel's first trade partner), and the EU has an interest in maintaining Israel's participation in Europe's research and development programs (because of Israel's technological expertise).

At the same time, Israel has been able to offset the European Commission's Middle East policy by upgrading its relations with the EU's "rebellious" governments of Eastern Europe. In July 2017 Prime Minister Netanyahu attended the Budapest summit of the Visegrád Group, a political alliance between Poland, Hungary, the Czech Republic, and Slovakia, which (along with other Eastern European governments) openly challenge traditional EU policies on the Middle East. In 2018, for example, the Czech Republic, Hungary, and Romania blocked an EU decision meant to condemn the transfer of the U.S. embassy to Jerusalem. The Czech president and the Romanian prime minister have both expressed support for the transfer of their countries' embassies to Jerusalem. When Prime Minister Netanyahu made an official visit to Lithuania in August 2018, addressing the transfer issue as well as Israel's perspective on the Iran nuclear agreement, Lithuania's prime minister declared, "Lithuania really has a better understanding of Israel and that understanding could be spread among other EU countries."[66]

For Israel, the governments of Eastern Europe have become useful and ad hoc counterweights to unwelcome EU votes. Its special ties with the governments of Eastern Europe have enabled Israel to use "divide and rule" tactics in the EU, thereby ruling out an EU consensus, led by Brussels, that would have condemned American decisions to transfer the U.S. embassy to Jerusalem and pull out from the nuclear agreement. The Visegrád Group is also making it harder for the EU to bypass the renewed U.S. sanctions on Iran.

Still, populist governments do have downsides. Many of them oppose free trade and are more inclined to align with Russia than with the United States. Since the EU is Israel's first trade partner and Israel is a U.S. ally, Israel would not benefit from a Europe dominated by pro-Russian mercantilists. But ad hoc and calculated links with the governments of Eastern Europe do serve Israel's national interests for the time being.

Israel has also seen improved relations with Greece and Italy as a by-product of its emergence as an energy exporter. Israel's November 2018 memorandum of understanding with Cyprus, Greece, and Italy to build a pipeline shall enable Israel to export its natural gas to Europe.

Some commentators and politicians have suggested that Israel should become a formal member of the EU.[67] The prospect of a full Israeli membership is highly unlikely, however, and would be counterproductive. Israel is not a European country. Even if it were, full EU membership would hardly serve its interests. Indeed, not all European countries are EU members, because they do not think that full membership would best serve their interests. Norway, Switzerland, and Lichtenstein never joined, and Britain left in 2020. These countries have their own association and trade agreements with the EU (as

Israel does). As a small country, Israel's influence would be completely diluted in EU decision-making. Full EU membership also entails the predominance of European law over domestic law, and laws related to Israel's Jewishness (such as the law of return or the status of religious courts in the realm of family law) might be deemed incompatible with EU law. There is also the issue of free movement of EU citizens among member states (within the Schengen area). Add to this list Europe's growing Muslim population and the radicalization of some European Muslims, and full Israeli membership is unrealistic.

While Europe's growing Muslim population casts doubts on long-term prospects for Israel's relations with Europe, the 2008 financial crash, mass immigration, and ISIS-claimed terrorist attacks in Europe have contributed to new intelligence and military partnerships between the Old Continent and the Jewish state. Since 2015, Israel's military sales to Europe have grown significantly to over $1.5 billion a year.[68] Rising, meanwhile, are governments set on reclaiming full sovereignty over economic and immigration policies (in Poland, Hungary, Austria, Italy, and Greece) as well as parties such as Alternative for Germany and Marine Le Pen's National Rally in France — governments and parties that largely view Israel favorably for its economic, defense, and anti-terrorism achievements.

Conclusion

Theodor Herzl wrote *Der Judenstaat*, the Zionist manifesto, in Paris. He sought support for the establishment of a Jewish state among European leaders. The League of Nations granted a European country, Great Britain, the mandate to establish a Jewish national home in Palestine. Israel fought its war of independence with weapons bought in Europe (from Czechoslovakia). After independence, Israel's only military and diplomatic ally was European (France), and so was its main source of financial support (Germany). Over the years, however, relations between Israel and Europe often soured and became increasingly complex.

The friendly relationship between Israel and France had developed into an alliance in the mid-1950s because of Nasser's support for the Algerian nationalists. With de Gaulle's return to power in 1958 and the end of the Algerian War in 1962, France lost interest in Israel. The 1967 Six-Day War sealed the divorce between the two nations. With Britain, by contrast, relations improved in the 1960s because Israel turned out to be a useful and discreet partner to help pro-British forces in Yemen and Oman. As for relations with (West) Germany, they were overshadowed by the scars of recent history, as well as collaborations between German scientists and Egypt in the 1950s. Yet pragmatism eventually prevailed: Israel and Germany signed a reparations agreement, established full diplomatic relations, and became military partners. And with the establishment of the EEC in 1957, Israel's relations with Europe acquired a new, and multilateral, dimension.

After the 1973 Yom Kippur War and the ensuing oil embargo, the EEC started demanding from Israel a total withdrawal to the pre-1967 lines. In 1980 the EEC officially backed the PLO, which had just been sidelined by the U.S.-brokered Camp David Agreements. Despite political disagreements between the EEC and Israel, trade and research ties were maintained and even expanded. In recent years, however, the EU (the EEC's successor) has excluded the West Bank and the Golan Heights from all EU-Israel trade and science agreements. Israel has been able to break the EU consensus over issues such as the nuclear deal with Iran and the transfer of embassies to Jerusalem by developing special ties with member states that also resent Brussels, such as Greece, Hungary, Poland, the Czech and Slovak republics, and Lithuania. Israel, moreover, is increasingly leveraging its assets vis-à-vis Europe, especially its expertise in counterterrorism, its technological edge, and its natural gas resources.

14. The American Alliance

RICHARD NIXON: "We both have a Jewish foreign minister
[Henry Kissinger and Abba Eban]."
GOLDA MEIR: "Yes, but mine speaks English without an accent."

From Diplomatic Liability to Strategic Asset

Franklin D. Roosevelt was not in favor of the creation of a Jewish state. David Niles, who served the FDR administration as an advisor on ethnic issues and unofficial liaison to the Jewish community, wrote that Israel would not have been established had Roosevelt been in power during the critical postwar years (Roosevelt died on April 12, 1945). Roosevelt emerged from his meeting with Saudi king Ibn Saud on February 14, 1945, declaring that "I learnt more about the Middle East in a single hour with Ibn Saud than in all previous years."[1]

Roosevelt was not alone in his hostility to an independent Jewish state. When the UN partition plan was brought to a vote at the General Assembly on November 29, 1947, American oil companies, dependent on Middle Eastern oil fields, lobbied desperately for anti-partition votes.[2] The military and foreign policy establishment in Washington (the State Department, the Pentagon, and the CIA) were not in favor of the partition plan: now that the Cold War had begun, the United States and the Soviet Union were competing over influence and allegiances in the Middle East and in the world. Secretary of Defense James Forrestal proclaimed, "No group in this country should be permitted to influence our policy to the point where it could endanger our national security."[3] Secretary of State George Marshall, too, voiced opposition to the UN partition plan. Marshall, and most of the State Department, were in favor of prolonging British rule under a United Nations trusteeship. As Marshall explained to Harry Truman (who succeeded Roosevelt), recognizing a Jewish state would alienate the Arab world. Yet Truman decided to make a personal decision against the advice of his foreign policy and defense advisors.

His decision was influenced by his old friend Edward Jacobson. Truman and Jacobson (a Jew whose family had immigrated from Lithuania to Kansas City) had become close while serving together in the army during World War I. After the war, the two opened a business that went bankrupt during the Depression. They remained close friends, and when Truman became president, Jacobson had an open door to the Oval Office.

Jacobson played a critical role in convincing Truman to back the UN partition plan and to recognize Israel. Truman had become so irritated by Zionist lobbyists that he had given instructions not to let them into the White House. This decree applied to all, Chaim Weizmann included. This is when Jacobson intervened and told Truman, "Your hero is Andrew Jackson. I have a hero too. He's the greatest Jew alive. I'm talking about Chaim Weizmann. He's an old man and very sick, and he has traveled thousands of miles to see you. And now you're putting him off. This isn't like you, Harry." Truman replied, "You baldheaded son-of-a-bitch. You win. I'll see him."[4]

The November 19, 1947, meeting with Weizmann lasted for about two hours, and at the end Truman promised his support. Truman would later vividly describe how he acted against State Department will on the question of Palestine:

> Those State Department fellows were always trying to put it over on me about Palestine, telling me that I really didn't understand

what was going on there, and that I ought to leave it to the experts. Some were anti-Semitic, I'm sorry to say. Dealing with them was as rough as a cob. The last thing they wanted was American recognition of Jewish statehood. I had my own thoughts and doubts, too. But I'd made my commitment to Dr. Weizmann. And my attitude was that as long as I was president, I'd see to it that I was the one who made policy, not the second or third echelons at the State Department. So, on the day the Jewish State was declared, I gave those officials about thirty minutes notice what I intended to do, no more, so that they couldn't throw a spanner into the works. And then, exactly eleven minutes after the proclamation of independence, I had my Press Secretary, Charlie Ross, issue the announcement that the United States recognized Israel de facto.[5]

Among the issues discussed by Truman and Weizmann during their fateful meeting was the Negev desert. In early November 1947, the State Department (having been lobbied by the British government) had asked the Jewish Agency to abandon claims over the southern Negev. American representatives at the UN were even hinting that without this concession, they would abandon their support for the partition plan. Weizmann explained to Truman that the Arab states already had access to the Red Sea via Transjordan, Egypt, and Saudi Arabia. The Jewish state also needed such access as a gateway to Africa and Asia. Truman gave his consent and again imposed his will on his recalcitrant diplomats.

Yet the State Department tried to undo the president's decision. In March 1948 U.S. ambassador to the UN Warren Austin suggested the establishment of a trusteeship over Palestine instead of partition, and U.S. secretary of state George Marshall warned Britain not to end its mandate on May 15. As Abba Eban explained, "By early May [1948], Britain was 'only' attempting to diminish the size of the Jewish state, whereas the United States was still attempting to prevent the state from even coming into existence."[6] Marshall also warned Moshe Sharett (who managed the *Yishuv*'s foreign relations prior to independence) that if the Jews went ahead with their declaration of independence on May 15, 1948, the United States would not assist the Jewish state militarily. Marshall proved true to his word. Despite Truman's decision to recognize Israel in May 1948, the United States imposed a military embargo on Israel during its War of Independence.

Marshall was unswerving in his attacks on the Jews. Shortly after Israel had declared independence, a meeting in the president's office to discuss recognition turned into a bitter argument, with Marshall reportedly shouting, "They don't deserve a state, they have stolen that country! If you give this recognition, Mr. President, I may not vote for you in the next election!"[7] Even after the assassination of UN mediator Count Folke Bernadotte in September 1948, Marshall continued to advocate Bernadotte's idea of removing the Negev desert from Israel's territory.

Other Truman critics viewed his choice to recognize Israel as a zero-sum game in which Truman had been unduly influenced to uphold Jewish national aspirations at the cost of American interests. Dean Acheson, Truman's secretary of state between 1949 and 1953, wrote, "From Justice Brandeis, whom I revered, and from Felix Frankfurter, my intimate friend, I have learned to understand but not to share the mystical emotion of the Jews to return to Palestine and end the diaspora. In urging Zionism as an American government policy, they had allowed, so I thought, their emotion to obscure the totality of American interests."[8]

The State Department did not consider the 1949 armistice lines to be legitimate and final borders. It called for Israel's return to the 1947 partition lines and denied Israel's right to territorial gains after the war (it was willing, at most, to consider agreed-upon land swaps). The

State Department also demanded that Israel repatriate at least half of the seven hundred thousand Palestinian refugees from the 1948 war.[9]

When Dwight Eisenhower became president in 1953, his administration tried to undo the "damages" they deemed the Truman administration had caused in the Arab world. Many in the administration thought that U.S. recognition of Israel had alienated the Arab states and helped the Soviet Union make progress in the Middle East. The U.S. embassy in Amman urged the Eisenhower administration to extort from Israel territorial concessions (i.e., a compromise between the 1947 partition plan and the 1949 armistice lines), the repatriation and/or compensation of Palestinian refugees, and the internationalization of Jerusalem.[10] Other American ambassadors throughout the Arab world warned the White House and the State Department that U.S. support for Israel would throw Arab countries into the arms of the Soviet Union.[11] Henry Byroade, the assistant secretary of state for the Middle East, South Asia, and Africa, told Israel to accept territorial concessions, since it had conquered territories beyond the UN partition plan.[12] In 1953 the Eisenhower administration strongly opposed Jewish immigration from the Soviet Union, claiming that such immigration would alienate the Arabs and would not be economically sustainable.[13]

The Eisenhower administration amply demonstrated its "more balanced approach" on at least two occasions: during the crisis of the Bnot Yaakov Bridge in 1953, and in the wake of the Suez Crisis in 1956. The first crisis resulted from a water conflict between Israel and Syria. Israel had chosen the site known as Bnot Yaakov Bridge as a water intake for Israel's national water carrier. Syria opposed Israel's decision, claiming it breached the armistice agreements of 1949, since the bridge was in the demilitarized zone between Israel and Syria. When Syria brought its claim against Israel to the UN Security Council, the U.S. government sided with Syria. As for the Suez Crisis of 1956, the U.S. government threatened Israel with sanctions and retaliation (including Israel's removal from the UN) were Israel not to pull out from Sinai (see chapter 11).

In addition, the U.S. government pressured Israel into withdrawing from some of the territories it had acquired during its 1948 War of Independence. After U.S. secretary of state John Foster Dulles toured the Middle East in the summer of 1953, he hinted to Israel's ambassador to the United States, Abba Eban, that Israel should offer territorial concessions to Egypt and to Jordan for the sake of reaching a peace agreement. In August 1955 Dulles declared that the boundaries between Israel, Jordan, and Egypt "were fixed by the Armistice Agreements of 1949. They were not designed to be permanent frontiers in every respect."[14] Technically, Dulles was correct. But his statement meant that his government was now trying to buy Egyptian goodwill through Israeli territorial concessions.

In November 1954 the State Department conceived a plan code-named "Alpha." Designed to reach a "settlement" between Israel, Egypt, and Jordan, the Alpha Plan called for some Israeli territorial withdrawals from the 1949 armistice lines so as to increase the size of the West Bank—to Jordan's benefit—and also create a corridor between Egypt and Jordan in the southern Negev (see chapter 9, map 11, for the Alpha Plan map). Israel was also expected to accept seventy-five thousand Palestinian refugees and to let Jordan use its port of Haifa. As for Egypt, it was supposed to open the Suez Canal to Israeli shipping. In addition, both Egypt and Jordan were expected to end the boycott of Israel.[15] The Alpha Plan, however, was shelved in 1955 because Nasser asked for the entire Negev south of Beersheba, not only the small corridor the Americans had suggested.[16]

Despite the Eisenhower administration's appeasement policy, Egypt announced in September 1955 a military alliance with the Soviet Union (via Czechoslovakia). Since the Soviets now had a foothold in Egypt, Abba Eban tried to convince the Eisenhower administration to sell weapons to Israel, but the administration decided that supporting

Israel was "not essential."[17] Eban would subsequently accuse the Eisenhower administration of indirectly catalyzing the 1956 Suez War by refusing to compensate Israel for the Soviet armament of Egypt: "If anyone could have prevented Israel's Sinai War, it was the United States. . . . If Eisenhower and Dulles had supplied us with a minimal jet force, there would have been little temptation for us to go to Paris and make common cause with France."[18] After the 1956 war, however, Israel's prime minister Ben-Gurion realized that a declining France could not be a reliable and long-term ally, and he tried to build a strategic relationship with the United States, notwithstanding Eisenhower administration reservations.

Eisenhower seemingly thought that he could halt Soviet advances in the Middle East by brokering an agreement between Israel and Egypt. In January 1956 Eisenhower announced that he was sending his emissary, Robert B. Anderson, to the Middle East to mediate between the two nations. Yet Anderson's three-month mission failed: Nasser was actively backing pro-Soviet rebellions in the Middle East, and Ben-Gurion rejected the proposition that Israel was an occupier in the territories it had conquered beyond the 1947 UN partition plan. Meanwhile, the Soviet Union kept making progress in the Middle East. In November 1956 Syria signed a pact with the Soviet Union. In July 1958 a pro-Nasserist coup in Iraq eliminated the royal family and aligned with the Soviet Union. Nasser was also encouraging rebellion against the Christian government in Lebanon and the Hashemite monarchy in Jordan. America was losing the Middle East. Eisenhower and Dulles's strategy had obviously failed.

After the coup in Iraq, the United States sent marines to Beirut, and the United Kingdom reinforced its military presence in Jordan. American foreign policy toward Israel and the Middle East started to change. From 1958 onward, Abba Eban remarked, Israel was "now being treated not as burden to be chivalrously borne, but as a friend whose cooperation was worthy of respect."[19]

The Eisenhower administration's reassessment of its Israel policy was not unanimously approved in Washington, however. There were still, in fact, two schools of thought about Israel and the Middle East: one saw in Israel an obstacle to U.S. influence in the Middle East; the other believed that since the Arab states would be unstable and unreliable no matter what, the United States had nothing to lose by supporting Israel. By 1958 the second school of thought was gaining in influence, but it was not dominant.[20]

With the new Kennedy administration in 1962, the United States further reassessed its Middle East policy. John F. Kennedy was the first American president who spoke of a "special relationship" between the United States and Israel. He was also the first president to end the military embargo his predecessors had imposed on Israel. Kennedy approved the sale of Hawk missiles to Israel—something Eisenhower had refused to do.

Some historians have claimed that Kennedy allowed the supply of U.S. weaponry to Israel to dissuade it from pursuing its suspected nuclear program, but this does not seem to be backed up by empirical evidence.[21] In any case, the United States failed to block Israel's alleged nuclear program. Israel agreed to American inspections at its French-built nuclear reactor in Dimona, but Israel also kept fooling U.S. inspectors during their visits. President Kennedy was so frustrated by Israel's cat-and-mouse game with U.S. inspectors that he warned Ben-Gurion in the summer of 1963 with a strongly worded letter: "The United States' commitment to Israel would be imperiled . . . were the U.S. government to fail to obtain reliable information on Israel's nuclear activities."[22] Yet Kennedy never took strong practical measures to stop Israel's alleged nuclear program, which became a matter of public speculation on June 14, 1967, with the publication of the *New York Times* article "Israel Said to Plan to Make Atom Bomb."[23]

When Lyndon Johnson became president after Kennedy's assassination in November 1963, he increased America's military supplies to

Israel in response to the strengthening of military relations between the Soviet Union and Egypt (in June 1963, the Soviet Union and Egypt had signed an additional $500 million military deal). In December 1963 the Pentagon wrote that previous U.S. policies in the Middle East had not prevented the flow of Soviet weaponry to Egypt, Syria, and Iraq, and therefore U.S. military supplies to Israel were now justified.[24]

Nasser became so involved in supporting anti-American forces in the Middle East (especially in Yemen, from 1962 onward) that the United States decided to sever its diplomatic relations with Egypt in 1965. It was in this context that Israel's prime minister, Levi Eshkol, paid an official visit to the United States in June 1964. Eshkol was the first Israeli prime minster to be officially invited to the White House.

During Eshkol's visit to the United States, President Johnson invited him to tour his Texas ranch. The Israeli diplomat Yehuda Avner, who was also present, wrote of that experience in his book *The Prime Ministers*, "The President . . . gunned his vehicle down rutted dirt tracks, causing us to bounce crazily about. As we approached one particular pasture, a cluster of cows bolted in alarm at the sight of us, leaving just one cow that stubbornly refused to move. The president honked his horn and nudged it with his vehicle's fender until it, too, skedaddled. 'That's Daisy,' Johnson roared with laughter. 'She's as pigheaded as a Texan senator with colic.' Holding firmly onto his homburg for fear it might fly off, Eshkol looked inquiringly at Dr. Herzog, and above the growl of the engine, asked, *'Vus rett der goy?'* —Yiddish for 'What's the goy talking about?'"[25]

For Israel, Eshkol's visit to the United States was timely, since the alliance with France was by now reaching its limits. In 1965 the United States decided to supply Israel with advanced weapons while cutting down its wheat supplies to Egypt. By the time the Six-Day War erupted in June 1967, Israel and the United States had become allies. In September 1969 the first U.S. Phantom fighter jets arrived in Israel. France was no longer selling Israel its Dassault-made jets, due to the embargo de Gaulle had imposed; thus the transition in the Israeli Air Force from French fighter jets to American ones had begun. Johnson would also eventually abandon his demand that Israel sign the nuclear nonproliferation treaty as a condition for their supply.

An Alliance Reassessed

Richard Nixon became president in 1969, the year of the pro-Soviet coup in Libya. This major event was a reminder of the danger of Soviet expansionism in North Africa and in the Middle East. While Nixon maintained the alliance with Israel, there were two opposing approaches in his administration regarding the Arab-Israeli conflict. Secretary of State William Rogers blamed the Arab-Israeli conflict for Soviet involvement in the Middle East, while National Security Advisor Henry Kissinger blamed Soviet involvement in the Middle East for the continuation of the Arab-Israeli conflict. For Rogers, solving the Arab-Israeli conflict would reduce the Arab temptation to invite Soviet influence into the Middle East. The Rogers Plan (made official in December 1969) called for an Israeli withdrawal to the 1967 lines (including in the West Bank), but only in exchange for some "commitment to peace." Countering this plan, Kissinger contended that in order to improve the chances of reaching an agreement between Israel and its Arab neighbors, the United States first had to reduce Soviet influence in the Middle East. This could be achieved, Kissinger argued, by convincing Arab states such as Egypt that they would only recover their land via U.S. pressures on Israel and not via Soviet weaponry.[26] Unlike Rogers, Kissinger wanted to make Israeli concession concomitant to a reduced Soviet influence in the Middle East.

The September 1970 war between Jordan and the PLO (also known as Black September) was a reminder of the Middle East's Cold War polarization: the United States and Israel backed Jordan, while the Soviet Union and Syria supported the PLO. President Nixon personally thanked Israeli prime minister Golda Meir for Israel's key role in helping King Hussein thwart the Soviet-backed Syrian takeover of his kingdom.[27] The 1970 crisis in Jordan tended to confirm Kissinger's analysis that Soviet influence was a major obstacle to Middle East peace, and Kissinger gained the upper hand when he replaced Rogers as secretary of state in September 1973. Within two weeks of Kissinger's swearing in, the Yom Kippur War broke out, and the Middle East was ablaze.

The Yom Kippur War was a regional and international watershed that modified the United States' attitude to the Middle East and to Israel. Until the Yom Kippur War, U.S. diplomacy was mostly focused on ending the war in Vietnam, on negotiating arms control agreements with the Soviet Union, and on establishing relations with Communist China. The Yom Kippur War was a painful reminder of how deeply U.S. interests could be affected by the Middle East conflict. The war turned into a proxy conflict between the two superpowers: both the United States and the Soviet Union supplied their Middle East allies during the war, and both put their own forces on high alert. The war also generated an oil embargo that skyrocketed oil prices, thus disrupting the world economy and vital U.S. economic interests.

In fact, most of America's assumptions on the Middle East were challenged by the Yom Kippur War. The United States had presumed that Israel's military superiority would deter any Arab attack, that the Arab states would not use their oil cartel as a tool for political extortion, and that Soviet influence was in decline. Yet all these assumptions were proved wrong.

After the war, Egyptian president Anwar Sadat fully understood that Israel could be dealt a blow but could not be defeated militarily. He was therefore willing to explore the diplomatic option via the United States, which might be more useful to Egypt than the military alliance with the Soviet Union. For the sake of recuperating the Sinai Peninsula, Sadat was willing to switch Egypt's Cold War alliance from the Soviet Union to the United States. But he wanted to be certain the United States could deliver.

A master of realpolitik, Kissinger needed no further explanation. The October 24, 1973, ceasefire agreement between Israel and Egypt had left Israeli troops on the western shore of the Suez Canal. Sadat wanted an additional agreement that would involve a significant Israeli withdrawal from the Sinai Peninsula. While Israeli prime minister Yitzhak Rabin was willing to cooperate with Kissinger in order to pull Egypt out of the Soviet sphere of influence, he was not willing to pay the territorial price demanded by Sadat and acquiesced to by Kissinger. Yet this is what Rabin ended up accepting under the pressure of President Gerald Ford (who had replaced Nixon after the latter's resignation in August 1974). Ford even threatened to "reassess" the U.S.-Israel relationship if Israel were to reject the U.S. demand for an Israeli redeployment in the Sinai Peninsula.

Ford and Kissinger were determined to impose a second disengagement agreement on Israel because they were convinced that the United States needed to (at least partially) end the oil embargo. In addition, the United States was encountering major international setbacks—Turkey's invasion of Northern Cyprus in 1974; Communist North Vietnam's invasion of South Vietnam in 1975, and the corresponding collapse of the Vietnam peace accords—and Kissinger thought he had to prove to Sadat that America could deliver.

Israel and Egypt signed the "Sinai 2" agreement in September 1975. Egypt regained full control of the Suez Canal, the Gidi and Milta Passes, and the Abu Rudeis oil fields. A UN-supervised buffer zone was established between the two countries.

Rabin had been coerced into the 1975 interim agreement with Egypt, but at least he shared Kissinger's objective and subscribed to his strategy. With the election of Jimmy Carter in November 1976, however, Kissinger's realpolitik was replaced by a different approach. Unlike his predecessors, Carter was willing to engage the Soviet Union, including in the Middle East. In addition, Carter's approach to foreign policy was influenced by his religious beliefs and by his commitment to human rights. During his meeting with Yitzhak Rabin at the White House in March 1977, Carter insisted that he considered the Palestinian issue to be one of human rights and that, in his view, negotiating with the PLO was inevitable.[28] This was the first time that a U.S. president called for negotiations between Israel and the PLO. On borders, Carter was of the opinion that Israel should withdraw to the 1949 armistice lines, thus allowing for the establishment of a Palestinian state in the West Bank and the Gaza Strip, with minor territorial changes. Finally, Carter considered the Palestinian issue to be the core source of the Arab-Israeli conflict.

Rabin strongly disagreed with all of Carter's positions and proposals. As he would later write about his encounter with Carter, "I left the United States with the feeling that we were up against a grave problem."[29]

Three months after the Carter-Rabin meeting in Washington, Menachem Begin won the 1977 election and became prime minister of Israel. Carter and Begin's personalities and respective stances could not have been more at odds. Their meeting at the White House in July 1977 was tragicomic. According to Begin's advisor Yehudah Avner, Begin spoke with a lot of pathos about the Holocaust and about the Jews' historical rights in the biblical Land of Israel. Carter had other ideas in mind: the PLO and the 1949 armistice lines. The clash between the two leaders reached a climax as "silence settled on the chamber. The tick of the antique clock on the marble mantelpiece became audible. An eternity seemed to hang between each tick. All the president's men lowered their eyes."[30] When Carter finally asked Begin if he'd be willing to negotiate with the PLO if the PLO were to recognize Israel and fully endorse Resolutions 242 and 338, Begin shouted back, "No! Absolutely No!"[31] Pressed on the recognition issue by U.S. national security advisor Zbigniew Brzezinski, Begin retorted, "The United

States' affirmation of Israel's right to exist is not a favor, nor is it a negotiable concession. I shall not negotiate my existence with anybody, and I need nobody's affirmation of it."[32]

Although Egyptian president Anwar Sadat initiated direct negotiations with Israel, the Carter administration became actively involved in the negotiations, which culminated in the Camp David conference of September 1978. For thirteen days (between September 5 and September 17), the Israeli and Egyptian delegation teams negotiated at Camp David. Jimmy Carter's personal and intensive involvement in the negotiations would prove critical. When the talks reached an impasse on the question of Israeli settlements, Carter decided on a trade-off: Israel would dismantle all its settlements in the Sinai Peninsula (Sadat's demand), but the fate of the West Bank would only be decided in future negotiations (Begin's demand). This trade-off, as well as the pressure Carter exercised on both sides, made the agreement possible.

While the Carter administration was widely credited for the peace agreement, this achievement was overshadowed by three international fiascos for the United States, all of which occurred in 1979: the Islamic revolution in Iran accompanied by the assault on the American embassy in Tehran, the Soviet invasion of Afghanistan, and the Communist coup in Nicaragua. Carter was defeated in the 1980 presidential elections.

By the time Carter left office in January 1981, the Camp David Agreement had been implemented with regard to Egypt, but not with regard to Palestinian autonomy. For Begin, Ronald Reagan's electoral victory was a relief because, unlike Carter, Reagan wanted to defeat the Soviet Union, and he had no intention of engaging with Soviet allies such as the PLO.

Yet Begin overestimated the change. In 1981 the Reagan administration signed a "Memorandum of Understanding on Strategic Cooperation" with Israel, an agreement that established joint military exercises aimed at deterring Soviet threats, but it also sold AWACS fighter jets to Saudi Arabia. Israel was concerned by America's delivery of technologically advanced fighter jets to Saudi Arabia, an Arab country officially at war with Israel. Yet Saudi Arabia was a U.S. ally against the Soviet Union, and thwarting Soviet influence was Reagan's priority. U.S. interests in the Middle East did not rely on Israel alone.

When the United States condemned Israel for annexing the Golan Heights in 1981, Begin summoned the U.S. ambassador, literally yelling at him, "What do you mean the U.S. is considering punishing Israel for annexing the Golan? Are we a vassal state of yours or a banana republic? Or a misbehaved child who deserves spanking?"[33]

The 1982 Lebanon War would genuinely foment tensions between the Reagan administration and the Begin government. On August 12, 1982, Reagan expressed "outrage" over Israel's latest bombing raids in Beirut, saying the attacks had resulted in "needless destruction and bloodshed."[34] The Lebanon War also affected Israel's image in the United States; it was the first Middle East war to be covered by CNN, with devastating effects on Israel's public image.

In September 1982 Reagan announced his administration's peace initiative for the Middle East, declaring, "The departure of the Palestinians from Beirut dramatizes more than ever the homelessness of the Palestinian people. Palestinians feel strongly that their cause is more than a question of refugees. I agree."[35] Because the Reagan announcement hinted at Palestinian statehood, an angry Begin rejected Regan's initiative. Six years later, in the wake of the failed London Agreement and the beginning of the first intifada (see chapter 12), the Reagan administration initiated contacts with the PLO, despite Israel's vocal protest.

At the same time, Reagan was a staunch advocate of the right of Soviet Jews to immigrate to Israel. He broached the issue of Soviet Jewry during his meeting with Gorbachev in Reykjavik in October 1986 and would continue to do so in subsequent discussions with the Soviet leader.[36]

And despite these and other disagreements, the Cold War made Israel an indispensable U.S. ally in the Middle East. Thus, as the Soviet threat withered, so did Israel's strategic importance. Hence was the Bush administration (1989–93) less forgiving toward Israel. When, in 1990 Israeli prime minister Yitzhak Shamir formed a narrow right-wing coalition, U.S. secretary of state James Baker publicly accused Israel of not wanting peace. In June 1990 Baker told the House of Representative's Foreign Affairs Committee that were Shamir interested in peace, he should call the White House: "I have to tell you that everybody over there should know that the telephone number [of the White House] is 1-202-456-1414. . . . When you're serious about peace, call us."[37]

As the Baker-Shamir relationship was deteriorating, the unexpected happened: Iraq invaded Kuwait in August 1990, and the ensuing Gulf War began in early 1991. Iraq launched thirty-nine Scud missiles at Israel, and all the while the United States requested that Israel not retaliate. The Bush administration feared that an Israeli retaliation would undermine its military coalition that encompassed Arab countries such as Saudi Arabia, Egypt, and Syria—a coalition the United States had painfully built. Going against his own principles and ideology, Shamir decided to accede to the administration's request and not retaliate—an uneasy act of political realism that Shamir described thus in his memoirs: "I can think of nothing that went more against my grain as a Jew and a Zionist, nothing more opposed to the ideology on which my life has been based, than the decision I took in the crisis preceding the Gulf War . . . to ask the people of Israel to accept the burden of restraint in the face of attack."[38]

The Bush administration had been able to build up an international coalition against Iraq, together with Arab states, because it had committed to dealing with the Israeli-Palestinian conflict immediately after the war. Once the war ended, the United States enjoyed a hegemonic status in the Middle East, and the Bush administration was determined to leverage its power.

While the Madrid Peace Conference (October 30–November 1, 1991) was formally co-hosted by the United States and the Soviet Union, it was under U.S. pressure that Israel and the Palestinians agreed to attend. At the same time, Israel asked the U.S. government to sign a guarantee for a $10 billion loan needed to absorb the massive and sudden immigration from the Soviet Union. For its part, the Bush administration asked the Shamir government to commit not to use the loan to build beyond the green line, to freeze settlement constructions, and to "lay aside, once and for all, the unrealistic vision of a Greater Israel."[39] U.S. officials argued that America could not host a Middle East peace conference and, at the same time, allow the pursuit of settlement construction, which U.S. governments had always opposed as a matter of principle. Shamir, however, refused to meet the administration's demand, thus forfeiting the loan guarantee Israel needed.

Israel's Labor Party, which undoubtedly benefited from this crisis and from the bewilderment of many Israeli voters, won the general election of June 1992. A senior aide to Yitzhak Shamir claimed that Labor leader Shimon Peres had asked the Bush administration not to unconditionally agree to the loan guarantee in order to improve the Labor Party's chances in Israel's 1992 elections.[40] Foreign Minister Moshe Arens then accused the Bush administration of "interfering in the Israeli domestic political arena in an undisguised attempt to bring down the democratically elected government of Israel" in order "to further a policy of its own."[41] The tension between the Bush administration and the Shamir government was unprecedented. So was James Baker's decision to bar Benjamin Netanyahu (then serving as deputy foreign minister) from the State Department.[42] At the same time, George Bush had always willingly used his influence as vice president and as president to convince Ethiopian as well as Soviet leaders to let their Jewish citizens emigrate to Israel.

The animosity between George Bush and Yitzhak Shamir was replaced in 1993 by a close friendship between Bill Clinton and Yitzhak

Rabin. While the Oslo Agreements were initially brokered by Norway, they were officially signed in Washington. The Declaration of Principles was originally supposed to be signed in Washington between Israeli foreign minister Shimon Peres and PLO official Mahmoud Abbas (Abu Mazen), but the Clinton administration decided to invite both Rabin and Arafat. Rabin first demurred but then decided to fly to Washington. Arafat flew to Washington on a plane donated by Saddam Hussein. The aircraft was hurriedly repainted with Algerian colors, since Iraqi planes were banned from the United States. President Clinton personally orchestrated the historic handshake between Rabin and Arafat, and he built a unique friendship with Yitzhak Rabin. Clinton, whose eulogy of Rabin (*Shalom haver*—"Goodbye, friend") was heartfelt and memorable, would later describe the announcement of Rabin's assassination as "maybe the worst day I had at the White House."

Bill Clinton's personal involvement in the negotiations between Israel and the Palestinian Authority culminated in the failed Camp David conference of July 2000 (see chapter 12). The defeat was personally humiliating to Clinton. When Arafat called Clinton to wish him well before the end of his presidency, he praised him as a great president—to which Clinton replied, "I'm a colossal failure, and you made me one."[43]

In light of Bill Clinton's Middle East setback, his successor George W. Bush (who took office in January 2001) was not eager to risk his own credibility by brokering the Arab-Israeli conflict. Yet the 9/11 terrorist attacked forced him to deal with this complicated region. Meanwhile, administration officials strongly disagreed about how to handle the Middle East. Secretary of State Colin Powell thought the United States needed to solve the Arab-Israeli conflict in order to tame the Arab world's anti-Americanism. Secretary of Defense Donald Rumsfeld, on the other hand, argued that the United States could not bridge the gap between Israel and the Palestinians without defeating radical Islamism and without neutralizing the Iranian nuclear threat, because in his view the Palestinians were unlikely to make concessions as long as they could rely on Iranian support and might. As then national security advisor Condoleezza Rice would write of the tensions within the Bush administration, "The differences in the administration between the decidedly pro-Israel bent of the White House and the State Department's more traditional pro-Arab view percolated beneath the surface."[44]

The competing views produced a somewhat awkward compromise expressed in President Bush's speech on June 24, 2002. On the one hand, the president explicitly called for the establishment of a Palestinian state. On the other hand, he also declared that the establishment of a Palestinian state had to be preceded by the total democratization of Palestinian society and of its political institutions and by the Palestinians' struggle against terrorism. The establishment of a Palestinian state was now conditional: the Palestinians would have to earn it by fighting terrorism and by building democratic institutions. "The Arabists in the State Department were appalled," recalled Condoleezza Rice.[45] Indeed, this was the dream speech for Israeli prime minister Ariel Sharon, since asking Arafat to fight terrorism was like asking Al Capone to fight the mafia.

Then came the Iraq War in 2003. Just as in 1991 George Bush had convinced Arab countries to join the U.S.-led coalition against Saddam Hussein by committing to a peace initiative on the Israeli-Palestinian conflict immediately following the Gulf War, George W. Bush promised Arab leaders he would undertake a serious effort on the Israeli-Palestinian conflict after the ousting of Saddam Hussein.[46] After the invasion of Iraq and the fall of Saddam Hussein in 2003, Bush did indeed show determination about handling the Israeli-Palestinian conflict. In April 2003 the Bush administration released the final draft of the "Middle East Roadmap for Peace," which called for the establishment of a Palestinian state by 2005. In May 2003 the Israeli government announced its acceptance of the Roadmap, but with preconditions: the establishment of a Palestinian state had to be preceded by a proven Palestinian commitment to an eradication of terrorism and to functioning institutions.

In December 2003, however, Ariel Sharon announced that Israel would unilaterally withdraw from the Gaza Strip and tried to convince the Bush administration to endorse his initiative (for reasons explained in chapter 12). Upon hearing of Sharon's intention to unilaterally withdraw from Gaza, Condoleezza Rice said she was "stunned."[47]

Sharon's successor, Ehud Olmert, had won the 2006 elections on a platform to pursue unilateral withdrawal from most of the West Bank. Yet Olmert's tenure began with a war against Hezbollah in Lebanon—which reminded Israelis of the dangers of unilateralism. Israel had unilaterally withdrawn from southern Lebanon in 2000, Hezbollah had filled the vacuum, and Israel was now paying the price of that policy.

Olmert subsequently abandoned the pursuit of unilateralism and agreed to renew negotiations with the Palestinian Authority in 2007. The negotiations were hosted by the Bush administration in Annapolis, thus bringing President Bush to the point he had wanted to avoid upon his inauguration in January 2001: direct U.S. involvement in the Israeli-Palestinian conflict.

The "Israel Lobby" and the Iranian Nuclear Deal

In December 2006 *The Iraq Study Group Report* was published. Co-chaired by former secretary of state James Baker and by former congressman Lee Hamilton, the report claimed that the United States could not win the war in Iraq and preserve its interests in the Middle East without solving the Arab-Israeli conflict. In August 2007 two American scholars, John Mersheimer and Stephen Walt, published *The Israel Lobby and U.S. Foreign Policy*, a book that accused the American Israel Public Affairs Committee (AIPAC) of having excessive and damaging influence on U.S. foreign policy. This accusation was somewhat reminiscent of the Eisenhower administration's allegation back in 1953: U.S. foreign policy had to defend the national interest and could not let itself be influenced by the pro-Israel lobby.

While President Barack Obama (who assumed office in 2009) did not necessarily subscribe to the Mersheimer-Walt theory, he did adopt a more critical approach to Israel and its policies. Obama believed that full U.S. support made Israel less peace-prone and that throwing "daylight" on the relationship would contribute to peace. Aiming to reset America's relations with the Arab world, he spoke in Cairo in June 2009, calling for improved understanding between the West and Islam and reaffirming his administration's commitment to Palestinian statehood. Soon, however, the Arab world unraveled; what seemingly started as an "Arab Spring" in January 2011 turned into a general implosion of Arab states and to the expansion of the Islamic State in Iraq and in Syria.

During his second term in office (2013–17), President Obama focused on reining in Iran's nuclear ambitions through diplomacy. His administration initiated negotiations for a nuclear deal with Iran. Meanwhile, Israel's prime minister Benjamin Netanyahu vociferously criticized the planned Iran deal, based on three arguments: (1) the agreement did not block Iran's path to the nuclear bomb, but only bought time by pushing off by ten years Iran's "break-out time" (i.e., its ability to acquire a nuclear weapon); (2) the agreement did not curb Iran's development of long-range missiles; and (3) the agreement did not curb Iran's support for terrorist militias throughout the Middle East. In March 2015 Netanyahu openly made his case before the two houses of Congress. "Why should Iran's radical regime change for the better," Netanyahu asked, "when it can enjoy the best of both worlds: aggression abroad, prosperity at home?" That an Israeli prime minister addressed Congress to criticize the president's policy was unprecedented, and the Obama administration perceived it as an affront. At the same time, Netanyahu failed to convince two-thirds of Congress to block the deal Obama had negotiated. The Iran nuclear deal was signed on July 14, 2015.

A year and a half later, in December 2016, the Obama administration did not veto UN Security Council Resolution 2334 (see chapter 12). This resolution constituted a serious drawback for Israel, as it undermined the flexibility of the earlier Resolution 242 by denying the legitimacy and legality of any Israeli sovereignty beyond the 1949 armistice line.

Unsurprisingly, Israel was relieved by the change of guard at the White House in January 2017. President Donald Trump made three dramatic decisions that were warmly welcomed by the Israeli government: in May 2018 he announced the transfer of the U.S. embassy from Tel Aviv to Jerusalem, as well as the U.S. withdrawal from the Iran nuclear deal, and in March 2019 he recognized Israel's sovereignty over the Golan Heights.

Despite ups and downs, over the last five decades the U.S.-Israel relationship has largely been stable in two areas: military aid and public opinion. Each year the United States provides Israel with financial assistance of $3 billion, three-quarters of which must be spent on U.S. military equipment and services. As valuable as this is to Israel's economy, the assistance also benefits the American military industry and helps the United States improve its defense capabilities in the Middle East. Another constant in U.S.-Israel relations is the support of public opinion. A Gallup poll published in March 2018 found that 74 percent of Americans have a favorable opinion of Israel—the highest figure since the early 1990s. This favorable opinion is higher among Republicans (83 percent) than among Democrats (64 percent). According to the poll report, "Republicans have consistently shown greater support than Democrats for Israel, partly because of conservative Christians' beliefs about the biblical significance of Israel."[48] The poll also found that two-thirds of Americans sympathize more with Israel than with the Palestinians.

Conclusion

President Truman decided to support partition and to recognize Israel in 1948 despite the State Department and the oil lobby. The Eisenhower administration (1953–61) was so eager to prevent Arab defections to the Soviet Union that it sided with Syria in 1953, pressured Israel into territorial concessions in 1955, condemned Israel in 1956, and refused to sell weapons to Israel. Despite this policy, the Soviet Union did acquire new allies in the Middle East. President Kennedy subsequently reassessed U.S. foreign policy in the Middle East and allowed minor arms sales to Israel. Under President Johnson, the United States and Israel became de facto allies. The alliance with Israel proved valuable in 1970, when Israel helped the United States prevent pro-Soviet forces from overthrowing the Jordanian monarchy.

But the 1973 Yom Kippur War and the ensuing oil embargo induced the United States to pressure Israel into making concessions to Egypt. Israel was both an asset and a burden to the United States: an asset because it countered Soviet influence in the Middle East, a burden because the unsolved Arab-Israeli conflict nurtured Arab resentment of the United States.

With the end of the Cold War, the United States was more willing and more able to extract concessions from Israel. Yet, despite those concessions, the 2000 Camp David summit failed, and peace was not achieved. The Obama administration's signing of a nuclear agreement with Iran instigated tensions with the Israeli government, and the U.S. decision not to veto UN Security Council Resolution 2334 was a serious blow for Israel. By contrast, the Israeli government warmly welcomed President Trump's decisions to transfer the U.S. embassy to Jerusalem, to leave the nuclear deal with Iran, and to recognize Israel's sovereignty over the Golan Heights.

15. The Russian Enigma

> The struggle which is now beginning between the
> Zionist and Bolshevik Jews is little less than a strug-
> gle for the soul of the Jewish people.
>
> WINSTON CHURCHILL

Stalin's Gamble

Relations between Israel and Russia were overshadowed from day one
by the ideological incompatibility between Zionism and Marxism-
Leninism. In the year 1917 the British government issued a charter for
Jewish national self-determination (the Balfour Declaration), and a
Communist revolution swept Russia. Both were competing solutions
to "the Jewish problem": national self-determination for the former;
the replacement of nationalism by communism for the latter.

Considering the large number of Jews involved in the Bolshevik
revolution, the contradiction between Zionism and bolshevism could
not go unnoticed. In February 1920 Winston Churchill published an
article titled "Zionism versus Bolshevism," which praised the Jews as
"the most formidable and the most remarkable race which has ever
appeared in the world" and credited them for "a system of ethics
which, even if it were entirely separated from the supernatural, would
be incomparably the most precious possession of mankind, worth in
fact the fruits of all other wisdom and learning put together."[1] At the
same time, however, Churchill pointed out that many Jews were to be

blamed for the conception and spread of communism, a "system of morals and philosophy as malevolent as Christianity was benevolent." Churchill strongly condemned the disproportionate role atheistic and anti-nationalist Jews had played in the Bolshevik revolution all the while he praised the efforts of other Jews to reclaim their identity and rights as a nation. Hence, Churchill understood that the struggle between Zionism and Marxism was not only an ideological battle, but also an inter-Jewish feud—and hence his support for Zionism:

> Zionism has already become a factor in the political convulsions of Russia, as a powerful competing influence in Bolshevik circles with the international communistic system. Nothing could be more significant than the fury with which Trotsky has attacked the Zionists generally, and Dr. Weizmann in particular. The cruel penetration of his mind leaves him in no doubt that his schemes of a world-wide communistic State under Jewish domination are directly thwarted and hindered by this new ideal, which directs the energies and the hopes of Jews in every land towards a simpler, a truer, and a far more attainable goal. The struggle which is now beginning between the Zionist and Bolshevik Jews is little less than a struggle for the soul of the Jewish people.[2]

As Churchill correctly noticed, the fiercest opposition to Zionism came from Jewish Bolsheviks. Leon Trotsky (aka Lev Bronstein) was an internationalist who wanted a worldwide socialist revolution. Joseph Stalin, on the other hand, was a Russian nationalist (even though he was Georgian) who wanted "socialism in one country." Stalin eventually sidelined Trotsky and had him exiled (in 1929) and assassinated (in 1940). In his November 7, 1941, war speech, Stalin evoked Russian national history and even figures of the Orthodox church. He praised "our glorious motherland" and extolled ancient Russian leaders (such as Alexander Nevsky and Dmitry Donskoy) the Russian Orthodox

Church had canonized as saints. Indeed, Stalin officially named World War II "the Great Patriotic War," not "the Great Marxist Struggle."

Stalin was not only a nationalist. He was also a man of realpolitik who had no problem signing a pact with Hitler in August 1939 and then allying with the "capitalists" after the Nazi invasion of Russia in June 1941. His foreign policy was devoid of ideological considerations, and he approached the question of Zionism accordingly. Had Trotsky prevailed over Stalin after Lenin's death in 1924, the Soviet Union would not have encouraged the partition of Palestine, and it likely would not have recognized Israel.

For Stalin, a Jewish state established and run by socialist Russian Jews was likely to be a useful ally to drive Britain out of the Middle East. A Soviet document published in 1948 said explicitly that "the exit of Britain from Palestine will deal a blow to British colonial interests, for this exit will not end with the Middle East. Britain will lose an important link in the chain of countries it controls in the Middle East, and therefore its continuity between the Mediterranean and the Persian Gulf will come to an end."[3] Hence Stalin's decisions to support the partition of Palestine at the UN in 1947; hence his decision to immediately recognize Israel upon its independence in 1948 (the Soviet Union was the first country to recognize Israel de jure, on May 17, 1948); and hence his decision to arm Israel (via Czechoslovakia) during the critical hours of the Arab-Israeli war of 1948. Stalin's decision to arm Israel in March 1948 was crucial, since Jewish military forces were on the defensive and the United States was maintaining a strict arms embargo on the Middle East.

Zionist representatives were stunned to hear the Soviet ambassador to the UN, Andrei Gromyko, declare on May 15, 1948, that "both Arabs and Jews have historical roots in Palestine and it would be unjust to deny the rights of the Jewish people to realize their aspirations to establish their own state."[4] Gromyko's deputy, Semyon Tsarapkin, conveyed a similar and no less clear message: "Every people, and that includes the Jewish people, has a full right to demand that their fate should not depend on the mercy or goodwill of a particular state. The members of the United Nations can help the Jewish people by acting in accordance with the principles of the Charter which call for the guaranteeing to every people their right to independence and self-determination."[5]

The Cold War between the Soviet Union and the United States began shortly after the end of the Second World War. Europe had been divided between the two new superpowers. Other regions, especially the Middle East, were up for grabs. In 1947 the Middle East was still mostly under British influence. Syria and Lebanon had gained their formal independence from France. There was still a strong British military presence in Egypt. The Iraqi monarchy was loyal to Britain. Jordan, though officially independent, was a de facto British dominion, and a British officer was in command of the Jordanian army. Given the intensifying conflict between the Zionist underground and the British government, Stalin had no doubt that a Jewish state would be more useful than yet another Arab one in driving Britain out of the Middle East.

From Support to Confrontation

Once the goal of ending the British Mandate in Palestine had been achieved, Stalin had little reason to maintain his support for Israel. With a progressive British retreat from the Middle East, Soviet influence would be achieved via Arab nationalist regimes, not via tiny Israel. Indeed, anti-Western nationalists had overthrown the pro-British Egyptian monarchy in 1952, making Egypt a potential Soviet ally.

Moreover, the enthusiasm Soviet Jews displayed for the new State of Israel and its first ambassador to the Soviet Union — Golda Meir — embarrassed the Soviet leadership. When Meir arrived in the Soviet Union as Israel's first ambassador in September 1948, Moscow's Jewish community gave her a hero's welcome. After she attended Rosh Hashanah and Yom Kippur services at the Moscow Choral Synagogue, thousands of Jews surrounded her and chanted her name. Meanwhile, the State of Israel's Declaration of Independence openly called upon Jews to immigrate to Israel for the "Ingathering of the Exiles." Since the Soviet Union was supposedly the happy homeland of all workers, and since socialism was supposed to erase religion and nationalism, cheering crowds of Muscovite Jews publicly displaying pro-Israel sentiments was an affront to Soviet dogma.

Stalin had supported the creation of Israel, and he had immediately recognized the Jewish state. How could he now justify his policy in light of Israel's popularity among Soviet Jews, about three million of whom were now living in the Soviet Empire? In an ostensible attempt to answer this question, the renowned Jewish writer Ilya Ehrenburg published "Support for Israel, Yes! Jewish Immigration from the Soviet Union to Israel? No!" in *Pravda* on September 21, 1948. "The Soviet Union stood by Israel in its war against the Arab invaders," he wrote. "The solution to the Jewish problem does not depend on Israel's military success but on the victory of socialism over capitalism. . . . Soviet Jews are proud of their country and consider it their motherland. They have no intention of immigrating to Israel, nor do their brethren in Eastern Europe." Ehrenburg would later admit that the article had been dictated to him.[6]

The tone was set: yes, the Soviet Union had helped the Jews protect their lives in 1948, but Soviet Jews' allegiance was solely to the Soviet Union and to socialism, not to Israel and to Zionism. Indeed, Israeli leaders would subsequently call upon Jews, including Soviet Jews, to move to Israel—a threat to the Soviet regime. According to official Soviet ideology, socialism had supplanted nationalism as well as religion. The Soviet government informed Israel that it considered its encouragement of *aliyah* among Soviet Jews an unacceptable intrusion in domestic Soviet matters.[7] Ben-Gurion, however, rejected the Soviet demand, declaring, "The Jewish people, which has rebuilt its national independence, will not give up on the right of any Jew to move to Israel and to join the effort of national reconstruction."[8]

The official Soviet tone toward Israel had started to change even six months after the creation of the state. On December 16, 1948, the Soviet weekly *Novoye Vremya* wrote that Israel was thankless and hostile to Moscow despite the help it had received from the Soviet Union.[9] And in 1950, after Israel broke from its neutrality policy and sided with the United States during the Korean War (see chapter 9), Stalin pointed to Israel's support for South Korea as evidence that the Jewish state had joined the "imperialist" camp. "At most," Israeli scholar Aharon Klieman says, "the Korean War provided the catalyst and pretext for revising the [Soviet] policy adopted in 1947."[10]

In November 1952 the Soviet Union accused eleven Jewish founding members of the Czech Communist Party (whose policy was dictated by Moscow) of taking part in a "Zionist-imperialistic conspiracy." The "Slánský Trial," as it became known, aroused an international outcry after Rudolf Slánský, the secretary general of the Czech Communist Party, was hanged together with the other falsely accused suspects. In 1952–53 the Soviet government arrested and tortured hundreds of Jewish doctors whom it accused of trying to poison Stalin. The Soviet regime also arrested dozens of other Jewish doctors and dismissed them from their jobs. International outcries against the Soviet Union followed, with anti-Stalin demonstrations held around the world (including in Israel). During a February 1953 demonstration in Tel Aviv in front of the Soviet embassy, a demonstrator threw an explosive device at the embassy, damaging the building. As a result of this incident, the Soviet Union severed its diplomatic relations with Israel.

Following Stalin's death in March 1953, the Jewish doctors were released, and diplomatic relations with Israel were renewed in July 1953.

Yet the renewal of diplomatic relations did not signal any significant change in Soviet Union policy toward Israel. In 1954 the Soviet

Union used its veto at the UN Security Council against a resolution that would have enabled Israel to pursue its irrigation work near the Bnot Yaakov Bridge at the Syrian border. This first Soviet veto against Israel marked a new trend that would not abate during the Cold War.

Since the 1956 Suez War was directed at a Soviet ally (Egypt), the Soviet Union condemned and threatened Britain, France, and Israel (see chapter 9). Soviet prime minister Nikolai Bulganin warned David Ben-Gurion that Moscow was likely to take military action against Israel if it did not withdraw from Sinai. The threat had a chilling effect on Ben-Gurion, who had declared after conquering Sinai that Israel was there to stay and that Sharm el-Sheikh (a town in southern Sinai) had been the seat of an ancient Jewish kingdom.[11]

Following the British retreat from the Middle East, the Soviet Union tried to build alliances with Arab countries. This Soviet policy bore fruit, as Arab countries progressively joined the Soviet camp: Egypt (1955), Syria (1956), and Iraq (1958). Still, the United States was able to halt Soviet expansionism into Latin America with the Cuban Missile Crisis of 1962. The Soviet Union had tried to introduce ballistic missiles in Cuba, a Soviet ally, but backed down after President Kennedy demanded the removal of those missiles at the risk of war. By 1964, when Leonid Brezhnev replaced Nikita Khrushchev as Soviet leader, the lessons of 1962 had been internalized: the United States was determined not to let any Latin American country become a Soviet ally. The Soviet Union abandoned the prospect of expanding its influence in Latin America.

It could not expand to Western Europe either, because of the NATO military alliance between the United States and Western Europe meant to deter the Soviet Union. In Asia, China had become the self-proclaimed leader of the Communist revolution in the Third World. Africa was formally independent, but in fact still under French and British influence. Alone among those "sealed" regions stood the Middle East.

The year Brezhnev came to power (1964), Israeli prime minister Levi Eshkol paid an official visit to the United States, thus marking the beginning of strategic relations between the United States and Israel. Just as the Soviet Union was marking the Middle East as its top geopolitical priority, Israel was in the process of becoming a U.S. ally. In 1965 the United States severed diplomatic relations with Egypt because of Nasser's support for pro-Soviet forces in Yemen. In 1966 the coup in Syria produced the most radical (and pro-Soviet) regime in the country's history. That same year, Britain ended its military presence in Yemen, and France left NATO's military command. Meanwhile, domestic and international public opinion was getting increasingly hostile to the war in Vietnam, and the United States was on the defensive.

These sequential events convinced Soviet leaders that the Middle East was now ripe for increased Soviet influence. Yet the June 1967 Six-Day War produced the very opposite effect: Soviet allies were humiliated by a triumphant Israel.

The Soviets' first reaction was to sever diplomatic relations with Israel. All Eastern European countries followed suit, except Romania. By defying the Soviet Union and breaking ranks with the other members of the Warsaw Pact, Romania's dictator Nicolae Ceaușescu would now benefit from good ties with Washington. Some historians have since speculated that Moscow wanted Bucharest to maintain diplomatic relations with Israel so as to use the Romanian embassy in Tel Aviv for Soviet espionage,[12] but this theory does not explain Ceaușescu's dissidence from the Communist bloc on other issues. Romania did not always vote with the Communist bloc in condemning Israel; for example, Romania did not support the UN resolutions condemning the Camp David Agreements or defining Zionism as a form of racism. And Romania's policy toward Jews was generally more liberal than that of other Eastern European countries; Romanian Jews were mostly free to practice their religion, and they were allowed to immigrate to Israel within quotas and under the official policy of "family reunification."

Meanwhile, the Soviet Union's ability to spread further in the Middle East was hampered by its conflict with China. The "Sino-Soviet Split" (a geopolitical contest between the world's two largest Communist countries), begun in 1956, culminated in territorial clashes in Manchuria in 1969. The Soviet Union was now compelled to send more troops and military material to its eastern border.

While Israel indirectly benefited from the Sino-Soviet Split, the United States actively took advantage of it. China's support for the Vietnamese Communists was an obstacle to a U.S.-Chinese rapprochement, but the Vietnam War was finally coming to an end, and U.S. national security advisor Henry Kissinger initiated contacts with the Chinese government. President Nixon's visit to China in February 1972 symbolized and officialized America's new policy toward the Communist country.

In the Middle East, Kissinger strategized to end the historical alliance between Egypt and the Soviet Union; hence did he broker the 1975 interim agreement between Israel and Egypt, which eventually led to the 1979 peace agreement and to Egypt's abandonment of its Soviet ally (see chapter 11). Soviet leaders realized by then that severing diplomatic relations with Israel in 1967 had been counterproductive.[13] In 1975 the Soviet government asked Israeli prime minister Yitzhak Rabin to return to the Geneva conference (in which the Soviet Union had taken part after the 1973 Yom Kippur War) and to stop cooperating with Henry Kissinger's Middle East strategy.[14]

The "loss" of Egypt was a serious diplomatic blow to the Soviet Union. The Camp David Agreements had officialized Egypt's new status as a U.S. ally. That same year, the Soviet Union invaded Afghanistan. The Soviet regime tried to market its invasion of Afghanistan as a legitimate act of solidarity with an embattled Communist government, but hardly anyone bought into this argument. The Soviet Union had in fact invaded a Muslim country, and its "anti-imperialist" rhetoric now sounded more hollow and disingenuous than ever. As Israel's ambassador to the UN Yehuda Blum commented, "My delegation has noted with profound satisfaction the statement made by the representative of the Soviet Union in which he pledged his country to the principle of the inadmissibility of acquisition of territory by war. In compliance with this principle, the Soviet Union will no doubt wish to announce the timetable for its withdrawal from, *inter alia*, Lithuania, Latvia, Estonia, the Kurile Islands and, last but not least, Afghanistan."[15]

In 1979, seven years after Nixon had been a guest in China, the United States and China established full diplomatic relations, and China's new leader, Deng Xiaoping, initiated a policy of economic liberalization and modernization. As the Soviet Union was overreaching beyond the capacity of its deeply troubled economy, China was starting the slow rehabilitation of its economic system.

The Chinese decision was as wise as the Soviet adventure was foolish. When Mikhail Gorbachev inherited the Soviet leadership in 1985, it was already too late for him to rescue a sinking ship. Yet Gorbachev also understood that the Soviet Union could no longer afford its confrontational and expansionist foreign policy. He admitted that the absence of relations with Israel was absurd and outdated.[16]

Gorbachev was conciliatory toward the United States, but the Reagan administration demanded the release of Jewish political prisoners. In 1986 Gorbachev agreed to free the famous refusenik Anatoly (Natan) Sharansky. Eventually, in 1989 Gorbachev allowed the Jews to leave the Soviet Union.

A massive wave of Russian *aliyah* began. Between 1989 and 2006, about 979,000 Soviet (and former Soviet) citizens immigrated to Israel. While not all Soviet Jews and their immediate relatives immigrated to Israel—many moved to the United States and Germany—nearly two-thirds of those who left moved to Israel. Indeed, Gorbachev himself declared in June 1992 that in the ideological struggle between Zionism and communism, Zionism had prevailed and even triumphed.[17]

The End of the Cold War and Its Paradoxes

Gorbachev did not exercise his veto at the UN Security Council in 1991 to stop the U.S.-led coalition against Iraq. In 1991 the Soviet Union co-hosted the Madrid Peace Conference with the United States, and it renewed diplomatic relations with Israel.

These renewed diplomatic relations were short-lived, however, since the Soviet Union was dissolved in 1991. Soviet ambassador Alexander Bovin had presented his credentials to Israeli president Chaim Herzog just two weeks before the dissolution of the Soviet Union.

In the twilight of the Cold War, Israel had full diplomatic relations with Russia. After the dissolution, it also developed strategic ties with the former Soviet republics of Central Asia and the Caucasus, aimed at three objectives: pre-empting Iran's influence in these newly independent Muslim states, foiling the export of nuclear technology to other Muslim states, and benefiting from these republics' oil and natural gas resources.

To date, Israel's policy in Central Asia and the Caucasus has mostly been successful. Azerbaijan, for example, has become a major customer of Israel's military industry.[18] Israel was able to establish strong ties with Kazakhstan, including full diplomatic relations in 1992, thanks to its advanced water-related technologies, dearly needed in Kazakhstan's arid climate. Netanyahu's official visit to Azerbaijan and Kazakhstan in December 2016 was indicative of Israel's special ties with those two former Soviet republics. Israel reportedly imports 40 percent of its oil from Azerbaijan[19] and 20 percent from Kazakhstan.[20]

As for Russia itself, despite the renewal of diplomatic relations with Israel, Russian and Israeli interests often continue to clash. Russia's main Middle East allies are Israel's primary foes, Iran and Syria.

Russian geopolitical interests and calculations have not significantly changed. Though Russia cannot afford the military and financial support for the Arab states the Soviet Union once offered, Russia continues to regard the Arab states as allies. And precisely because Russia was bankrupt in the 1990s, it tried to take advantage of its energy-related assets, including its expertise in nuclear power—hence the sale of Russian nuclear technology to Iran. Despite Israel's warnings that Iran might use its nuclear technology for military purposes, Russia has maintained its policy.

Vladimir Putin's election as Russia's president in 2000 added to the complexity of Russia's relations with Israel. Committed to avenging the humiliation of the Soviet collapse (an event he described as "the worst geopolitical catastrophe of the twentieth century") and to restoring Russia's international influence and prestige, Putin retook control of Russia's oil and natural gas producers. He replenished Russia's coffers by selling hydrocarbons as well as nuclear technology (including to Iran), and he became more and more confrontational vis-à-vis the United States.

At the same time, Israel and Russia coordinate their respective moves in Syria. The confrontational days of the Cold War have been replaced by regular meetings between Russian and Israeli leaders. In the early months of 2018, it seemed that Israel and Russia were on a collision course as Russia let Iran overtake Syria, despite Israel's protests, and as Israel commenced bombing of Iranian targets in Syria, to Russia's dismay. Yet after Israel threatened to target Syrian dictator Bashar Assad, Putin eventually agreed to meet Israel's requests and to address its concerns. In May 2018 Putin seemed to be giving carte blanche to Israel for its airstrikes against Iranian targets in Syria.[21] On May 9, 2018, Netanyahu was Putin's guest of honor for the ceremonies marking the seventy-third anniversary of the Russian army's victory in the Second World War (an admittedly dubious honor, since most Western leaders had boycotted the ceremonies in protest of Russia's annexation of Crimea). At the end of the ceremony, the Russian military orchestra played "Hatikvah" (Israel's national anthem) on the

Red Square. Those symbols and images were a far cry from the hostile days of the Cold War.

Conclusion

Stalin had supported the establishment of Israel because he wanted to drive Britain out of the Middle East. Once this goal was achieved, Soviet support for Israel lost its raison d'être. The sight of Soviet Jews giving a hero's welcome to Israel's first ambassador to Moscow was a PR disaster for the Communist regime, and Israel's decision to side with South Korea in 1950 provided Stalin with the perfect excuse to justify a turnabout on Israel. To advance Soviet influence and interests in the Middle East, Stalin needed to build alliances with Arab states, and so he ended his short-term support for Israel.

The gradual rapprochement between Israel and the United States in the 1960s widened the gap between Israel and the Soviet Union. Humiliated by the 1967 Six-Day War, Moscow severed diplomatic relations with Israel.

Gorbachev realized that the Soviet Union's Middle East policy had become counterproductive and renewed diplomatic relations with Israel in 1991. Despite the renewal of relations, however, Russian and Israeli interests often continue to clash. Russia's main Middle East allies are Israel's primary foes, Iran and Syria.

At the same time, Israel has managed in recent years to establish relations of mutual trust and understanding with Russia. These relations enable the two countries to defend their conflicting interests while coordinating their respective moves in Syria.

16. The Long March to Asia

> PLO people come to me all the time asking for advice on how to
> get rid of Israel. After all, we Vietnamese defeated both France
> and the United States. My answer is always the same: the French
> went back to France and the Americans went back to Amer-
> ica. The Jews have nowhere to go. So you can't beat them.
>
> Vietnamese general VO NGUYEN GIAP to
> Israeli general MEIR DAGAN

China: In Search of a Common Ground

When Israel declared its independence in 1948, the world was already
divided by the Cold War. Not all countries identified with the United
States or with the Soviet Union, however. The French geographer and
demographer Alfred Sauvy coined the expression *Tiers Monde* (Third
World) in the early 1950s to describe newly independent nations that
identified with neither bloc.[1] This "Third World" was less important
to Israel than to the United States, the Soviet Union, and Europe,
all of which could offer critical diplomatic, economic, and military
support. Yet Israel took notice of the Third World's potential geopolitical weight with the 1955 Bandung Conference — an international
gathering, in Indonesia, of newly independent Asian and African
nations. Originally, Burma (today's Myanmar) had invited Israel to
the conference, and India had confirmed the invitation, but then the
invitation was rescinded; Egyptian president Nasser had threatened

to boycott the conference and to convince other Arab and Muslim states to do the same.

Until the Bandung Conference, which symbolized Israel's isolation in Asia, diplomatic relations between Israel and China seemed possible. Back in December 1918, the Chinese government had expressed its support for the Balfour Declaration.[2] After Nazi Germany annexed Austria in 1938, Chinese president Chiang Kai-shek and other Chinese officials held that China should help the Jews since they were barred from immigrating to other countries. In 1939 the government formulated a plan to settle European Jews in the Yunnan province close to the Burmese border,[3] but the plan was ultimately scrapped, most likely because Chiang Kai-shek feared alienating Germany.[4] Still, China did provide a haven to Jews during the Holocaust. In the late 1930s and early 1940s, some twenty thousand Jews from Germany, Austria, and Poland immigrated to Shanghai, building upon the already well-established Jewish community there. During World War II, Jews were able to immigrate to Shanghai when the rest of the world had shut its doors to Jewish refugees. (Jewish immigration to China had begun nearly half a century earlier. With the Russian invasion of Manchuria in 1895 and the construction of the Eastern Railway, the czar had encouraged Russian Jews to immigrate to the conquered region. Most of them settled in the city of Harbin, including the family of former Israeli prime minister Ehud Olmert.)

Despite the presence of Jews in China, certain Chinese officials were ignorant about the Jewish people. During the San Francisco Conference on the establishment of the UN (April–June 1945), a member of the Chinese delegation, Wu Yi-Fang, asked the president of the American Jewish Congress if Jews were Catholic or Protestant.[5]

China nearly voted in favor of the UN partition plan in 1947. The Chinese ambassador to the UN announced on November 22, 1947, that his government would support partition — but upon hearing this announcement, the Chinese defense minister (who was Muslim) warned Chiang Kai-shek that were China to vote for partition, it would alienate its Muslim neighbors (especially Pakistan and Afghanistan).[6] In the end, Chiang Kai-shek decided to abstain.

Yet Chiang Kai-shek recognized Israel and voted in favor of its admission to the UN in 1949. That same year, however, Mao Zedong's Communist forces defeated him, and he retreated to the island of Taiwan.

When China became Communist, Israel's foreign policy was officially neutral, and therefore diplomatic relations with China could have been established. Yet the opportunity was missed. Israel did recognize Mao Zedong's government de jure in January 1950—in fact, Israel was the first Middle East country to recognize China's Communist government—and in September 1950 Israel voted in favor of a resolution (jointly sponsored by the Soviet Union and India) calling for the recognition of Mao Zedong's government as the legitimate and legal representative of China.[7] By that same time, however, Israel also expressed support for the UN-led coalition against the Communist invasion of South Korea (see chapter 9), voted in favor of all UN resolutions against North Korea, and sent food and medicine to South Korea. David Ben-Gurion even offered to send Israeli troops to fight in Korea under the UN flag (though his cabinet outvoted him on that matter). China thus perceived Israeli policy on Korea as hostile and pro-Western.

Once the Korean war ended in 1953, Mao's China was isolated internationally. That same year, the Soviet Union renewed its diplomatic relations with Israel after a short interruption (see chapter 15). These two developments seem to have influenced China's decision to unofficially approach Israel about the possibility of establishing diplomatic relations.[8]

The behind-the-scene negotiations between Israel and China put Israel in a dilemma. On the one hand, Israel wanted to establish diplomatic relations with the world's largest country (population-wise); on the other hand, Israel feared alienating the United States by establishing full diplomatic relations with a Communist government ostracized by the Eisenhower administration. Israel's ambassador to the United States and to the UN, Abba Eban, warned in 1953 that establishing diplomatic relations with Communist China would alienate both the United States and France, whose soldiers were being killed by Chinese forces in Korea and Indochina.[9] When the war in Indochina ended in 1954, however, Eban favored establishing diplomatic relations with China.[10] Some of Israel's Foreign Ministry officials argued that establishing diplomatic relations with Communist China would have devastating and irreparable effects on Israel's relations with the United States; others maintained otherwise.

Diplomatic archives indicate that Israel tried to upgrade relations with China immediately after the end of the Korean War in July 1953.[11] In February 1954 Israel informed China that it was interested in increasing trade relations, but Israel was evasive regarding diplomatic relations. In February 1955 an official Israeli delegation visited China to discuss bilateral relations, but by that point China seemed to be less interested in establishing full diplomatic relations.[12] As China was trying to break its diplomatic isolation, Israel was only one option among others. In fact, China was also making contacts with Arab countries, especially Egypt and Syria.

At the time, China's foreign policy was still mostly aligned with that of the Soviet Union (the conflict between the two, known as the Sino-Soviet Split, would begin in 1956). The Soviet Union's pro-Arab foreign policy, adopted in 1953, seems to have influenced China's attitude toward Israel. In 1953 Chinese official publications had started describing Israel as an agent of "American imperialism" in the Middle East.[13]

The 1955 Bandung Conference was also a turning point for China in realizing the geopolitical weight of the Arab world. Discussions between Chinese premier Zhou Enlai and Nasser at Bandung led China to rally to the Arab cause: the Chinese leadership decided to become the advocate of the Third World against "imperialism." Realizing it was losing ground to Nasser, Israel submitted a request for full diplomatic relations to China on April 29, 1955, five days after the close of the Bandung Conference, but at this point China had changed its mind and was evasive. Not formally rejecting Israel's request, China sent a noncommittal reply.

In 1956 China established diplomatic relations with Egypt, Syria, and Yemen. By then (even before the Suez Crisis), China's tone vis-à-vis Israel had started becoming hostile. In January 1956 China's prime minister declared in Cairo that Israel is "an artificial state created to serve imperialism."[14] China then strongly condemned the 1956 Suez War as an "imperialist collusion" between Britain, France, and Israel. In 1959, when Israel renewed its offer to establish diplomatic relations with China, the Chinese government did not even bother to reply.[15] Relations between the two countries became so tense that in the 1962 conflict between China and India over a disputed border, Israel provided military support to India.

Chinese premier Zhou Enlai reiterated during a Middle East tour in June 1965 that China was "against any compromise over Palestine."[16] In 1965 China allowed the opening of an official PLO office in Beijing. In March 1965 Mao Zedong declared that "Israel and Formosa [Taiwan] are the basis of imperialism in Asia."[17] In 1966 (i.e., one year before the Six-Day War), the Afro-Asian Bureau of the Chinese Foreign Ministry declared Zionism to be "intrinsically a colonialist movement, aggressive in its aims, founded on racism, and fascist in its means." The statement added that China "considers Israel as a base for colonialism . . . ; condemns the Zionist movement and Israeli presence in occupied Palestine; considers that the Palestine people's right to liberate their homeland is a natural extension of self-defense and self-determination; demands that all political, economic, and cultural relations be severed with Israel . . . ; condemns strongly continuous Jewish immigration to Palestine."[18]

This hostile rhetoric, however, masked a complex set of conflicting interests. Since the beginning of the Sino-Soviet Split in 1956, China and the Soviet Union competed over the leadership of the Communist camp—a Communist family feud shrewdly exploited by Henry Kissinger (see chapter 15). The 1969 war between the Soviet Union and China brought the conflict to its apex. Israel benefited from the Sino-Soviet Split, because Moscow's deployment of forces to its eastern border impeded Soviet military involvement in the Middle East. Furthermore, by this point China also considered the Soviet Union its biggest enemy, and Israel was at the forefront of the struggle against the Soviet Union in the Middle East.

Hence, China started reassessing its policy toward Israel in the early 1970s. In December 1973, the CIA estimated that "Beijing's vital interest is to block the Soviet penetration from Southeast Asia to Europe, and to the extent that Israel stands in the way of Soviet dominance in the Middle East, China supports Israeli efforts."[19] In addition, China became interested in Israel's military expertise. With the Sino-Soviet Split, China had lost its one and only military supplier. Despite U.S. recognition of China in the early 1970s, military ties between Washington and Beijing were out of the question; the United States was still committed to Taiwan's independence and security. Moreover, the Soviet military material China had was outdated, and Israel was known for its expertise in upgrading outdated Soviet military equipment, having captured Soviet rifles and tanks in the wars of 1956, 1967, and 1973.[20] In a first sign of China's interest in Israeli military technology, Chinese officials visited Israel's booth at the 1975 Paris Air Show.[21]

With the death of Mao Zedong in 1976 and the consolidation of Deng Xiaoping's leadership in 1979, China's foreign policy became more pragmatic. In July 1977 China's foreign minister Huang Hua made a statement that would have been unconceivable under Mao: "We do not endorse the one-sided idea of certain ultra-leftists that Israel should be eliminated. Since Jews in Israel are also one of the peoples of the world, they have a right to national survival."²² Around the time formal diplomatic relations between China and the United States were established (1979), China started developing secret contacts with Israel to upgrade and improve Chinese military equipment.²³

This was also the year of the Sino-Vietnamese War, in which China proved unsuccessful in ending Vietnam's presence in Cambodia, yet another reminder of China's antiquated military equipment. Israel was one of the only countries in the world able and willing to help China modernize its army.

Israeli businessman Shaul Eisenberg made the first contacts between China and Israel's military industry. In the 1980s newspapers started reporting about military ties between China and Israel—an alliance both countries officially denied.²⁴ By the late 1980s hundreds of Israeli military technicians were reportedly in China, upgrading and modernizing Soviet-made tanks and artillery.²⁵ In November 1991 *Ha'aretz* asserted that Israel's arms deals with China amounted to "billions of dollars."²⁶ Finally, on March 14, 1992, Israeli defense minister Moshe Arens openly admitted that Israel was selling military technology to China.²⁷

Israel had also helped China with nonmilitary technologies. In 1983 and 1984 China had secretly invited Israeli agronomic engineers to improve crop yields. In 1986 the Chinese government had also secretly invited Israeli hydrologists and geologists to advise on irrigation projects.²⁸

Overall, rapprochement between China and Israel had been gradual and unofficial, until three geopolitical upheavals of 1991—the collapse of the Soviet Union, the Gulf War, and the Madrid Peace Conference—convinced China to establish full diplomatic relations with Israel in 1992. The collapse of the Soviet Union, China's main geopolitical rival, enabled China to finally claim leadership among Communist countries. The Gulf War had seen Israel act with restraint to Iraq's unprovoked attacks. And the Madrid Peace Conference had raised hopes about an imminent end to the Arab-Israeli conflict.

At the same time, however, America was dismayed that Israel had become a major provider of military technology to China. In March 1992 the U.S. government accused Israel of transferring American military technology to China. In 2000 America stopped Israel from selling its airborne early warning and control radar system (AEW&C) to China. Although this system had been developed exclusively by Israel and did not include American technology, the U.S. government feared the sale would alter the military balance in the Strait of Taiwan to China's advantage. In December 2004 the U.S. government asked Israel not to sell drones to China. Again, the technology was Israeli, but the United States feared it might provide too much of a qualitative military advantage to China. The same year, Israel and the United States signed an agreement in which Israel committed not to sell any military equipment to China that might include American technology.[29]

While Israel had to downgrade its military ties with China, economic relations between the two countries flourished. In 2013 it was announced that China would be involved in building the "Med-Red" project, a commercial railway planned to run from the Red Sea to the Mediterranean. In 2015 Israel became one of the founding members of China's Asian Infrastructure Investment Bank (AIIB), despite strong American reservations. In March 2016 Israel and China announced the negotiation of a free trade agreement. In 2016 as well, China invested $21.5 billion in infrastructures in the Middle East and Africa.[30] Its "Belt and Road Initiative" (BRI), partly financed by AIIB, involves investing heavily in transportation infrastructures (such as roads, railroads, and seaports) to connect China to European and African markets. China is also involved in building infrastructures in Israel, such as the Carmel tunnels in Haifa, the light rail in Tel Aviv, and the expansion of the Ashdod and Haifa ports.

China's interest in Israel is related to Israel's scientific excellence and innovation, especially in high-tech, agriculture and water technologies, and biotech. Shouguang's Water City, for instance, incorporates Israeli water technologies. Since 2013, there has been a steady increase in Chinese business delegations to Israel. China's total investments in Israel amounted to half a billion dollars in 2015.[31] In 2016 the Israeli embassy in Beijing issued more than ten thousand visas to Chinese businessmen.[32] The Chinese businessman Li Ka-sing (estimated worth: $34 billion) is heavily invested in Israeli companies and made a $130 million donation to Israel's Technion Institute of Technology in 2013. In 2018 Israeli exports to China grew by 56 percent.[33]

Even though Israel's deepening ties with China are now mostly commercial and technological, they are still a source of concern for the United States. Since the United States perceives China as an economic rival in the global sphere, senior U.S. officials have warned their Israeli counterparts that trade and technological relations between Israel and China are going too far. In January 2019, for example, U.S. national security advisor John Bolton expressed to Israeli leaders his government's discomfort that the Chinese companies Huawei and ZTE are investing in Israel and that a Chinese company is building the new Haifa port.

India: From Rejection to Partnership

The nineteenth-century Hindu monk Swami Vivekananda took pride in the fact that Jews had found a safe haven in India "the very year in which their holy temple was shattered to pieces by Roman tyranny."[34] Many Indian Jews claim descent from the ten lost tribes of Israel (the ten of the twelve tribes that were deported from the Kingdom of Israel after its conquest by the Neo-Assyrian Empire in 722 BCE). According to some accounts and traditions, traders from the Kingdom of Judea reached the southern Indian city of Cochin in 562 BCE and were joined by Jewish refugees after the destruction of the Second Temple in 70 CE. Those early migrants are known as Cochin Jews. Other categories of Indian Jews include Madras Jews (Jewish immigrants of Portuguese descent who arrived in India in the mid-seventeenth century), Bene Israel (who claim descent from the lost tribes of Israel), Baghdadi Jews (Iraqi Jews who settled in India in the eighteenth century), as well as Bene Menashe (Indians who practice Judaism and claim descent from the lost tribe of Menashe) and Bene Efraim (Indians who practice Judaism and claim descent from the lost tribe of Efraim).

In the early 1900s an estimated thirty thousand Jews lived in India under British rule; most of them immigrated to Israel after 1948. While India was indeed tolerant of its Jewish refugees, Indian leaders were not always sympathetic to Jewish national aspirations. Gandhi (who led India to its independence in August 1947 and was assassinated in January 1948), for example, opposed Zionism.[35] "Palestine belongs to the Arabs," he wrote in November 1938,[36] adding that the Jews should be tolerated as a religious minority in the Arab state of Palestine. Gandhi admitted that "the cry for a national home for the Jewish people does not have much appeal to me." He could not understand why the Jews should not "make that country their home where they are born and where they earn their livelihood."[37] Meetings between Gandhi and Zionist leaders in the 1930s failed to change his mind on the question of Jewish self-determination.

Jawaharlal Nehru (India's prime minister from 1947 to 1964) held similar views. In 1936, for example, Immanuel Olsvanger (a Polish-born Palestinian Jew whose many linguistic skills included knowledge of Sanskrit) visited India and met with Nehru, who was adamant about his opposition to Zionism.[38] Even Chaim Weizmann, meeting with Nehru in July 1938, did not manage to convince him of the Jews' national rights in Palestine. Instead, Nehru offered to allow German Jews to immigrate to India.[39] Hence Nehru went out of his way to dissuade Jews from immigrating to British Palestine.

In April 1939 Hebrew University professors Martin Buber and Yehuda Magnes sent letters to Gandhi making the case for the Jews' national rights in Palestine, but both letters remained unanswered. Gandhi maintained his opposition to Zionism even after the Holocaust. Nehru gave the instruction to vote against the UN partition plan in November 1947, despite a last-minute plea by Chaim Weizmann.

It is not entirely clear if Gandhi's and Nehru's opposition to Zionism was more a matter of conviction or political calculation. They did want to rally as many Muslims as possible to their Congress Party and could not afford to alienate Indian Muslims by siding with Israel.[40]

Not all Indian political and spiritual leaders shared Gandhi's and Nehru's stance on Zionism. Rabindranath Tagore (the first non-European to win the Nobel Prize for literature), for example, was well-disposed toward Zionism.[41] So was Indian author and diplomat Kavalam Madhava Panikkar, himself a senior figure in the Congress Party.

Nehru recognized Israel de jure in 1950, but he refrained from establishing full diplomatic relations. He was reportedly in favor of establishing full diplomatic relations with Israel, but his government's Muslim ministers opposed the move, and Nehru did not insist.[42] On the whole, the Indian government felt it had to be cautious with Israel. India's population was about 15 percent Muslim, and the ruling Congress Party had no intention of alienating Indian Muslims by developing close relations with Israel. In addition, India was embroiled in a conflict with Pakistan (over the Muslim-dominated Kashmir region) and could not afford to further complicate its relations with Arab and Muslim countries.

Like China, India realized after the Bandung Conference of 1955 and the Suez Crisis of 1956 that it had nothing to gain from a closer official relationship with Israel. On the contrary, its leadership status in the Third World depended on its relations with the Arab and Muslim worlds. India strongly condemned Israel over the 1956 Suez campaign.

Still, even though India officially kept its distance from Israel, Nehru secretly asked Ben-Gurion for military aid during the border war between India and China, Ben-Gurion agreed, and Israel supplied India with weaponry in 1962. The IDF chief of staff even visited India during the conflict.[43] Israel also provided India with military equipment and advice during its war with Pakistan in 1965. Yet the Indian government tried to keep this short-lived cooperation secret, and when it was revealed, India strongly denied it.

During the Cold War, India aligned with the Soviet Union, despite its officially "non-aligned" foreign policy. (Nehru had proclaimed India's neutrality at the beginning of the Cold War, but his foreign policy, and that of his successors, was effectively pro-Russian.) This diplomatic alignment further widened the rift between India and Israel, especially after the 1967 Six-Day War, at which point the Soviet Union severed its diplomatic relations with Israel. Under Indira Gandhi's premiership (1966–77 and 1980–84), India's pro-Soviet foreign policy was institutionalized. The Indian government expelled Israel's consul to Bombay in 1982, in protest of the Lebanon War.

This event probably marked the lowest point in the relations between the two countries. At the same time, members of India's opposition party questioned the benefit of this pro-Arab policy, pointing out that India had barely benefited from the support of Arab countries in its territorial disputes and border conflicts in 1962 (between India and China), in 1965 (between India and Pakistan), and in 1971 (between India and Pakistan). Indeed, in the 1965 and 1971 conflicts between India and Pakistan, the Arab states had sided with Pakistan.

The end of the Cold War and the establishment of full diplomatic relations between the Soviet Union and Israel (in 1991) influenced India's Middle East policy. The general director of the Indian Foreign Ministry, Jyotindra Nath Dixit, wrote in his memoirs that India realized with the end of the Cold War that the absence of relations with Israel no longer made sense.[44] The 1991 Madrid Peace Conference was another factor influencing India's reconsideration of Israel, as Israel had insisted on not inviting to the conference countries that had full diplomatic relations with the Arab states but not with Israel.[45] The post–Cold War international system offered new opportunities for an emerging power like India, but for such opportunities to be seized India needed to improve its relations with the now dominant United States. In 1991 India voted in favor of repealing the UN's 1975 resolution defining Zionism as a form of racism. After China established diplomatic relations with Israel in 1992, India felt that it was losing diplomatic ground to the benefit of China.[46] Moreover, India's prime minister Narashima Rao needed financial help from the United States to implement his ambitious economic reforms, and many U.S. leaders (as well as World Jewish Congress chairman Isi Leibler)[47] made it clear to Rao that he had to abandon India's hostility to Israel to benefit from America's support.[48]

Eventually, in 1992, India established full diplomatic relations with Israel. India announced its decision on the eve of Prime Minister Rao's visit to the United States. The Indian government thus abandoned its original precondition that Israel withdraw to the borders of the 1947 UN partition plan for the normalization of relations with Israel (and not merely to the 1949 armistice lines, as expected by most countries).[49]

In the post–Cold War international system, the relationship between India and the United States was transformed as well. India no longer had the backing of the Soviet Union, and it needed an international ally for its struggle against Pakistan and for its geopolitical contest with China. The United States, for its part, saw in India a necessary counterweight to the rising power of China. The United States also started losing patience with Pakistan, its former Cold War protégé, because it showed little sign of fighting Islamic terrorism. In fact, a Pakistani scientist, Abdul Qadeer Khan, had sold his country's nuclear knowledge to countries such as Iran and North Korea. This shift in U.S. foreign policy was made manifest by a 2008 Congress bill that allowed India to use nuclear technology.

The India-Pakistan conflict acquired a global dimension with the spread of nuclear knowledge and Islamic terrorism. In this context, India sought military and intelligence assistance from both the United States and Israel. India's conflict with Pakistan over Kashmir had entered a danger zone when Pakistan detonated its first nuclear bomb in 1998 (India had been a military nuclear power since 1974). As opposed to the Arab states, Israel consistently supported India's position on Kashmir. A strategic and military partnership soon developed between the two countries. In 1998 alone, military contracts between Israel and India were worth hundreds of millions of dollars.[50] In 1999 Israel provided India with surveillance drones and laser-guided missiles for the "Kargil war" with Pakistan.

India's rapprochement with Israel was also influenced by Indian domestic politics. In fact, the political histories of the two countries bore striking similarities. Both countries gained their independence from Britain after being partitioned (India in 1947, Israel in 1948). During the first three decades of their independence, both India and Israel were uninterruptedly ruled by a socialist party—the Congress Party in India and Mapai in Israel. Both countries had a marginalized and ostracized nationalist right—the Janata Party in India (today's Bharatiya Janata Party, BJP) and the Herut party in Israel (today's Likud). Both the Indian and Israeli right-wing parties won their first elections in 1977, though in India the nationalist government only lasted for two years and barely modified India's Middle East policy. Yet BJP's win in the 1998 general election led to a diplomatic realignment, which included a rapprochement with Israel. The Indian right was always staunchly pro-Israel and critical of the Congress Party's pro-Soviet and pro-Arab foreign policy. When Narendra Modi brought BJP to power again in 2014, he renewed his party's pro-American and pro-Israel foreign policy. In July 2017 Modi became the first Indian prime minister to pay an official visit to Israel, and in January 2018 Israeli prime minister Netanyahu followed suit with an official visit to India.

Today it seems that fear of "Muslim reprisals" no longer deters India from deepening its ties with Israel — at least as long as BJP is in power. As an Indian commentator wrote in January 2018, Israel "is a friend worth having," and "Israel has been among the most consistent of India's friends in international fora, something that the foes of Israel in the Islamic world can hardly boast of. The decades of bankrolling and support for the Palestinian cause does not appear to have earned India any additional diplomatic goodwill when it came to the crunch."[51]

Today, India is Israel's largest client of military equipment, and Israel is India's third provider of military equipment after the United States and Russia. Prime Minister Modi has approved a $250 billion multiyear plan to modernize the Indian army (against threats posed by India's two major regional rivals, Pakistan and China), and India has made Israel a key player in the modernization plan. In April 2017, for example, India's Defense Ministry signed a $2 billion contract with Israel Aircraft Industries for the supply of missile defense systems.[52]

Israel's Special Relationships in Asia and Oceania

JAPAN

During the 1904–5 war between Russia and Japan, an American Jewish financier by the name of Jacob Schiff helped fund Japan's war effort as a personal contribution to the struggle against antisemitic czarist Russia.[53] American Jews raised money to help Japan buy a battleship, which they insisted be named *Kishinev* (the Russian city in which the 1903 pogrom took place).[54] Japan supported the Balfour Declaration and the idea of Jewish national self-determination, and the Japanese ambassador to London wrote to Chaim Weizmann in January 1919 that his government fully supported the idea of a Jewish national home in Palestine.[55] In December 1927 the Japanese chief of staff sent a high-ranking officer by the name of Yasue Norihiro to Palestine to find out how the Jewish national home was developing. Full of praise for the *Yishuv*, Norihiro wrote in his report that Japan should support Jewish self-determination in Palestine.[56]

Yet as the Japanese came into contact with Russia, they also started translating Russian antisemitic pamphlets, including *The Protocols of the Elders of Zion*. During the military alliance between Japan and Germany (1940–45), Nazi propaganda, including Hitler's *Mein Kampf*, was translated into Japanese. The Japanese tried to convince the Muslim peoples they had conquered in Southeast Asia (today's Malaysia and Indonesia) of their anti-British and anti-Zionist credentials. The trick worked, since Hadj Amin al-Husseini called upon the Muslims of Southeast Asia to accept Japanese rule.[57]

Despite Japan's military alliance with Germany during World War II, Japan was not complicit in the Holocaust. Japan provided refuge to Jews in Manchuria and Shanghai (two Chinese territories Japan occupied during the Second World War) and even in Japan itself. Japan's consul to Lithuania, Chiune Sugihara, helped thousands of Jews flee Europe by granting them Japanese visas (Israel honored Sugihara as a "Righteous Among the Nations" in 1985).

In the 1940s two large religious movements were founded in Japan: Makuya (founded in 1948 by Ikurō Teshima) and Beit Shalom (founded in 1946 by Ōtsuki Takeji). Both are strongly pro-Israel. Yet also in the 1940s, the myth of "Jewish world domination" became widespread in Japan and has never fully dissipated since. Many Israeli diplomats and statesmen have reported their Japanese counterparts' convictions that Israel's population is far larger than its actual size and that the Jews control the United States. When Abba Eban explained in Tokyo back in 1966 that Israel had a population of 2.5 million, his hosts burst into laughter.[58] Yitzhak Shamir wrote in his memoirs so hearing from Japanese officials: "You people are so fortunate with your unlimited access and boundless influence everywhere. You are so powerful. See how you hold the United States in the palms of your hands."[59] The

Japanese businessman Den Fujita (who opened and ran the McDonald's™ chain in Japan) authored the 1972 book *Jewish Business Methods: Controlling the Economy of the World*, a fundamentally antisemitic work that nonetheless argues that the Jews should be emulated and their worldwide success be seen as a source of inspiration.

Israel was the first Middle East country to open a legation in Tokyo upon Japan's full independence from U.S. occupation in 1952. In the next decades, Japan's foreign policy toward Israel was mostly aligned with that of the United States. As the United States upgraded its relations with Israel in the 1960s, so did Japan. In 1963 Israel and Japan established full diplomatic relations.

However, because Japan was heavily dependent on Middle East oil imports, its policy toward Israel was very much influenced by the 1973 oil embargo. Back in the 1950s Japan had become Asia's largest consumer of Middle Eastern oil. In the 1960s Japan imported over 80 percent of its fuel, of which 70 percent came from the Middle East, and in the 1970s Japan was importing 90 percent of its fuel.[60] After 1973, Japan was caught between Arab states' demands to cut ties with Israel and U.S. warnings not to do so.

In the end, Japan rejected the Arab demand to sever diplomatic ties with Israel, but it also issued strongly worded statements demanding an Israeli withdrawal from all the territories conquered in 1967. The Japanese government also allowed the opening of a PLO office in Tokyo in 1976. In 1980 the Japanese agricultural cooperative Zenno ended its potassium imports from Israel, admitting that it had to choose between potassium and oil.[61]

By the 1980s, however, Japan came to question whether its diplomatic kowtowing to Arab pressures for the sake of its oil dependency was fully in its best interests. Oil prices dropped in the 1980s, thus reducing OPEC's political leverage. Japan attracted America's ire for not condemning the assault on the U.S. embassy in Tehran (in 1979) and for not demonstrating support for the U.S. bombing of Libya (in

1986). It became increasingly clear to Japanese decision makers that they had to choose between their privileged relation with the United States and their favored status in the Arab world. Meanwhile, Eli Stern, a Jewish American businessman, was also playing an important and discreet role in convincing Japanese officials to loosen their unofficial economic boycott of Israel.

The 1991 Gulf War was also a turning point. The U.S. government made it clear to Japan, as well as Kuwait and Saudi Arabia, that it was unconceivable that U.S. soldiers would die in the Gulf War to free Kuwait, protect Saudi Arabia, and safeguard oil deliveries to Japan while those three countries continued boycotting U.S. companies doing business with Israel. Japan subsequently and progressively ended its de facto economic boycott of Israeli companies. In 1995, for the first time, a Japanese prime minister (Tomiichi Murayama) paid an official visit to Israel.

Today, more than forty years after the 1973 oil embargo, Japan has reduced its dependency on oil, but its economy has been stagnating for nearly two decades. These two trends have increasingly modified Japan's attitude toward Israel. The "oil blackmail" is no longer an efficient diplomatic weapon. Additionally, with a sluggish economy and an aging population, Japan needs Israel's technological innovation to produce economic growth. The consequence is economic synergy: Japanese companies are heavily invested in Israeli high-tech.

MYANMAR

Myanmar (formerly Burma) was the first Asian country to ask for Israel's assistance in agriculture. Close economic relations soon developed between the two countries, and they established full diplomatic relations in 1953. Ties were also military; in 1954 Myanmar purchased old Spitfire airplanes from Israel.[62] In 1955 Myanmar's prime minister U Nu was the first foreign leader to pay an official visit to Israel. A senior British diplomat commented at the time that "the Burmese

Prime Minister's refusal to be railroaded by Arab pressure into an anti-Israeli policy has further strengthened the admiration of the country for U Nu as Israel's lone champion in the Asian world."[63]

Following the 1988 military coup in Myanmar, the country was under a military embargo imposed by Western countries. Approached by the junta, Israel was asked to fill the military void left by the United States and Europe. In the 1990s Israel became a major provider of military equipment for Myanmar.[64] In 2017 the Israeli newspaper *Ha'aretz* reported that Israel had sold weapons to Myanmar despite the violent repression of the Rohingya minority.[65] Israel reportedly suspended its military ties with Myanmar in 2019.

SOUTH KOREA AND NORTH KOREA

Israel's support for South Korea during the 1950–53 war created special ties between the two countries, including close cooperation between the Mossad and South Korea's intelligence community.[66]

In 1962 Israel and South Korea established full diplomatic relations. In the early 1960s, as South Korean leaders toiled to turn their country into one of Asia's "economic tigers," they looked at Israel as a source of inspiration. South Korean president Park Chung Hee declared in 1965 that "Israel, made of a nation which wandered throughout the world for two thousand years, turned in ten years into the richest and most powerful nation in the Middle East."[67] South Korea started purchasing Israeli military equipment and learning from Israeli defense strategies in the late 1960s.[68]

North Korea, by contrast, has shown enmity toward Israel since its inception—a by-product not only of Pyongyang's Stalinist regime (since 1946), but, more recently, mostly because of North Korea's sale of missiles and nuclear technology to Syria and Iran. The nuclear reactor Israel destroyed in Syria in 2007 had been built by North Korea. Back in 1999 Pyongyang had conveyed to Israel that it would be willing to stop supplying Iran with nuclear technology in exchange for $1 billion in cash. Israel declined the offer.[69]

SINGAPORE

When Singapore, a city-state with a predominantly Chinese population, seceded from the Muslim nation of Malaysia to become independent in 1965, it asked for Israel's assistance and advice to build its army.[70] Singapore's military was built with the help of Israeli advisors and was modeled on the IDF.[71] Impressed by the outcome of the Six-Day War, Singapore intensified its military cooperation with Israel after June 1967.

Not surprisingly, Malaysia fiercely criticized Singapore over its close ties with Israel. Yet Singapore's prime minister Lee Kuan Yew was adamant and defiant. To his critics in the Muslim world, he candidly explained the rationale of his policy: "We made a study of what small countries surrounded by large neighbors with big populations do for their own survival. The study eventually led us to compare. . . . Switzerland, Finland and Israel. In the end, Singapore opted for the Israeli pattern."[72] Singapore's ruling People's Action Party would typically describe Singapore as the "Israel in South-East Asia."[73]

At the same time, Singapore was not insensitive to pressures from the Arab world. Hence were forty-five IDF officers in Singapore officially registered as "Mexican agricultural advisors."

In 2010 Israel was reported to have sold Singapore sea-to-sea missiles and to have upgraded Singapore's air force.[74]

TAIWAN

Israel's policy toward Taiwan was and continues to be influenced by the complex relationship between Israel and China. When relations between Israel and China were hostile, such as in the 1960s, Israel developed close ties with Taiwan.

A small island-state threatened by invasion from mainland Communist China, Taiwan tried to develop its own nuclear deterrent—hence its interest in Israel's nuclear know-how. In 1961 and 1965 the president of Israel's Atomic Energy Commission (Prof. Ernest David Bergman) visited Taiwan upon the invitation of the Taiwanese government. Israel's Foreign Ministry, however, successfully lobbied the government to block the sharing of nuclear technology with Taiwan.[75] The Foreign Ministry also stopped Israel's planned sale of Gabriel missiles to Taiwan, asserting that Israel should not provoke China.[76] Israel did agree to Taiwan's purchase of basic military equipment.

Once Israel and China established diplomatic relations (in 1992), Taiwan tried to follow suit but was rejected. Israel did not want to damage its new official relations with Beijing.

Despite the absence of diplomatic relations between Israel and Taiwan, the two countries have strong trade and military ties.

VIETNAM, LAOS, AND CAMBODIA

Israel's relations with Vietnam were complicated by the country's division until its forced "unification" by the North in 1975, because North Vietnam, being a Communist country at war with the United States, considered Israel an enemy country.

Once all of Vietnam became Communist, it turned hostile to Israel, as was de rigueur during the Cold War. Yet relations between the Vietnamese Communists and Israel were complex. Ho Chi Minh, the Vietnamese Communist leader, was no anti-Zionist. He admired the Zionists' struggle against Great Britain, and in 1946 he offered David Ben-Gurion the opportunity to establish a government-in-exile in Hanoi.[77] Ho Chi Minh's personal sympathy, however, could not resist the constraints of Cold War politics. Israel and the United States had become allies in the mid-1960s, the very time when the Johnson administration was intensifying the war against the Vietcong in North Vietnam. As a Vietcong diplomat put it bluntly, "Those who are being supported by the United States are our enemies. This is why we are in favor of the Arabs."[78] Vietcong leaders started developing close ties with the PLO. By the late 1960s, the PLO had learned and imitated the guerilla tactics of Vietcong military strategist Võ Nguyên Giáp.[79]

In 1975 the Vietcong invaded South Vietnam, and the Communists took over neighboring Laos and Cambodia as well. The new Communist governments of Laos and Cambodia severed diplomatic relations with Israel. This came as a blow, since Israel had developed close ties with both nations.

With the end of the Cold War, the establishment of diplomatic relations with the Soviet Union (in 1991) and with China (1992), as well as the signature of the Oslo Agreements between Israel and the PLO (1993), Vietnam started mitigating its dogmatic approach to the Middle East. In addition, Vietnam wanted the Clinton administration to lift its economic embargo, and Vietnamese leaders were convinced that recognizing Israel would help mend fences with Washington. Vietnam and Israel established full diplomatic relations in 1993, and flourishing economic ties ensued. Cambodia and Laos also restored their diplomatic ties with Israel in 1993.

THAILAND AND THE PHILIPPINES

The Philippines was the only Asian country to vote in favor of the 1947 UN partition plan. Over the years Israel developed close ties with both the Philippines and Thailand, two countries whose foreign policy was anti-Communist during most of the Cold War. Israel established diplomatic relations with Thailand in 1954 and with the Philippines in 1958.

Still, both countries' attitude to Israel has been a constant balancing act between their closeness to the United States and the pressures of their significant (and sometimes unruly) Muslim populations (5 percent in Thailand, 6 percent in the Philippines). Libyan dictator Muammar Gaddafi used to support Muslim dissidents in the Philippines, which had the effect of strengthening ties between the Philippines and Israel. In addition, the Philippines' eagerness to reduce its military dependence on the United States led to the purchase of

Israeli weaponry starting in the 1960s.[80] This military relationship has been maintained over the years. In 2018, for example, the Philippines bought surface-to-surface missiles from Israel.[81] In September 2018 the Philippines' president visited Israel to sign large oil and arms contracts.[82]

Thailand is one of the most popular tourist destinations for Israelis. At the same time, some twenty thousand Thai migrant workers are employed in Israel, in agriculture and as cooks in Asian restaurants.

MALAYSIA, INDONESIA, AND PAKISTAN

Israel has managed to establish diplomatic relations with almost all Asian countries, except for Asia's Muslim states (Indonesia, Malaysia, Pakistan, and Bangladesh) and Communist North Korea.

In the case of Indonesia and Malaysia, their Muslim identity continues to constitute an obstacle to diplomatic relations. While Malaysia's first prime minister, Tunku Abdul Rahman (1955–70), was personally well-disposed toward Israel, he headed the government of a Muslim country whose leadership was strongly opposed to recognizing Israel. Abdul Rahman criticized his opponents for blocking Israel's recognition, but he did not overcome them.[83] A senior Malaysian official privately admitted in 1959 that his country's Muslim majority (about 60 percent) would not allow the establishment of diplomatic relations with Israel.[84] During the Indonesia-Malaysia Confrontation (1963–66), Malaysia sought international support and could not afford to alienate the Arab world by establishing diplomatic relations with Israel.

Malaysia's relations with Israel turned from distant to hostile under the premiership of Mahathir bin Mohamad (1981–2003, and 2018–20). In his 1970 book *The Malay Dilemma*, Mahathir described the Jews as "hooked-nosed" people who instinctively understand finance.[85] Two years after his election, *The Protocols of the Elders of Zion* was translated into Malay and distributed in Malaysia. In 1984 Mahathir ordered the cancellation of the New York Philharmonic

Orchestra's performance in Kuala Lumpur because the orchestra's director refused to remove *Hebrew Rhapsody for Cello and Orchestra* by the Jewish composer Ernest Bloch from the program. In an August 1986 speech, Mahathir claimed that the *New York Times* and the *Wall Street Journal* were controlled by the Jews and the Zionists; two months later he accused "the Zionists" of secretly trying to undermine the Malaysian economy.[86] In 1994 Mahathir banned *Schindler's List* from Malaysia, claiming it was a film of Jewish propaganda. He blamed the 1997 Asian financial crisis on the Hungarian-born American financier Georges Soros, explicitly referring to Soros's Jewishness. At the 2003 Organization of the Islamic Conference summit, Mahathir declared that "1.3 Muslims cannot be defeated by a few million Jews. . . . Today, the Jews rule this world by proxy. They get others to fight and die for them. . . . They have now gained control of the most powerful countries and they, this tiny community, have become a world power."[87] In June 2016 Mahathir reiterated in a TV interview that "Jews are ruling the world by proxy."[88] In recent years, many Palestinian students have relocated to Malaysia, where Hamas is actively trying to recruit them to its cause. Hamas has used Malaysia to train its members for terrorist attacks against Israel.[89]

Even though Israel did not have, and still doesn't have, formal diplomatic relations with Asia's main Muslim countries, Israel's "arms sales diplomacy" has extended to those countries as well. Israel sells military hardware to Indonesia, and Indonesia sells coal to Israel.[90] Indonesia agreed to a secret Mossad presence in Jakarta, and by the early 1980s there were significant military deals between Israel and Indonesia.[91] Despite the absence of formal diplomatic relations with Indonesia, an Indonesia-Israel trade bureau was established in 2010, and large Israeli companies operate in Indonesia.[92]

Regarding Pakistan, relations were not always hostile. In September 1956 Pakistan's foreign minister declared that "Israel is a reality," and after the 1956 Suez War a Pakistani diplomat praised Israel for its military success.[93] There were also unofficial contacts between Israel and Pakistan in the 1980s regarding the Pakistani nuclear program. Fearing an Israeli raid on its nuclear sites, the Pakistani government assured Israel that it would not transfer nuclear technology to Arab countries.[94]

Pakistani society itself was divided on how to relate to Israel. In August 1992, for example, the Pakistani ambassador to the United States suggested that her country should recognize Israel, just as India did. Pakistan's religious leaders and Islamist parties harshly condemned the ambassador's statement and demanded her resignation.[95] A Pakistani official attended the funeral of Yitzhak Rabin in Jerusalem in November 1995. However, as Israel's military and intelligence cooperation with India increased after 1992, so did Pakistan's resentment at the India-Israel partnership.

AUSTRALIA, NEW ZEALAND, OCEANIA

Australian forces fought in the Middle East alongside Britain in the two world wars. During the UN debates on Palestine in 1947—thanks to Australian foreign minister Herbert Vere Evatt—Australia voted in favor of the partition plan, despite British pressures to the contrary. Evatt's strong Zionist sympathies overrode British and Arab pressures on Australia, which then recognized Israel in 1949.

In recent years, Australia has been a staunch supporter of Israel—especially under conservative governments. The Australian government fully backed Israel during the 2006 Lebanon War. In December 2016 Australian foreign minister Julie Bishop declared that her country would have voted against UN Security Council Resolution 2334, which the United States did not veto (see chapter 12). In July 2018 the Australian government decided to redirect $10 million away from the World Bank's Multi-Donor Trust Fund over concern that the Palestinian Authority was using the money to pay terrorists.[96]

Like Australia, New Zealand sent troops to the Middle East in the two world wars, and like Australia, it voted in favor of the partition of Palestine despite British pressures and recognized Israel in 1949. Unlike Australia, however, New Zealand supported UN Security Council Resolution 2334, which prompted Israel to call back its ambassador and to downgrade relations with Wellington in 2016. Full bilateral relations were restored after the New Zealand government expressed regret for supporting Resolution 2334.

In Oceania, Israel also enjoys strong bilateral ties with the Marshall Islands, Micronesia, Nauru, and Palau. These reliable allies have consistently voted against anti-Israel resolutions at the UN General Assembly. In December 2017, for example, all four countries voted against a resolution that condemned the transfer of the U.S. embassy to Jerusalem.

Conclusion

China became Communist the year Israel joined the United Nations (1949). Israel, however, had a neutral foreign policy at the time, and therefore diplomatic relations with China could have been established—a missed opportunity, as China's foreign policy turned hostile to Israel after the Bandung Conference (1955) and the Suez War (1956). The Sino-Soviet Split and America's recognition of Communist China led to a behind-the-scenes rapprochement between China and Israel. China started purchasing Israeli military technology and equipment way before the two countries established full diplomatic relations in 1992. Those military ties—and, later, growing economic ties— generated friction between Israel and the United States.

India has become a major importer of Israel military equipment and technology. Originally India had kept its distance from Israel; the Congress Party did not want to alienate Muslim voters and sought to mollify Muslim countries that were better disposed toward Pakistan.

India's de facto alignment with the Soviet Union during the Cold War further widened the rift with Israel. With the end of the Cold War, India sought to amend relations with the United States, and it established diplomatic relations with Israel in 1992. India's protracted conflict with Pakistan acquired a new dimension when Pakistan became nuclear in 1998. India subsequently upgraded its military ties with Israel, especially under governments led by the pro-Israel BJP.

As for Japan, relations were temporarily overshadowed by the oil embargo, but they bloomed again with Israel's emergence as a technology powerhouse and with the decline of the Arab oil weapon.

Israel's military expertise and technological edge contributed to the strengthening of ties with most Asian countries. Though full diplomatic ties have never been established with Asia's Muslim countries, Israel has informal trade and even military relations with most of them.

17. The Scramble for Africa

I have lived to see the restoration of the Jews; I should like to pave the way for the restoration of the Africans.

THEODORE HERZL, *Altneuland*

From Diplomatic Irrelevance to Strategic Importance

When in 1947 the Jewish Agency was struggling to gather international support for Jewish statehood at the United Nations, Africa was still under colonial rule and therefore voiceless at the UN. At the time only two African countries were independent, Liberia and Ethiopia (the former voted in favor of partition; the latter abstained).

Liberia had been founded a hundred years earlier (in 1847) by former African American slaves, and Liberians sympathized with the idea of formerly exiled people returning to their homeland. Edward Wilmot Blyden, a nineteenth-century Liberian politician and author, saw in Zionism a model for African Americans' return to their ancestral continent. U.S. civil rights activist William Edward Burghardt Dubois said that the Pan-Africanist movement was inspired by Zionism, and that the Pan-African Congress drew its inspiration from the Zionist Congress.[1]

Only with the decolonization and independence of African countries did Africa became a factor in Israel's foreign policy. In the late 1950s through the early 1970s, Israel's "periphery strategy" included Ethiopia (see chapter 10). With the decolonization of Africa, from the early 1960s onward, the periphery strategy started expanding to the rest of the continent.

After the Tiran Straits reopened in the wake of the 1956 Suez War, Israel had physical access to eastern Africa, enabling trade between Israel and the African continent. Golda Meir, who served as foreign minister from 1956 to 1966, initiated a proactive policy vis-à-vis Africa. She would quote from Herzl's book *Altneuland* ("I have lived to see the restoration of the Jews; I should like to pave the way for the restoration of the Africans"), but her African policy was primarily motivated by realpolitik. Israel needed to strengthen its international stance and bypass its regional isolation; therefore, Africa's newly independent countries were important to Israel.

Israel's diplomacy in Africa benefited from an admiration for Israel's prowess, but also from the Africans' historical resentment toward their former Arab enslavers. When Saudi Arabia's ambassador to the UN, Ahmed Shukairi, accused the ambassador of Côte d'Ivoire of being "bought by the Jews," the latter replied that it was the Arabs, not the Jews, who had sold Africans into slavery.[2]

It was only natural that Israel's Africa policy had begun with Ethiopia. Ethiopia's emperor Haile Selassie claimed descent from King Solomon; his dynasty was called the Solomonic Dynasty, and his seal included Jewish symbols such as the Lion of Judah. After Mussolini's Italy invaded Ethiopia in 1935, Emperor Selassie made a pilgrimage to Jerusalem before temporarily settling in England. When British forces drove out the Italian army from Ethiopia in April 1941, they were assisted by Haganah soldiers who had been recruited by the pro-Zionist British officer Orde Wingate. There was a significant Jewish community in Ethiopia (roughly estimated at fifty thousand in the mid-twentieth century), and even some Christian Ethiopians had adopted Jewish customs such as circumcision, the prohibition of pork consumption, and refraining from working in the fields on Saturdays.[3]

Israel would waste no time in establishing contacts and relations with newly independent African states.

The Rise and Fall of Israel's African Diplomacy

Paradoxically, one of the first targets of Israel's African diplomacy was Sudan — a Muslim, and mostly Arab, country. When a Sudanese official declared in the fall of 1956 that "Sudan perceives the Egyptian military empowerment [as] a direct danger for its independence," decision makers in Jerusalem raised the possibility of developing ties with Sudan, based on a common enmity to Nasser's Egypt. British intelligence (MI6) helped establish unofficial contacts between Israel and Sudan, and in August 1956 a senior Sudanese official made a secret trip to Israel.[4] A year later, Israeli foreign minister Golda Meir met with Sudanese prime minister Abdallah Khalil in Paris.[5] Those early contacts, however, were cut short by the 1958 military coup in Sudan. The new Sudanese leader decided to align his country with Nasser's Egypt.

Golda Meir officially inaugurated her proactive African policy with a 1958 tour that took her to Liberia, Senegal, Nigeria, Ghana, and Côte d'Ivoire. New opportunities opened for Israel in 1960 with the independence of French Equatorial Africa and French West Africa. Nigeria was of special importance, both because of its size (45 million people in 1960, 186 million today) and its oil resources. Israel established diplomatic relations with Nigeria upon its independence in 1960 despite the opposition of Nigerian Muslims.[6]

Israel also developed strong ties with Côte d'Ivoire upon its independence in 1960. Côte d'Ivoire's president Félix Houphouët-Boigny, a great friend and admirer of Israel, saw in Israel a model of economic development, national cohesion, and success[7] and would systematically oppose anti-Israel resolutions at the Organization of African Unity (an organization established in 1963 to promote political and economic integration in Africa; its name would change to African Union in 2002). One of Houphouët-Boigny's first foreign visits as head of state was to Israel, in July 1962.

Israeli president Itzhak Ben-Zvi paid an official visit to western African countries in 1962, and Prime Minister Levi Eshkol followed in 1966. In the 1960s Israel had diplomatic relations with all the countries of sub-Saharan Africa, except for Mauritania and Somalia, two Arab League members. By 1972 the number of Israeli embassies and consulates in Africa had grown from six in 1960 to thirty-two. Indeed, by the early 1970s, Israel had established diplomatic relations with all of Africa's non-Arab countries and had even became an observer state of the Organization of African Unity (not a formal member, but allowed to attend the organization's meetings). Israel had more embassies in Africa at the time than any other country, except the United States.[8]

In the 1960s African countries had resisted pressures from Arab states (especially from Egyptian president Nasser) to sever or at least downgrade relations with Israel. By 1968 twenty-two African states had signed economic cooperation agreements with Israel. Israel provided African countries with training and technical assistance in agriculture and medicine, and military training as well. Israel trained the first air force pilots of Kenya, Uganda, Tanzania, Zaïre, and Ghana. In the 1960s more than seven thousand Africans received professional training in Israel. Some twenty cooperation agreements were signed between Israel and African countries, and Israel was one of the world's most sought-after partner for agriculture, health care, and defense.[9] Even the Six-Day War of 1967, and the ensuing pressures from Arab countries, did not undo these strong relations. In fact, it was thanks to the votes of African states that Israel was then able to block a resolution calling for a total and unconditional withdrawal of Israel from its conquered territories.[10]

Later, in the 1970s, however, Israel's special status in Africa began to deteriorate. When small countries switched allegiances in the global

geopolitical contest of the Cold War, increasingly more African countries became Soviet allies: Bénin in 1972; Angola, Mozambique, and
Madagascar in 1975; Ethiopia in 1977; and Congo-Brazzaville in 1979.
Upon becoming Soviet allies, these countries cut their ties with Israel;
the Soviet Union had severed its diplomatic relations with Israel in 1967,
and it expected its new allies to follow suit. In addition, having failed
to put an end to Israel's ties with Africa after the Six-Day War, Arab
countries started investing diplomatic efforts in Africa. In 1968 Egypt
declared that it intended to isolate Israel in Africa. That same year, Egypt
opened eight new embassies in Africa. By 1972 there were more than
one hundred Arab embassies in Africa, up from seventy-eight in 1967.

Of all the Arab leaders attempting to sever Israel's ties with Africa,
the Libyan dictator Muammar Gaddafi was the most proactive. Right
after becoming Libya's new leader in 1969, he tried to undo Israel's ties
in Africa. Between 1970 and 1973, eight African leaders visited Tripoli
to obtain financial and military aid from Gaddafi.[11] One of Gaddafi's
main successes in Africa was Uganda. Until Idi Amin seized power
in Uganda in 1971, the country was a close ally of Israel. Under Amin,
Uganda switched alliance to Libya, becoming violently anti-Israel and
even taking part in the hijacking of the Air France flight to Entebbe
in 1976. In fact, the erratic Amin was himself an Israel fan until his
"conversion." He had taken an (uncompleted) paratrooper course in
Israel and was friendly with Colonel Baruch Bar-Lev, Israel's military attaché in Uganda. (Bar-Lev was suspected of having advised
Amin prior to his 1971 military coup,[12] though Bar-Lev denied any
involvement and said that Amin's coup had taken him by surprise.[13])
Once in power, Amin had asked Israel to give him a £10 million loan
and to sell him Phantom fighter planes to conquer parts of Tanzania
(Amin sought direct access to the Indian Ocean).[14] Israel declined,
and Amin subsequently turned to Muammar Gaddafi. The Libyan
dictator obliged, but with conditions that Amin eagerly accepted.
Amin severed diplomatic relations with Israel, expelled all Israelis

from Uganda, installed the PLO in the former Israeli embassy, and undertook the construction of a giant mosque in Kampala. He also instructed his foreign minister to cable Golda Meir (then Israel's prime minister) to "pick up your knickers and go back to America where you came from" (Uganda's foreign minister thankfully disobeyed).[15] Both Libya and Saudi Arabia responded with generous grants and loans to the Ugandan government.[16]

Saudi Arabia also tried to sever Israel's ties with Africa by buying goodwill with petrodollars. In November 1972 King Faisal of Saudi Arabia paid visits to Uganda, Chad, Niger, Senegal, and Mauritania, offering money and the instruction to cut ties with Israel. Soon after this visit, Chad severed its relations with Israel. When President Idi Amin of Uganda severed his country's ties with Israel, he was promised $30 million from Libya and $15 million from Saudi Arabia. Likewise, Libya offered a $92 million loan to Chad and a $50 million loan to Senegal.[17] Gaddafi boasted that "Libya has succeeded within two years in isolating Israel from Africa."[18]

The 1973 Yom Kippur War also led Arab countries to coax African states into severing their diplomatic relations with Israel. Now convinced that they could not vanquish Israel militarily, the Arab states decided to isolate Israel internationally, by leveraging their oil resources. Promising lower oil prices, they persuaded oil-importing countries to cut ties with Israel or at least to condemn Israel (see chapter 11). Additionally, Egyptian president Anwar Sadat personally asked African leaders to cut ties with Israel — such efficient and devastating pressure that by the end of the war, all but four African states (Lesotho, Malawi, Swaziland, and Mauritius) had severed their diplomatic relations with Israel.[19] Altogether, thirty African countries broke their ties with Israel in the wake of the war, twenty-one of them between October 4 and October 12, 1973. Even the pro-Israel Houphouët-Boigny succumbed to the pressure; in November 1973 Côte d'Ivoire severed relations with Israel. This was a serious blow to Israel's diplomacy and international standing. Abba Eban condemned the African turn-around as a "gross betrayal of international friendship." The Israeli newspaper *Ha'aretz* characterized the reversion as a "mad rush" that did "not reflect honor on the African states."[20]

Chad's president François Tombalbaye vividly explained Gadda-fi's key role in severing relations between Israel and Africa to Israeli diplomat David Kimche. Rebels in Chad were supported by Gaddafi and had an office in Tripoli. "One day," Tombalbaye said, "a Gaddafi emissary arrived in N'Djamena. He told me that Gaddafi was willing to end his support for the rebels and evict them from Libya, and even to donate money to Chad, but on the condition that we sever our dip-lomatic relations with Israel. Our situation was so dire that I didn't really have a choice."[21]

Even though diplomatic relations were officially severed, economic and military relations were maintained. In fact, Israel's trade with Africa doubled between 1973 and 1977.[22] Israel maintained nondiplo-matic offices in Ghana, Côte d'Ivoire, and Kenya. Military ties, main-tained with Kenya, enabled the successful completion of the Entebbe rescue operation in 1976.

Furthermore, with time, African leaders realized that they had not gained what they had been promised for ending their diplomatic rela-tions with Israel. The reduced oil prices promised by Arab countries had failed to materialize. At the 1974 Organization of African Unity summit in Mogadishu (Somalia), African countries complained of high oil prices and that Arab states did nothing to relieve their eco-nomic burden.[23] As Joel Peters (an expert on Israel-Africa relations) quipped, "The Africans found the Arabs willing to share enemies but not energy."[24] Moreover, Gaddafi hardly ever kept his promises. Chad, for example, had severed its diplomatic relations with Israel because Gaddafi had promised to provide financial support and to stop supporting its anti-regime rebels. Yet when Chad's president asked Gaddafi to honor his commitment, the latter laid down a new demand: Chad's president had to convert to Islam and change the name of his country to the Islamic Republic of Chad. Chad rejected the ultimatum, and Gaddafi never honored his commitment.[25]

The disappointment of African leaders brought back memories of the Arabs' slave trade in Africa—memories that had made Africans sympathetic to Israel in the first place. The *Zambian Daily Mail* wrote that the "refusal by Arab countries to sell oil to African states at a reduced price is a tacit example that the Arabs, our former slave masters, are not prepared to abandon the rider and horse partnership. We have not forgotten that they used to abuse us like herds and sell us as slaves."[26] Furthermore, Zambia and Kenya, among other African countries with Christian majorities, were becoming increasingly concerned by the Islamic radicalism encouraged in their nations by Libya, Sudan, and Iran. President Houphouët-Boigny of Côte d'Ivoire protested that the only "investment" of Arab petrodollars in Africa was in mosques and madrasas.[27] When, in September 1983, the Arab Bank for African development published a report claiming that it had invested $58 million in Côte d'Ivoire, Houphouët-Boigny declared that this was a lie; his country had never received any money from the bank.[28]

Israel arguably could have been more proactive in exploiting the disappointment of African countries with the Arab states. Yet Israel felt betrayed and isolated, and it reacted to the post-1973 diplomatic divorce with Africa by upgrading its relations with South Africa, a country whose apartheid regime was officially based on racial discrimination and was therefore boycotted by the rest of Africa. The new policy was motivated both by disappointment and realpolitik, as an Israeli official explained: "For years we spent millions in Black Africa on various projects, including building up their armies. . . . What was the result? In the course of less than two years, 1972 and 1973, one after the other broke relations with us. Bought off by Arab money. So today we make friends where we can and however we can."[29]

In 1974 Israel sent its first ambassador to Pretoria (the administrative capital of South Africa), something it had refrained from doing until then, so as not to offend African countries. In April 1976 the Rabin government officially hosted South Africa's prime minister John Vorster in Jerusalem. Israel and South Africa developed close military ties, with the tacit consent and even support of the United States, because of South Africa's anti-Communist foreign policy. In 1980 South Africa purchased 35 percent of Israel's military exports.[30] In 1981 Israel sold South Africa the rights to manufacture the Israeli Galil rifle, as well as the Reshef and Dabur gunboats and the Gabriel missile. Israel was also suspected of having assisted South Africa in its invasion of Angola in 1983.[31] Military cooperation between Israel and South Africa included nuclear technology. In June 1980 the CIA claimed that Israel and South Africa had jointly tested a nuclear bomb in the South Atlantic.[32]

Israel's military cooperation with South Africa was not an isolated practice among Western countries: the United States, UK, France, and West Germany had strong military ties with South Africa as well. In 1980 France supplied over half of Pretoria's military imports.[33] The West tacitly supported the apartheid regime, fearing that its toppling by the African National Congress—which had Marxist and pro-Soviet leanings—would turn South Africa into a Soviet ally.

Pretoria also enjoyed strong economic ties with the United States, Britain, West Germany, and France. Only after Pretoria's 1985 proclamation of a state of emergency did the United States and Britain impose sanctions on South Africa in 1986. Israel followed suit by joining the sanctions regime against Pretoria in 1987.

By the late 1970s, many African leaders viewed Israel as an important partner against Marxist guerrillas supported by the Soviet Union and against Islamic forces encouraged by Gaddafi. And beyond not having gained much from Gaddafi's blackmail, African countries now felt threatened by him. Gaddafi had tried to conquer Chad and topple its government on several occasions between 1978 and 1987. Gaddafi was also supporting Islamic rebels, destabilizing governments in Uganda, Nigeria, Chad, and Burkina Faso. African countries with Christian majorities grew increasingly concerned by his efforts at Islamic expansionism—a fear that became ever more acute after the 1979 Islamic revolution in Iran.

Since the 1973 Yom Kippur War, African statesmen had claimed that their boycott of Israel was motivated by solidarity with Egypt, itself an African country partially occupied by Israel (in the Sinai Peninsula). With the 1979 peace agreement between Israel and Egypt and Israel's subsequent withdrawal from Sinai, this argument fell flat. Indeed, when African countries started renewing their diplomatic relations with Israel in the 1980s, they systematically referred to the Israel-Egypt peace agreement to justify their move. When, by contrast, the Nigerian government refused to renew diplomatic relations with Israel even after the peace agreement, a Nigerian academic criticized the decision thus: "When Egypt decided that it was in its national interest to make peace with Israel it did so without asking the permission of Nigeria or of the Organization of African Unity. . . . It is right to condemn occupation and Israel's intrusion in Lebanon. But what about the Soviet invasion of Afghanistan or the Vietnamese invasion of Laos? Nigeria didn't sever its diplomatic relations with these countries even though it condemned them. Renewing relations with Israel will not only make it easier for Nigerian Christians to visit the Holy Land, but it will also benefit Nigeria's agricultural and technological development."[34]

By the early 1980s, Israel was ready to realize the opportunity to build on Africa's disappointment with Gaddafi and fear of communism. Ariel Sharon, serving as defense minister, advocated for strengthening strategic and military ties with anti-Soviet and anti-Gaddafi regimes throughout Africa.[35] Israel's foreign ministry general director David Kimche, who had worked for the Mossad in Africa, convinced the

Israeli government to rebuild Israel's ties with Africa, and he helped implement the policy.

The first country to renew ties with Israel was Zaïre (today's Democratic Republic of Congo, or DRC), in 1982. Zaïre's dictator, Mobutu Sese Seko, had taken a short paratrooper course in Israel back in 1963, and he had always maintained military ties with Israel despite the severance of diplomatic relations in 1973.[36] Mobutu was also convinced that renewing relations with Israel would help him obtain U.S. financial aid. Arab countries strongly condemned Zaïre's decision, but Mobutu dismissively replied that his country had no intention of following "slave caravans with its whips and turbans"—a clear historical reference to the Arab slave trade in Africa.[37]

Zaïre was followed by Liberia in 1983, Côte d'Ivoire in 1985, Cameroon in 1986, Togo in 1987, Kenya in 1988, Ethiopia in 1989, Zambia in 1991, Nigeria in 1992, Uganda and Eritrea in 1993, and Tanzania in 1994. In the case of Zambia, the renewal of diplomatic relations was due not only to geopolitics, but also to a regime change. Zambia's new president, Frederick Chiluba, insisted on renewing diplomatic relations with Israel immediately after his election. A devout Christian, he explained to Israel's ambassador to Kenya that he believed in the verse from Genesis 12:3, "I will bless those who bless you, and curse him that curses you" and that Zambia had been cursed since it had severed diplomatic relations with Israel. He also expressed his fear of radical Islam in Africa and his eagerness to benefit from Israel's intelligence and military expertise.[38]

As for Eritrea, establishing relations with Israel was not self-evident. It was a Muslim nation. The Arab world had supported Eritrea's secession from Ethiopia, while Israel had sided with Ethiopia (Israel did not want an additional Muslim country on the shores of the Red Sea). Nonetheless, Eritrea's first president, Isaias Afewerki, decided to establish diplomatic relations with Israel in 1993 after his life was saved by Israeli doctors.[39]

Israel also started distancing itself from South Africa after joining the sanctions movement against Pretoria in 1987. With the Soviet Union's collapse in 1991, pro-Soviet African countries (such as Angola, Mozambique, Ethiopia, and Congo-Brazzaville) toned down their anti-Israel rhetoric. When the apartheid regime in South Africa ended in 1994, African countries could no longer use Jerusalem's relations with Pretoria as an excuse for not renewing relations with Israel. Ultimately, the 1993 Oslo Agreements between Israel and the PLO and the 1994 peace agreement between Israel and Jordan removed the final obstacles to the renewal of diplomatic relations with reticent African countries (such as Uganda and Tanzania).

In October 1999 Nelson Mandela (who was now no longer president of South Africa) paid a visit to Israel, where he met the son of the Johannesburg Jewish lawyer who had given Mandela his first full-time job as a lawyer half a century before. Mandela had close ties with Jewish South Africans who opposed apartheid, and he always felt indebted to them. At the same time, he also remembered the special ties between Jerusalem and Pretoria under the apartheid regime. While in Israel, Mandela conveyed a message that was both accusatory and conciliatory: "Israel worked very closely with the apartheid regime. I say: I've made peace with many men who slaughtered our people like animals. Israel cooperated with the apartheid regime, but it did not participate in any atrocities."

Mandela's successors at the African National Congress (ANC) were not as conciliatory; South African foreign policy became increasingly antagonistic toward Israel. With the outbreak of the second intifada in September 2000, successive ANC governments systematically sided with the Palestinians and harshly criticized Israel. The movement for the academic boycott of Israel was founded in South Africa following the 2001 Durban Conference. In May 2018 South Africa recalled its ambassador to Israel, protesting Israel's reprisals to the shooting of rockets from Gaza.

Overall, however, Israel was able to rebuild its relations with Africa in the 1980s and 1990s. Yet this diplomatic achievement was soon to be challenged by Iran's influence on the African continent.

Rebuilding Bridges with Africa: Successes and Challenges

In 2008, then Iranian president Mahmoud Ahmadinejad declared that his country intended to develop ties with Africa. One year later he traveled with Iranian diplomats and generals to many African countries, signing commercial, diplomatic, and defense deals.

Today Iran's influence in Africa relies on Lebanon's rich and influential Shia diaspora in countries such as Congo, Guinea, and Senegal, which donates money to Hezbollah, the anti-Israel Shia militia operating in southern Lebanon. At the same time, given the Jihadist threats in Mali and Niger, increasingly more African countries are becoming fearful of Iran and its Islamic allies. Ethiopia, faced with Islamic militias backed by rebels in neighboring Somalia, has become one of Israel's closest African allies, as well as a major buyer of Israeli defense equipment.[40] Kenya, which also faces Islamic terrorism, is strengthening its military ties with Israel. Even Nigeria reportedly spent about $500 million on Israeli military equipment in recent years.[41]

Shortly after France's military intervention in Mali in January 2013, the president of Mali voiced his anger at Arab countries, especially Egypt (then ruled by Mohamed Morsi and the Muslim Brotherhood), for condemning France but not the Jihadists who were planning on overtaking the country. The Malian president was expressing a wider African fear of Islamic influence, the Jihadist threat, and Iranian meddling, all intended to topple governments throughout the continent. In November 2011 both Kenya's prime minister and Uganda's president visited Israel to discuss cooperation in fighting against the penetration of radical Islam in their countries.

In another painful reminder of the Jihadist threat in Africa, the Islamic group al-Shabab perpetrated a terrorist attack in Nairobi in September 2014. Africa's growing concerns opened a window of opportunity for Israel, which leveraged its counterterrorism expertise among African countries targeted by Islamic terrorism. This, in turn, translated into increased military sales. In 2016 alone, Israel's military sales to Africa grew by 70 percent.[42]

Al-Shabab ("the youth" in Arabic), which carried out the Nairobi attack, was founded in 2005 in Somalia. When military rule ended in 1991, Somalia was left without an official government and central authority. The country sank into chaos, with gangs and militias competing for power. By 2009 some five thousand Islamic al-Shabab fighters had gained control over the southern half of the country (including the capital, Mogadishu). Al-Shabab thus became the first al-Qaida ally to partially rule over a Muslim country. In 2011 al-Shabab lost Mogadishu to the troops of the Transitional Federal Government, and since then, al-Shabab has lost about two-thirds of the territory it used to control in southern Somalia, but it is lethally active in other parts of Africa, including Nairobi.

Al-Shabab collaborates with AQIM (al-Qaida in the Islamic Maghreb) in the Sahel (African zone of transition between the Sahara to the north and the Sudanese Savanna to the south) and with Boko Haram in Nigeria. AQIM, operating from Mali, aims to overthrow the Algerian government and replace it with an Islamic state. Boko Haram (whose meaning is "Western education is sinful") aims at establishing Sharia law in Nigeria, Cameroon, and Niger. The former chief of the U.S. Africa Command, General Carter F. Ham, has warned that al-Shabab, AQIM, and Boko Haram collaborate throughout Africa in coordination with al-Qaida.[43] Geographically, the three terrorist organizations span from East to West Africa via the Maghreb (northwest Africa). This "Islamic Arc" goes through three countries that are of strategic importance to both Africa and the world economy: Mali is Africa's third largest gold producer (after South Africa and Ghana); Nigeria is Africa's top oil producer and has Africa's largest proven natural gas reserves; Somalia borders a major sea passage for international trade.

Africa's Islamic Arc serves Iran's interests. In February 2013 UN monitors overseeing the arms embargo in Somalia reported that al-Shabab was receiving arms from both Iran and Yemen.[44] Iran is also an active supporter of its ally Hezbollah in Africa. In May 2013, partly thanks to Israel, the Nigerian government uncovered a Hezbollah cell and arms cache in the city of Kano in northern Nigeria. The cooperation between Israel and Nigeria is part of a wider Israeli activity aimed at countering Hezbollah's presence in western Africa. Israel has been offering security training and equipment to western African governments that oppose Hezbollah's activities on their territory.

According to Abel Assadina, a former senior Iranian diplomat who defected in 2003, Iran is establishing local power bases in Africa for the purpose of influencing local governments and inducing them to act against Western interests. Back in November 2010, Iran's foreign minister openly declared that Iran's "African outreach" was a top priority.

In Nigeria, in addition to Hezbollah and Boko Haram, Islamic operators include the Islamic Movement in Nigeria (IMN), an organization founded in the early 1980s with Iranian financial and logistical support. Nigerian students from the Muslim Student Society and trained by the Islamic Republic of Iran post-1979 had started IMN in order to produce an Iranian-style Islamic revolution in Nigeria. IMN's founding leader, and also the current leader of the Shiites in Nigeria, Ibrahim Zakzaky, typically sits under a portrait of Ayatollah Khomeini when addressing his supporters. His speeches are virulently antisemitic.

The consequences of the Islamic infiltration in Africa have been lethal, starting with the 1997 al-Qaida terrorist attack against the U.S. embassy in Nairobi. Then came the 2002 al-Qaida terrorist attack against Israeli tourists in Mombasa.

Israel is also assisting Kenya in rooting out Islamic terrorism. When in May 2013 a Kenyan court convicted two Iranians for planning terrorist attacks against Western targets in Kenya, Israeli investigators interrogated the Iranian defendants in a Kenyan prison. Israel has also provided the Kenyan government with anti-terror intelligence. This assistance is likely to increase, and not only in Kenya.

In a way, a by-proxy war is being waged between Israel and Iran in Africa. Throughout the African continent, more and more countries are the victims of Islamic terrorism, but not all of them are ready to abandon the economic benefits of doing business with Iran.

After years of diplomatic neglect, Israel is now more proactive in Africa. Declaring that "Israel has returned to Africa," Prime Minister Netanyahu flew four times to Africa between 2015 and 2019.[45] In January 2019 Chad renewed diplomatic relations with Israel—relations Chad had severed in 1972 under the pressure of Muammar Gaddafi. Chad, a Muslim country, has common borders with Libya and Sudan, two dysfunctional states in which jihadists act with impunity. Today Chad sees in Libya a threat and in Israel a partner to fight jihadism and border infiltrations.

Conclusion

Israel gained access to the Red Sea only after the 1956 Suez War and shortly before independent African states started emerging from European colonialism. Popular in Africa because of its achievements in economic development and nation building (whereas Africans associated the Arabs with the former perpetrators of Africa's Arab slave trade), Israel swiftly established relations with the new African countries. Israel developed a strong diplomatic and economic presence throughout Africa in the 1960s, but this success was undermined in the 1970s due to the economic blackmail of Saudi Arabia and Libya and to Marxist coups that turned some African countries into Soviet allies.

Nearly all African countries severed their diplomatic relations with Israel following the 1973 Yom Kippur War, but they did not reap the benefits they had expected from kowtowing to Arab pressures. After Egypt signed a peace agreement with Israel in 1979, African countries lost what had been their official excuse for not renewing relations with Israel. Ties were progressively restored in the 1980s. Today Iran tries to undermine Israel's ties with African countries. On the other hand, the threats of radical Islam and terrorism in sub-Saharan Africa make Israel an indispensable ally for African countries.

18. Latin American Dilemmas

Somoza is a son of a bitch, but he's our son of a bitch.

FRANKLIN D. ROOSEVELT

Diplomatic Salvation from Nazi Hideouts

Unlike Africa, Latin America was already independent by the mid-twentieth century. Moreover, three of the eleven countries that composed the United Nations Special Committee on Palestine (UNSCOP) were Latin American: Guatemala (represented by Jorge García Granados), Peru (represented by Arturo García Salazar), and Uruguay (represented by Enrique Rodríguez Fabregat). When the Jewish Agency tried to gather diplomatic support for the 1947 UN partition plan, Latin America became a crucial focus of Zionist diplomacy.

Jorge García Granados, a pro-Zionist, insisted on meeting with Menachem Begin. Two meetings between Granados and Begin took place in a secret location, to the horror and dismay of the British authorities (Begin was on top of the "wanted" list). Both Granados and Fabregat recommended the partition of Palestine between a Jewish and an Arab state. Granados declared at the UN, "The establishment of a Jewish state is a reparation that humanity owes to an innocent and defenseless people that has been persecuted and subjugated for two thousand years."[1] For his part, however, Salazar (who was also his country's ambassador to the Vatican) insisted on the internationalization of Jerusalem.

The president of the General Assembly at the time of the partition vote was Oswaldo Aranha from Brazil. Like Granados, Aranha had strong Zionist sympathies. The vote had been scheduled for November 27, 1947, but as the date approached, it became clear that there was no majority for the approval of partition. More time was needed to gather support, especially among Latin American countries. Aranha conceived an idea that saved the day: November 28 was Thanksgiving, he reminded delegates, and since it would be unfair to keep American workers at the UN, he suggested that the final deliberations and vote be postponed until after Thanksgiving. His proposal was accepted, and the extra forty-eight hours enabled the Jewish Agency to gather more support among UN delegations.

When the UN General Assembly vote on partition took place on November 29, the support of Latin American countries proved critical. Thirty-three countries voted yes, thirteen voted no, and ten abstained. Of the thirty-three "yes" votes, thirteen—equivalent to 40 percent—were from Latin America. Furthermore, half of the twenty-two countries that recognized Israel in 1948 were Latin American. And in May 1949, eighteen out of Latin America's twenty countries voted in favor of admitting Israel as a member of the United Nations.

How can the decisive support of Latin America for partition be explained? Not by U.S. pressures, since the Washington establishment was mostly against partition (see chapter 14). In February 1948 U.S. secretary of state George Marshall had asked the newly formed Organization of American States (a trans-regional organization established to foster cooperation among nations of the northern and southern American continents) to abandon the principle of partition and endorse America's proposal of a trusteeship regime in Palestine instead.[2] Nor can the vote be construed as resulting from some powerful Jewish lobby within Latin America. Most of the countries voting yes were not democratic and therefore not influenceable by electoral pressure groups. Indeed, most of the Latin American countries that voted in favor of partition had small or insignificant Jewish communities. Latin America's largest Jewish communities at the time were in Argentina, Mexico, Brazil, and Chile, all countries that abstained during the vote.

What tilted the balance in favor of Israel was the intensive lobbying of the Jewish Agency. Latin American countries did not have much to lose by voting for partition because, unlike the great powers, they did not have strategic interests in the Middle East. As opposed to countries such as India, Latin American states did not need to worry about the possible unrest of large Muslim minorities. Finally, Latin American countries favored an independent Jewish state because they were not interested in welcoming Holocaust survivors as refugees.

Despite this widespread support at the UN, however, relations between Israel and Latin America were overshadowed by the fact that many Nazi war criminals found hideouts in Latin America. Argentina's president, Juan Perón, adopted a policy of "friendly neutrality" toward Germany while helping Nazi fugitives. Assisted by the Vatican, the Argentinian Catholic Church, and the Swiss government, Perón actively provided cover for Nazi war criminals, allowing them to lead prosperous and safe lives after the war.[3] In 1946 operatives from Heinrich Himmler's secret service, planning escape routes, established their headquarters in the presidential palace in Buenos Aires. Nazi war criminals hiding in Latin America would include, among others, Adolf Eichmann (Argentina), Klaus Barbie (Bolivia), and Joseph Mengele (Argentina, Paraguay, and Brazil).

In the case of Adolf Eichmann, his capture by the Mossad in May 1960 created a diplomatic crisis between Israel and Argentina. Strongly protesting the violation of its sovereignty, the Argentinian government demanded Eichmann's return to Argentina and the indictment of his capturers.[4] When Israel reminded Argentina that Eichmann had entered the country illegally on forged papers, Argentina's ambassador to the UN replied that many Jewish Holocaust survivors had done the same.[5]

Argentina would not have extradited Eichmann had it been asked to. The Argentinian government had already rejected West Germany's extradition requests to judge former Nazi criminals such as Joseph Mengele and Karl Klingenfuss (a former German foreign office official who played an active role in the mass murder of Jews). Moreover, Argentinian law stated that all crimes related to World War II could no longer be judged fifteen years after the end of the war. In other words, Argentina could not have legally extradited Eichmann after May 7, 1960.[6] Other Nazis lived a happy life in Argentina and died in old age. Erich Priebke, an ss commander who took part in a mass killing in Rome in March 1944 and never stood trial, died in October 2013 at age one hundred. For years he ran a deli in the Argentinian ski resort of Bariloche, where Joseph Mengele took his driving test. The deli was said to be the best in town, and customers used to call it "the Nazi deli."[7]

The Moral Hazards of International Isolation

While most Latin American countries voted in favor of partition in 1947, their voting patterns at the General Assembly became unfavorable to Israel from the 1960s onward. In 1964 a voting group of Third World countries (known as the Group of 77) formed at the General Assembly to leverage the voting power of Third World countries. Latin American countries were part of this bloc, which was very much influenced by its Arab and Muslim members because of the General Assembly's horse-trading practices: countries would support resolutions related to conflicts in which they had no or little stake, based on the understanding that they would secure future votes of other group members when needed. To Israel, Latin America was now "lost" diplomatically, but it still mattered economically because of its oil reserves.

Yet Latin America became diplomatically relevant to Israel once again after the 1973 Yom Kippur War. After that war, Israel had become isolated internationally; most African countries cut their diplomatic ties, Israel had no diplomatic relations with China or India, and Western Europe and Japan had become outspokenly critical of Israel. Latin America thus became the last bastion of Israel's presence in the Third World. Trying to bypass its isolation, Israel leveraged common interests with whoever was interested, without asking too many questions. In the case of Latin America, that meant selling weapons to anti-Soviet and morally questionable regimes such as Argentina and Chile and sticking to the "our son of a bitch" policy of supporting anti-Communist dictators.[8] This was a change of course for Israel, which hadn't become an arms supplier until the 1970s. In the past, Israel had been the one purchasing weapons from Latin America (in April 1948, for example, Nicaragua delivered weapons purchased by the Haganah).[9]

Of all Latin American states, only Cuba and Guyana severed their diplomatic relations with Israel after the Yom Kippur War. Except for Cuba after 1959 and Nicaragua after 1979, Latin America did not become "red" during the Cold War (Guyana was run by a Socialist party but was not a Communist country). The United States was eager to prevent a Communist "domino effect" in what it considered its backyard. When, in 1973, the Socialist Salvador Allende was elected president of Chile, he was eliminated by the CIA. Meanwhile, the United States was selling military weaponry largely carte blanche to Latin America's anti-Communist dictators. Latin American leaders knew they could count on the United States to keep Communists at bay and at any price.

When this policy temporarily changed under Jimmy Carter's presidency (1977–81), it opened up an arms-selling opportunity for Israel. Carter had stopped giving a free pass to anti-Communist dictators in Latin America, demanding they clean up their human rights record first. In 1977 Carter vetoed granting a loan to Argentina for the purchase of U.S. weapons. Under Carter, the U.S. share in Latin America's military imports dropped from 70 percent to 20 percent.[10] Filling the gap temporarily left by America, Israel became a major arms supplier to most Latin American countries, among them Argentina, Ecuador, Guatemala, and Honduras.[11] In 1980 Israel was reportedly providing 80 percent of El Salvador's military hardware.[12]

Except for Nicaragua after the 1979 Sandinista Revolution, all Central American countries bought weapons from Israel. This was a win-win relationship, since Latin America needed Israel's weapons as much as Israel needed Latin America's oil. Especially after the 1979 Iranian revolution, when Israel lost Iran as a major oil supplier, and the final, 1982 retrocession of Sinai to Egypt (which had oil fields in Abu Rudeis), Israel presumably turned to oil exporters such as Venezuela, Mexico, Brazil, and Ecuador as valuable alternatives.[13]

Strengthening the Israel–Latin American relationship, meanwhile, were the close ties between their common enemies: anti-regime Communist guerillas, the PLO, and anti-Western Arab leaders. The Sandinistas in Nicaragua, for example, had cooperated with the PLO since 1969 and enjoyed military and financial support from Libyan dictator Muammar Gaddafi. Conversely, Israel had quietly supported the deposed Nicaraguan dictator Somoza, and it would later cooperate with the anti-Sandinista "contras" rebels. Ties between Israel and Central American states became so close that most Central American countries voted against the 1975 UN resolution defining Zionism as racism and did not condemn Israel's invasion of Lebanon in 1982. Until 1980, sixteen countries had embassies in West Jerusalem, eleven of them Latin American.[14] In 1980 only two of these sixteen countries (Costa Rica and El Salvador) did *not* move their embassies from Jerusalem to Tel Aviv to protest Israel's new law declaring Jerusalem the "eternal capital" of Israel.

In the early 1980s, Latin America purchased between one-third and one-half of Israel's arms exports.[15] Although Israel's Latin American customers were known to be human rights violators, the Argentinian junta was especially gruesome, and therefore Israel's arms sales to

Buenos Aires drew criticism and even outcry. Israel sold weapons to the Argentinian junta (1976–83), under which Jews (like the rest of their fellow Argentinians) suffered from repression. According to one estimation, Israel provided 13 percent of Argentina's military imports from 1976 to 1981 (the top suppliers during that period being West Germany, the United States, and France).[16] During the 1982 Falklands War, Israel continued to sell weapons to Argentina.[17] Furthermore, Israel defied NATO's embargo on Argentina by supplying advanced missile systems and helping the Argentinian air force maintain its strike capability.[18]

Some Israeli politicians and commentators expressed discomfort with Israel's foreign policy in Latin America—a policy that admittedly pushed realpolitik to its limits. Yet even the liberal Abba Eban admitted that Israel was short of options during the lean years of diplomatic isolation. "For many years," he wrote, "Israel was so starved for friendship that it had to look for it wherever it could be found. We could not have maintained even a restricted foothold in world diplomacy if we had made the acceptance of Israel's social ideals a condition of our friendship."[19]

For its part, Argentina's established Jewish community had welcomed the overthrow of President Isabel Perón, under whose leadership (1974–76) antisemitism had turned violent.[20] During the following junta years, Argentinian Jews were allowed to emigrate to Israel (though few of them did), the Nazi publisher Milicia was shuttered in 1976, and the antisemitic weekly *Cabildo* was suspended in 1977.[21] The focus of the junta's struggle was not the Jews, but Marxist guerillas. On the other hand, Jews constituted about 10 percent of the estimated thirty thousand victims of the "Dirty War" (the junta's systematic elimination of suspected Marxist militants), even though Jews only represented 1 percent of the total Argentinian population.[22] In addition, the junta arrested and tortured Jacobo Timerman, editor of the left-leaning *La Opinion*. Israel's foreign minister Moshe Dayan conveyed to the junta that if it freed Timerman, Israel would refrain from publicly criticizing Argentina and would continue its supply of military equipment, including fighter jets to the Argentinian air force. When Argentinian dictator Jorge Rafael Videla turned down the offer, Israel continued to press for Timerman's liberation, and eventually, in 1979, Timerman was freed.[23] In addition, the Israeli embassy in Buenos Aires systematically tried to free Argentinian Jews who had been arbitrarily arrested by the junta.[24] Israel's military ties with the junta were decried as cynical, but they did grant Israel some leverage to ease the plight of Argentinian Jews.

Israel's "arms sales diplomacy" in Latin America became less of a moral dilemma as many Latin American countries democratized in the 1980s and 1990s. It also became less of a necessity, as the end of the Cold War broke Israel's international isolation.

The Shadow of Iranian Influence

On July 18, 1994, the Jewish community center of Buenos Aires was bombed, killing eighty-five people. It was revealed in October 2006 that Iran had ordered the bombing and that Hezbollah had carried it out. In June 2013 Alberto Nisman, Argentina's special prosecutor, issued a five-hundred-page report showing that Iran had been building a network in Argentina for thirty years. Nisman's report disclosed that Iranian officials had been conducting Iran's intelligence activities in Latin America through Hezbollah. Nisman was found dead in January 2015. In December 2017 an Argentinian court ruled that Nisman had been murdered, and an Argentinian judge called for the arrest of former president Cristina Fernandez Kirchner for covering up Iran's involvement in the Jewish community center bombing.[25]

Hezbollah had started to infiltrate Latin America in the mid-1980s, establishing its first major stronghold in the Tri-Border Area, a relatively lawless region along the borders of Argentina, Brazil, and Paraguay. Known in Spanish as La Triple Frontera, the Tri-Border Area (TBA) had become home to a large community of Shia Lebanese businessmen who settled there in the 1950s. Construction of the Friendship Bridge connecting Paraguay and Brazil in 1965 and the Itaipu Dam in 1984 boosted the economy of the region, and Paraguay's dictator Alfredo Stroessner encouraged more Lebanese to immigrate and make the area prosper. Shia Lebanese would later serve as a conduit for Hezbollah's infiltration on the continent, with the backing of the Islamic Republic of Iran. To this day, Paraguay, Brazil, and Argentina have large Arab diasporas that have mostly assimilated into Latin American life and culture, and the Arab inhabitants of TBA maintain strong ties with Lebanon and Hezbollah. The Shia mosques of TBA are affiliated with Hezbollah, and the Shia school on the Brazilian side of TBA is run by Hezbollah.[26] TBA's links to Hezbollah are both financial and logistical. When Iran ordered the 1994 bombing of the Jewish community center, Hezbollah operatives in the TBA provided the needed logistical support.[27]

These days, from its base deep in the heart of South America, Hezbollah runs illicit enterprises—money laundering, counterfeiting, piracy, and drug trafficking—to fund its operations in the Middle East and elsewhere. The Tri-Border Area constitutes Hezbollah's most significant source of independent funding. A 2004 Naval War College study determined that Hezbollah's operations in the Tri-Border Area generate about $10 million annually. A 2009 Rand Corporation report said Hezbollah netted around $20 million a year in the area.[28]

Meanwhile, Hezbollah's presence in Latin America is growing, both in economic capacity and in its placing of operatives in the region, through the rapid expansion of Iran's diplomatic and intelligence missions, businesses, and investments. Iran's strengthened economic ties with Venezuela, Bolivia, Ecuador, and Nicaragua have coincided with these Latin American countries' distancing themselves from Israel; Venezuela severed diplomatic relations in 2009, Nicaragua and Bolivia did so in 2010, and Ecuador recalled its ambassador to Israel in 2010.

In December 2017 the U.S. magazine *Politico* reported that the Obama administration had put "an increasingly insurmountable series of roadblocks" before a Drug Enforcement Agency effort to combat Hezbollah drug trafficking from Latin America, so as not to unravel the 2015 nuclear deal with Iran.[29] In January 2018 U.S. attorney general Jeff Sessions ordered a review of decisions made by the Obama Department of Justice and established an interagency task force to monitor and fight Hezbollah's activities in South America.[30]

Latin American governments that are concerned about Iranian and Hezbollah-sponsored terror have been upgrading their cooperation with Israel. Mexico is fighting Hezbollah cells on its soil. Colombia has long struggled against the FARC, a terrorist organization with strong ties to both Hezbollah and Iran. With the election of the conservative Mauricio Macri as Argentina's president in 2015, Argentina reversed the pro-Iranian policy of Cristina Fernández de Kirchner. It is no coincidence that Argentina, Mexico, and Colombia were the three Latin American countries visited by Israeli prime minister Netanyahu in September 2017, the first official visit of an Israeli head of government to Latin America.

Brazil also became an ally of Israel with the election of Jair Bolsonaro in October 2018. Bolsonaro's January 2019 swearing-in was attended by Benjamin Netanyahu, the first Israeli prime minister to pay an official visit to Brazil. As opposed to his predecessors, who had developed close ties with the Iranian regime and had turned a blind eye on Hezbollah's presence in Brazil, Bolsonaro has declared his intention to isolate Iran and fight Hezbollah's activities in the Tri-Border Area.

Conclusion

Most Latin American countries voted in favor of the partition of Palestine in 1947, thanks partly to the diplomatic activism of the Jewish Agency. Latin American countries had no vested interests in the Middle

East, and they did not want to share the burden of the Jewish refugee crisis after the Holocaust. Still, Israel's relations with Argentina and other Latin American countries were overshadowed by the visas the nations officially granted to Nazi war criminals. In the 1970s and 1980s, the Communist threat in Latin America, combined with Israel's international isolation, created a new synergy: Israel sold weapons to Latin America (especially under the Carter administration, which blocked U.S. arms sales to many Latin American countries because of their human rights violations), and Latin America sold oil to Israel (Israel had lost two major oil sources after the Islamic revolution in Iran in 1979 and the retrocession of Sinai to Egypt). Israel's critics around the world, as well as Israeli intellectuals, decried Israel's realpolitik policy toward Latin America as immoral.

Today, Israel's ties with Latin American countries are very much influenced by their stances on Iran. Countries that have close ties with Iran (such as Venezuela) are antagonistic to Israel, but countries that fight the influence of Iran and Hezbollah in their midst (such as Argentina after 2015 and Brazil since 2019) cooperate closely with Israel.

19. The United Nations Saga

After the final destruction of the Nazi tyranny, they [the United States and Great Britain] hope to see established a peace which will afford to all nations the means of dwelling in safety within their own boundaries, and which will afford assurance that all the men in all lands may live out their lives in freedom from fear and want.

THE ATLANTIC CHARTER, August 14, 1941

From Celebration to Castigation

The United Nations (UN), founded in 1945 by the Allied powers that had fought against Nazi Germany and Imperial Japan, was initially favorable toward Israel, not least because Palestinian Jews took part in the war effort that had led to the establishment of the UN (as explained in chapter 7, a Jewish Brigade composed of Palestinian Jews had fought under the Union Jack in northern Italy in 1944), and because the UN had played a role in the birth of Israel (although, as explained in chapter 9, the UN did not establish the state). In 1947 a majority of member nations voted for partition at the UN General Assembly (thirty-three in favor, thirteen against, and ten abstentions). Among the UN Security Council's five permanent members, the United States, the Soviet Union, and France voted in favor; Britain and China abstained. When Israel raised its flag at the UN upon becoming a member in May 1949, Israeli foreign minister Moshe Sharett declared that the Jews had finally become free and equal among the nations. Israel looked at the Isaiah Wall, proclaiming the Jewish ideal of beating swords into plowshares, sited across the street from the UN building on First Avenue in Manhattan, and felt comfortable being part of the United Nations.

The favorable constellation changed over time, however. While in theory the UN was a world body committed to universal principles and to lofty ideals, in reality it was (and remains) an organization of sovereign states with their own interests. Like the operations of any other parliament, General Assembly decisions were (and remain) based on coalitions built by voting blocs that promoted their respective agendas. Voting patterns at the UN necessarily fluctuated depending on the organization's membership and on the members' changing interests.

After Israel's independence, the UN underwent many changes, both at the Security Council and at the General Assembly. The first change happened at the Security Council. Whereas the Soviet Union had been supportive of Israel in 1947–48, it became hostile in the wake of the Korean War (see chapter 15). China, neutral in 1947, came to engage in a pro-Arab foreign policy after the 1955 Bandung Conference and the 1956 Suez Crisis (see chapter 16). France, an ally of Israel in the 1950s, downgraded its relations after the Algerian War (1954–62), and it became confrontational after the 1967 Six-Day War (see chapter 13). Britain became fiercely critical of Israel after the 1973 Yom Kippur War. The United States, which became Israel's ally in the mid-1960s, remained its only and last support at the Security Council.

Israel lost its support not only at the Security Council, but also at the General Assembly. In 1947 the UN had 51 members, only 6 of which were Arab countries. (By contrast, today the UN has 193 member-states, 57 of which belong to the Organization of Islamic Cooperation, and 22 of which belong to the Arab League.) Decolonization brought new member states to the UN, many of them Muslim; Indonesia joined the UN in 1950, Jordan and Libya in 1955, Morocco and Tunisia in 1956, Malaysia in 1957, Algeria in 1962, Kuwait in 1963, North Yemen in 1967, and Bahrain, Qatar, and the United Arab Emirates in 1971. By the early 1970s, the UN had 120 member-states, 16 of which were Arab, 6 Muslim, and 37 from Africa and Asia. What soon became an Arab and Muslim bloc at the General Assembly joined forces with the Soviet Union, which had embarked on a pro-Arab foreign policy in 1953. This voting bloc would also come to include China, India, Latin America, and, after 1973, Africa.

The UN and the Arab-Israeli Conflict

After the 1973 Yom Kippur War, the Arab and Muslim blocs built majorities with Third World and Communist countries, thus leveraging the General Assembly's "automatic majority" to isolate Israel. The "Group of 77," a coalition of developing and supposedly nonaligned countries established in 1964 (which now includes two-thirds of the UN's members), could generally be counted on to support political resolutions promoted by the Arab and Muslim blocs. With the end of the Vietnam War in 1973, Soviet propaganda needed a new cause célèbre to rally the Third World, and it picked the "Palestinian cause" as a target to be promoted via the UN General Assembly.[1] Thus it was that after the Yom Kippur War, the Soviet Union gave its full support to the PLO. In the global geopolitical contest of the Cold War, the Soviet Union skillfully exploited the anti-Western sentiments among Third World nations to pass General Assembly resolutions against the United States and its allies. As a result, the number of one-sided and often absurd resolutions on Israel grew exponentially and culminated with the 1975 resolution that defined Zionism as a form of racism (see below). Abba Eban quipped at the time that if the Arab world wanted to pass a General Assembly resolution declaring the world to be flat, the automatic majority would oblige.

Since the General Assembly elected the ten non-permanent and rotating members of the Security Council, the new makeup of the assembly had an impact on the council. By the 1970s, General Assembly voting patterns started influencing those of the Security Council. For example, for lack of a majority, the Security Council never condemned the PLO's terrorist attacks in the 1970s: against Israeli children killed in the northern Israeli town of Avivim in 1970; against Israel's athletes killed in Munich in 1972; against Israeli children killed in the Ma'alot kibbutz in 1974; against a two-year-old killed in front of her father on the Naharya beach in 1979; and against the children of the Misgav Am Kibbutz killed in 1980. The Security Council condemned Israel's annexation of the Golan Heights in 1981 but said nothing about the Soviet invasion of Afghanistan, Vietnam's invasion of Cambodia, Iraq's invasion of Iran, Libya's invasion of Chad, or the violent repression of the pro-independence Solidarność movement by the Soviet-backed Polish government that same year. The Security Council condemned Israel's invasion of Lebanon in 1982, though not the shelling that triggered the invasion, and had not condemned Syria's invasion of Lebanon six years earlier in 1976. Indeed, in the 1980s, the Security Council spent altogether more time condemning Israel than addressing all of the world's conflicts.[2] As international law scholar Leo Gross wrote then about this double standard, "The members of the United Nations now seem to be moved to moral indignation only in selected cases, which deprives indignation of its moral basis."[3]

It was at the General Assembly, however, that the automatic majority produced the most disturbing results. By invitation, on November 13, 1974, at the height of PLO terrorist attacks conducted against Israeli civilians, PLO leader Yasser Arafat addressed the General Assembly; there he received a warm welcome from Secretary General (and former Wehrmacht intelligence officer) Kurt Waldheim. In his speech, Arafat said that the 1947 UN partition plan was null and void and that Israel should be dismantled and replaced by an exclusively Arab state in which only Jews who lived in Palestine before the late nineteenth century would be allowed to stay (even though there was no Palestine at the time, only Ottoman provinces called sanjaks). It was the first time that the leader of a terrorist organization had addressed the UN General Assembly and that a speaker had called for the elimination of a UN member state from the General Assembly podium. Arafat received a standing ovation. Commenting on the disgraceful scene, Abba Eban was to write, "We had the feeling that the world belonged to our enemies."[4]

A year later, on November 10, 1975, the General Assembly passed a resolution defining Zionism as a form of racism. Israel's ambassador to the UN, Chaim Herzog, declared that this vote was the first international assault against the Jewish people since the Second World War. It was a sad coincidence, Herzog pointed out, that November 10 also marked the anniversary of Kristallnacht—the 1938 German-wide pogrom against its Jewish citizens. "I stand here not as a supplicant," Herzog had said to his fellow General Assembly members prior to the vote. "Vote as your moral conscience dictates to you. For the issue is neither Israel nor Zionism. The issue is the continued existence of this organization, which has been dragged to its lowest point of discredit by a coalition of despots and racists." At the end of his speech, Herzog tore up the resolution in front of the General Assembly. This gesture was symbolic: Chaim Herzog's father, Rabbi Yitzhak Herzog (the first Ashkenazi chief rabbi of Israel), had torn up in public the 1939 White Paper (published by the British government to curtail Jewish immigration and land purchase). The U.S. ambassador to the UN, Daniel Patrick Moynihan, also gave a powerful and dignified speech. "How will the people of the world feel about racism and the need to struggle against it, when they are told that it is an idea as broad as to include the Jewish national liberation movement?" he asked, before declaring that the United States "does not acknowledge, it will not abide by, it will never acquiesce in this infamous act."

In addition to the Zionism equals racism resolution, on the very same day the General Assembly established the Committee on the

Exercise of the Inalienable Rights of the Palestinian People. One of the committee's first decisions was to endorse (in 1976) the PLO Charter, which denied Israel's right to exist and called for its replacement by an exclusively Arab state. In addition, in 1977 the General Assembly established the Special Unit on Palestinian Rights, to promote the PLO's messages at the UN.

All these new bodies cost money, yet to this day nearly a quarter of the UN's funding comes from the United States, a country that opposed the politization of the UN by the Soviet-backed PLO. Member states contribute to the UN budget proportionally, based on the size of their gross domestic product. In the 1970s and 1980s, at the height of the Arab states' political hijacking of the UN, those states contributed marginally to the UN budget, whereas the United States contributed 25 percent of the UN budget (and today funds 22 percent of the UN budget).[5] In other words, the United States was funding a pro-Soviet apparatus used against one of its closest allies, Israel (as well as against itself).

The automatic majority also affected the composition and agenda of the General Assembly's commissions. Infamous among them was the Commission on Human Rights, which the French legal scholar René Cassin had argued for establishing in 1946 and whose first chairperson was Eleanor Roosevelt. Fifty-seven years later, in 2003, the commission was chaired by Libyan dictator Muammar Gaddafi. From the mid-1970s, the Commission on Human Rights repeatedly condemned Israel for building settlements but said nothing, for example, about the Iraqi dictator Saddam Hussein gassing Kurds in 1988.

Israel's isolation at the UN was amplified by its exclusion from regional voting blocs. Originally, UN member states had been unofficially grouped into regions for the sake of fair representation in UN bodies (such as the Security Council, the General Assembly's commissions, and the International Court of Justice), but in 1966 regional groups were reorganized so as to reflect the soaring number of new member states as a result of decolonization.[6] All Middle East countries belong to the Asian group, except for Turkey (which belongs to the Western group, known as Western European and Others Group, or WEOG) and Israel. Israel was blocked from the Asian group because of the Arab states' veto, yet it was not accepted to WEOG either; its members argued that Israel should apply to the Asian group. This exclusion, which lasted until 2000, barred Israel from being elected to UN bodies such as the Security Council, the International Court of Justice, and the commissions of the General Assembly. In 2000, after many years of lobbying, Israel was temporarily accepted to WEOG. Its membership became final in 2004 for UN institutions in New York (such as the Security Council) and in 2013 for UN institutions in Geneva (such as the Human Rights Council).

The automatic majority at the UN has had a particularly negative impact on the issue of refugees—an open sore of the Arab-Israeli conflict. After Israel's independence in 1948, about 700,000 (between 580,000 and 760,000) Arabs of British Palestine fled, and about 900,000 Jews were expelled from Arab and Muslim countries. This double refugee problem, largely resulting from the Arab League's rejection of the 1947 UN partition plan and its unprovoked war against the newly proclaimed Jewish state, is part of a wider world phenomenon. Since the end of World War I, ethnic conflicts have often produced refugees and displaced persons. In 1919 Greece and Bulgaria agreed to end their border conflict by transferring 46,000 ethnic Greeks from Bulgaria to Greece and 96,000 ethnic Bulgarians from Greece to Bulgaria. Greece's similar agreement with Turkey in 1923 forced 1.2 million ethnic Greeks to move from Turkey to Greece and 600,000 Turks to move from Greece to Turkey. After World War II, 12 million ethnic Germans were expelled from east German territories annexed by Poland, as well as from central European countries such as Czechoslovakia and Hungary. A million Poles were also expelled from the Ukraine and from Belarus, and some 300,000 Italians were forced to leave Yugoslavia. Following the partition of the Indian subcontinent in 1947, there were about 15 million refugees and displaced persons between India and Pakistan; the split between East Pakistan and West Pakistan in 1971 added about 10 million refugees and displaced persons to those gruesome figures.

Yet today, the Palestinians are the only refugees for whom there is a special UN agency, the United Nations Relief and Works Agency for Palestine Refugees in the Near East (UNRWA). By contrast, the United Nations High Commissioner for Refugees (UNHCR) is responsible for all refugees in the world, except for Palestinian refugees.

UNRWA was created in December 1949, when UNHCR did not yet exist. Once UNHCR was established, UNRWA was not abolished—as it should have been. The merger between the two agencies never took place precisely because the Arab states refused to integrate the Arab refugees of British Palestine. Back in December 1948, General Assembly Resolution 194 had established a Conciliation Commission for the Palestine conflict. In August 1949 the Conciliation Commission created its own economic subcommission for the Middle East, chaired by the former director of the Tennessee Valley Authority, Gordon Clapp. After touring the Middle East in his new capacity, Clapp concluded that the repatriation of seven hundred thousand Arab refugees to Israel was unrealistic and unpractical, and he recommended their integration in their host countries, with which they shared the same ethnicity, language, and religion. He subsequently decided to create a special fund for the integration of refugees. Arab governments were willing to take the money to help support the refugees in their midst, but not to integrate them. Clapp decided to go along, figuring that with time Arab governments would integrate the refugees from the former British Mandate. He also initiated the establishment of an agency for the distribution and the management of the UN's aid to the refugees. This agency was meant to be temporary, lasting for a couple of years. Yet Arab governments agreed to the agency's creation only on condition of making its mandate renewable by decision of the General Assembly. Clapp agreed, and the new agency, UNRWA, was established. The General Assembly would renew UNRWA's mandate for the next seventy years.

Unlike UNRWA, UNHCR was created as a permanent institution in December 1950. Once UNHCR was established, Arab governments blocked the merger of the two organizations precisely because UNHCR seeks "permanent or durable solutions" to the plight of refugees, including "local integration" (in which refugees legally, economically, and socially integrate in the host country, availing themselves of the national protection of the host government) and "resettlement" (in which refugees are selected and transferred from the country of refuge to a third state, which has agreed to admit them as refugees with permanent residence status).[7] UNHCR explains that "local integration is an important facet of comprehensive strategies to develop solutions to refugee situations, particularly those of a protracted nature. . . . Overall, ethnic, cultural, or linguistic links with the local community can increase the chances of successful local integration."[8] UNWRA does not apply this principle.

No other population of refugees has ever benefited from such special treatment, and there is no precedent at the UN for a separate refugee agency that has existed for so long. The only comparable case is that of UNKRA (United Nations Korean Reconstruction Agency), an agency created to relieve the fate of Korean refugees and displaced persons from the Korean War (1950–53). Yet UNKRA was dismantled in 1958, after outliving its purpose. When the U.S. government pushed for dismantling UNKRA, it suggested doing the same for UNRWA. By that time, however, the Arab and Muslim states had a large voting bloc at the General Assembly, which enabled them to block the dismantling of UNRWA.

UNRWA has also set its own rules in ways that artificially inflate the number of Palestinian refugees. In 1954 UNRWA decided to keep records of all births in its camps to distribute aid to the refugees' children.

Since then, UNRWA has systematically applied refugee status to the refugees' descendants—a practice that is not consistent either with UN Resolution 194 (which led to its creation) or with UNHCR practice. Resolution 194 refers to the 1948 refugees themselves, not to their descendants. For its part, UNHCR only transfers refugee status to refugees' descendants after verifying their actual status, making sure, for example, that they have not acquired a country's citizenship. UNHCR also has a "cessation clause," which applies to "situations where refugee status ceases, generally because the refugees have found a durable solution or because the events that led refugees to leave their countries of origin have ceased to exist."[9] UNHCR thus does not have in its records refugees that have been defined as such for seventy years; UNHCR's longest recorded refugees are Afghan refugees from the early 1980s.

There were about 1.3 million Arabs in British Palestine in 1947. Only 250,000 of them—about 20 percent—left the borders of the British Mandate for neighboring Arab countries. The remaining 450,000 who left their villages remained within the borders of British Palestine—in what would become the West Bank and the Gaza Strip after the 1949 armistice agreements—and have therefore been considered "internally displaced persons" according to the criteria and definition of the UN Refugee Convention (1951). About 2.2 million of the 5.4 million people UNRWA defines as Palestinian refugees live in the West Bank and the Gaza Strip, but UNHCR would not count these internally displaced persons as refugees.

Another 2.2 million people that UNRWA alone counts as refugees are internally displaced persons who had settled in the West Bank and were granted Jordanian citizenship after 1950—as well as their descendants. UNHCR, however, would not recognize them as refugees because they are citizens of Jordan (at least until 1988, when Jordan waived its claim over the West Bank).

Thus, among the 5.4 million Palestinian "refugees" registered by UNRWA, 4.4 million are not refugees by UNHCR's standards.

In short, because of its separate status, definitions, and practices, UNRWA produces the false impression that there are 5.4 million Palestinian refugees today. In fact, there were approximately 250,000 Palestinian refugees and 450,000 Palestinian internally displaced persons in 1948. The transfer of refugee status to descendants of internally displaced persons and descendants of those who have acquired citizenship have substantially elevated the figures beyond UNHCR's protocols for tallying refugees.

Hence, by perpetuating and aggravating the Palestinian refugee question, the UN has become part of the problem rather than part of the solution.

The Hopes and Disappointments of the "New World Order"

With the end of the Cold War, the prospect of reforming the dysfunctional UN seemed to be within reach. In 1991 the Soviet Union had not vetoed the UN-led military coalition against Iraq, and the General Assembly had repealed the 1975 resolution that had condemned Zionism as a form of racism. In 1993 Israel and the PLO recognized each other. Many then believed an end to the Arab-Israeli conflict was in sight. If so, the Arab states' diplomatic war against Israel in the halls of the UN would finally cease as well.

Optimists who hoped the UN would recover its credibility were soon to be disappointed, however. Although the UN Security Council did act against Saddam Hussein in 1991 by allowing the use of force to drive him out of Kuwait, in 1994 the UN sat idle while a million Tutsis were massacred in Rwanda. In July 1995 the UN peacekeepers in Srebrenica, Bosnia, ran away, letting eight thousand Muslims be massacred. In 2003 Syria was elected to the Security Council, and Libya was elected to chair the Commission on Human Rights.

As for Israel, none of the agencies set up on behalf of the PLO in the 1970s were abolished, and despite the negotiations between Israel and the PLO, the defamatory rhetoric at the UN — especially at the UN Commission on Human Rights — remained mostly unchanged. On March 11, 1997, for example, the Palestinian delegate to the UN's Human Rights Commission, Nabil Ramlawi, accused Israel of spreading the AIDS virus among Palestinian children and of perpetuating a genocide against the Palestinians.[10] On February 8, 1991, the Syrian representative at the Human Rights Commission claimed that Jews kill Christian children to use their blood for the baking of Passover bread.[11]

With the outburst of the second intifada in the fall of 2000, the PLO redoubled its use of the UN as a diplomatic tool against Israel. The 2001 Durban Conference (hosted by the UN) made Israel the focus of world condemnation, with accusations of racism and apartheid.

The UN never recovered its lost credibility. Reforms were patchy and often counterproductive. The Human Rights Commission had included countries such as Idi Amin's Uganda, Saddam Hussein's Iraq, and Hafez al-Assad's Syria before Gaddafi's Libya was elected chair of the Human Rights Commission in 2003. At that point, UN secretary general Kofi Annan admitted that something was fundamentally wrong, and he called for reform. In 2006 the Human Rights Commission was abolished and replaced by a Human Rights Council (HRC), but its members have included many human rights abusers: Saudi Arabia (a country that practices flogging and amputations), China, Russia, Cuba, Mauritania, Venezuela (under Hugo Chavez), and Libya again (under Gaddafi).

The HRC is also a forum of disproportionate condemnation of Israel. The HRC's founding charter has a special article (Article 7) that stipulates that any conference on human rights must hold a separate discussion on Israel. This article applies to no other country in the world, certainly not to the human rights violators represented at the HRC. In March 2017 the United Kingdom notified the HRC that it would vote against any future HRC resolution on Israel because of the council's bias against Israel. Britain's representative at the HRC declared:

Nowhere is the disproportionate focus on Israel starker and more absurd than in the case of today's resolution on the occupation of Syria's Golan. . . . Syria's regime butchers and murders its people on a daily basis. But it is not Syria that is a permanent standing item on the Council's agenda; it is Israel. . . . We cannot accept the perverse message sent out by a Syria Golan resolution that singles out Israel, as Assad continues to slaughter the Syrian people. . . . Israel is a population of eight million in a world of seven billion. Yet since its foundation, the Human Rights Council has adopted 135 country-specific resolutions; 68 of which are against Israel. . . . Israel is the only country permanently on the Human Rights Council's agenda.[12]

The Kafkaesque HRC sometimes unintentionally produces entertaining moments, though. In November 2013, for example, a UN interpreter, unaware that her microphone was on, said to her colleague that there had to be something wrong with an organization that only condemns Israel. The video of the delegates' embarrassed laughter went viral.

In September 2017 former Hamas member Mosab Hassan Yousef castigated the Palestinian Authority for its human rights violations on the HRC floor. This was a rare exception to the rule of a body whose members protect one anther from human rights condemnations, while disproportionally castigating Israel.

Several months later, in May 2018, Syria chaired the UN disarmament forum (which produced the treaty banning chemical weapons)— one month after Syrian dictator Bashar al-Assad had reportedly used chemical weapons against Syrian civilians in the city of Douma.

Conclusion

Although the United Nations did not establish Israel, its 1947 vote on partition was a landmark. Israel was welcomed to the UN in 1949, and at the time it enjoyed widespread support both at the Security Council and at the General Assembly. This situation did not last, however. Decolonization and the Cold War swelled UN membership and created voting blocs at the General Assembly. Those blocs were manipulated by the Arab and Muslim states to isolate Israel, especially after the 1973 Yom Kippur War. The hijacking of the UN's automatic majority by the Arab states culminated in the 1975 General Assembly resolution that equated Zionism with racism. The end of the Cold War offered an opportunity to reform the UN, and the 1993 Oslo Agreements between Israel and the PLO should have ended the anti-Israel propaganda at the UN. Yet none of those hopes materialized. The UN failed in Rwanda, in Yugoslavia, and in Iraq. Replacing the Human Rights Commission with a Human Rights Council did not end the legitimization of human rights abusers by the UN, nor the disproportionate condemnations of Israel. As for anti-Israel propaganda, it redoubled in 2001 with the Durban Conference. Despite those failures and shattered illusions, however, there have been some changes for the better. Israel finally integrated a regional group in 2000, and the abuses of the Human Rights Council have caused the United States to walk out and other Western countries (such as the UK) to denounce the disproportionate and politicized condemnation of Israel.

20. The Diaspora Challenge

> Jews should be granted everything as individuals
> but nothing as a nation.
>
> STANISLAS DE CLERMONT-TONNERRE

Between Uneasiness and Pride

From the outset, the new State of Israel made a clear statement about its strong connection with the Jewish Diaspora. Israel's Declaration of Independence proclaimed, "The State of Israel will be open for Jewish immigration and for the Ingathering of the Exiles. . . . We appeal to the Jewish people throughout the Diaspora to rally around the Jews of Israel in the tasks of immigration and of building, and to stand by them in the great struggle for the realization of the age-old dream of the redemption of Israel." In 1950 Israel passed the Law of Return, which grants to every (qualifying) Jew an automatic right to immigrate to Israel, and in 1952 it passed the Citizenship Law, which automatically grants Israeli citizenship to Jewish immigrants. With the passage of those two laws, all Jews around the world became potential citizens of the newly proclaimed State of Israel.

At the same time, this policy created diplomatic frictions with countries that had large Jewish minorities and whose governments opposed Jewish immigration for ideological reasons. First and foremost (as explained in chapter 15), Jews were not allowed to practice their religion or to leave the Soviet Union—even applying for immigration to Israel was viewed as an affront to Soviet propaganda—yet Israel openly advocated their religious and national freedom. Thus the Zionist aspect of Israel's foreign policy constituted a challenge to Soviet Communism and became a source of friction with the Soviet Union.

In May 1950 Israeli prime minister David Ben-Gurion asked Moscow to let Soviet Jews immigrate to Israel. The Israeli government then made that request official in December 1951.[1] Over the years, Israeli leaders continued to demand the free immigration of Soviet Jews, something the Soviet Union rejected as interference in its domestic affairs. The Kremlin strongly condemned the September 1960 international conference in Paris to support Soviet Jews, claiming that the Jews did not constitute a nation and that Soviet Jews were citizens who enjoyed equal rights and had no connection to Israel.[2] In 1966 Israel's prime minister Levi Eshkol expressed his hope that "the pressure of the Jewish people and of the world's enlightened public opinion would change the position of the Soviet regime on the Jewish issue."[3] In October 1974 Israeli foreign minister Yigal Allon declared from the UN General Assembly podium, "Granting permission to go to Israel, to those who want to go, will not only solve an agonizing Jewish problem which is unique in human history, but, I believe, will also provide the solution for a Soviet problem with which the Soviet Union has struggled for many years."[4] A few years later, Moshe Dayan proclaimed from the same podium, "The Government of Israel once again calls on the Soviet Union to permit those Jews who wish to do so to leave in order to join their people and their families."[5] The Soviet leadership perceived these calls as provocative.

Israel's commitment to the fate of Soviet Jews also constituted an obstacle to the renewal of diplomatic relations between Israel and the Soviet Union, which had been severed in 1967. In September 1977 Menachem Begin told Soviet diplomats that he would not renew diplomatic relations before the release of the "prisoners of Zion."[6] When the question of renewing diplomatic relations between the two countries was raised again in 1985, Israel insisted on the Soviets' lifting the ban on the emigration of Soviet Jews. Addressing the General Assembly in October 1985, Prime Minister Shimon Peres declared, "Let our people go! Empty the prisons of people whose sole crime is loyalty to Jewish tradition and pursuit of the Zionist dream! This call exceeds ordinary political considerations."[7]

Israel's advocacy on behalf of Jewish communities worldwide also generated unease in France. Since the French Revolution, Jews had been granted citizenship, but they were expected to abandon their self-identification as a people. As the question of Jewish emancipation was debated at the French National Assembly during the revolution, the conservative parliamentarian Count Stanislas de Clermont-Tonnerre declared that Jews should be granted everything as individuals but nothing as a nation. As mentioned in chapter 5, Napoléon Bonaparte might have been sympathetic to Jewish national renaissance during his Egyptian expedition, but once he became emperor, he convened a Sanhedrin and asked France's rabbis to officially declare that the Jews' only national allegiance was to France. Republican France had granted Jews civil rights, but it was also at pains to deny the Jews' self-identification as a people. Thus, by declaring Jews a nation and by calling for their *aliyah*, Israel challenged the status of French Jews since the French Revolution. This issue was so sensitive that at the height of the two countries' military alliance in the late 1950s, France asked Israel not to publicly encourage the *aliyah* of Algerian Jews (who had been French citizens since 1870).[8]

Even as Israel's self-proclaimed custodian role for all Jews created frictions with the Soviet Union and France, it hardly produced significant *aliyah* from those countries; in the 1950s and 1960s the Soviet Union barred Jewish immigration, and most French Jews were not interested in leaving their country. During the early years of Israel's independence, most Jewish immigrants came from Eastern Europe, North Africa, and the Middle East. Only a third of the nine hundred thousand Jewish refugees from Arab and Muslim lands immigrated to Israel. In some cases, Israel coordinated the emigration of Jews from Arab countries, such as with Operation Ezra and Nehemiah (1950), which brought Iraqi Jews, and Operation Magic Carpet, also known as "On Eagles' Wings" (1949–50), which brought Jews from Yemen.

Iraqi Jews had become the victims of persecutions and of pogroms in the early 1940s. In June 1941 hundreds of Iraqi Jews were killed after the failed pro-Nazi coup of Rashid Ali al-Gaylani. Following this pogrom, the *Yishuv* began sending emissaries to Iraq to organize clandestine immigration to British Palestine. After Israel declared independence in 1948 the persecution of Iraqi Jews intensified, but the Iraqi government forbade them to emigrate to Israel. In March 1950, however, the Iraqi government reversed its policy, allowing Jews to leave, but on condition that they renounce their Iraqi citizenship and abandon their property. Hence did the Israeli government organize the airlift operation known as Operation Ezra and Nehemiah (named after the two biblical figures who had brought Jewish exiles back from Babylon in the fifth century BCE), bringing some 120,000 Iraqi Jews to the State of Israel.

As for Operation Magic Carpet, it brought to Israel most— approximately 47,000—Yemenite Jews as well as Jews from Aden, Djibouti, and Eritrea between June 1949 and September 1950. According to their tradition, Yemenite Jews descended from refugees whom the Babylonians had expelled from the Kingdom of Judah in 587 BCE. A few Yemenite Jews had immigrated to the Land of Israel, on their own initiative, in 1862, 1881, and 1920, out of religious belief in Israel's soon-to-be redemption. After Israel's independence, however, Yemenite Jews started suffering from persecution because Israel was a red herring in the Arab world. The Israeli government secretly flew them to Israel with national El Al planes as well as planes from America's Alaska Airlines. Elgen Long, a young Alaska Airlines pilot who took part in the operation, later described the experience:

The company sent us a cable and it said: "Go to Aden and the commander there will meet you there." We landed and he told us of the plight of the Yemenite Jews who had found their way to Aden after crossing the desert, on foot. . . . They were dying of diseases and they had to get to Israel and get out of there as soon as possible. . . . Because it was a matter of life and death, we flew on the Sabbath, we did not stop, back and forth. . . . Twelve flights, 1,800 people, that was before Operation Magic Carpet (had officially begun), a few months earlier. . . . Actually Magic Carpet was with benches and seats, they could carry about 107 passengers and rarely did they fit in 120. But that continued for over a year after we left. I was one of a crew of about six men. I just did my job as a navigator; we could not land in an Arab country because of the war, which was just ending. We did not file any flight plan, it was all secret, nothing was in the papers or the radio. We just flew up the middle of the Red Sea and up the Gulf of Aqaba until Um Rushrush (now Eilat), then turned towards Be'er Sheva, then to Lydda.⁹

The larger wave of 47,000 Yemenite Jews (1949–50) and 120,000 Iraqi Jews (1950) was followed, starting in 1956, by smaller waves of Jewish immigration from Morocco and Tunisia, two countries that had gained independence from France that year. That same year, some 15,000 Egyptian Jews were forced to leave Egypt following the war with Israel, and most of them immigrated to Israel; some 9,000 Hungarian Jews immigrated to Israel as well, following the Soviet invasion of Hungary. By contrast, when Algeria gained its independence from France in 1962, most of its Jews immigrated to France. Unlike Moroccan and Tunisian Jews, Algerian Jews had been French citizens since 1870, and they primarily identified as French.

The 1967 Six-Day War brought a major change in Israel-Diaspora relations. After Israel's unexpected victory, there was widespread relief and pride among Jews around the world. Until that time, most Jewish immigrants to Israel had been refugees, but after the Six-Day War, an ideologically motivated *aliyah* from the United States started taking shape (albeit in small numbers).

The Six-Day War also awakened feelings of pride and self-awareness among Soviet Jews. In the Soviet Union, Jews who had previously hidden their identity started to proudly assert their Jewishness and apply for immigration to Israel. As former refusenik Natan Sharansky was to recall in his memoirs:

> The Six Day War had made an indelible impression on me as it did on most Soviet Jews, for, in addition to fighting for her life, Israel was defending our dignity. On the eve of the war, when Israel's destruction seemed almost inevitable, Soviet anti-Semites were jubilant. But a few days later even anti-Jewish jokes started to change, and throughout the country, in spite of pro-Arab propaganda, you could see a grudging respect for Israel and for Jews. A basic, eternal truth was returning to the Jews of Russia—that personal freedom wasn't something you could achieve through assimilation. It was available only by reclaiming your historical roots.[10]

The Years of Unity

If the 1967 Six-Day War created a momentum of Jewish pride and ideological *aliyah*, the 1973 Yom Kippur War and Israel's ensuing international isolation reinforced the feeling of being "a people that dwells alone." Two dramatic events in the 1970s—the 1975 UN resolution equating Zionism with racism (see chapter 19) and the Entebbe rescue operation of 1976—hardened those sentiments. The UN resolution aroused outrage in Israel and among Diaspora Jewry. As for the Entebbe operation a year later, it brought back dark memories from the past (as German terrorists separated Jewish hostages from non-Jewish ones) and also symbolized Israel's responsibility for Jews regardless of their citizenship. On June 27, 1976, Arab and German terrorists (belonging respectively to the Popular Front of the Liberation of Palestine and the Baader-Meinhof terrorist organization) had hijacked an Air France flight from Tel Aviv to Paris and demanded the liberation of fifty-three terrorists, forty of whom were jailed in Israel. The diverted plane eventually landed in Entebbe, the main airport of Uganda, whose dictator, Idi Amin, welcomed the hijackers. Over the following days, most of the non-Israeli passengers were released and flown to Paris, while the Israeli and non-Israeli Jewish hostages were threatened with death. On July 4, 1976, in a spectacular military operation, the IDF rescued the hostages. The Entebbe operation (renamed Operation Yonatan in memory of its fallen commander, Yonatan Netanyahu) symbolized Israel's status as the guarantor of Jews' safety regardless of their citizenship.

Feelings of solidarity also intensified in the 1980s and 1990s with Israel's dramatic rescue of Ethiopian Jews in Operation Moses (1984–85) and Operation Solomon (1991). The American Jewish community took pride in assisting the successful completion of both operations by lobbying for U.S. support and raising funds.

Menachem Begin had initiated the rescue of Ethiopian Jewry in June 1977 when he asked the Ethiopian dictator Mengistu Haile Mariam to let Ethiopian Jews leave for Israel.[11] In the mid- and late 1970s, in the midst of a civil war, thousands of Ethiopian Jews had fled Ethiopia on foot and become refugees in southern Sudan. Many had died on the way, and many of those who had made it to the refugee camps were perishing from disease and malnutrition. The Israeli government decided to rescue them, but doing so required cooperation from the Sudanese government, with which Israel had no diplomatic relations. Israel asked and obtained U.S. help to secure Khartoum's cooperation; then vice president George Bush was personally involved with this endeavor. Between November 1984 and January 1985, thirty-five flights between Khartoum and Tel Aviv brought some seventy-five hundred Ethiopian Jews to Israel. Sudan secretly acquiesced to their evacuation by Israel.

In 1991 Ethiopian dictator Mengistu Haile Mariam was about to be toppled, and Ethiopian Jews were at risk due to the ongoing violence between Mengistu's opponents and supporters. The Israeli government drew plans to airlift Ethiopia's Jews to Israel. Israel's Operation Solomon, overseen by Prime Minister Yitzhak Shamir and kept secret by military censorship, proceeded to rescue 14,440 Ethiopian Jews.

A Relation at Risk?

While the struggle for the freedom of Soviet Jews and the rescue of Ethiopian Jews brought Israel and U.S. Jewry together, there also were — and still are — fundamental disagreements between the Jewish state and the world's largest Jewish Diaspora. The gap between Palestinian Jews (as they were called before 1948) and U.S. Jewry was palpable even before Israel's independence. When David Ben-Gurion traveled to the United States in October 1940 to promote the idea of a Jewish army, he realized the depth of the divide. Most American Jews saw in Zionism a threat to their hard-earned status as full-fledged Americans. Zionism "spoiled the party" by proclaiming that Jews were not only a religious community but also a national one. The conflict between Zionism and the Arabs added insult to injury; if U.S. Jewry was going to show support for a movement it did not approve of in the first place, at least that movement should not cause trouble. It was therefore "imperative" to solve the conflict between Arabs and Jews in Palestine, to spare American Jews the embarrassment of being identified with warmongering Jewish nationalists. Upon his arrival in New York, Ben-Gurion was lectured about how to achieve peace in Palestine: establish an Arab-Jewish federation and a joint Jewish-Arab army to fight Hitler—never mind that at this point, Palestinian leader Hadj Amin al-Husseini had already pledged allegiance to Nazi Germany. Ben-Gurion would write in his diary that he thought American Jews had no idea what they were talking about.[12]

The divide between American and Palestinian Jews reemerged after World War II, although for different reasons. While the Holocaust had converted much of U.S. Jewry to Zionism, still, some of the new "converts" to Zionism thought they knew better. When the World Zionist Congress convened in Basel in December 1946, the catastrophic scope of the Holocaust by now known to all, the question of rebellion against Britain was in the air. Zionists everywhere resented Great Britain for having restrained Jewish immigration to Palestine when it was most needed and for keeping the gates of the Mandate sealed even as Holocaust survivors tried to reach the Promised Land. At the congress, an American Zionist leader declared, "Palestine Jewry should revolt against Britain while American Jews would give full political and moral support," to which Chaim Weizmann dryly replied, "Moral and political support is very little when you send other people to the barricades to face tanks and guns." He added that "the eleven new settlements just established in the Negev have much a greater weight than a hundred speeches about resistance, especially when the speeches are made in New York while the proposed resistance is to be made in Tel Aviv and Jerusalem."[13]

At the same time, leading American Jews did express their support for Zionism even as they became more integrated into American society. Prominent among them were Louis Brandeis and Stephen Wise. Brandeis was the first Jew to be nominated to the U.S. Supreme Court (by President Woodrow Wilson, in 1916). In 1912 Brandeis became active in the Federation of American Zionists; in 1914 he was elected president of the Provisional Executive Committee for Zionist Affairs, thus becoming the leader and spokesman of Zionism in the United

States. Unlike most of his fellow liberal American Jews, Brandeis argued that a reborn Jewish homeland was the solution to antisemitism and to what was then called the "Jewish problem" in Europe and in Russia. As he explained to American Jews who feared that by supporting Zionism they would be accused of dual allegiance:

> Let no American imagine that Zionism is inconsistent with Patriotism. Multiple loyalties are objectionable only if they are inconsistent. . . . Every American Jew who aids in advancing the Jewish settlement in Palestine, though he feels that neither he nor his descendants will ever live there, will likewise be a better man and a better American for doing so.

Brandeis used his personal relation with President Wilson to promote the Balfour Declaration at the Paris Peace Conference and its inclusion in the British Mandate on Palestine (which Brandeis visited in 1919). In the 1930s Brandeis advocated Jewish immigration to Palestine and criticized Britain's restrictive immigration policy.

Another atypical American Zionist was Stephen Wise. Unlike most Reform rabbis in the late nineteenth and early twentieth centuries, Wise was a Zionist. In 1897 he founded the New York Federation of Zionist Societies, which eventually became the Zionist Organization of America. Wise attended the Second Zionist Congress of 1898 as an American delegate, though he did not consistently help the cause of Zionism.[14]

When Israel was fighting for its life in 1948, it also benefited from the precious help of American volunteers. Among them was Mickey Marcus (known in Israel as David Marcus). An attorney by trade and a U.S. army officer during World War II, Marcus was named chief of the U.S. Army's War Crimes Division. In that capacity, he planned the legal procedures for the Nuremberg Trials, and he thoroughly documented Nazi war crimes. After visiting the Dachau concentration camp, Marcus decided to dedicate himself to the rebirth of Israel. He volunteered to serve as an advisor to the nascent Jewish army. Marcus obtained the unofficial approval of the U.S. War Department, but he had to change his name to Michael Stone so as not to get into trouble with the British government. Ben-Gurion appointed him as a general (*aluf*), and he was given command of the Jerusalem front. He built the famous "Burma Road" to Jerusalem, which opened an alternative route to the besieged city. Killed due to the tragic mistake of an Israeli soldier, Marcus is the only American buried at West Point Cemetery who was killed fighting under the flag of another country. The memorial plaque in his honor at the Union Temple of Brooklyn reads, "Killed in action in the hills of Zion while leading Israeli forces as their supreme commander in the struggle for Israel's freedom."

Another heroic volunteer was Al Schwimmer. A U.S. pilot and aerospace engineer during World War II, Schwimmer decided to smuggle warplanes to the IDF during Israel's War of Independence and to recruit pilots to fly the smuggled planes. In 1950 Schwimmer was convicted for violating the U.S. Neutrality Acts, stripped of his voting rights and veteran benefits, and fined $10,000. Schwimmer pleaded guilty and declared that smuggling airplanes to Israel against U.S. law was the right moral decision and a proper form of moral civil disobedience. Schwimmer subsequently settled in Israel, where he founded the Israel Aircraft Industries. President Bill Clinton pardoned him in 2001.

Marcus, Schwimmer, and other Diaspora Jews saw it as their duty and calling to help secure Israel's independence. After Israel's independence, however, the ideological gap between Israeli and American Jews resurfaced. For David Ben-Gurion, Jews who did not make *aliyah* lived in exile and therefore in an abnormal condition. Jacob Blaustein, president of the American Jewish Committee, saw things differently, as he made clear to Ben-Gurion in August 1950:

We must, in a true spirit of friendliness, sound a note of caution to Israel and its leaders. Now that the birth pains are over, and even though Israel is undergoing growing pains, it must recognize that the matter of good will between its citizens and those of other countries is a two-way street: that Israel also has a responsibility in this situation—a responsibility in terms of not affecting adversely the sensibilities of Jews who are citizens of other states by what it says or does. I would be less than frank if I did not point out to you that American Jews vigorously repudiate any suggestion or implication that they are in exile. . . . To American Jews, America is home.

In the 1950s there was little criticism of Israel among American Jews. The main contentious issue was the claim, generally made by Israeli leaders, that all Diaspora Jews were living in exile. Yet the 1956 Suez War was the first war fought by Israel without the full support of American Jews, because this war was not unanimously perceived as defensive. Abba Eban noted that with the 1956 war, "for the first time in our history there was reluctance to justify Israel's actions without reserve."[15]

Unease and criticism widened with subsequent military conflicts. Images of the first Lebanon War in 1982 and then of the first intifada in 1988 made many American Jews uncomfortable and increasingly critical of Israel. Among the many examples of this "family feud" was an exchange of letters, in January 1988, between the president of the Union of American Hebrew Congregations (the Reform movement's congregational arm), Rabbi Alexander M. Schindler, and the president of Israel, Chaim Herzog. In his response to Schindler, who criticized Israel's handling of the intifada, Herzog wrote that "Jewish ethics and morals, which you evoke, are very clear as to one's duty to defend oneself when facing possible mortal danger."[16]

Israel and U.S. Jewry have also been at odds on religious matters. Most American Jews are not Orthodox, and the United States, which by and large upholds church-state separation, recognizes life-cycle ceremonies officiated by representatives of all the major Jewish movements. By contrast, in Israel, the Orthodox rabbinate currently wields a monopoly over religious matters, and as a result the state only recognizes Orthodox conversions and marriages; Reform and Conservative marriages and conversions in Israel are deemed invalid. Meanwhile, many Israelis also contest and criticize the Orthodox religious monopoly, which does not reflect the pluralism of Israeli society.

Prayer at the Western Wall (or Wailing Wall) has also become contentious. The Orthodox rabbinate, which runs the Western Wall and its plaza, only allows services according to Orthodox customs, including only permitting men to pray according to customary Jewish rites. The police forcibly remove women who wear tefillin (phylacteries) or a tallit (prayer shawl) or who read from a Torah scroll at the plaza, because Israeli law states that worshipers and visitors at holy sites (whether Jewish, Muslim, or Christian) must respect the customs and practices of these sites. Only in recent years have some women, known as the Women of the Wall, tried to introduce new practices at the Western Wall, something the ultra-Orthodox perceive as a violation of the site's customs and practices and, therefore, of the law. Furthermore, ultra-Orthodox onlookers often verbally and physically attack the Women of the Wall. To most American Jews, as well as many Israelis, images of police forcefully removing Jewish women from the Wall plaza are intolerable. Even some American Orthodox rabbis have protested the Orthodox rabbinate's heavy-handed policy. In July 2010, for example, Rabbi Shmuel Herzfeld, of the Modern Orthodox Ohev Shalom synagogue in Washington DC, declared that he fully supported the Women of the Wall (who want to read from a Torah scroll at the Wall's women's section) and that their arrest by the Israeli police "doesn't represent Orthodoxy and the Orthodox Jews I know."[17] Likewise, many in Israel have raised their voice against the banning of Women of the Wall. In March 2013, for example, female members of Knesset (MKs) joined the Women of the Wall, thus preventing police arrests.[18]

Compounding this, since the early 1990s, the fate of Soviet refuseniks has ceased to be a unifying cause for Israeli and American Jewry. Once the Soviet government lifted the ban on their emigration, there has been no need for the two to fight together for the "prisoners of Zion."

The second intifada (2000–2004) and the global demonization of Israel (exemplified by the 2000 Al Dura Affair and the 2001 Durban Conference) temporarily restored unity between Israel and the Diasporas. Eventually, however, American Jewry's attitudes toward Israel became mostly partisan: right-wing Jews generally circled the wagons around Israel, while left-wing Jews advocated for a Palestinian state alongside the State of Israel and became increasingly vocal in their criticism of Israel's settlement policy. The 2008 creation of the liberal Jewish advocacy organization J Street exemplified the growing divide within U.S. Jewry. According to Dov Waxman, professor of Jewish Historical and Cultural Studies at Northeastern University, "Israel used to bring American Jews together. Now it is driving them apart."[19] In the summer of 2015, Israel drove American Jews apart as never before: as Congress was to vote on President Obama's controversial nuclear deal with Iran, American Jews were torn between the call of the U.S. president to support the deal and the call of the Israeli prime minister to oppose it.

The Israel-Diaspora relationship is characterized not only by a widening political divide among American Jews, but also by demographic differences between Israel and U.S Jewry. When Israel declared its independence in 1948, its population constituted only a small fraction of what remained of the Jewish people after the Holocaust. Today most Jews still live outside of Israel (about 58 percent), but Israel has the world's largest Jewish community (over six million). Israel is the only country in the world where the Jewish population is growing, because of high birth rates, *aliyah,* and a near absence of intermarriage. In the rest of the world, by contrast, the Jewish population is shrinking, because of assimilation and intermarriage. This tendency is especially true in the United States, where 40 percent of world Jewry lives, and it influences the relationship between Israel and U.S. Jewry because, as shown by recent surveys, support for Israel among American Jews tends to be proportional to their level of religious observance — the more Orthodox they are, the more they support Israel, and vice versa.[20] At the same time, Reform, Conservative, and other liberal Jews have strong ties with Israel, individually as well as organizationally (e.g., Association of Reform Zionists of America, or ARZA), and their criticism is meant to be constructive.

In June 2017 the Israeli government, pressured by ultra-Orthodox parties, backed down from an agreement with the American Conservative and Reform movements to expand a non-Orthodox prayer area at the Western Wall — a decision that appalled most American Jews. (Israeli governments are composed of multiparty coalitions, something that often forces Israeli prime ministers to cave in to the pressures of coalition partners for fear of losing one's government.) In April 2018, following the harsh criticism of his hard-core electorate, Prime Minister Netanyahu scrapped a deal — which had been partially motivated by a willingness to assuage the criticism of American Jewry — that would have legalized the status of some illegal African migrants and asylum seekers in Israel. Jewish organizations in the United States also highly criticized the Knesset's August 2018 "nation-state" basic law, which specifies that the State of Israel is the nation-state of the Jewish People. These developments point to an ever-widening ideological gap between Israel and U.S. Jewry. In January 2019 veteran Washington journalist Jonathan Weisman openly expressed this concern in a *New York Times* op-ed titled "American Jews and Israeli Jews Are Headed for a Messy Breakup." Pointing out that most Israelis are supportive of Donald Trump, while most American Jews are not, Weisman also suggested that Israel seems to have given up on liberal American Jews:

> Israeli politicians—and citizens—are increasingly dismissive of the views of American Jews anyway. Evangelical Christians, ardently pro-Israel, give Jerusalem a power base in Washington that is larger and stronger than the American Jewish population. And with Orthodox American Jews aligned with evangelicals, that coalition has at least an interfaith veneer—even without Conservative and Reform Jews, the bulk of American Jewry.[21]

Weisman mentioned that his rabbi had recently asked his congregation to act and save Israel from itself, to which U.S.-born Israeli author Daniel Gordis replied, "If American Jewish progressives want Israelis to be in dialogue with them, it is time to end the assumption that the repository of morality, wisdom and decency resides exclusively on the Western edge of the Atlantic."[22]

Still, other U.S.-born Israeli rabbis and thinkers have kept their original outlook. For example, years after the preeminent Conservative rabbi Reuven Hammer made *aliyah*, he served on Netanyahu's Neeman Commission, charged with recommending a solution to the controversy over conversions conducted by Conservative and Reform groups in Israel that threatened to bring down the government. (Ultimately the chief rabbinate rejected the Neeman Commission's proposal of a new institute, to be run jointly by all groups, that would have prepared conversion candidates, while the actual conversion would have been performed by special Orthodox courts consisting of rabbis selected for their willingness to be moderate and understanding in their requirements.) Moreover, Orthodox Judaism in Israel is itself not monolithic; many Orthodox rabbis—prominent among them Rabbis Shlomo Riskin and Aryeh Stav—have challenged the rigidity of the Orthodox rabbinate on issues such as conversions.

For most Israelis, these social and religious issues are less important than security. Even secular Israelis are generally indifferent to the monopoly of Orthodox customs at the Western Wall, and they tend to see the Woman of the Wall as a needless and even provocative challenge to an Israeli consensus. When it comes down to security, mainstream Israelis are still willing to consider a two-state solution, but they also believe that this solution is not feasible in the foreseeable future because of Palestinian rejectionism. In theory, then, mainstream Israelis would not take issue with the 2013 statement of the Union for Reform Judaism and Central Conference of American Rabbis (the Reform rabbinic body) that "the ongoing failure to establish a viable peace poses security and other risks to Israel and is a disservice to those Palestinians who desire a peaceful future for their children and grandchildren." But the same mainstream Israelis would point to what is missing in this statement: that for the past eight decades, from the 1937 Peel plan to the 2008 Olmert proposal, Palestinian leaders have rejected territorial compromise with Zionism in any shape or form regardless of the size and location of Jewish settlements. Hence the inattentive dialogue between Israeli and American Jews: the latter tend to think that Israelis are not truly interested in peace, while the former strongly feel that they are the ones suffering from the absence of peace and that their past efforts to achieve peace are too often overlooked.

Conclusion

By calling upon Diaspora Jews to join "the great struggle for the real-ization of the age-old dream of the redemption of Israel" (as stated in the Declaration of Independence) and by making all Jews potential citizens of Israel (with the passing of the Law of Return), Israel cre-ated a challenge for its foreign policy by complicating its relations with countries opposed to Jewish emigration—first and foremost the Soviet Union. The struggle to free Soviet Jews brought Israel and

U.S. Jewry together. This feeling of togetherness was reinforced by the 1975 UN vote against Zionism and by the 1976 Entebbe operation. Yet Israel-Diaspora relations—especially between Israel and U.S. Jewry—became strained with the 1982 Lebanon War, the first intifada, Israel's non-recognition of Conservative and Reform Judaism, and Israel's continued building of settlements in the West Bank (a policy denounced by its critics as incompatible with a two-state solution). Israel always valued its relationship with American Jews, not least because of their political influence in the United States. This influence, however, is increasingly split along religious and political lines.

21. Israel and the Geopolitics of Energy

> In the field of Energy, we [Israel, Greece, and Turkey]
> reconfirm our support and commitment for the imple-
> mentation of the East-Med Pipeline Project, a project that
> represents a viable and strategic option of common inter-
> est, both to our countries and to the European Union.
>
> JOINT DECLARATION of the trilateral summit between Israel,
> Greece, and Cyprus, in Beersheba, Israel, December 20, 2018

The Rise and Fall of the Oil Weapon

Israel had an "oil problem" at birth. In 1947 the American oil industry lobbied against the partition of Palestine for fear of alienating Saudi Arabia. In October 1955 U.S. secretary of state John Foster Dulles argued against threatening Egypt after it signed a military agreement with the Soviet Union, via Czechoslovakia, for fear of affecting oil supplies to the West.[1] The oil embargo imposed by OPEC (Organization of Petroleum Exporting Countries) after the 1973 Yom Kippur War seriously damaged Israel's international standing; Western Europe and Japan were now demanding a full and unconditional Israeli with-drawal from all territories conquered in 1967, and nearly all African countries severed diplomatic relations with Israel.

OPEC was able to blackmail oil importers and isolate Israel because of the geographic concentration of oil resources and the cartel structure of the oil market. The Middle East and North Africa generate more than one-third of global oil production, and OPEC controls about 80 percent of the world's crude oil reserves and 40 percent of global production—a virtual monopoly that has enabled OPEC to manipulate oil prices and thus maintain political pressure on oil importers.

In short, energy resources have long been vital to national interests. Energy assets enabled Putin's Russia to pursue an aggressive foreign policy and to rebuild alliances with former Soviet allies (including in the Middle East). Iran's nuclear program was built thanks to Russian technology. Iran was able to conclude a nuclear deal with the great powers in 2015 partially thanks to China's need for Iranian oil and natural gas.

Following the shock of the 1973 embargo, the United States initiated a policy designed to reduce its dependence on Middle Eastern oil. Four decades later, America has almost reached this goal and is nearly energy independent. The "shale boom" (i.e., production of oil and natural gas by fracking) has reduced U.S. dependence on fossil fuel imports (i.e., oil, natural gas, and coal) by 64 percent since 2005.[2] Today, the United States only imports 13 percent of its fossil fuel consumption—a third of what it imported a decade ago[3]—and only 5 percent from outside North America. As for oil, the United States produces 40 percent of its domestic needs and imports the rest from Canada, Mexico, Venezuela, Nigeria, and the Persian Gulf, but the Persian Gulf countries (including Saudi Arabia) provide only 13 percent of U.S. oil imports and only 7 percent of total U.S. oil needs.[4] Thus, U.S. reliance on Middle Eastern oil is minor. Middle Eastern oil exporters cannot blackmail America, especially since the U.S. economy is expected to further reduce its oil imports over time.

Since 2014, moreover, oil prices have plummeted (from $110 a barrel in June 2014 to $45 in August 2017, going as low as $30 in January 2016), driven by Saudi Arabia's November 2014 decision to flood the global oil market in order to drive out fracking firms and thwart Iran (by reducing oil prices). At the same time, Saudi Arabia's gamble has failed; the fracking industry has proved resilient, and the increase in Saudi production did not affect Iranian oil sales (Iran rejoined the oil market in January 2016 when sanctions were lifted).

All in all, even as energy has traditionally been Israel's Achilles' heel, recent trends in the world energy market, as well as Israel's emergence as a natural gas exporter, have transformed and improved Israel's position. Whereas at the time of the 1973 embargo, oil's share in the global energy supply was 46 percent, today, oil's share is 31 percent (as opposed to 29 percent for coal and 21 percent for natural gas)[5]—a significant (albeit not dramatic) change. The Paris Agreement on the environment, sealed in December 2015, compels signatory countries to reduce their carbon dioxide emissions and, therefore, their oil consumption—a policy choice that, when combined with the afore-mentioned structural changes, makes it harder if not impossible for OPEC nations to manipulate the oil market for political purposes—also good news for Israel. And even though oil will continue to be a central source of energy in the foreseeable future, natural gas is emerging as a favorite source of energy, because of its abundance and relative cleanliness. Shale gas turned the United States into a net exporter of natural gas in 2017, the first time in sixty years. The global LNG (lique-fied natural gas) market is growing by 4–6 percent per year, LNG is the fastest growing way of trading gas, and LNG demand stands at about 265 million tons per year.[6] Therefore, Israel's natural gas resources are turning out to be economic and geopolitical assets.

Israel's Emergence as a Natural Gas Exporter

In January 2009 the Texan firm Noble Energy discovered gas in the Tamar field in the eastern Mediterranean, transforming Israel's econ-omy and international stature overnight. This field is estimated to contain 200 billion cubic meters (BCM) of natural gas—representing over half of what the European Union's twenty-seven nations consume annually. Two years later, in December 2010, Noble Energy discovered an even larger gas field, named Leviathan, which is now estimated to contain 500 BCM of gas. The Tamar and Leviathan deposits are expected to provide Israel with enough natural gas for decades and transform the country into an energy exporter.

The Tamar and Leviathan discoveries have already transformed Israel's international standing and its relations with Egypt, Jordan, Turkey, Greece, and Cyprus. Jordan imports 97 percent of its energy needs at a cost of 20 percent of its GDP, and 88 percent of the energy it consumes comes from natural gas.[7] In October 2016 the Leviathan gas field partners signed a $10 billion contract to sell gas to Jordan's National Electric Power Company over fifteen years. In January 2017 Israel started exporting natural gas to Jordan after connecting the state-owned Jordanian companies Arab Potash and Jordan Bromine to Israel's national gas pipeline network.[8]

Israel's gas resources have also helped mend fences with Turkey. While Israel and Turkey were close allies in the 1990s, the relationship deteriorated after Turkey's Islamic leader Recep Tayyip Erdoğan became prime minister in 2002, and even more so after the 2010 *Mavi Marmara* incident (see chapter 10). While in recent years, Erdoğan has adopted a hostile and offensive rhetoric toward Israel, the two countries did reach a reconciliation agreement in December 2015, in large part because of Turkey's desire to reduce its significant dependence on Russia for its gas imports. Of the 99 percent of its natural gas that Turkey imports (generating half of its electricity), 60 percent of it comes from Russia.[9] Israel and Turkey are discussing an agreement for natural gas supply, but the talks have not progressed smoothly due to serious political issues (among them Erdoğan's continued support for Hamas, close ties with Iran and Russia, and aggressive anti-Israel rhetoric).[10]

Natural gas resources have improved Israel's relations with Greece, a country with a traditionally pro-Arab foreign policy, which only established diplomatic relations with Israel in 1990 (see chapter 13). In June 2017 Israel, Greece, and Cyprus announced their planned cooperation in the construction of a pipeline linking the three countries aimed at delivering natural gas to the EU. Since Cyprus has its own large gas field (Aphrodite), this partnership can turn Cyprus into a mega gas exporter. For Greece, the prospect of becoming a transiting country for the export of eastern Mediterranean gas to the European continent is a welcome and much needed means of strengthening its weak economy. Israel, in turn, has been happy to further improve its relations with Greece, especially given the deterioration of the Israel-Turkey relationship after 2010.

Israel sees in Europe an important potential customer for its natural gas, not least because Europe is trying to reduce its dependency on Russian gas. Yet building gas pipelines from Israel to Europe is logistically challenging. An overland pipeline would have to go through Lebanon and Syria, two war-torn and failed states with which Israel is technically at war. An underwater pipeline to Turkey is technically possible, but it would have to go through Cypriot territorial waters and thus involve Israel in the conflicting claims of the Turkish-occupied Northern Cyprus and the Republic of Cyprus in the southern part of the island. Cyprus will not allow a pipeline to Turkey through its territorial waters until an agreement has been reached on reunification of the island. Cyprus, with its own gas fields, is interested in a partnership with Israel for export to Europe. Yet Turkey is opposed to such a partnership unless Turkish Cypriots also benefit from it.

Israel is promoting the building of an undersea pipeline directly to Europe. Such a pipeline, connecting Israel to Italy via Cyprus and Greece—if completed—would be the world's longest (2,200 kilometers, or 1,367 miles). This pipeline project, signed by Israel, Italy, Greece, Cyprus, and the EU in April 2017, would be completed by 2025 and cost $7 billion. Most energy experts, however, dismiss both estimations as too optimistic,[11] calling the project a "pipe dream" that will take decades and require more proven reserves.[12]

An alternative strategy, which also carries risks, would be to focus on an energy partnership between Israel, Turkey, Jordan, and Egypt. So far, however, talks about an undersea gas pipeline between Israel and Turkey have not made significant progress.

A partnership with Egypt was unthinkable when the country was ruled by the Muslim Brotherhood between 2012 and 2013, and it might still be risky due to Egypt's political instability. As of this writing, Egyptian president Abdel-Fattah al-Sisi has restored and expanded Israel's security cooperation with Egypt. Moreover, Israel and Egypt have common interests when it comes to natural gas. While, like Israel, Egypt has large natural gas reserves—in fact its Zohr gas field, discovered off its northern coast in 2015, is the largest in the Mediterranean, nearly twice the size of Israel's Leviathan—because Egypt has ninety-five million inhabitants and a high population growth, it will likely need even more natural gas for domestic consumption than Zohr will be able to supply once it becomes operational. Those needs can be met by Israel's exports. In August 2017 the Egyptian president signed a law that allows private companies to import natural gas. In February 2018 the Tamar and Leviathan fields signed a $15 billion contract with Egypt's Dophinus Holdings for the export of sixty-four billion cubic meters of natural gas from Israel to Egypt.[13] Even beyond this, it makes sense for Israel to develop an energy partnership with Egypt because Egypt has two natural gas liquefaction terminals (which Israel lacks), via which Israel could export LNG to Europe.

In January 2019 the Eastern Mediterranean Gas Forum (EMGF) was established between Israel, Egypt, Greece, Cyprus, Italy, Jordan, and the Palestinian Authority. This significant move formalizes a new energy partnership in the Eastern Mediterranean that gives stronger impetus to a double geopolitical interest shared by Israel and the United States: (a) curtail Russia's domination of the European energy market; and (b) counterbalance Iran's access to the Eastern Mediterranean via Syria. By linking Egypt to Israel via natural gas, EMGF is frustrating Iran's regional ambitions. During the brief (2012–13) regime of Mohamed Morsi and the Muslim Brotherhood in Egypt, Iran had hoped to turn Egypt into a client state for natural gas. Such a scenario was not unlikely after the signature of the nuclear deal (JCPOA) in 2015 and the lifting of sanctions on Iran. EMGF is an indication that (at least for the time being) the United States has convinced Egyptian president al-Sisi to remain in the realm of U.S. allies and to downgrade Egypt's ties with Iran.

Israel's Role in the Energy Transition

Western economies were taken by surprise when the OPEC cartel quadrupled the price of oil after the Yom Kippur War. While the "oil weapon" proved effective in the short term, it also boomeranged in the long term because oil importers progressively reformed their energy markets and partially reduced their dependency on oil. This reduction was achieved in electricity production. At the time of the 1973 oil embargo, 25 percent of the world's electricity was produced from oil; today, this percentage has dropped to 4 percent.[14] And yet the world economy continues to be oil dependent, because oil still enjoys a quasi-monopoly in transportation. Oil still fuels 93 percent of global transportation.[15]

So far, this monopoly has been broken only in isolated cases. Brazil set up a large-scale sugar-cane-based ethanol industry in the wake of the 1973 oil embargo. Today most Brazilian cars have engines that can run on either petroleum or ethanol (gas stations in Brazil offer both options to their customers). Furthermore, sugar cane ethanol is not the only biofuel available on the market. Research over the years has produced "second generation" biofuels based on nonconsumable crops, organic waste, and algae.

Unlike countries such as China, the United States, or Brazil, Israel cannot compete with the massive production of biofuels. (Israel could theoretically produce biofuels in sub-Saharan Africa, but doing so would present major logistical and financial challenges.) Rather, Israel's comparative advantage lies in its technological edge. Israel has world-renowned researchers who specialize in second-generation biofuels and other technologies that can produce alternatives to petroleum.

Given Israel's interest in contributing to the progressive dethroning of oil's monopoly in transportation, in January 2011 the Israeli government launched an ambitious multiyear program to promote "technologies to reduce the global use of oil in transportation."[16] This led to generous funding for scientific research, incentives for investment in local companies developing oil alternatives, a scheme for implementing these alternatives in Israel as a preliminary application site, and cooperation with multinational organizations and countries seeking to reduce oil dependency (such as China and India).

Alternatives to oil for transportation include natural gas and electricity. The gradual replacement of the internal combustion engine by electric vehicles (at least for ground transportation) is no longer utopian. Electric cars' performances have improved dramatically thanks to lithium-ion batteries. In 2019 Tesla, a leading U.S. manufacturer of electric cars, released a model that can drive for 1,000 kilometers (620 miles) on a single charge. UBS, a global investment bank, predicts that electric cars will comprise 14 percent of global car sales by 2025, as opposed to 1 percent in 2019.[17] Electric cars are getting not only more efficient but also cheaper: their cost per kilowatt-hour has dropped from $1,000 in 2010 to less than $200 in 2019.[18] Battery costs have been cut by 80 percent in the past decade.[19] Both France and Britain have declared that by 2040, they will make it illegal to manufacture cars that rely solely on internal combustion engines.[20]

Israeli technology is making significant contributions to the reliability and autonomy of electric vehicles. The French car maker Peugeot, for example, is testing battery-powered cars that recharge with an on-board generator designed by Aquarius Engines, an Israeli start-up.[21] In May 2017 StoreDot, an Israeli start-up, unveiled a vehicle battery that can be charged in five minutes and can run for about 300 kilometers (186 miles).[22] The Israeli government is collaborating with ElectRoad, another start-up, to install public transportation lines in Tel Aviv, using an under-road wireless technology that eliminates the need for plug-in recharging stations.[23]

Israeli technology also has a contribution to make to the energy transition required by the Paris Agreement and implemented by Germany's ambitious *Energiewende* (energy transition). Germany's 2010 legislation on energy transition requires that the country produce 60 percent of its energy from renewables by 2050. Renewable energy sources (such as wind and solar power) only produce 7 percent of the electricity generated worldwide.[24] Expanding the share of renewables in electricity production will largely depend on reducing the cost of renewable energies through further research and development. About 270 Israeli companies currently operate in the field of renewable energies, and many of them are world leaders.[25]

In essence, Israel's "oil problem" has turned into an asset, but one that can and must be fully leveraged through wise and proactive policies. Israel's energy policy will also need to manage risks. Those include political instability in Egypt and Turkey (hence the need for diversification) and the "Dutch disease" (the appreciation of the national currency resulting from the massive export of natural resources). Moreover, energy markets are admittedly unpredictable. Oil prices might stabilize and even surge again, and new natural gas discoveries in the Mediterranean Sea might affect Israel's market value.

Nonetheless, as a whole, the transformation of the energy factor from liability to asset in Israel's foreign policy is no less than revolutionary. Despite the uncertainties inherent in the global energy market, Israel's status as a powerful player is now recognized by its allies and foes alike.

Conclusion

Energy used to be the Achilles' heel of Israel's foreign policy because of the Arab world's domination of the oil market. This was epitomized by the oil embargo imposed after the 1973 Yom Kippur War. Today, however, the world's leading economies have significantly reduced their oil consumption, Israel's emergence as a natural gas exporter has transformed its regional and international status, and Israel's technological edge is a sought-after boon in the energy transition being implemented throughout Europe. The establishment of the Eastern Mediterranean Gas Forum in January 2019 corroborates that the energy factor that was once a liability has remarkably become an asset for Israel's foreign policy.

Conclusion

As explained in chapter 1, the name Israel did not irreversibly replace that of Jacob in the Hebrew Bible. Even after the announcement that "your name shall no longer be Jacob, but Israel" (Gen. 32:29), the biblical text continues to interchangeably use both names. The verse quoted at the beginning of this book (which inspired its title) makes two correlations: that of a star with Jacob, and that of a scepter with Israel. The star symbolizes faith (the Star of David is the symbol of Judaism), while the scepter symbolizes power (in the book of Esther, King Ahasuerus's scepter is the expression of his absolute power). This duality is part of the Jews' very identity, as they are both a religion and a nation. Ernest Renan's definition of a nation — "a soul, a spiritual principle" — certainly applies to the Jews. Yet there is something unique in the congenital link between the Jewish religion and the Jewish nation. Other nations have special religious allegiances: Shinto is a Japanese religion; Catholicism is hardly separable from Polish national identity; the British monarch is both head of state and head of the Anglican Church. Yet one can be Japanese and Christian, Polish and Protestant, British and Catholic. A Jew belongs concomitantly and inseparably to a religion and to a nation, even if an atheist, a convert, or an Israel basher.

Over their long history, the Jews were deprived, more often than not, of a scepter. Their statelessness left them with the star — the spiritual message that Jacob inherited from Abraham and Isaac. Yet, in the real world, a defenseless Jacob was in constant danger of physical demise. Hence the trial of the nighttime combat with the angel before Jacob's encounter with a menacing Esau: only after displaying strength, and a willingness to use it, was Jacob renamed Israel. Strength, however, is not an end in itself, but a means to serve and preserve an ideal. The Hebrew Bible repetitively warns that the Jews' national sovereignty is conditional upon their faithfulness to the Sinai covenant. Without a scepter, the star is in danger of extinction; without a star, the scepter is purposeless.

Nineteenth-century German Jewish philosophers thought that the Jews were no longer in need of a scepter. Hermann Cohen claimed the Jews had a spiritual and moral mission that was inherently incompatible with sovereignty and power — hence his strong opposition to Zionism. Franz Rosenzweig was critical of Zionism precisely because, for him, Judaism had to be divorced from power. Yet the genocide of European Jews was initiated and operated by the German state under the Nazis. Cohen and Rosenzweig were tragically proved wrong. The dialectic between spirituality and power, between the star and the scepter, is not over.

As Jews started rebuilding political power in the late nineteenth century, they discovered a new type of dilemma: their ideals encountered uncooperative realities. Zionist leaders soon came to realize that diplomacy and foreign policy are about striking compromises between aspirations and constraints. The 1903 Uganda proposal and the 1937 partition plan were early and painful tests of statesmanship. The evolution of the international system during the British Mandate (1920–48) had a strong impact on Zionist leaders. As the post–World War I League of Nations system crumbled in the 1930s, and as Britain reneged on her commitments to the Jewish "national home" out of political expediency, Zionist leaders learned realpolitik the hard way. The Ribbentrop-Molotov Pact finally shattered the illusions of those Socialist Zionists who had still put their hopes in the Soviet Union. An idealist Socialist Zionist in his youth, Ben-Gurion became a Bismarck-type statesman, *faute de mieux*. Precisely because it makes ungenerous assumptions about human nature, he came to see political realism as a safer bet. As former Italian premier Giulio Andreotti used to quip, "When you assume the worst of people you commit a sin; but you generally get it right."

Historically, Jews "got it right" in their relations with the nations by combining faith with pragmatism. The Hebrew Bible produced a unique eschatology that holds the key to Jewish survival: armed with a strong sense of historical mission, the Jews saw their setbacks as a well-deserved punishment ahead of a brighter future. Under Greek and Roman rule, hellenized Jews eventually vanished and Bar Kokhba's followers were crushed. In exile, both messianism and assimilation led to a dead end: Sabbatai Zevi converted to Islam, and Alfred Dreyfus was singled out as a Jew despite having embraced the French nation. Zionism was a response to the unkept promises of Emancipation: if Jews were still considered an alien nation despite their assimilation, then they should revert to their nationhood. In essence, Zionism was a pragmatic *retour aux sources*, opposed on both sides of the spectrum, by both assimilated Jews and religious rigorists.

Zionist diplomats soon faced the dilemma of choosing between realism and ideology. They rejected the 1903 Uganda proposal but were willing to consider the 1937 partition plan. It was by combining an unwavering faithfulness to the past ("If I forget thee Jerusalem, may my right hand forget me," the Jews had sworn throughout the centuries) with a pragmatic adaptability to the present ("Biltmore, Shmiltmore, we need a Jewish state," said Ben-Gurion prior to state-hood) that Israel prevailed in 1948.

A frail and threatened state in its early days, Israel eventually became a powerful country with global clout. Today, despite the unsolved imbroglio with the Palestinians, Israel has gained the upper hand in its conflict with the Arab world. Despite a history of ups and downs, Israel's alliance with the United States is now stronger than ever. Despite political differences, Israel has become a significant partner for Europe in trade, research, energy, and security. Despite often incompatible geopolitical interests, Israel has established a strong working relationship with Russia. Israel also has significant ties with China and India, as with most Asian nations; has rebuilt its presence in Africa, where it is often seen as the bulwark against radical Islam; and has made itself indispensable in Latin America in the fight against Iranian influence and Hezbollah's misdeeds. Even at the United Nations, Israel's stance has improved in recent years: Israel is now part of a regional group and has somewhat tamed the tyranny of the majority. Israel continues to enjoy the support and political power of Diaspora Jews, even if relations with American Jews have become strained in recent years. Energy, which used to be a liability in Israel's foreign policy, has become an asset.

At the same time, however, Israel faces unresolved problems and challenges in the coming decades, especially the unresolved conflict with the Palestinians and the weakening political support of American Jewry.

Israel's diplomatic achievements and challenges can only be understood in the wider context of Jewish history. Israel will continue to thrive by remembering the ultimate lesson of its unique past: it must always keep a sense of historical purpose in the real world by striking a never-ending balance between faith and power—between the star and the scepter.

Glossary

aliyah: Immigration (literally: "ascent") of Jews to the Land of Israel.

Ashkenazi: Jew of Central or Eastern European descent.

Conversos: Jews forcibly converted to Catholicism in Spain and Portugal in the fourteenth and fifteenth centuries.

dhimmi: A non-Muslim, second-class citizen under Muslim rule.

fatwa: A ruling of Islamic law.

fedayeen: "Those who sacrifice themselves" in Arabic. Arab guerillas who crossed Israel's borders with Gaza and the West Bank in the 1950s to perpetuate terrorist attacks in Israel.

green line: The armistice line that separated Israel from Cis-Jordan (the "West Bank") between 1949 and 1967.

Haganah: A Jewish paramilitary organization in the British Mandate of Palestine, which became the core of the Israel Defense Forces.

Irgun (or Etzel): A Jewish paramilitary organization in the British Mandate of Palestine, which declared war on Britain in 1944.

jihad: "Holy war" in Arabic. Islam's struggle against "infidels."

Lehi (or Stern Group/Gang): A radical Jewish paramilitary organization in the British Mandate of Palestine.

Mapai: A center-left political party that dominated Israeli politics from the pre-independence days to the mid-1970s; precursor of Israel's Labor Party.

midrash: Interpretations and commentaries on the Hebrew Bible.

Mishnah: Written version of Jewish oral laws and traditions.

Mossad: Israel's national intelligence agency.

Ostjude (plural: *Ostjuden*): "Eastern Jew" in German; a derogatory expression used by German Jews to refer to Jews of Eastern Europe who immigrated to Germany and Austria.

refuseniks: Soviet Jews who were denied permission to emigrate to Israel.

Sanhedrin: Ancient Jewish court of law. The "Grand Sanhedrin" was a modern version of the old one, convened in 1806 by Emperor Napoléon Bonaparte to clarify the legal status of French Jews.

Sephardi: Jew of Spanish and Portuguese descent and, by extension, of North African and Middle Eastern origin.

Talmud: The central text of Rabbinic Judaism.

Wakf: Islamic trust that controls and manages the Temple Mount in Jerusalem.

Yishuv: The Jewish population of British Mandatory Palestine.

Notes

Introduction

1. Poliakov, *The History of Anti-Semitism*, 104–5.
2. Wisse, *Jews and Power*, 2 (Kindle™ edition).
3. Y. Herzog, *A People That Dwells Alone*, 45.
4. Jon D. Levenson, "The Contrast between the Bible's Idea of History and the Modern Idea," *Mosaic*, August 13, 2018.

1. The Pentateuch

1. The text says that Jacob lived seventeen years in Egypt and that he arrived there two years after the seven-year famine started; Jacob, therefore, died twelve years after the famine had ended.

4. From Kingdom to Serfdom

1. The Bar Kokhba revolt (also known as the third Jewish-Roman war or the third Jewish revolt) was a rebellion of the province of Judea against the Roman Empire. Led by Simon bar Kokhba, it was fought between 132 and 136 CE.
2. Eban, *Personal Witness*, 115.
3. Johnson, *A History of the Jews*, 59–64.
4. Bar-Kochva, *The Image of the Jews in Greek Literature*, 470.
5. Bar-Kochva, *The Image of the Jews in Greek Literature*, 506.
6. Naim, "Operation Solomon," 650.
7. Hence the large number of places called Hirbet (Arabic for "ruins of") in today's Israel. Interestingly, the Mishnah (Tractate Bava Kamma 7:7) forbids the breeding of goats in the Land of Israel.

5. Between Powerlessness and Empowerment

1. Ayoun, *Les Juifs de France, de l'émancipation à l'intégration*, 66–70.
2. Milka Levy-Rubin, "The Plan Submitted to Napoléon Revealed: A State for the Jews, Funded by the Jews," *Ha'aretz* [Hebrew edition], February 4, 2017.

3. Milka Levy-Rubin, "The Plan Submitted to Napoléon Revealed: A State for the Jews, Funded by the Jews," *Ha'aretz* [Hebrew edition], February 4, 2017.

4. Kissinger, *Diplomacy*, 155.

5. Beker, *The Chosen*, 82.

6. Beker, *The Chosen*, 82–83.

7. Beker, *The Chosen*, 86.

8. Beker, *The Chosen*, 83–84.

9. Beker, *The Chosen*, 85.

10. Wisse, *Jews and Power*, 83.

11. In 1941 Hitler ordered the destruction of Heinrich Heine's grave at Paris's Montmartre cemetery. Johnson, *A History of the Jews*, 348–49.

6. The Zionist Controversy

1. Morris, *Righteous Victims*, 16.

2. Bergmann, "Dühring, Engen Karl," 191.

3. Wisse, *Jews and Power*, 91.

4. Wisse, *Jews and Power*, 89.

5. Weizmann, *Trial and Error*, 61–62.

6. Weizmann, *Trial and Error*, 73.

7. Weizmann, *Trial and Error*, 359.

8. Morris, *Righteous Victims*, 30.

9. Morris, *Righteous Victims*, 57.

10. Ben-Ami, *Scars of War, Wounds of Peace*, 5.

7. Diplomacy in Post-WWI System

1. Weizmann, *Trial and Error*, 272–73.

2. Eban, *Personal Witness*, 20.

3. A famed and iconic hero of the Jewish Legion was the Russian-born Joseph Trumpeldor, who had lost his left arm in the 1904–5 Russo-Japanese War and was the most decorated soldier in Russia. Trumpeldor was also the first Jew to receive an officer's commission in the Russian army. In 1911 he emigrated to the Land of Israel and joined Kibbutz Degania. In 1920 he died in combat while defending the Jewish settlement of Tel-Hai from southern Lebanese Shiites. The last words attributed to him ("Never mind, it is good to die for our country") made him a national hero.

4. Ben-Ami, *Scars of War, Wounds of Peace*, 15.

5. Eban, *Personal Witness*, 108.

6. Morris, *Righteous Victims*, 116.

7. Morris, *Righteous Victims*, 133.

8. Weizmann, *Trial and Error*, 501.

9. Yegar, *In the Foreign Service and Afterwards*, 332.

10. "British White Paper of 1939," Avalon Project, Yale Law School, http://avalon.law.yale.edu/20th_century/brwh1939.asp.

11. Eban, *Personal Witness*, 48.

12. Eban, *Personal Witness*, 23.

13. Morris, *Righteous Victims*, 155.

14. Sandler, *The Jewish Origins of Israeli Foreign Policy*, 94–95.

15. Johnson, *A History of the Jews*, 450.

16. Johnson, *A History of the Jews*, 453.

17. The Twenty-First Zionist Congress took place in 1939 in Geneva, Switzerland, and was not able to convene thereafter because of the war and the Nazi occupation of Europe.

18. Beker, *The Chosen*, 109.

19. Daladier, *Journal de captivité*, 349.

20. Rick Richman, "Jabotinsky's Lost Moment: June 1940," *Tower Magazine*, December 2013.

21. Rick Richman, "Jabotinsky's Lost Moment: June 1940," *Tower Magazine*, December 2013.

22. Rick Richman, "Jabotinsky's Lost Moment: June 1940," *Tower Magazine*, December 2013.

23. Rick Richman, "Jabotinsky's Lost Moment: June 1940," *Tower Magazine*, December 2013.

24. Tari, "Remarks on Fifty Years of Relations between Israel and France," 369.

25. Tari, "Remarks on Fifty Years of Relations between Israel and France," 369.

26. Eban, *Personal Witness*, 25.

27. Sofer, *Zionism and the Foundations of Israel Diplomacy*, 253–54.

28. Morris, *Righteous Victims*, 157.

29. Wasserstein, "New Light on the Moyne Murder," 30–38.

30. Eban, *Personal Witness*, 62.

31. Weizmann, *Trial and Error*, 536.

32. Weizmann, *Trial and Error*, 538.

33. Hoffman, *Anonymous Soldiers*, 3777 (page location in Kindle™ edition).

34. Hoffman, *Anonymous Soldiers*, 3943 (page location in Kindle™ edition).

35. Hoffman, *Anonymous Soldiers*, 3943 (page location in Kindle™ edition).

36. Wasserstein, "New Light on the Moyne Murder," 30–38.

37. Eban, *Personal Witness*, 101.

8. The British Mandate

1. Eban, *Personal Witness*, 52.
2. Weizmann, *Trial and Error*, 111.
3. Weizmann, *Trial and Error*, 114.
4. Weizmann, *Trial and Error*, 115.
5. Weizmann, *Trial and Error*, 193.
6. Morris, *Righteous Victims*, 73.
7. Morris, *Righteous Victims*, 74.
8. Sasson, "On Negotiations with Our Neighbors," 105.
9. Weizmann, *Trial and Error*, 307.
10. Morris, *Righteous Victims*, 82.
11. Morris, *Righteous Victims*, 82.
12. Owen, "Israel's Foreign Policy from a British Viewpoint," 113.
13. Weizmann, *Trial and Error*, 413.
14. Weizmann, *Trial and Error*, 469.
15. Sheffer, "Conflict Resolution vs. Conflict Management in the Arab-Israeli Conflict," 119.
16. Eban, *Personal Witness*, 56.
17. Eban, *Personal Witness*, 57.
18. Eban, *Personal Witness*, 108–9.
19. Weizmann, *Trial and Error*, 485.
20. Weizmann, *Trial and Error*, 485–86.
21. Eban, *Personal Witness*, 50.
22. Eban, *Personal Witness*, 23.
23. Sofer, *Zionism and the Foundations of Israeli Diplomacy*, 119.
24. Sofer, *Zionism and the Foundations of Israeli Diplomacy*, 142.
25. Sofer, *Zionism and the Foundations of Israeli Diplomacy*, 153.
26. Sofer, *Zionism and the Foundations of Israeli Diplomacy*, 159.
27. Sofer, *Zionism and the Foundations of Israeli Diplomacy*, 216.
28. Sofer, *Zionism and the Foundations of Israeli Diplomacy*, 227.
29. Weizmann, *Trial and Error*, 214.
30. Sofer, *Zionism and the Foundations of Israeli Diplomacy*, 256.
31. Sofer, *Zionism and the Foundations of Israeli Diplomacy*, 258.
32. Sofer, *Zionism and the Foundations of Israeli Diplomacy*, 286.

9. Israel and the Middle East

1. Eban, *Personal Witness*, 99.

2. Eban, *Personal Witness*, 101.

3. Eban, *Personal Witness*, 104.

4. Eban, *Personal Witness*, 88.

5. Eban, *Personal Witness*, 88–89.

6. Eban, *Personal Witness*, 115.

7. Eban, *Personal Witness*, 106.

8. Eban, *Personal Witness*, 107.

9. Eban, *Personal Witness*, 131.

10. Morris, *Righteous Victims*, 187.

11. Morris, *Righteous Victims*, 201.

12. Eban, *Personal Witness*, 110.

13. Crawford, "The Criteria for Statehood in International Law," 93–182.

14. "Mahmoud Abbas: The PLO Should Reexamine Its Agreements with Israel; We Will No Longer Accept the U.S. as Mediator," MEMRI, January 15, 2018, https://www.facebook.com/memri.org/videos/10156092669729717/.

15. Opaz, *Israel's Foreign Relations*, 35.

16. Rosenne, "Israel's First Letter of Credence," 30–31.

17. Eytan, *Between Israel and the Nations*, 189.

18. Eban, *Personal Witness*, 132.

19. C. Herzog, *The Arab-Israeli Wars*, 17–108.

20. Morris, *Righteous Victims*, 242.

21. Morris, *Righteous Victims*, 243.

22. Morris, *The Birth of the Palestinian Refugee Problem Revisited*.

23. Gilbert, *In Ishmael's House*; Fischbach, *Jewish Property Claims against Arab Countries*.

24. Morris, *Righteous Victims*, 221.

25. Morris, *Righteous Victims*, 231.

26. At the "Grande Albergo delle Rose" hotel.

27. Eban, *Personal Witness*, 187.

28. Eytan, "The First Year," 15.

29. Morris, *Righteous Victims*, 262–65.

30. Kahana, "Israel in the Arena of the United Nations," 796.

31. Kahana, "Israel in the Arena of the United Nations," 795.

32. Eytan, *Between Israel and the Nations*, 109.

33. Berkowits, *The Battle for the Holy Places*, 41–47; Berkowits, *How Dreadful Is This Place*, 50–61.

34. Bialer, *Between East and West*.

35. Guvrin, "Israel-USSR Relations from Israel's Independence (1948) to the Demise of the Soviet Union (1991)," 449.

36. Shlaim, "Israel between East and West, 1948–1956," 660.

37. Klieman, *Israel and the World after 40 Years*, 193.

38. Ma, "Israel's Rule in the UN during the Korean War," 83.

39. Eban, *Personal Witness*, 242.

40. Eban, *Personal Witness*, 245.

41. Eban, *Personal Witness*, 245.

42. Eban, *Personal Witness*, 242–43.

43. Sasson, "On Negotiations with Our Neighbors," 122.

44. Sasson, "On Negotiations with Our Neighbors," 122.

45. Eban, *Personal Witness*, 261.

10. The Periphery Strategy

1. Gilead, "Israel's Efforts to Connect with NATO (1957–1959)," 363.

2. De Gaulle, *Mémoires d'Espoir*, 285.

3. Alpher, *Periphery*, 5.

4. Alpher, *Periphery*, 5.

5. Alpher, *Periphery*, 52–53.

6. Alpher, *Periphery*, 53.

7. Gilead, "Relations between Israel and Iran (1949–1979)," 251.

8. Sasson, "On Negotiations with Our Neighbors," 124.

9. Gazit, "The Iranian Who Established the Oil Trade with Israel," 255–56.

10. Bialer, "The Power of the Weak," 83.

11. Abadi, *Israel's Quest for Recognition and Acceptance in Asia*, 41.

12. Sasson, "On Negotiations with Our Neighbors," 124.

13. Gilead, "Relations between Israel and Iran (1949–1979)," 254.

14. Alpher, *Periphery*, 22.

15. Abadi, *Israel's Quest for Recognition and Acceptance in Asia*, 45.

16. Alpher, *Periphery*, 22.

17. Klieman, *Israel's Global Reach*, 159.

18. Bergman, *The Secret War with Iran*, 45.

19. Klieman, *Israel's Global Reach*, 159.

20. Abadi, *Israel's Quest for Recognition and Acceptance in Asia*, 49.

21. Alpher, *Periphery*, 81.

22. Abadi, *Israel's Quest for Recognition and Acceptance in Asia*, 55–56.

23. Ben-Ya'acov, "Two Stories," 415.

24. Turkey took control of the Alexandretta province from French Syria in 1939. France did not try to reverse this annexation because of the looming war with Germany, but Syria (which formally became independent in 1946) never recognized Turkey's sovereignty over the Alexandretta.
25. Alpher, *Periphery*, 11.
26. Gilead, "Our Neighbors," 372.
27. Shlaim, *The Iron Wall*, 196.
28. Alpher, *Periphery*, 11.
29. Alpher, *Periphery*, 15.
30. Inbar, "Regional Implications of the Israeli-Turkish Strategic Partnership," 54.
31. Alpher, *Periphery*, 17.
32. Alpher, *Periphery*, 17.
33. Chris McGreal, "Turkish PM Accuses Israel of Practicing State Terrorism," *Guardian*, June 4, 2004.
34. "Turkey PM: Israel War Crimes Worse Than Sudan," *Ha'aretz*, November 8, 2009.
35. "Rachel's Tomb War Never Jewish," *Jerusalem Post*, March 7, 2010.
36. Inbar, "The Deterioration on Israeli-Turkish Relations and Its International Ramifications," 4.
37. Raphael Ahren, "Erdogan Calls Zionism 'A Crime against Humanity,'" *Times of Israel*, February 28, 2013.
38. Gavriel Fiske, "Turkish PM Accuses Israel of Engineering Egyptian Coup," *Times of Israel*, August 20, 2013.
39. "Turkey Revealed Israeli Spy Ring to Iran-Report," *Reuters*, October 17, 2013.
40. In May 2010, the *Mavi Marmara* Turkish ship, filled with armed militants from the IHH Islamic organization, tried to break the military sea blockade of the Gaza Strip. It was intercepted by Israeli naval commandos, who were violently attacked by the IHH militants. Acting in self-defense, the Israeli commandos killed nine of the Turkish Islamic militants.
41. Inbar, "The Deterioration on Israeli-Turkish Relations and Its International Ramifications," 11.
42. Sharon Udasin, "Report: Majority of Israeli Oil Imported from Kurdistan," *Jerusalem Post*, August 24, 2015.
43. Alpher, *Periphery*, 106.
44. Alpher, *Periphery*, 108.
45. "The Ambitious United Arab Emirates," *Economist*, April 6, 2017.

46. Henderson, "From Bahrain to Jerusalem."
47. Yaalon and Friedman, "Israel and the Arab States."
48. "Saudi Arabia Purchased Iron Dome Missile Defense System from Israel: Report," *i24News*, September 13, 2018.

11. Israel and the Arab States

1. Sasson, "On Negotiations with Our Neighbors," 119.
2. Sasson, "On Negotiations with Our Neighbors," 120–21.
3. Sasson, "On Negotiations with Our Neighbors," 111–14.
4. Sasson, "On Negotiations with Our Neighbors," 114.
5. Sasson, "On Negotiations with Our Neighbors," 114.
6. Sasson, "On Negotiations with Our Neighbors," 116.
7. Morris, *Righteous Victims*, 267.
8. Eban, *Personal Witness*, 281.
9. Eban, *Personal Witness*, 291–92.
10. Eban, *Personal Witness*, 330.
11. Eban, *Personal Witness*, 346.
12. Eban, *Personal Witness*, 352.
13. Eban, *Personal Witness*, 348.
14. Eban, *Personal Witness*, 352.
15. Eban, *Personal Witness*, 353.
16. Eban, *Personal Witness*, 353.
17. Eban, *Personal Witness*, 354.
18. Oren, *Six Days of War*, 55.
19. Heller, *Israel and the Cold War from the War of Independence to the Six Day War*, 558.
20. Raviv, "The Six Day War," 91.
21. Eban, *Personal Witness*, 362.
22. Eban, *Personal Witness*, 444.
23. Eban, *Personal Witness*, 364.
24. Eban, *Personal Witness*, 372.
25. Eban, *Personal Witness*, 374.
26. Eban, *Personal Witness*, 388–89.
27. Eban, *Personal Witness*, 455.
28. Eban, *Personal Witness*, 366.
29. Eban, *Personal Witness*, 383.
30. Eban, *Personal Witness*, 400–401.
31. Raviv, "The Six Day War," 99.

32. Morris, *Righteous Victims*, 324.
33. Raviv, "The Six Day War," 93.
34. Eban, *Personal Witness*, 444.
35. Eban, *Personal Witness*, 435.
36. Lapidoth, "The Security Council in the May 1967 Crisis," 534–50.
37. Sasson, "On Negotiations with Our Neighbors," 125.
38. Sasson, "On Negotiations with Our Neighbors," 124.
39. Sasson, "On Negotiations with Our Neighbors," 126.
40. Eban, *Personal Witness*, 439.
41. Eban, *Personal Witness*, 452–53.
42. Eban, *Personal Witness*, 456.
43. Security Council Official Records, 1382nd Meeting, 22 November 1967, Paragraph 88.
44. Security Council Official Records, 1382nd Meeting, 22 November 1967, Paragraph 90.
45. Eban, *Personal Witness*, 457–58.
46. Eban, *Personal Witness*, 458–59.
47. Security Council Official Records, 1382nd Meeting, 22 November 1967, Paragraph 111.
48. Rosenne, "On Multi-lingual Interpretation," 360–66.
49. Lapidoth, "The Misleading Interpretation of Security Council 242 (1967)," 11.
50. B. Jones, "The Council and the Arab-Israeli Wars," 308.
51. Brown, *In My Way*, 233.
52. Lapidoth, "UNSC Resolution 242 from 1967," 845.
53. UN Press Release SG/SM/4718, March 19, 1992, 11.
54. Lapidoth, "UNSC Resolution 242 from 1967," 842.
55. Kissinger, *Years of Upheaval*, 847.
56. Morris, *Righteous Victims*, 359.
57. Eban, *Personal Witness*, 517.
58. Eban, *Personal Witness*, 517.
59. Eban, *Personal Witness*, 518.
60. Eban, *Personal Witness*, 518.
61. Kissinger, *Years of Upheaval*, 220–21.
62. Eban, *Personal Witness*, 516.
63. Morris, *Righteous Victims*, 395.
64. Ben-Ami, *Scars of War, Wounds of Peace*, 135.
65. Eban, *Personal Witness*, 535.
66. Eban, *Personal Witness*, 589.

67. Morris, *Righteous Victims*, 434.
68. Kissinger, *Crisis*, 352–54.
69. Morris, *Righteous Victims*, 454.
70. Eban, *Personal Witness*, 655.
71. Eban, *Personal Witness*, 543.
72. Kissinger, *Crisis*, 11.
73. Eban, *Personal Witness*, 560.
74. Rabin, *The Rabin Memoirs*, 256.
75. Nisan, "The PLO and Vietnam," 181–210.
76. Schwartz and Wilf, *The War of Return*, 154.
77. Karsh, *Arafat's War*, 154.
78. Morris, *Righteous Victims*, 454.
79. Medzini, *Israel's Foreign Relations*, vol. 3, *Selected Documents 1974–1977*, 552.
80. Shlaim, *The Iron Wall*, 359.
81. Dayan, *Breakthrough*, 53.
82. Gefen, "Ceauşescu's Independent Policy toward Israel," 493.
83. Eldad, *Things You See from Here.*
84. Inbar, *Rabin and Israel's National Security*, 21.
85. Medzini, *Israel's Foreign Relations*, vol. 6, *Selected Documents 1979–1980.*
86. Eban, *Personal Witness*, 592.
87. Kissinger, *Observations*, 94.
88. Morris, *Righteous Victims*, 460.
89. Ross, *The Missing Peace*, 691 (Kindle™ Edition).
90. Sher, *Just Beyond Reach*, 141.

12. Israel and the Palestinians

1. Medzini, *Israel's Foreign Relations*, vol. 8, *Selected Documents 1982–1984*, 161–63.
2. Morris, *Righteous Victims*, 496.
3. Morris, *Righteous Victims*, 498.
4. Schiff and Ya'ari, *Israel's Lebanon War.*
5. Eban, *Personal Witness*, 610.
6. Alpher, *Periphery: Israel's Search for Middle East Allies*, 48.
7. Medzini, *Israel's Foreign Relations*, vols. 9–10, *Selected Documents 1984–1988*, 231.
8. Medzini, *Israel's Foreign Relations*, vols. 9–10, *Selected Documents 1984–1988*, 427.
9. Pazner, *I Was in Paris and in Rome*, 218.

10. Shultz, *Turmoil and Triumph*, 948.

11. Morris, *Righteous Victims*, 587.

12. Lapidoth and Hirsch, *The Arab-Israeli Conflict and Its Resolution*, 340.

13. Shlaim, *The Iron Wall*, 458.

14. Medzini, *Israel's Foreign Relations*, vols. 9–10, *Selected Documents 1984–1988*, 1046–47.

15. Medzini, *Israel's Foreign Relations*, vols. 9–10, *Selected Documents 1984–1988*, 1047.

16. PLO agents shot the mayor of Nablus, Zafer al-Masri, because of his open support for negotiations with Israel and without the PLO.

17. Baker, *The Politics of Diplomacy*, 464.

18. Indyk, "Peace without the PLO," 33–37.

19. Ben-Ami, *Scars of War, Wounds of Peace*, 164.

20. Said, *Peace and Its Discontents*, 193–94.

21. Noa Landau, "After a Quarter of a Century, Rabin's Man in Oslo Analyzes the Failures and the Successes," *Ha'aretz* [Hebrew], September 4, 2018.

22. Said, *Peace and Its Discontents*, 79.

23. Said, *Peace and Its Discontents*, 118.

24. Ross, *The Missing Peace*, 766 (Kindle™ edition).

25. Ben-Ami, *Scars of War, Wounds of Peace*, 207.

26. Sher, *Just Beyond Reach*, 32.

27. "Arafat Compares Oslo Accords to Muhammad's Hudaybiyyah Peace Treaty, Which Led to Defeat of the Peace Partners," Palestinian Media Watch, May 10, 1994, http://palwatch.org/main.aspx?fi=711&doc_id=486.

28. Rubin, *Yasir Arafat*, 125–27.

29. Shlaim, *The Iron Wall*, 609.

30. Morris, *Righteous Victims*, 621.

31. Karsh, *Arafat's War*, 138.

32. Karsh, *Arafat's War*, 5.

33. *MEMRI Special Dispatch No. 7676*, September 18, 2018.

34. Karsh, *Arafat's War*, 61.

35. Ben-Ami, *Scars of War, Wounds of Peace*, 214.

36. Karsh, *Arafat's War*, 148.

37. Ben-Ami, *Scars of War, Wounds of Peace*, 210–11.

38. "Faysal Husseini in His Last Interview: The Oslo Accords Were a Trojan Horse; The Strategic Goal Is the Liberation from the [Jordan] River to the [Mediter-

ranean] Sea," MEMRI, July 6, 2001, https://www.memri.org/reports/faysal-al
-husseini-his-last-interview-oslo-accords-were-trojan-horse-strategic-goal.

39. Karsh, *Arafat's War*, 78.

40. Karsh, *Arafat's War*, 80.

41. Karsh, *Arafat's War*, 81.

42. Ben-Ami, *Scars of War, Wounds of Peace*, 217–18.

43. Karsh, *Arafat's War*, 182.

44. Karsh, *Arafat's War*, 182.

45. Ross, *The Missing Peace*, 760 (Kindle™ edition).

46. Ben-Ami, *Scars of War, Wounds of Peace*, 265.

47. Sher, *Just Beyond Reach*, 210.

48. Ben-Ami, *Scars of War, Wounds of Peace*, 252.

49. Ross, *The Missing Peace*, 676 (Kindle™ edition).

50. Sher, *Just Beyond Reach*, 163.

51. Ross, *The Missing Peace*, 694 (Kindle™ edition).

52. Ross, *The Missing Peace*, 699 (Kindle™ edition).

53. Ross, *The Missing Peace*, 704–5 (Kindle™ edition).

54. Sher, *Just Beyond Reach*, 191.

55. Sher, *Just Beyond Reach*, 193.

56. Sher, *Just Beyond Reach*, 194.

57. Sher, *Just Beyond Reach*, 231.

58. Ben-Ami, *Scars of War, Wounds of Peace*, 250–51.

59. Ben-Ami, *Scars of War, Wounds of Peace*, 263.

60. Ben-Ami, *Scars of War, Wounds of Peace*, 251.

61. Ross, *The Missing Peace*, 714–15 (Kindle™ edition).

62. Ben-Ami, *Scars of War, Wounds of Peace*, 233.

63. Ben-Ami, *Scars of War, Wounds of Peace*, 235.

64. Karsh, *Arafat's War*, 193.

65. Karsh, *Arafat's War*, 194.

66. Benny Morris, "Camp David and After: An Exchange," *New York Review of Books*, June 13, 2001.

67. State of Israel, Ministry of International Affairs and Strategy, *The France 2 Al Dura Report, Its Consequences and Implications*, May 19, 2013.

68. Sher, *Just Beyond Reach*, 357.

69. Ross, *The Missing Peace*, 754 (Kindle™ edition).

70. Sher, *Just Beyond Reach*, 375.

71. Ross, *The Missing Peace*, 756 (Kindle™ edition).

72. Ross, *The Missing Peace*, 757 (Kindle™ edition).

73. Sher, *Just Beyond Reach*, 295–96.

74. Sher, *Just Beyond Reach*, 386.

75. Sher, *Just Beyond Reach*, 388–89.

76. Ross, *The Missing Peace*, 757 (Kindle™ edition).

77. Sher, *Just Beyond Reach*, 397–98.

78. Karsh, *Arafat's War*, 210.

79. Ari Shavit, "The Day Peace Died" (interview with Shlomo Ben-Ami), *Ha'aretz* (Friday magazine), September 14, 2001.

80. Sher, *Just Beyond Reach*, 408.

81. Sher, *Just Beyond Reach*, 413.

82. Sher, *Just Beyond Reach*, 396.

83. Ben-Ami, *Scars of War*, 210.

84. Ben-Ami, *Scars of War*, 257.

85. Gold, *The Fight for Jerusalem*, 112.

86. Berkowits, *How Dreadful Is This Place*, 255.

87. Berkowits, *How Dreadful Is This Place*, 253.

88. Berkowits, *How Dreadful Is This Place*, 254.

89. Berkowits, *How Dreadful Is This Place*, 257.

90. Berkowits, *How Dreadful Is This Place*, 258.

91. Berkowits, *How Dreadful Is This Place*, 258.

92. Ross, *The Missing Peace*, 771 (Kindle™ edition).

93. Ben-Ami, *Scars of War, Wounds of Peace*, 247.

94. Rice, *No Higher Honor*, 54 (Kindle™ edition).

95. Rice, *No Higher Honor*, 135 (Kindle™ edition).

96. Arieli, *A Border between Us and You*, 163.

97. Ben-Ami, *Scars of War, Wounds of Peace*, 240.

98. William Safire, "The Sharon Plan of Disengagement," *New York Times*, April 16, 2004.

99. A catch-22 is a dead-end situation with no way out due to unsolvable contradictions. The expression became colloquial following the publication in 1961 of Joseph Heller's novel *Catch-22*, in which a pilot wants to be exempted from a dangerous mission by feigning to be insane; yet he cannot possibly submit an exemption request without being sane.

100. Sher, *Just Beyond Reach*, 256.

101. "Exchange of Letters between PM Sharon and President Bush," Israel's Ministry of Foreign Affairs, April 14, 2004, https://mfa.gov .il/mfa/foreignpolicy/peace/mfadocuments/pages/exchange%20of %20letters%20sharon-bush%2014-apr-2004.aspx.

102. Closing address of the Sixth Herzliya Conference.
103. Rice, *No Higher Honor*, 650 (Kindle™ edition).
104. Rice, *No Higher Honor*, 652 (Kindle™ edition).
105. Rice, *No Higher Honor*, 723 (Kindle™ edition).
106. "Ehud Olmert: When Peace Was within Arm's Reach, I Was Politically Assassinated," *Times of Israel*, March 26, 2018.
107. Rice, *No Higher Honor*, 723 (Kindle™ edition).
108. Arieli, *A Border between Us and You*, 171.
109. "Ehud Olmert: When Peace Was within Arm's Reach, I Was Politically Assassinated," *Times of Israel*, March 26, 2018.
110. "Ehud Olmert: When Peace Was within Arm's Reach, I Was Politically Assassinated," *Times of Israel*, March 26, 2018.
111. Rice, *No Higher Honor*, 724 (Kindle™ edition).
112. Caspit, *The Netanyahu Years*, 447–448 (Kindle™ edition).
113. Caspit, *The Netanyahu Years*, 455 (Kindle™ edition).
114. Amir Tibon, "Obama's Detailed Plans for Mideast Peace Revealed— And How Everything Fell Apart," *Ha'aretz*, June 7, 2017.
115. Caspit, *The Netanyahu Years*, 472 (Kindle™ edition).
116. Amir Tibon, "Obama's Detailed Plans for Mideast Peace Revealed—and How Everything Fell Apart." *Ha'aretz*, June 7, 2017.
117. Caspit, *The Netanyahu Years*, 473 (Kindle™ edition).
118. "Mahmoud Abbas: The PLO Should Reexamine Its Agreements with Israel; We Will No Longer Accept the U.S. as Mediator," MEMRI, January 15, 2018, https://www.facebook.com/memri.org/videos/10156092669729717/.
119. Sheffer, "Conflict Resolution vs. Conflict Management in the Arab-Israeli Conflict," 128.
120. Morris, *Righteous Victims*, 669.
121. Ben-Ami, *Scars of War, Wounds of Peace*, 351.

13. The European Paradox

1. Morris, *Righteous Victims*, 165.
2. Patterson, *A Genealogy of Evil*, 26.
3. Eban, *Personal Witness*, 24.
4. Weiler, *Ernest Bevin*, 170–71.
5. Eban, *Personal Witness*, 169–70.
6. Weizmann, *Trial and Error*, 512.
7. Eban, *Personal Witness*, 86.

8. Weizmann, *Trial and Error*, 535.
9. Eban, *Personal Witness*, 184–85.
10. Eban, *Personal Witness*, 324.
11. Alpher, *Periphery*, 5.
12. Alpher, *Periphery*, 38.
13. Alpher, *Periphery*, 39.
14. Bermant, *Margaret Thatcher and the Middle East*, 118.
15. Bermant, *Margaret Thatcher and the Middle East*, 11.
16. Bermant, *Margaret Thatcher and the Middle East*, 81.
17. Bermant, *Margaret Thatcher and the Middle East*, 88.
18. After invading Kuwait, Saddam Hussein said he would be willing to pull out on condition of a full Israeli withdrawal from "all occupied Arab territories in Palestine, Lebanon, and Syria."
19. Robin Simcox, "Jeremy Corbyn Has a Soft Spot for Extremists," *Foreign Policy*, October 3, 2018.
20. George Eaton, "Corbyn's 'Zionist' Remarks Were 'Most Offensive' since Enoch Powell, Says Ex–Chief Rabbi," *New Statesman*, August 28, 2018.
21. "Momentum for Strengthening US-Israel Relationship?," ELNET, July 2, 2018, https://elnetwork.eu/country/uk/warming-uk-israel-ties-on-the-eve-of-brexit/.
22. Tari, "Remarks on Fifty Years of Relations between Israel and France," 368.
23. Eban, *Personal Witness*, 123.
24. Tzur, "How Israel Was Compelled to Withdraw from Sinai in 1957," 84.
25. Charbit, "France-Israel Relations, 1948–2008," 1034.
26. Charbit, "France-Israel Relations, 1948–2008," 1035.
27. De Gaulle, *Mémoires d'Espoir*, 284.
28. Charbit, "France-Israel Relations, 1948–2008,"1029.
29. Charbit, "France-Israel Relations, 1948–2008," 285.
30. Wilson, *The Chariot of Israel*, 358.
31. Eban, *Personal Witness*, 374.
32. Eban, *Personal Witness*, 372.
33. Eban, *Personal Witness*, 376.
34. "Conférence de Presse du 27 novembre 1967," Institut national de l'audiovisuel, https://fresques.ina.fr/de-gaulle/fiche-media/Gaulle00139/conference-de-presse-du-27-novembre-1967.html.
35. The French caricaturist Tim (pen name for Louis Mitelberg) published in the December 3–4, 1967, issue of *Le Monde* a cartoon depicting an

arrogant and defiant Jewish prisoner in a Nazi concentration camp with the subtitle "Self-assured and domineering."

36. "Conférence de Presse du 27 novembre 1967," Institut national de l'audiovisuel, https://fresques.ina.fr/de-gaulle/fiche-media/Gaulle00139 /conference-de-presse-du-27-novembre-1967.html.

37. "Conférence de Presse du 27 novembre 1967," Institut national de l'audiovisuel, https://fresques.ina.fr/de-gaulle/fiche-media/Gaulle00139 /conference-de-presse-du-27-novembre-1967.html.

38. Eban, *Personal Witness*, 279.

39. Meroz, "Europe in the State's Foreign Policy System," 336.

40. Sher, *Just Beyond Reach*, 299.

41. Ross, *The Missing Peace*, 735 (Kindle™ edition).

42. Neuberger, "Feelings, Realpolitik and Morals in Israel's Policy toward Germany," 270.

43. Levavi, "Konrad Adenauer Visits Israel," 360.

44. Dan Raviv and Yossi Melman, "The Nazi Who Became a Mossad Hitman," *Forward*, March 27, 2016.

45. Ronen Bergman, "Why Did Israel Let Mengele Go?," *New York Times*, September 6, 2017.

46. Ronen Bergman, "Why Did Israel Let Mengele Go?," *New York Times*, September 6, 2017.

47. Shapiro, "Shadow Interests," 172.

48. Neuberger, "Feelings, Realpolitik and Morals in Israel's Policy toward Germany," 276.

49. Eban, *Personal Witness*, 334.

50. Shapiro, "Shadow Interests," 180.

51. Lorch, "Israel-Spain," 398.

52. Hadas, "Israel and Spain," 407.

53. Lirio Abbate, "L'Espresso Reveals the Secret Diaries of Arafat," *L'Espresso*, February 2, 2018.

54. Greilsammer and Weiler, *Europe's Middle East Dilemma*, 73.

55. Yegar, "Israel-Sweden," 431.

56. Yegar, "Israel-Sweden," 436.

57. "Margot Wallström," Wikipedia (English), accessed February 24, 2020, https://en.wikipedia.org/wiki/Margot_Wallstr%C3%B6m.

58. Ben-Horin, "Israel-Vatican Relations," 994.

59. Ben-Horin, "Israel-Vatican Relations," 996.

60. Ben-Horin, "Israel-Vatican Relations," 998.

61. Ben-Horin, "Israel-Vatican Relations," 1013.

62. Pazner, *I Was in Paris and in Rome*, 295.

63. Rafael, *Destination Peace*, 358.

64. Before the launching of the "Fifth Framework Programme" in 1998, however, Israel's membership had to be fought for, due to political disagreements over the Middle East peace process.

65. Inbar, *Rabin and Israel's National Security*, 50.

66. "After Meeting Netanyahu, Lithuanian Leader Proposes Closer EU Ties," *Times of Israel*, August 24, 2018.

67. Herb Keinon, "Berlhusconi Dreams of Israel Joining EU," *Jerusalem Post*, February 2, 2010.

68. Ora Coren and Gili Cohen, "Record Europe Sales Push Israeli Defense Exports to $6.5 Billion in 2016," *Ha'aretz*, March 29, 2017.

14. The American Alliance

1. Eban, *Personal Witness*, 80.

2. Eban, *Personal Witness*, 123.

3. Johnson, *A History of the Jews*, 525.

4. Avner, *The Prime Ministers*, 121.

5. Avner, *The Prime Ministers*, 122.

6. Eban, *Personal Witness*, 136.

7. Eban, *Personal Witness*, 149.

8. Eban, *Personal Witness*, 213.

9. Sasson, "On Negotiations with Our Neighbors," 119.

10. Heller, *Israel and the Cold War from the War of Independence to the Six Day War*, 126.

11. Heller, *Israel and the Cold War from the War of Independence to the Six Day War*, 127.

12. Heller, *Israel and the Cold War from the War of Independence to the Six Day War*, 128.

13. Heller, *Israel and the Cold War from the War of Independence to the Six Day War*, 132.

14. Eban, *Personal Witness*, 245.

15. Heller, *Israel and the Cold War from the War of Independence to the Six Day War*, 144–45.

16. Heller, *Israel and the Cold War from the War of Independence to the Six Day War*, 147.

17. Heller, *Israel and the Cold War from the War of Independence to the Six Day War*, 149.

18. Eban, *Personal Witness*, 286.

19. Eban, *Personal Witness*, 290.

20. Heller, *Israel and the Cold War from the War of Independence to the Six Day War*, 272.

21. Gazit, "Early Warnings on the Way to the Strengthening of Security Ties between Israel and the United States," 295.

22. Gazit, "Early Warnings on the Way to the Strengthening of Security Ties between Israel and the United States," 295.

23. A. Cohen, *Israel and the Bomb*, 359.

24. A. Cohen, *Israel and the Bomb*, 359.

25. Avner, *The Prime Ministers*, 167.

26. Bar-On, "Five Decades of Israel-US Relations," 272.

27. Bar-Siman-Tov, "Israel and the United States (1948–1998)," 54.

28. Rabin, *The Rabin Memoirs*, 296.

29. Rabin, *The Rabin Memoirs*, 300.

30. Avner, *The Prime Ministers*, 422.

31. Avner, *The Prime Ministers*, 426.

32. Avner, *The Prime Ministers*, 440.

33. Medzini, *Israel's Foreign Relations*, vol. 7, *Selected Documents 1981–1982*, 239.

34. Bernard Weinraub, "Reagan Demands End to Attacks in Blunt Telephone Call to Begin," *New York Times*, August 13, 1982.

35. Medzini, *Israel's Foreign Relations*, vol. 8, *Selected Documents 1982–1984*, 167.

36. Lou Cannon, "Reagan-Gorbachev Summit Talks Collapse as Deadlock on SDI Wipes Out Other Gains," *Washington Post*, October 13, 1986.

37. Thomas L. Friedman, "Baker Rebukes Israel on Peace Terms," *New York Times*, June 14, 1990.

38. Shamir, *Summing-Up*, 217.

39. Medzini, *Israel's Foreign Relations*, vols. 11–12, *Selected Documents 1988–1992*, 169.

40. Ben-Aharon, "Political Struggles, 1981–1992," 172.

41. Arens, *Broken Covenant*.

42. Baker, *The Politics of Diplomacy*, 129.

43. Michael Hirsch, "Clinton to Arafat: It's All Your Fault," *Newsweek*, June 26, 2001.

44. Rice, *No Higher Honor*, 55 (Kindle™ edition).

45. Rice, *No Higher Honor*, 145 (Kindle™ edition).

46. Ross, *The Missing Peace*, 789 (Kindle™ edition).

47. Rice, *No Higher Honor*, 280 (Kindle™ edition).

48. Amir Tibon, "Poll: American Support for Israel at Highest Rates Since Early 1990s as Partisan Gap Widens," *Ha'aretz*, March 14, 2018.

15. The Russian Enigma

1. Winston Churchill, "Zionism versus Bolshevism: A Struggle for the Soul of the Jewish People," *Illustrated Sunday Herald*, February 8, 1920.

2. Winston Churchill, "Zionism versus Bolshevism: A Struggle for the Soul of the Jewish People," *Illustrated Sunday Herald*, February 8, 1920.

3. Palmor, "Israel, the Soviet Union and East European Countries," 522.

4. Eban, *Personal Witness*, 95.

5. Eban, *Personal Witness*, 112.

6. Guvrin, "Israel-USSR Relations from Israel's Independence (1948) to the Demise of the Soviet Union (1991)," 447–48.

7. Guvrin, "Israel-USSR Relations from Israel's Independence (1948) to the Demise of the Soviet Union (1991)," 448.

8. Guvrin, "Israel-USSR Relations from Israel's Independence (1948) to the Demise of the Soviet Union (1991)," 449.

9. Guvrin, "Israel-USSR Relations from Israel's Independence (1948) to the Demise of the Soviet Union (1991)," 448.

10. Klieman, *Israel and the World after Forty Years*, 193.

11. Eban, *Personal Witness*, 275.

12. Guvrin, "Israel-Romania Relations in the Twilight of Ceauşescu's Regime," 501.

13. Roi, "Relations between Israel and the Soviet Union/Russia, 1948–2008," 920.

14. Roi, "Relations between Israel and the Soviet Union/Russia, 1948–2008," 920.

15. Medzini, *Israel's Foreign Relations*, vol. 6, *Selected Documents 1979–1980*, 312.

16. Roi, "Relations between Israel and the Soviet Union/Russia, 1948–2008," 922.

17. Medzini, *Israel's Foreign Relations*, vols. 11–12, *Selected Documents 1988–1992*, 735.

18. Ora Coren and Gili Cohen, "Record Europe Sales Push Israeli Defense Exports to $6.5 Billion in 2016," *Ha'aretz*, March 29, 2017.

19. Herb Keinon, "Top Aide to Azerbaijan President: Israel Important Strategic Partner," *Jerusalem Post*, January 27, 2015.

20. Yossi Melman and Herb Keinon, "Netanyahu in Kazakhstan Seeks Help in Winning Israel Spot on UN Security Council," *Jerusalem Post*, December 14, 2016.

21. Raphael Ahren, "After Putin Meet, PM Indicates Moscow Won't Curtail Israeli Strikes in Syria," *Times of Israel*, May 9, 2018.

16. The Long March to Asia

1. *Tiers Monde* was an adaptation of *Tiers État* (Third Estate), i.e., French subjects who belonged neither to the nobility nor to the clergy before the 1789 revolution.

2. Yegar, *In the Foreign Service and Afterwards* [Hebrew], 181.

3. Aharon Shai, "Revealed: In 1939, China Planned to Settle Persecuted European Jews in Remote Part of Country," *Ha'aretz*, August 5, 2017.

4. Aharon Shai, "Revealed: In 1939, China Planned to Settle Persecuted European Jews in Remote Part of Country," *Ha'aretz*, August 5, 2017.

5. Yegar, *In the Foreign Service and Afterwards* [Hebrew], 215.

6. Yegar, *In the Foreign Service and Afterwards* [Hebrew], 223.

7. Shichor, "The Middle East in China's Foreign Policy," 968.

8. Sufott, "Israel's China Policy, 1950–1992," 582.

9. Sufott, "Israel's China Policy, 1950–1992," 582.

10. Sufott, "Israel's China Policy, 1950–1992," 585.

11. Yegar, *In the Foreign Service and Afterwards* [Hebrew], 230.

12. Shichor, "The Middle East in China's Foreign Policy," 972–973.

13. Shichor, "The Middle East in China's Foreign Policy," 970.

14. Sufott, "Israel's China Policy, 1950–1992," 586.

15. Sufott, "Israel's China Policy, 1950–1992," 586.

16. Shichor, *The Middle East in China's Foreign Policy, 1949–1977*, 111.

17. Shichor, "The Middle East in China's Foreign Policy," 987.

18. Kumaraswamy, *Israel's China Odyssey*, 31.

19. Melman and Sinai, "Israeli-Chinese Relations and the Future Prospects," 403.

20. Segal, "China and Israel," 207.

21. Sufott, "Israel's China Policy, 1950–1992," 588.

22. Abadi, *Israel's Quest for Recognition and Acceptance in Asia*, 80.

23. Calabrese, *China's Changing Relations with the Middle East*, 136.

24. Sobin, "The China-Israel Connection," 118–20.

25. Abadi, *Israel's Quest for Recognition and Acceptance in Asia*, 82.

26. Abadi, *Israel's Quest for Recognition and Acceptance in Asia*, 83.

27. Abadi, *Israel's Quest for Recognition and Acceptance in Asia*, 88.

28. Siegel, *Let There Be Water*, 198 (Kindle™ edition).

29. Ben-Meir, *Foreign Policy* [Hebrew], 634.

30. Galia Lavi, Assaf Orion, and Matan Vilnai, "Israel and China: Toward a Comprehensive Innovative Partnership," *INSS Insight* 906 (March 19, 2017).

31. Galia Lavi, Assaf Orion, and Matan Vilnai, "Israel and China: Toward a Comprehensive Innovative Partnership," *INSS Insight* 906 (March 19, 2017).

32. Galia Lavi, Assaf Orion, and Matan Vilnai, "Israel and China: Toward a Comprehensive Innovative Partnership," *INSS Insight* 906 (March 19, 2017).

33. Amos Harel, "US Opposition to Tightening of Ties between Israel and China Is Becoming Open and Constraining," *Ha'aretz* [Hebrew], January 7, 2019.

34. "Full Text of Swami Vivekananda's Chicago Speech of 1893," *Business Standard*, September 11, 2017.

35. G. Shimoni, *Gandhi, Satyagraha and the Jews*.

36. Yegar, *In the Foreign Service and Afterwards* [Hebrew], 200.

37. Abadi, *Israel's Quest for Recognition and Acceptance in Asia*, 258.

38. Yegar, *In the Foreign Service and Afterwards* [Hebrew], 192–93.

39. Yegar, *In the Foreign Service and Afterwards* [Hebrew], 198–200.

40. Yegar, *In the Foreign Service and Afterwards* [Hebrew], 190–91.

41. Yegar, *In the Foreign Service and Afterwards* [Hebrew], 256–61.

42. Y. Shimoni, "India," 540.

43. Y. Shimoni, "India," 541.

44. Yegar, *In the Foreign Service and Afterwards* [Hebrew], 249.

45. Yegar, *In the Foreign Service and Afterwards* [Hebrew], 231.

46. Bachar, "Normalization in India-Israel Relations," 547.

47. Yegar, *In the Foreign Service and Afterwards* [Hebrew], 243.

48. Yegar, "Basic Factors in Relations between Israel and Asia," 535.

49. Yegar, *In the Foreign Service and Afterwards* [Hebrew], 248.

50. Yegar, *In the Foreign Service and Afterwards* [Hebrew], 248.

51. Swapan Dasgupta, "Modi Ends Hypocrisy on India's Israel Policy," *Pioneer*, January 21, 2018.

52. Efraim Inbar, "Modi Is Coming to Jerusalem," BESA *Center Perspective Papers* 515 (July 1, 2017).

53. Y. Cohen, "Israel-Japan," 553.

54. Yegar, *In the Foreign Service and Afterwards* [Hebrew], 176.

55. Y. Cohen, "Israel-Japan," 552.

56. Yegar, *In the Foreign Service and Afterwards* [Hebrew], 179–80.

57. Yegar, *In the Foreign Service and Afterwards* [Hebrew], 180.

58. Eban, *Personal Witness*, 344.

59. Shamir, *Summing-Up*, 194.

60. Y. Cohen, "Israel-Japan," 553.

61. Y. Cohen, "Israel-Japan," 557.

62. Abadi, *Israel's Quest for Recognition and Acceptance in Asia*, xvii.

63. Abadi, *Israel's Quest for Recognition and Acceptance in Asia*, 153.

64. Ben-Meir, *Foreign Policy* [Hebrew], 603.

65. Gili Cohen, "Israel Sold Advanced Weapons to Myanmar During Anti-Rohingya Ethnic Cleansing Campaign," *Ha'aretz*, October 24, 2017.

66. Abadi, *Israel's Quest for Recognition and Acceptance in Asia*, 125.

67. Abadi, *Israel's Quest for Recognition and Acceptance in Asia*, 126.

68. Yegar, *The Long Journey to Asia* [Hebrew], 322–323.

69. Raphael Ahren, "North Korea Offered Israel a Halt to Its Missiles Sales to Iran for $1b-Report," *Times of Israel*, July 9, 2018.

70. Friedfeld and Metoudi, *Israel and China*, 55.

71. Abadi, *Israel's Quest for Recognition and Acceptance in Asia*, 176.

72. Abadi, *Israel's Quest for Recognition and Acceptance in Asia*, 177.

73. Abadi, *Israel's Quest for Recognition and Acceptance in Asia*, 179.

74. Ben-Meir, *Foreign Policy* [Hebrew], 640.

75. Yegar, *The Long Journey to Asia* [Hebrew], 288.

76. Yegar, *The Long Journey to Asia* [Hebrew], 290.

77. Abadi, *Israel's Quest for Recognition and Acceptance in Asia*, 200.

78. Abadi, *Israel's Quest for Recognition and Acceptance in Asia*, 203.

79. Sharon, *Warrior*, 248.

80. Abadi, *Israel's Quest for Recognition and Acceptance in Asia*, 238.

81. Gabriel Dominguez, "Philippine Navy Receives Spike ER Missile Systems," *Jane's Defense Weekly*, May 3, 2018.

82. Noa Landau, "The Quiet Side of Duterte's Visit to Israel: Large Oil and Arms Deals" [Hebrew], *Ha'aretz*, September 2, 2018.

83. Abadi, *Israel's Quest for Recognition and Acceptance in Asia*, 390.

84. Yegar, *In the Foreign Service and Afterwards* [Hebrew], 274.

85. Yegar, *In the Foreign Service and Afterwards* [Hebrew], 278.

86. Yegar, *In the Foreign Service and Afterwards* [Hebrew], 279–80.

87. Manfred Gerstenfeld, "Mahathir, 10 Years Ago: Jews Rule the World," *Jerusalem Post*, November 27, 2013.

88. Ishaan Tharoor, "Former Asia Leader Won't Stop Claiming 'Jews Rule the World,'" *Washington Post*, June 27, 2016.

89. Avi Issacharoff, "Israel-Hamas Shadow War Follows Palestinian Expats to Malaysia," *Times of Israel*, April 22, 2018.

90. Ben-Meir, *Foreign Policy* [Hebrew], 662.

91. Abadi, *Israel's Quest for Recognition and Acceptance in Asia*, 374.

92. Friedfeld and Metoudi, *Israel and China*, 60.

93. Abadi, *Israel's Quest for Recognition and Acceptance in Asia*, 337.

94. Abadi, *Israel's Quest for Recognition and Acceptance in Asia*, 343.

95. Abadi, *Israel's Quest for Recognition and Acceptance in Asia*, 345.

96. "No Paying for Slaying," editorial, *Jerusalem Post*, July 5, 2018.

17. The Scramble for Africa

1. Oded, "Israel and Africa," 617.

2. Inor, "Relations with Côte d'Ivoire," 682.

3. Inor, "Ethiopia and Israel," 646.

4. Ronen, "Israel's Clandestine Diplomacy with Sudan," 157.

5. Ronen, "Israel's Clandestine Diplomacy with Sudan," 158.

6. Gilboa, "Israel and Nigeria," 631.

7. Ojo, *Africa and Israel*, 11–12.

8. Neuberger, "Israel's Relations with African, Asia, and Latin America (1948–2008)," 1058.

9. Oded, "Israel and Africa," 618.

10. Oded, "Israel and Africa," 618.

11. Peters, *Israel and Africa*, 45.

12. Helen Epstein, "Idi Amin's Israeli Connection," *New Yorker*, June 27, 2016.

13. Oded, "Relations with Uganda," 676.

14. Oded, "Relations with Uganda," 676.

15. Helen Epstein, "Idi Amin's Israeli Connection," *New Yorker*, June 27, 2016.

16. Oded, "Relations with Uganda," 677.

17. Peters, *Israel and Africa*, 46.

18. Peters, *Israel and Africa*, 47.

19. Mauritius eventually severed diplomatic ties with Israel in 1976, under Gaddafi's pressures.

20. Ojo, *Africa and Israel*, 64.

21. Kimche, "Israel's Struggle against Its Isolation," 66.

22. Ojo, *Africa and Israel*, 69.

23. Oded, "Israel and Africa," 623.

24. Peters, *Israel and Africa*, 78.

25. Kimche, "Israel's Struggle against Its Isolation," 66.

26. Peters, *Israel and Africa*, 78–79.

27. Inor, "Relations with Côte d'Ivoire," 689.

28. Inor, "Relations with Côte d'Ivoire," 689.

29. Osia, *Israel, South Africa and Black Africa*, 31.
30. Klieman, *Israel's Global Reach*, 139.
31. Peters, *Israel and Africa*, 159.
32. Navon, *A Plight among the Nations*, 198.
33. Klieman, *Israel's Global Reach*, 152.
34. Gilboa, "Israel and Nigeria," 638.
35. Klieman, *Israel's Global Reach*, 34.
36. Alan Cowell, "Israel's Toehold in Africa Mat Falls Victim to War," *New York Times*, June 19, 1982.
37. Ojo, *Africa and Israel*, 96.
38. Oded, "Israel and Africa," 625.
39. Divon, "The Moves That Lead to the Establishment of Relations between Israel and Eritrea," 670.
40. "A Search for Allies in a Hostile World," *Economist*, February 4, 2010.
41. "A Search for Allies in a Hostile World," *Economist*, February 4, 2010.
42. Ora Coren and Gili Cohen, "Record Europe Sales Push Israeli Defense Exports to $6.5 Billion in 2016," *Ha'aretz*, March 29, 2017.
43. Lauren French, "African Extremist Groups Linking Up: U.S. General," *Reuters*, June 26, 2012.
44. Louis Charbonneau, "Exclusive: UN Monitors See Arms Reaching Somalia from Yemen, Iran," *Reuters*, February 11, 2013.
45. Herb Keinon, "Netanyahu Departs for Liberia: Israel Has Returned to Africa," *Jerusalem Post*, June 4, 2017.

18. Latin American Dilemmas

1. Lorch, "Israel-Latin American Relations until 1972," 726.
2. Lorch, "Israel-Latin American Relations until 1972," 727.
3. Goñi, *The Real Odessa*.
4. Lorch, "Israel-Latin American Relations until 1972," 739.
5. Lorch, "Israel-Latin American Relations until 1972," 742.
6. Arendt, *Eichmann à Jérusalem* [French], 459.
7. "Just Following Orders," *Economist*, October 24, 2013.
8. Franklin Roosevelt is said to have uttered, "He might be a son of a bitch, but he's our son of a bitch" (the quotation that opens this chapter) when referring to Nicaragua's dictator Anastasio Somoza García. There is no documented evidence that Roosevelt made such a statement regarding Somoza, but the expression has become apocryphal and has been attributed to other U.S. presidents in their dealings with anti-Communist Latin American dictators.

9. Lorch, "Israel-Latin American Relations until 1972," 734.

10. Klieman, *Israel's Global Reach*, 136.

11. Klieman, *Israel's Global Reach*, 133.

12. Klieman, *Israel's Global Reach*, 134.

13. This is almost a certainty, but the Israeli government is very secretive about its oil imports — something that has always constituted a challenge for researchers. Only when certain Israel state archives are released after forty years will researchers know for sure.

14. Bolivia, Chile, Colombia, Costa Rica, Dominican Republic, Ecuador, El Salvador, Guatemala, Panama, Uruguay, and Venezuela. The other countries that had embassies in Jerusalem were the Netherlands, Haiti, Côte d'Ivoire, Zaïre (today's Democratic Republic of Congo), and Kenya.

15. Klieman, *Israel's Global Reach*, 132.

16. Bar-Romi, "Argentina under the Junta, 1977–1983," 778.

17. Neuberger, "Israel's Relations with Africa, Asia, and Latin America (1948–2008)," 1060.

18. Klieman, *Israel's Global Reach*, 156.

19. Eban, *Personal Witness*, 544.

20. Bar-Romi, "Argentina under the Junta, 1977–1983," 771.

21. Bar-Romi, "Argentina under the Junta, 1977–1983," 772.

22. Bar-Romi, "Argentina under the Junta, 1977–1983," 777.

23. Bar-Romi, "Argentina under the Junta, 1977–1983," 773–75.

24. Bar-Romi, "Argentina under the Junta, 1977–1983," 776.

25. "Argentine Court Rules Prosecutor in AMIA Bombing Case was Murdered," *Times of Israel*, December 27, 2017.

26. Emanuele Ottolenghi, "The Mystery Martyr," *Weekly Standard*, February 23, 2018.

27. Emanuele Ottolenghi, "The Mystery Martyr," *Weekly Standard*, February 23, 2018.

28. Emanuele Ottolenghi, "Hezbollah in Latin America Is a Threat the U.S. Cannot Ignore," *The Hill*, June 11, 2017.

29. Josh Meyer, "The Secret Backstory of How Obama Let Hezbollah off the Hook," *Politico*, December 2017.

30. Emanuele Ottolenghi, "The Mystery Martyr," *Weekly Standard*, February 23, 2018.

19. The United Nations Saga

1. Kimche, "Israel's Struggle against Its Isolation," 67.

2. Blum, "Israel and the United Nations," 827.

3. Gross, "On the Degradation of the Constitutional Environment of the United Nations," 589.

4. Eban, *Personal Witness*, 576.

5. United Nations Secretariat, *Assessment of Member States' Contributions to the United Nations Regular Budget for the Year 2017*, ST/ADM/SER.B/955, December 28, 2016.

6. The five regional groups are Africa Asia-Pacific, Latin America and Caribbean, Eastern Europe (includes Russia), Western Europe and Others (which includes, besides Western Europe, the United States, Canada, Australia, and Turkey).

7. UNHCR *Resettlement Handbook* (United Nations High Commissioner for Refugees, 2011), 28.

8. UNHCR *Resettlement Handbook* (United Nations High Commissioner for Refugees, 2011), 35.

9. UNHCR *Resettlement Handbook* (United Nations High Commissioner for Refugees, 2011), 27.

10. Lamdan, "Blood Libels at the UN Human Rights Commission," 889.

11. Lamdan, "Blood Libels at the UN Human Rights Commission," 890–91.

12. "After UNHRC Adopts 5 Anti-Israel Resolutions, UK Vows to All Future Such Moves," *Times of Israel*, March 24, 2017.

20. The Diaspora Challenge

1. Guvrin, "Soviet Jews and Israel," 469.

2. Heller, *Israel and the Cold War from the War of Independence to the Six Day War*, 365.

3. Roi, "Relations between Israel and the Soviet Union/Russia, 1948–2008," 917.

4. Medzini, *Israel's Foreign Relations*, vol. 3, *Selected Documents 1974–1977*, 90.

5. Medzini, *Israel's Foreign Relations*, vols. 4–5, *Selected Documents 1977–1979*, 135.

6. Zak, *Forty Years of Dialogue with Moscow* [Hebrew], 428.

7. Medzini, *Israel's Foreign Relations*, vols. 9–10, *Selected Documents 1984–1988*, 281.

8. Charbit, "France-Israel Relations, 1948–2008," 1036.

9. Ahiya Raved, "Operations on Wings of Eagles Remembered by Volunteer Pilot," *Ynet News*, October 3, 2018.

10. Sharansky, *Fear No Evil*, xx.
11. Parfitt, *Operation Moses*, 37.
12. Rick Richman, "David Ben-Gurion's 1940 Mission to Rouse the Fighting Spirit of American Jews," *Mosaic*, January 17, 2018.
13. Eban, *Personal Witness*, 82.
14. Medoff, *The Jews Should Keep Quiet*.
15. Eban, *Personal Witness*, 263.
16. Medzini, *Israel's Foreign Relations*, vols. 9–10, *Selected Documents 1984–1988*, 844–45.
17. "Protest Over Women of the Wall Arrest Held Outside Israel's U.S. Embassy," *Forward*, July 22, 2010.
18. Jonathan Lis, "Female Israeli MKs Join Women of the Wall; No Arrests for First Time in Months," *Ha'aretz*, March 12, 2013.
19. Waxman, *Trouble in the Tribe*, 3.
20. Waxman, *Trouble in the Tribe*, 27.
21. Jonathan Weisman, "American Jews and Israeli Jews Are Headed for a Messy Breakup," *New York Times*, January 4, 2019.
22. Daniel Gordis, "The American 'Zionist' Assault on Israel," *Times of Israel*, January 9, 2019.

21. The Geopolitics of Energy

1. Heller, *Israel and the Cold War from the War of Independence to the Six Day War*, 152.
2. Liam Denning, "The Day after Energy Independence Day," *Bloomberg*, March 29, 2017.
3. Liam Denning, "The Day after Energy Independence Day," *Bloomberg*, March 29, 2017.
4. United States Energy Information Administration (www.eia.org).
5. "The Future of Oil," *Economist*, November 26, 2016.
6. "The Rapidly Expanding Global Liquefied Natural Gas Market," *Forbes*, July 9, 2017.
7. International Energy Agency (www.iea.org).
8. "Israel Quietly Begins Exporting Natural Gas to Jordan amid Political Sensitivities," *Ha'aretz*, March 2, 2017.
9. "Turkey's Rising Natural Gas Demand Needs U.S. LNG," *Forbes*, February 7, 2016.

10. "Turkey-Israel Natural Gas Deal Important Step for Regional Stability," *Daily Sabah*, April 27, 2017.

11. "Israel Has a Gas Conundrum," *Economist*, August 17, 2017.

12. "Israel Signs Pipeline Deal in Push to Export Gas to Europe," *Financial Times*, April 3, 2017.

13. Oded Eran, Elai Rettig, and Ofir Winter, "The Gas Deal with Egypt: Israel Deepens Its Anchor in the Eastern Mediterranean," *INSS Insight* 1033 (March 12, 2018).

14. *Key World Energy Statistics* (International Energy Agency, 2016), 24.

15. "The Future of Oil," *Economist*, November 26, 2016.

16. Kandel and Oded, "Staring Down the Barrel," 42.

17. "The Death of the Internal Combustion Engine," *Economist*, August 12, 2017.

18. "The Death of the Internal Combustion Engine," *Economist*, August 12, 2017.

19. "The Coming Revolution in Transport," *Economist*, November 24, 2016.

20. "After Electric Cars, What More Will It Take for Batteries to Change the Face of Energy?," *Economist*, August 12, 2017.

21. "Peugeot Tests Israeli Range-Extender Technology in Electric Car Push," *Reuters*, July 13, 2016.

22. "This Israeli Car Battery Can Charge in Five Minutes," *Jerusalem Post*, May 18, 2017.

23. Abigail Fagan, "Israel Tests Wireless Charging Roads for Electric Vehicles," *Scientific American*, May 11, 2017.

24. "A World Turned Upside Down," *Economist*, February 25, 2017.

25. "Israel Gears Up to Forge Renewable Energy Nation," *Ha'aretz*, November 27, 2015.

Bibliography

Abadi, Jacob. *Israel's Quest for Recognition and Acceptance in Asia*. New York: Frank Cass, 2004.

Alpher, Yossi. *Periphery: Israel's Search for Middle East Allies*. London: Rowman & Littlefield, 2015.

Arendt, Hannah. *Eichmann à Jérusalem: Essai sur la banalité du mal* [French]. Paris: Gallimard, 2006.

Arens, Moshe. *Broken Covenant: American Foreign Policy and the Crisis between the U.S. and Israel*. New York: Simon & Schuster, 1995.

Ariel, David. "Remarks on the Israel-South Africa Relation during the Collapse of Apartheid." In *Ministry of Foreign Affairs* [Hebrew], edited by Yossef Guvrin, Aryeh Oded, and Moshe Yeger. Jerusalem: Keter, 2002.

Arieli, Shaul. *A Border between Us and You* [Hebrew]. Tel Aviv: Yediot, 2013.

Avner, Yehuda. *The Prime Ministers: An Intimate Narrative of Israeli Leadership*. London: Toby, 2010.

Ayoun, Richard. *Les Juifs de France, de l'émancipation à l'intégration* [French]. Paris: L'Harmattan, 1997.

Bachar, Giora. "Normalization in India-Israel Relations." In *Ministry of Foreign Affairs* [Hebrew], edited by Yossef Guvrin, Aryeh Oded, and Moshe Yeger. Jerusalem: Keter, 2002.

Bahbah, Bishara, and Linda Butler. *Israel and Latin America: The Military Connection*. New York: Saint Martin's, 1986.

Baker, James. *The Politics of Diplomacy: Revolution, War and Peace 1989–1992*. New York: Putnam's Sons, 1995.

Bar-Kochva, Bezalel. *The Image of the Jews in Greek Literature: The Hellenistic Period*. Berkeley: University of California Press, 2016.

Bar-On, Hanan. "Five Decades of Israel-US Relations." In *Ministry of Foreign Affairs* [Hebrew], edited by Yossef Guvrin, Aryeh Oded, and Moshe Yeger. Jerusalem: Keter, 2002.

Bar-Romi, Yoel. "Argentina under the Junta, 1977–1983." In *Ministry of Foreign Affairs* [Hebrew], edited by Yossef Guvrin, Aryeh Oded, and Moshe Yeger. Jerusalem: Keter, 2002.

Bar-Siman-Tov, Ya'acov. "Israel and the United States (1948–1998): A Special Relationship." In *Israel's Foreign Relations* [Hebrew], edited by Haim Opaz. Jerusalem: Israel's Ministry of Foreign Affairs, 1999.

Beilin, Yossi. *Touching Peace* [Hebrew]. Tel Aviv: Yediot, 1997.

Beker, Avi. *The Chosen: The History of an Idea, the Anatomy of an Obsession.* London: Palgrave Macmillan, 2008.

———. *The United Nations and Israel: From Recognition to Reprehension.* Washington DC: Lexington, 1988.

Ben-Aharon, Yossef. "Political Struggles, 1981–1992." In *Ministry of Foreign Affairs* [Hebrew], edited by Yossef Guvrin, Aryeh Oded, and Moshe Yeger. Jerusalem: Keter, 2002.

Ben-Ami, Shlomo. *Scars of War, Wounds of Peace: The Israeli-Arab Tragedy.* Oxford: Oxford University Press, 2006.

Ben-Horin, Nathan. "Israel-Vatican Relations: Between Theology and Interest." In *Ministry of Foreign Affairs* [Hebrew], edited by Yossef Guvrin, Aryeh Oded, and Moshe Yeger. Jerusalem: Keter, 2002.

Ben-Meir, Dov. *Foreign Policy* [Hebrew]. Tel Aviv: Yediot, 2011.

Ben-Ya'acov, Yitzhak. "Two Stories." In *Ministry of Foreign Affairs* [Hebrew], edited by Yossef Guvrin, Aryeh Oded, and Moshe Yeger. Jerusalem: Keter, 2002.

Ben-Zvi, Avraham. *The United States and Israel: The Limits of the Special Relationship.* New York: Columbia University Press, 1993.

Benz, Wolfgang, ed. *Handbuch des Antisemitismus. Judenfeinschaft in Geschichte und Gegenwart* [German]. Berlin: Walter de Gruyter, 2009.

Bergman, Ronen. *The Secret War with Iran.* New York: Free Press, 2008.

Bergmann, Werner. "Dühring, Engen Karl." In *Handbuch des Antisemitismus. Judenfeinschaft in Geschichte und Gegenwart* [German], edited by Wolfgang Benz. Berlin: Walter de Gruyter, 2009.

Berkowits, Shmuel. *The Battle for the Holy Places: The Struggle over Jerusalem and the Holy Sites in Israel, Judea, Samaria and the Gaza District* [Hebrew]. Or Yehuda: Hed Arzi, 2000.

———. *How Dreadful Is This Place! Holiness, Politics and Justice in Jerusalem and the Holy Places in Israel* [Hebrew]. Jerusalem: Carta, 2006.

Bermant, Azriel. *Margaret Thatcher and the Middle East.* Cambridge: Cambridge University Press, 2016.

Biale, David. *Power and Powerlessness in Jewish History.* Tel Aviv: Schocken, 1986.

Bialer, Uri. *Between East and West: Israel's Foreign Policy Orientation 1948–1956.* Cambridge: Cambridge University Press, 1990.

———. "The Power of the Weak: Israel's Oil Diplomacy, 1948–57." In *Israel's Clandestine Diplomacies*, edited by Jones Clive and Tore Peterson. London: Hurst & Company, 2013.

Blum, Yehuda. "Israel and the United Nations." In *Ministry of Foreign Affairs* [Hebrew], edited by Yossef Guvrin, Aryeh Oded, and Moshe Yeger. Jerusalem: Keter, 2002.

Brecher, Michael. *Decisions in Israel's Foreign Policy*. Oxford: Oxford University Press, 1974.

———. *The Foreign Policy System of Israel: Settings, Images, Process*. New Haven: Yale University Press, 1972.

Brown, George. *In My Way: Political Memoirs*. New York: St. Martin's, 1971.

Calabrese, John. *China's Changing Relations with the Middle East*. London: Pinter, 1991.

Caspit, Ben. *The Netanyahu Years*. New York: St. Martin's, 2017.

Charbit, Denis. "France-Israel Relations, 1948–2008: From the Delight of and Alliance to Post-Divorce Bitterness." In *Foreign Policy Between Confrontations and Agreements: Israel 1948–2008* [Hebrew], edited by Benjamin Neuberger and Arieh Grunik. Ra'anana: Open University Press, 2008.

Cohen, Avner. *Israel and the Bomb* [Hebrew]. Tel Aviv: Shocken, 2000.

Cohen, Ya'acov. "Israel-Japan: Fifty Years of Relations." In *Ministry of Foreign Affairs* [Hebrew], edited by Yossef Guvrin, Aryeh Oded, and Moshe Yeger. Jerusalem: Keter, 2002.

Crawford, James. "The Criteria for Statehood in International Law." *British Yearbook of International Law* 48, no. 1 (1976): 93–182.

Curtis, Michael. "The United Nations against Israel." *Middle East Review* 13 (1981): 32–35.

Daladier, Édouard. *Journal de captivité (1940–1945)* [French]. Paris: Calmann-Lévy, 1991.

Dayan, Moshe. *Breakthrough: A Personal Account of the Egypt-Israel Peace Negotiations*. New York: Weidenfeld & Nicholson, 1981.

De Gaulle, Charles. *Mémoires d'espoir* [French]. Paris: Plon, 1970.

Divon, Haim. "The Moves That Lead to the Establishment of Relations between Israel and Eritrea." In *Ministry of Foreign Affairs* [Hebrew], edited by Yossef Guvrin, Aryeh Oded, and Moshe Yeger. Jerusalem: Keter, 2002.

Dror, Yehezkel. *Israeli Statecraft: National Security Challenges and Responses*. Abingdon-on-Thames: Routledge, 2011.

Eban, Abba. *Personal Witness: Israel through My Eyes*. New York: Putnam's Sons, 1992.

Eldad, Aryeh. *Things You See from Here: What Happens to Right-Wing Leaders When They Reach Power?* [Hebrew]. Tel Aviv: Kinneret Zmora Bitan, 2016.

Eytan, Walter. *Between Israel and the Nations* [Hebrew]. Tel Aviv: Massada, 1958.

———. "The First Year." In *Ministry of Foreign Affairs* [Hebrew], edited by Yossef Guvrin, Aryeh Oded, and Moshe Yeger. Jerusalem: Keter, 2002.

Fischbach, Michael. *Jewish Property Claims against Arab Countries.* New York: Columbia University Press, 2008.

Freedman, Robert. *Soviet Policy toward Israel under Gorbachev.* New York: Praeger, 1991.

———. *Soviet Policy toward the Middle East since 1970.* New York: Praeger, 1978.

Freilich, Charles. *Zion's Dilemmas: How Israel Makes National Security Policy.* Ithaca: Cornell University Press, 2012.

Friedfeld, Lionel, and Philippe Metoudi. *Israel and China: From Silk Road to Innovation Highway.* Bloomington IN: Partridge, 2015.

Gazit, Mordechai. "Early Warnings on the Way to the Strengthening of Security Ties between Israel and the United States." In *Ministry of Foreign Affairs* [Hebrew], edited by Yossef Guvrin, Aryeh Oded, and Moshe Yeger. Jerusalem: Keter, 2002.

———. "The Iranian Who Established the Oil Trade with Israel." In *Ministry of Foreign Affairs* [Hebrew], edited by Yossef Guvrin, Aryeh Oded, and Moshe Yeger. Jerusalem: Keter, 2002.

Gefen, Abba. "Ceauşescu's Independent Policy toward Israel: 1978–1982." In *Ministry of Foreign Affairs* [Hebrew], edited by Yossef Guvrin, Aryeh Oded, and Moshe Yeger. Jerusalem: Keter, 2002.

Gilbert, Martin. *The Atlas of Jewish History.* New York: William Morrow, 1992.

———. *Churchill and the Jews.* New York: Simon & Schuster, 2008.

———. *In Ishmael's House: A History of Jews in Muslim Lands.* New Haven: Yale University Press, 2010.

Gilboa, Moshe. "Israel and Nigeria: Relations in the Shadow of Crises." In *Ministry of Foreign Affairs* [Hebrew], edited by Yossef Guvrin, Aryeh Oded, and Moshe Yeger. Jerusalem: Keter, 2002.

Gilead, Baruch. "Israel's Efforts to Connect with NATO (1957–1959)." In *Ministry of Foreign Affairs* [Hebrew], edited by Yossef Guvrin, Aryeh Oded, and Moshe Yeger. Jerusalem: Keter, 2002.

———. "Our Neighbors: Turkey and Cyprus." In *Ministry of Foreign Affairs* [Hebrew], edited by Yossef Guvrin, Aryeh Oded, and Moshe Yeger. Jerusalem: Keter, 2002.

————. "Relations between Israel and Iran (1949–1979): Underground Diplomacy." In *Ministry of Foreign Affairs* [Hebrew], edited by Yossef Guvrin, Aryeh Oded, and Moshe Yeger. Jerusalem: Keter, 2002.

Golan, Galia. *Soviet Policies in the Middle East from World War Two to Gorbachev.* Cambridge: Cambridge University Press, 1990.

Gold, Dore. *The Fight for Jerusalem: Radical Islam, the West, and the Future of the Holy City.* Washington DC: Regnery, 2007.

————. *Tower of Babble: How the United Nations Has Fueled Global Chaos.* New York: Crown Forum, 2005.

Goñi, Uri. *The Real Odessa: Smuggling the Nazis to Peron's Argentina.* London: Granta, 2002.

Govrin, Moshe, Aryeh Oded, and Moshe Yeger, eds. *Ministry of Foreign Affairs: The First Fifty Years* [Hebrew]. Jerusalem: Keter, 2002.

Greilsammer, Ilan, and Joseph Weiler. *Europe's Middle East Dilemma.* Boulder CO: Westview, 1987.

Gross, Leo. "On the Degradation of the Constitutional Environment of the United Nations." *American Journal of International Law* 77 (1983): 569–84.

Guvrin, Yossef. "Israel-Romania Relations in the Twilight of Ceauşescu's Regime." In *Ministry of Foreign Affairs* [Hebrew], edited by Yossef Guvrin, Aryeh Oded, and Moshe Yeger. Jerusalem: Keter, 2002.

————. "Israel-USSR Relations from Israel's Independence (1948) to the Demise of the Soviet Union (1991)." In *Ministry of Foreign Affairs* [Hebrew], edited by Yossef Guvrin, Aryeh Oded, and Moshe Yeger. Jerusalem: Keter, 2002.

————. "Soviet Jews and Israel." In *Ministry of Foreign Affairs* [Hebrew], edited by Yossef Guvrin, Aryeh Oded, and Moshe Yeger. Jerusalem: Keter, 2002.

Hadas, Shmuel. "Israel and Spain: Split Ways." In *Ministry of Foreign Affairs* [Hebrew], edited by Yossef Guvrin, Aryeh Oded, and Moshe Yeger. Jerusalem: Keter, 2002.

Hammes, Thomas. *The Sling and the Stone: On War in the 21st Century.* St. Paul MN: Zenith, 2006.

Heller, Joseph. *Israel and the Cold War from the War of Independence to the Six Day War* [Hebrew]. Beer-Sheva: Ben-Gurion University Press, 2010.

————. *The Stern Gang: Ideology, Politics and Terror, 1940–1949.* London: Frank Cass, 1995.

Henderson, Simon. "From Bahrain to Jerusalem." *Foreign Policy,* December 2017.

Herzog, Chaim. *The Arab-Israeli Wars: War and Peace in the Middle East from the War of Independence through Lebanon*. New York: Vintage, 1984.

Herzog, Yaacov. *A People That Dwells Alone*. London: Weidenfeld & Nicolson, 1975.

Hoffman, Bruce. *Anonymous Soldiers: The Struggle for Israel, 1917–1947*. New York: Alfred Knopf, 2015.

Inbar, Efraim. "The Deterioration on Israeli-Turkish Relations and Its International Ramifications." *Begin-Sadat Center for Strategic Studies, Mideast Security and Policy Studies* 89 (February 2011): 1–26.

———. *Rabin and Israel's National Security*. Washington DC: Woodrow Wilson Center Press, 1999.

———. "Regional Implications of the Israeli-Turkish Strategic Partnership." *Middle East Review of International Affairs* 5, no. 2 (Summer 2001): 48–65.

Indyk, Martin. "Peace without the PLO." *Foreign Policy* 83 (1991): 30–38.

Inor, Hanan. "Ethiopia and Israel." In *Ministry of Foreign Affairs* [Hebrew], edited by Yossef Guvrin, Aryeh Oded, and Moshe Yeger. Jerusalem: Keter, 2002.

———. "Relations with Côte d'Ivoire." In *Ministry of Foreign Affairs* [Hebrew], edited by Yossef Guvrin, Aryeh Oded, and Moshe Yeger. Jerusalem: Keter, 2002.

Johnson, Paul. *A History of the Jews*. New York: Harper & Row, 1987.

Jones, Bruce D. "The Council and the Arab-Israeli Wars." In *The United Nations Security Council and War: The Evolution of Thought and Practice since 1945*, edited by Vaughan Lowe, Adam Roberts, Jennifer Welsh, and Dominik Zaum. Oxford: Oxford University Press, 2008.

Jones, Clive, and Tore Petersen. *Israel's Clandestine Diplomacies*. London: Hurst, 2013.

Kahana, Shamai. "Israel in the Arena of the United Nations." In *Ministry of Foreign Affairs* [Hebrew], edited by Yossef Guvrin, Aryeh Oded, and Moshe Yeger. Jerusalem: Keter, 2002.

Kandel, Eugene, and Netanel Oded. "Staring Down the Barrel: Israel's Oil Problem." *Azure* 45 (Summer 2011): 31–46.

Karsh, Efraim. *Arafat's War: The Man and His Battle for Israeli Conquest*. New York: Grove, 2003.

Katz, Yaacov, and Amir Bohbot. *The Weapon Wizards: How Israel Became a High-Tech Military Superpower*. New York: St. Martin's, 2017.

Kaufman, Edy, Yoram Shapira, and Joel Barromi. *Israel-Latin American Relations*. Piscataway NJ: Transaction, 1979.

Kimche, David. "Israel's Struggle against Its Isolation." In *Ministry of Foreign Affairs* [Hebrew], edited by Yossef Guvrin, Aryeh Oded, and Moshe Yeger. Jerusalem: Keter, 2002.

Kissinger, Henry. *Crisis: The Anatomy of Two Major Foreign Policy Crises.* New York: Simon & Schuster, 2003.

———. *Diplomacy.* New York: Simon & Schuster, 1994.

———. *Does America Need a Foreign Policy? Toward a Diplomacy for the 21st Century.* New York: Simon & Schuster, 2001.

———. *Observations.* London: Weidenfeld & Nicolson, 1984.

———. *Years of Upheaval.* Boston: Little, Brown, 1982.

Klein Halevi, Yossi. *Like Dreamers: The Story of the Israeli Paratroopers Who Reunited Jerusalem and Divided a Nation.* New York: HarperCollins, 2014.

Klieman, Aaron. *Israel and the World after Forty Years.* Oxford: Pergamon-Brassey's, 1990.

———. *Israel's Global Reach: Arms Sales as Diplomacy.* Oxford: Pergamon-Brassey's, 1985.

———. *Statecraft in the Dark: Israel's Practice of Quiet Diplomacy.* Boulder CO: Westview Press, 1988.

Klinghoffer, Arthur, and Judith Apter. *Israel and the Soviet Union: Alienation or Reconciliation?* Boulder CO: Westview, 1985.

Kowitt-Crosbie, Sylvia. *A Tacit Alliance: France and Israel from Suez to the Six Day War.* Princeton NJ: Princeton University Press, 1974.

Kumaraswamy, P. R. *India's Israel Policy.* New York: Columbia University Press, 2010.

———. *Israel's China Odyssey.* New Dehli: New Dehli Institute for Defense Studies and Analysis, 1994.

Lamdan, Yossef. "Blood Libels at the UN Human Rights Commission: A Chapter in the History of the UN, of the PLO, and of Anti-Semitism." In *Ministry of Foreign Affairs* [Hebrew], edited by Yossef Guvrin, Aryeh Oded, and Moshe Yeger. Jerusalem: Keter, 2002.

Lapidoth, Ruth. "The Misleading Interpretation of Security Council 242 (1967)." *Jewish Political Studies Review* 23, no. 3 (2011): 7–17.

———. "The Security Council in the May 1967 Crisis: A Study in Frustration." *Israel Law Review* 4, no. 4 (1969): 534–50.

———. "UNSC Resolution 242 from 1967." In *Ministry of Foreign Affairs* [Hebrew], edited by Yossef Guvrin, Aryeh Oded, and Moshe Yeger. Jerusalem: Keter, 2002.

Lapidoth, Ruth, and Moshe Hirsch. *The Arab-Israeli Conflict and Its Resolution: Selected Documents*. Leiden: Martinus Nijhoff, 1992.

Levavi, Aryeh. "Konrad Adenauer Visits Israel." In *Ministry of Foreign Affairs* [Hebrew], edited by Yossef Guvrin, Aryeh Oded, and Moshe Yeger. Jerusalem: Keter, 2002.

Lorch, Netanel. "Israel-Latin American Relations until 1972." In *Ministry of Foreign Affairs* [Hebrew], edited by Yossef Guvrin, Aryeh Oded, and Moshe Yeger. Jerusalem: Keter, 2002.

———. "Israel-Spain: The Establishment of Diplomatic Relations." In *Ministry of Foreign Affairs* [Hebrew], edited by Yossef Guvrin, Aryeh Oded, and Moshe Yeger. Jerusalem: Keter, 2002.

Ma, Young-sam. "Israel's Rule in the UN during the Korean War." *Israel Journal of Foreign Affairs* 4, no. 3 (2010): 81–89.

Medoff, Rafael. *The Jews Should Keep Quiet: FDR, Stephen S. Wise, and the Holocaust*. Philadelphia: The Jewish Publication Society, 2019.

Medzini, Meron, ed. *Israel's Foreign Relations*. Vol. 3, *Selected Documents 1974–1977*. Jerusalem: Israel's Ministry of Foreign Affairs, 1981.

———. *Israel's Foreign Relations*. Vols. 4–5, *Selected Documents 1977–1979*. Jerusalem: Israel's Ministry of Foreign Affairs, 1981.

———. *Israel's Foreign Relations*. Vol. 6, *Selected Documents 1979–1980*. Jerusalem: Israel's Ministry of Foreign Affairs, 1984.

———. *Israel's Foreign Relations*. Vol. 7, *Selected Documents 1981–1982*. Jerusalem: Israel's Ministry of Foreign Affairs, 1987.

———. *Israel's Foreign Relations*. Vol. 8, *Selected Documents 1982–1984*. Jerusalem: Israel's Ministry of Foreign Affairs, 1990.

———. *Israel's Foreign Relations*. Vols. 9–10, *Selected Documents 1984–1988*. Jerusalem: Israel's Ministry of Foreign Affairs, 1992.

———. *Israel's Foreign Relations*. Vols. 11–12, *Selected Documents 1988–1992*. Jerusalem: Israel's Ministry of Foreign Affairs, 1993.

Melman, Yossi, and Ruth Sinai. "Israeli-Chinese Relations and the Future Prospects: From Shadow to Sunlight." *Asian Survey* 27, no. 4 (April 1987): 395–407.

Meroz, Yohanan. "Europe in the State's Foreign Policy System." In *Ministry of Foreign Affairs* [Hebrew], edited by Yossef Guvrin, Aryeh Oded, and Moshe Yeger. Jerusalem: Keter, 2002.

Morris, Benny. *The Birth of the Palestinian Refugee Problem Revisited*. Cambridge: Cambridge University Press, 2004.

———. "Camp David and After: An Exchange." *New York Review of Books*, June 13, 2001.

————. *Righteous Victims: A History of the Zionist-Arab Conflict, 1881–2001.* New York: Knopf, 2001.

Naim, Asher. "Operation Solomon." In *Ministry of Foreign Affairs* [Hebrew], edited by Yossef Guvrin, Aryeh Oded, and Moshe Yeger. Jerusalem: Keter, 2002.

Navon, Emmanuel. *A Plight among the Nations: Israel's Foreign Policy between Nationalism and Realism.* Saarbrücken: VDM Verlag, 2009.

Neuberger, Benjamin. "Feelings, Realpolitik and Morals in Israel's Policy toward Germany." In *Foreign Policy between Confrontations and Agreements* [Hebrew], edited by Benjamin Neuberger and Arieh Grunik. Ra'anana: Open University Press, 2008.

————. "Israel's Relations with Africa, Asia, and Latin America (1948–2008)." In *Foreign Policy between Confrontations and Agreements* [Hebrew], edited by Benjamin Neuberger and Arieh Grunik. Ra'anana: Open University Press, 2008.

Neuberger, Benjamin, and Arieh Grunik, eds. *Foreign Policy between Confrontations and Agreements: Israel 1948-2008* [Hebrew]. Ra'anana: Open University Press, 2008.

Nisan, Mordechai. "The PLO and Vietnam: National Liberation Models for Palestinian Struggle." *Small Wars and Insurgencies* 4, no. 2 (1993): 181–210.

Oded, Aryeh. "Israel and Africa: Historical and Political Aspects." In *Ministry of Foreign Affairs* [Hebrew], edited by Yossef Guvrin, Aryeh Oded, and Moshe Yeger. Jerusalem: Keter, 2002.

————. "Relations with Uganda." In *Ministry of Foreign Affairs* [Hebrew], edited by Yossef Guvrin, Aryeh Oded, and Moshe Yeger. Jerusalem: Keter, 2002.

Ojo, Olusula. *Africa and Israel: Relations in Perspective.* Boulder CO: Westview, 1988.

Olmert, Ehud. *First Person* [Hebrew]. Tel Aviv: Yediot, 2018.

Opaz, Haim, ed. *Israel's Foreign Relations* [Hebrew]. Jerusalem: Israel's Ministry of Foreign Affairs, 1999.

Oren, Michael. *Six Days of War: June 1967 and the Making of the Modern Middle East.* Oxford: Oxford University Press, 2002.

Osia, Kunirum. *Israel, South Africa and Black Africa: A Study of the Primacy of the Politics of Expediency.* Lanham MD: University Press of America, 1981.

Owen, David. "Israel's Foreign Policy from a British Viewpoint." In *Israel's Foreign Relations* [Hebrew], edited by Haim Opaz. Jerusalem: Israel's Ministry of Foreign Affairs, 1999.

Palmor, Eliezer. "Israel, the Soviet Union and East European Countries: Concluding Remarks on Fifty Years of Unique Relations." In *Ministry of Foreign Affairs* [Hebrew], edited by Yossef Guvrin, Aryeh Oded, and Moshe Yeger. Jerusalem: Keter, 2002.

Parfitt, Tudor. *Operation Moses: The Story of the Exodus of the Falasha Jews from Ethiopia.* London: Weidenfeld & Nicolson, 1985.

Patterson, David. *A Genealogy of Evil: Anti-Semitism from Nazism to Islamic Jihad.* Cambridge: Cambridge University Press, 2011.

Pazner, Avi. *I Was in Paris and in Rome* [Hebrew]. Tel Aviv: ContentoNow, 2017.

Peters, Joel. *Israel and Africa: The Problematic Friendship.* London: British Academic Press, 1991.

Poliakov, Leon. *The History of Anti-Semitism.* London: Routledge and Kegan Paul, 1975.

Pryce-Jones, David. *Betrayal: France, the Arabs, and the Jews.* New York: Encounter, 2008.

Rabin, Yitzhak. *The Rabin Memoirs.* 3rd ed. Berkeley: University of California Press, 1996.

Radosh, Allis, and Ronald Radosh. *A Safe Haven: Harry S. Truman and the Founding of Israel.* New York: HarperCollins, 2009.

Rafael, Gideon. *Destination Peace: Three Decades of Israeli Foreign Policy.* London: Weidenfeld & Nicolson, 1981.

Rapoport, Louis. *Redemption Song: The Story of Operation Moses.* San Diego CA: Harcourt, 1986.

Raviv, Moshe. "The Six Day War." In *Ministry of Foreign Affairs* [Hebrew], edited by Yossef Guvrin, Aryeh Oded, and Moshe Yeger. Jerusalem: Keter, 2002.

Rice, Condoleezza. *No Higher Honor: A Memoir of My Years in Washington.* New York: Broadway Paperbacks, 2012.

Richman, Rick. *Racing against History: The 1940 Campaign for a Jewish Army to Fight Hitler.* New York: Encounter, 2018.

Roi, Yaacov. "Relations between Israel and the Soviet Union/Russia, 1948–2008." In *Foreign Policy between Confrontations and Agreements: Israel 1948–2008* [Hebrew], edited by Benjamin Neuberger and Arieh Grunik. Ra'anana: Open University Press, 2008.

———. *Soviet Decision-Making in Practice: The USSR and Israel, 1947–1954.* Piscataway NJ: Transaction, 1980.

Ronen, Yehudit. "Israel's Clandestine Diplomacy with Sudan: Two Rounds of Extraordinary Collaboration." In *Israel's Clandestine Diplomacies,* edited by Jones Clive and Tore Peterson. London: Hurst, 2013.

Rosenne, Shabtai. "Israel's First Letter of Credence." In *Ministry of Foreign Affairs* [Hebrew], edited by Yossef Guvrin, Aryeh Oded, and Moshe Yeger. Jerusalem: Keter, 2002.

———. "On Multi-lingual Interpretation: UN Security Council 242." *Israel Law Review* 6, no. 3 (1971): 360–66.

Ross, Dennis. *The Missing Peace: The Inside Story of the Fight for Middle East Peace.* New York: Farrar, Straus and Giroux, 2004.

Rubin, Barry. *Yasir Arafat: A Political Biography.* Oxford: Oxford University Press, 2003.

Said, Edward. *Peace and Its Discontents.* New York: Vintage, 1995.

Sandler, Shmuel. *The Jewish Origins of Israeli Foreign Policy: A Study in Tradition and Survival.* Abingdon-on-Thames: Routledge, 2018.

———. *The State of Israel, the Land of Israel: The Statist and Ethnonational Dimensions of Foreign Policy.* Santa Barbara CA: Greenwood, 1993.

Sasson, Moshe. "On Negotiations with Our Neighbors." In *Ministry of Foreign Affairs* [Hebrew], edited by Yossef Guvrin, Aryeh Oded, and Moshe Yeger. Jerusalem: Keter, 2002.

Savir, Uri. *The Process.* New York: Random House, 1998.

Schama, Simon. *Belonging: The Story of the Jews 1492–1900.* London: Bodley Head, 2017.

———. *The Story of the Jews: Finding the Words 1000 BCE, 1492 CE.* London: Bodley Head, 2013.

Sharansky, Natan. *Fear No Evil.* New York: Vintage, 1989.

Sharon, Ariel. *Warrior: An Autobiography.* New York: Simon & Schuster, 2002.

Schiff, Ze'ev, and Ehud Ya'ari. *Israel's Lebanon War.* New York: Simon & Schuster, 1984.

Schwartz, Adi, and Einat Wilf. *The War of Return* [Hebrew]. Tel Aviv: Dvir, 2018.

Segal, Gerald. "China and Israel: Pragmatic Politics." *SAIS Review* 7, no. 2 (1987): 195–210.

Shamir, Yitzhak. *Summing-Up.* Boston: Little, Brown, 1994.

Shapiro, Shlomo. "Shadow Interests: West German-Israeli Intelligence and Military Cooperation, 1957–82." In *Israel's Clandestine Diplomacies,* edited by Jones Clive and Tore Peterson. London: Hurst & Company, 2013.

Shavit, Ari. *My Promised Land: The Triumph and Tragedy of Israel*. Melbourne: Scribe, 2014.

Sheffer, Gabriel. "Conflict Resolution vs. Conflict Management in the Arab-Israeli Conflict: Reevaluating the Clash Between Moshe Sharett and David Ben-Gurion." In *Foreign Policy between Confrontations and Agreements: Israel 1948–2008* [Hebrew], edited by Benjamin Neuberger and Arieh Grunik. Ra'anana: Open University Press, 2008.

———. *Modern Diasporas in International Politics*. New York: Saint Martin's, 1986.

———. *Moshe Sharett: Biography of a Political Moderate*. Oxford: Clarendon, 1997.

Sher, Gilead. *Just Beyond Reach: The Israeli-Palestinian Peace Negotiations 1999–2001* [Hebrew]. Tel Aviv: Yediot, 2001.

Shichor, Yitzhak. "The Middle East in China's Foreign Policy." In *Foreign Policy between Confrontations and Agreements: Israel 1948–2008* [Hebrew], edited by Benjamin Neuberger and Arieh Grunik. Ra'anana: Open University Press, 2008.

———. *The Middle East in China's Foreign Policy, 1949–1977*. Cambridge: Cambridge University Press, 1979.

Shimoni, Gideon. *Gandhi, Satyagraha and the Jews: A Formative Factor in India's Policy toward Israel*. Jerusalem: Leonard Davis Institute for International Relations, Hebrew University, 1977.

Shimoni, Ya'acov. "India: The Years of Estrangement." In *Ministry of Foreign Affairs* [Hebrew], edited by Yossef Guvrin, Aryeh Oded, and Moshe Yeger. Jerusalem: Keter, 2002.

Shlaim, Avi. *The Iron Wall: Israel and the Arab World*. New York: Norton & Company, 2000.

———. "Israel between East and West, 1948–1956." *International Journal of Middle East Studies* 36, no. 4 (2004): 657–73.

Shultz, George. *Turmoil and Triumph: My Years as Secretary of State*. New York: Scribner's, 1993.

Siegel, Seth. *Let There Be Water: Israel's Solution for a Water-Starved World*. New York: St. Martin's, 2015.

Sobin, Julian M. "The China-Israel Connection: New Motivations for Rapprochement." *Fletcher Forum of World Affairs* 15, no. 1 (Winter 1991): 111–25.

Sofer, Sasson. *Zionism and the Foundations of Israeli Diplomacy*. Cambridge: Cambridge University Press, 1998.

Sufott, Zev. *A China Diary: Toward the Establishment of China-Israel Relations.* London: Frank Cass, 1997.

———. "Israel's China Policy, 1950–1992." In *Ministry of Foreign Affairs* [Hebrew], edited by Yossef Guvrin, Aryeh Oded, and Moshe Yeger. Jerusalem: Keter, 2002.

Tari, Ephraim. "Remarks on Fifty Years of Relations between Israel and France." In *Ministry of Foreign Affairs* [Hebrew], edited by Yossef Guvrin, Aryeh Oded, and Moshe Yeger. Jerusalem: Ketcr, 2002.

Timerman, Jacobo. *Prisoner without a Name, Cell without a Number.* New York: Knopf, 1981.

Tzur, Ya'acov. "Early Days." In *Ministry of Foreign Affairs* [Hebrew], edited by Yossef Guvrin, Aryeh Oded, and Moshe Yeger. Jerusalem: Keter, 2002.

———. "How Israel Was Compelled to Withdraw from Sinai in 1957." In *Ministry of Foreign Affairs* [Hebrew], edited by Yossef Guvrin, Aryeh Oded, and Moshe Yeger. Jerusalem: Keter, 2002.

Van Creveld, Martin. *The Land of Blood and Honey: The Rise of Modern Israel.* New York: St. Martin's, 2010.

Wasserstein, Bernard. "New Light on the Moyne Murder." *Midstream* 26, no. 3 (1980): 30–38.

Waxman, Dov. *Trouble in the Tribe: The American Jewish Conflict over Israel.* Princeton: Princeton University Press, 2016.

Weiler, Peter. *Ernest Bevin.* Manchester: Manchester University Press, 1993.

Weizmann, Chaim. *Trial and Error.* New York: Hamish Hamilton, 1949.

Wilson, Harold. *The Chariot of Israel.* London: Weidenfeld and Michael Joseph, 1981.

Wisse, Ruth. *Jews and Power.* Tel Aviv: Schocken, 2008.

Yaalon, Moshe, and Leehe Friedman. "Israel and the Arab States: A Historic Opportunity to Normalize Relations?" *Foreign Affairs*, January 2018.

Yegar, Moshe. "Basic Factors in Relations between Israel and Asia." In *Ministry of Foreign Affairs* [Hebrew], edited by Yossef Guvrin, Aryeh Oded, and Moshe Yeger. Jerusalem: Keter, 2002.

———. *In the Foreign Service and Afterwards* [Hebrew]. Tel Aviv: Yuvalim, 2014.

———. "Israel-Sweden: History of Complicated Relationships." In *Ministry of Foreign Affairs* [Hebrew], edited by Yossef Guvrin, Aryeh Oded, and Moshe Yeger. Jerusalem: Keter, 2002.

———. *The Long Journey to Asia: A Chapter in the Diplomatic History of Israel* [Hebrew]. Haifa: Haifa University Press, 2004.

Zak, Moshe. *Forty Years of Dialogue with Moscow* [Hebrew]. Tel Aviv: Maariv, 1988.

Index

Thatcher, Margaret, 251
Third World Congress of Betar, 119
Third World countries, 170, 177, 306,
    360–61
Thirty Years' War, xix, 58, 59
"Three No's," 182
Tiers État, 436n1
Tiers monde, 313
Timerman, Jacobo, 363, 364
Tito, Josip Broz, 157
Toi, king of Hamath, 18
Torah, 15, 24, 32, 34, 394. *See also*
    Pentateuch
Tornado fighter aircraft, 262
Toynbee, Arnold, xvi, 81
Transjordan, 46, 86, 106, 108, 109,
    118, 136, 138, 279
Treaty of Versailles, 110, 247. *See also*
    Paris Peace Conference
Treaty of Westphalia, 58
Treitscke, Heinrich von, 72
triangle, strategic, 150–57, 160–62
triangle of peace, 198
Tri-Border Area, 364–66
"Trident," 156–57
Tripoli, 344, 346
Trotsky, Leon, 91, 301, 302
Truman, Harry, 136, 143, 255, 278,
    280, 299
Trump, Donald, 239, 241, 298, 299,
    396–97
Trumpeldor, Joseph, 418n3
Tsarapkin, Semyon, 302
Tuhami, Hassan, 193
Tulkarm, 211
Tunis, 200, 203, 206, 208, 209, 213
Tunisia, 137, 200, 201, 265, 369, 386

Turkey: annexations by, 423n24; in
    anti-Soviet military alliance, 143,
    150, 156; diplomatic relationship
    with Israel, 157–59, 163, 266, 403;
    energy needs and production
    in, 161, 403, 405, 408; as German
    ally, 79, 82; invasion of Northern
    Cyprus, 288; Islamic militants
    from in Gaza, 423n40; land of,
    63; messianic claims in, 59; and
    occupation of Cyprus, 266; as
    part of strategic triangle, 151–53,
    156–62; position in UN, 374; ref-
    ugees in, 374; treatment of Jews
    in, xvii; vote on partition, 130.
    See also Ottoman Empire
Turkmenistan, 157
Tuscany, 58
Tyre, 18, 44

Uganda, 343, 345, 349–52, 379, 388
Uganda proposal (1903), 75, 79, 82,
    103, 114, 122, 412, 413
Ukraine, 58, 130, 374
Union for Reform Judaism and
    Central Conference of American
    Rabbis, 398
Union of American Hebrew Congre-
    gations, 393
Union of Revisionist Zionists, 108
Union Temple of Brooklyn, 392
United Arab Command, 169
United Arab Emirates (UAE), 162, 370
United Arab Republic (UAR), 151, 169
United Monarchy, xvi
United Nations: Arab representation
    in, 183; Ariel Sharon's address
    to, 232; Azerbaijan's position